OUTSTANDING FEATURES
OF THIS ACCLAIMED ANTHOLOGY

- Genres include poetry, biography, autobiography, essays, short stories, novels, diaries, and journals

- Helpful and fascinating biographical sketches for each author

- Critical and historical introductions to each of the book's four sections: Colonial period to the Civil War; Reconstruction to the end of the century; pre-World War I to the New Negro Movement; and the New Negro Movement (the Harlem Renaissance)

- A chronological listing of publications within each period follows the four general introductions

- Bibliographies of both the primary and selected secondary sources accompany the selections of each writer's works

- Appendix A includes brief biographies of notable Afro-American women writers of the New Negro Movement who did not publish books, or published them after 1933

- Appendix B lists additional sources about Afro-American women writers of the New Negro Movement

"A sensitive gathering of powerful works, for students of black literature or any serious reader."
—*Booklist*

ANN ALLEN SHOCKLEY is an associate librarian for special collections and university archivist and associate professor of library science at Fisk University in Nashville, Tennessee. She is the co-editor of *Handbook of Black Librarianship* and author of the novels *Loving Her, Say Jesus & Come to Me*, and *The Black & White of It*. Her short stories have been published in numerous anthologies and journals.

Afro-American Women Writers

1746-1933

An Anthology
and Critical Guide

ANN ALLEN SHOCKLEY

A MERIDIAN BOOK

NEW AMERICAN LIBRARY

A DIVISION OF PENGUIN BOOKS USA INC., NEW YORK
PUBLISHED IN CANADA BY
PENGUIN BOOKS CANADA LIMITED, MARKHAM, ONTARIO

To the family: Bessie L. Allen, mother, and foremother in her field; Tamara Ann Shockley, daughter; and William Leslie Shockley, Jr., son; as well as the extended family, Sylvia H. Moore, guardian; Jennie Ella Cobb Holland, foster sister; and to my dogs: Tiffany, who patiently watched me write for nineteen years, and Bianca, who still keeps vigil.

NAL BOOKS ARE AVAILABLE AT QUANTITY DISCOUNTS WHEN USED TO PROMOTE PRODUCTS OR SERVICES. FOR INFORMATION PLEASE WRITE TO PREMIUM MARKETING DIVISION, NEW AMERICAN LIBRARY, 1622 BROADWAY, NEW YORK, NEW YORK 10019.

"Grass Fingers" and "A Mona Lisa" by Angelina Weld Grimké from *Caroling Dusk* by Countee Cullen copyright 1927 by Harper & Row, Publishers, Inc.; renewed 1955 by Ida M. Cullen. Reprinted by permission of Harper & Row, Publishers, Inc.

"The Heart of a Woman" from *The Heart of a Woman*, Boston: Cornhill Press, 1918; "I Want to Die While You Love Me" from *An Autumn Love Cycle*, 1928; "Cosmopolite" from *Bronze* (B.J. Brimmer, Co., 1922); "Old Love Letters" from *Share My World* (Half-Way House, 1962), reprinted with permission of Henry Lincoln Johnson, Jr.

The Journal of Charlotte L. Forten, edited by Ray Allen Billington (New York: Dryden Press, 1953), reprinted with permission of Mabel C. Billington and Holt, Rinehart and Winston.

Letter from Georgia Douglas-Johnson to Angelina Grimké, December 6, 1955, reprinted by permission of Moorland-Spingarn Research Center.

This is an authorized reprint of a hardcover edition published by G.K. Hall & Co.

MERIDIAN TRADEMARK REG. U.S. PAT. OFF. AND FOREIGN COUNTRIES REGISTERED TRADEMARK—MARCA REGISTRADA
HECHO EN BRATTLEBORO, VT., U.S.A.

SIGNET, SIGNET CLASSIC, MENTOR, ONYX, PLUME, MERIDIAN and NAL BOOKS are published *in the United States* by New American Library, a division of Penguin Books USA Inc., 1633 Broadway, New York, New York 10019, *in Canada* by Penguin Books Canada Limited, 2801 John Street, Markham, Ontario L3R 1B4

LIBRARY OF CONGRESS CATALOGING-IN-PUBLICATION DATA

Afro-American women writers, 1746-1933 : an anthology and critical guide / [edited by] Ann Allen Shockley.

    p. cm.

    Reprint. Originally published: Boston, Mass. : G.K. Hall, c1988.

    Bibliography: p.

    ISBN 0-452-00981-2

    1. American literature—Afro-American authors. 2. American literature—Women authors. 3. Afro-American women—Literary collections. 4. American literature—Afro-American authors—Bio-bibliography. 5. American literature—Women authors—Bio-bibliography. 6. Women and literature—United States. 7. Afro-American women authors—Biography. 8. Women authors, American—Biography. 9. Authors, American—Biography. I. Shockley, Ann Allen.

    [PS508.N3A36 1989]

    810'.8'09287—dc 19

88-35328
CIP

First Meridian Printing, August, 1989

  3 4 5 6 7 8 9

PRINTED IN THE UNITED STATES OF AMERICA

Contents

CONTENTS

PART 2
RECONSTRUCTION TO THE END OF THE CENTURY
1868–1899

CONTENTS

CONTENTS

PART 3
PRE–WORLD WAR I TO THE NEW NEGRO MOVEMENT
1900–1923

CONTENTS

PART 4
THE NEW NEGRO MOVEMENT
1924–1933

Acknowledgments

I wish to express my appreciation to the following librarians, archivists, and academicians, as well as private, public, academic, and government repositories for providing information: Audie Myers, Library of Congress; Sharon Howard and Elizabeth Gubert, Schomburg Center for Research in Black Culture, New York Public Library; Daniel T. Williams, Hollis Burke Frissel Library Archives, Tuskegee Institute; Casper LeRoy Jordan, Atlanta Public Library; Florence Borders, Amistad Research Center; Oscar Sims, library, University of California, Los Angeles; Carole Taylor, Dillard University Library; Minnie Clayton, Robert W. Woodruff Library, Atlanta University; Wilson N. Flemister, the Interdenominational Theological Center, Religious Heritage of the Black World; Esme E. Bhan, Moorland-Spingarn Research Center, Howard University; Peter Dzwonkoski and Stephen L. Peterson, the Beinecke Rare Book and Manuscript Library, Yale University; Susan M. Eltscher, American Baptist Historical Society; Provident Public Library; Christine Lamar, Rhode Island Historical Society; Eva Slezack, Enoch Pratt Free Library; Beverly Feldman, Harvard College Library; Lysbeth Andrews-Zike, New Haven Colony Historical Society; *New Haven Register*; Mayme Clayton, Western States Black Research Center; Connie Harris and J. Richard Abell, Public Library of Cincinnati and Hamilton County; Katherine Phillips, Boston Public Library; Edna Carnegie; Afro-American Historical Society, New Haven, Connecticut; Ellen Lawson, Oberlin College; Katherine Emerson, University of Massachusetts Library, Amherst; Eleanor M. Richardson, South Caroliniana Library, University of South Carolina; Jualynne Dodson; E. J. Josey, University of Pittsburgh; Sam Cameron, Meharry Medical College; Rita B. Dandridge, Norfolk State University; Sandra Y. Govan, University of North Carolina at Charlotte; and End G. Brooks, Social Science Subject Specialist, Los Angeles Public Library.

Special thanks are extended to those relatives of the writers who shared their knowledge with me: Pauline Young, niece of Alice Dunbar-Nelson; Dorothy Fleming, daughter of Sarah Lee Brown Fleming; Bernice F. Guillaume, great-granddaughter of Olivia Ward Bush Banks; Henry Lincoln Johnson, son of Georgia Douglas Johnson; Marion Fauset, half sister to Jessie Redmon Fauset; Mrs. Benjamin J. Whipper, granddaughter of Samuel Parker Whipper, brother of William J. Whipper; and Dr. Frank M. Thomas, uncle of Effie Lee Newsome.

A very warm thanks to the writers and friends who offered private research data: Dorothy Sterling, Carolyn Wedin Sylvander, Pearl Creswell, Jean Fagan Yellin, Ethel Ray Nance, Regina Anderson Andrews, Nancy Loughridge, Dorothy Porter Wesley, James Abajian, and an old family friend, Blyden Jackson, an ardent supporter at the onset.

Special recognition is given to those who not only assisted with the gathering of resources but shared in my personal trials and tribulations as well as the joy of discovery: Tamara Ann Shockley, William Leslie Shockley, Jr., and Charles Blockson. At Fisk University: Sue P. Chandler, Anna P. Floyd, Dorothy Lake and particularly my assistant in Special Collections, Beth M. Howse, who encouraged me and cautioned patience during the entire project.

Finally my thanks to Bernard W. Bell who read the manuscript; my agent, Carole Abel, who advised me to "keep the faith"; a former editor, Susan Moldow, for getting the work off the ground; and editor Borgna Brunner who witnessed the end.

Preface

This anthology seeks to record the lives and works of Afro-American women writers from the eighteenth century to the early twentieth century. Some of the writers are well known, whereas others are obscure. Many have been either disregarded or lost to black literature.

All the authors here published books or serialized novels, save for Lucy Terry. Although Terry left only one surviving poem, "Bars Fight, August 28, 1746," her historical significance as the first black poet stands yet unchallenged. Slave narratives not authored by the narrators have been omitted. This anthology documents black women's contributions to Afro-American literature in particular, and to American literature in general. As such, and because of the periods it covers, it is the first of its kind. Because the work of so few Afro-American women writers was published in the past, it is important that those who did publish be located, identified, and resurrected to take their rightful places as foremothers of the black feminist literary tradition.

The work is divided into four sections: (1) colonial period to the Civil War; (2) Reconstruction to the turn of the century; (3) pre–

World War 1 to the New Negro Movement, and (4) the New Negro Movement.

At the outset, I intended to include only literary figures, but because of the paucity of black women's literary anthologies, writers who had published other than fiction or poetry were added. Thus the first section covers all the black women writers of the period. The second and third sections name additional authors in chronological listings for whom excerpts had to be excluded because of space. An appendix to the last section, the New Negro Movement, contains brief biographies of notable writers who either did not publish books at all or published at some other time; their contributions should not be overlooked.

Introductions to each section summarize the historical, social, political, economic, and racial climates of the periods as they affected the writers and their work. A few of the women bridge two periods; their place in the book was determined by their most productive and important years. An exception is Frances Ellen Watkins Harper, whose best work spanned two periods and is thus included in two sections.

Although the biographical sketches do not offer in-depth literary analyses of the writers, the portraits include some commentaries by critics and myself, as well as guides to others.

For many of these pioneer writers, biographical background was difficult to obtain; therefore a number of the sketches are brief. In some cases—for example, "Miss Garrison," Emma Dunham Kelley-Hawkins, Lillian E. Wood, Maria Louise Burgess, and others—nothing at all could be found. Book publication also helped determine the length of biographies.

Birth dates also posed problems, especially when slave or early family records were lost. Some writers preferred not to publicize them or, as in the case of Zora Neale Hurston, most likely chose a date to suit themselves. Through academic records, the true birth date of Georgia Douglas Johnson was verified, and proved to be contrary to printed sources. Accurate death dates were equally difficult to pinpoint in all cases and again like birth dates, led to inconsistencies with anthologies. To obtain the death date of Priscilla Jane Thompson, a former graduate school classmate of mine, Connie Harris, agreed to search a graveyard to authenticate a date, since church records were lost. Death certificates, church and family records, and obituaries in newspapers were consulted for accuracy.

But not only dates were fading into oblivion; the authors' works themselves were sometimes hard to find. A copy of *Clarence and Corinne; or, God's Way* (1890) by Amelia Etta Hall Johnson in the Library of Congress turned out to be missing; fortunately a microfilm of the book exists. A real discovery was the second novel of Emma Dunham Kelley, entitled *Four Girls at Cottage City* (1895). The book was found by chance in a secondhand bookstore by black book collector and friend, Charles Blockson, after being alerted by me—a rare find for documentation purposes.

Excerpts of writings are from the authors' books, except for Angelina Weld Grimké's play, *Rachel,* which was omitted because of length. Her poems, although uncollected, have been substituted here instead. The criteria for inclusion were (1) works of historical, social, or literary significance; (2) works of lesser-known writers and classic works of well-known authors; (3) works of progenitors of the black feminist literary tradition; and (4) works of artistic merit.

The chronological lists of authors and publications should not be considered inclusive, for there are surely additional women of letters who have been inadvertently overlooked or will be rediscovered in the future. Books on the selected reference lists are the ones actually used. Reprints and other editions are not specified unless utilized.

The idea for this anthology germinated in 1978 and was begun the following year. It grew into a mammoth undertaking, lengthened by discoveries and the amount of reading required. I did my own typing on a manual typewriter, so I have no one to thank for this task but myself.

The work was done during weekends, holidays, vacations, and summer months. Because grant funding could not be secured for visits to repositories, basic readings and research were done mostly in the Fisk University Library's Special Collections and through mail inquiries.

The anthology was a labor of love filled with the pleasure of discovery, as well as some feelings of sadness for those women whose creative works had been lost to posterity or whose creative impulses had been thwarted altogether. I shared a personal empathy with many of those women whose problems mirrored my own and those of women writers throughout the centuries: the absence of what Virginia Woolf called "a room of one's own" and the money to support it.

The anthology is designed to be of use in Afro-American literature courses, women's studies, and American literature courses, as well as serving as a reference tool for librarians. It should also provide individual reading enjoyment and a treasure of writings for personal library shelves.

Ann Allen Shockley

NOTE TO THE READER

Where two names are given, the symbol ✒ indicates the name under which the writer most frequently wrote.

Introduction

It was a black woman, Lucy Terry, who gave birth to Afro-American literature with her poem "Bars Fight" in 1746. Thereafter, other women followed and contributed a variety of genre firsts to the body of literature.

Phillis Wheatley's *Poems on Various Subjects, Religious and Moral* (1773) was the first book of poems published by a black. Ann Plato's *Essays; Including Biographies and Miscellaneous Pieces in Prose and Poetry* (1841) was the first collection of essays by a black. Harriet E. Wilson, author of *Our Nig; or Sketches from the Life of a Free Black, In A Two-Story White House, North. Showing That Slavery's Shadows Fall Even There* (1859) is reputed to be the first novel by either a black woman or a black man in America. Frances Ellen Watkins Harper's "The Two Offers," of the same year, was the first short story published by a black. Frances Anne Rollins Whipper had to resort to a male pseudonym, Frank A. Rollin, to bring out her book, *Life and Public Services of Martin R. Delany* (1868), the first biography of a free black. And finally, Angelina Weld Grimké's drama, *Rachel* (1916), was the first to be published by a black woman (1920) and to be performed professionally by blacks.

Despite Afro-American literature's enormous debt to these women writers, however, it is rarely acknowledged—only a handful of black women writers have been recognized or entered in the canon. These are the ones black critic Mary Burgher aptly terms the "stepchildren of Black American literature." They are stepchildren, indeed, for these foremothers have been relegated to backstage or offstage, and have been ignored altogether in literary anthologies, particularly in sections pertaining to the eighteenth, nineteenth, and early twentieth centuries. In early Afro-American collections, Wheatley and Harper were the most anthologized for the beginning periods, and Jessie Redmon Fauset, Georgia Douglas Johnson, and Zora Neale Hurston took precedence for the early twentieth century.

James Weldon Johnson's ground-breaking *The Book of American Negro Poetry* (1922), designed to make the public aware of "American Negro poets," featured thirty-one blacks. Out of these, four women were given space—Georgia Douglas Johnson, Jessie Fauset, Anne Spencer, and Alice Dunbar-Nelson. The book prompted a series of such poetry anthologies. Robert T. Kerlin, a poet like Johnson, came out the next year with *Negro Poets and Their Poems,* and he did better by the women than had Johnson. Phillis Wheatley and Frances Ellen Watkins Harper assumed their usual places in "The Earlier Period of Art." The third chapter grouped seven female poets under the genteel heading "The Heart of Negro Womanhood," profiling Eva A. Jessye (better known as a musician), Mrs. J. W. Hammond, Alice Dunbar-Nelson, Georgia Douglas Johnson, Angelina W. Grimké, Anne Spencer, and Jessie Fauset. A miscellaneous section introduced the fresh names of Charlotte Forten Grimké, Mae Smith Johnson, H. Cordelia Ray, and Corinne E. Lewis.

A third anthology was compiled by two editors, Norman Ivey White and Walter Clinton Jackson, who readily identified themselves as "Southern white men." In their *An Anthology of Verse by American Negroes* (1924), they claimed that the work gave representation to the older poets and introduced contemporary ones. Clara Ann Thompson, H. Cordelia Ray, and Sara Collins Fernandis were the contemporary women who joined the familiar names of Wheatley, Harper, Fauset, and Johnson. The "Bibliographical and Critical Notes" also launched Mary Weston Fordham, Priscilla Jane Thompson (sister of Clara Ann), and Myra Viola Wilds.

Three years later, the Renaissance poet Countee Cullen edited *Caroling Dusk: An Anthology of Verse by Negro Poets*, which contained "new voices" of the previous "three to five years." Cullen added female poets who had published in *Crisis* and *Opportunity*, Mary Effie Lee Newsome, Blanche Taylor Dickinson, Clarissa Scott Delany, Gwendolyn B. Bennett, Lucy Ariel Williams, Helene Johnson, and Lula Lowe Weeden.

Another white man, V. F. (Victor Francis) Calverton, expanded on the series of poetry anthologies with his *Anthology of American Negro Literature* (1929). Calverton's preface touted it as "the first anthology of Negro literature, which in terms of historical background as well as diversity of forms, has endeavored to be so inclusive." His inclusiveness embraced six already known women poets, along with Nella Larsen and Jessie Fauset as novelists and Georgia Douglas Johnson as playwright with *Plumes*.

The advent of black females as editors of anthologies initiated a broader spectrum of Afro-American women writers. In 1931, Otelia Cromwell, Lorenzo Dow Turner, and Eva B. Dykes published *Readings from Negro Authors, for Schools and Colleges, with a Bibliography of Negro Literature*. Women were represented not only as poets but as writers of other genres as well, including Zora Neale Hurston, Florence Marion Harmon, and Caroline Bond Day as short-story writers, and Jessie Fauset and Clarissa Scott Delany as essayists.

Beatrice M. Murphy, lamenting that previous Negro poetry anthologies always included the same names, attempted to introduce "promising newcomers to the field" in her *An Anthology of Contemporary Verse: Negro Voices* (1938). Her "new voices" were young, many published for the first time, and pleasant to hear were the voices of over thirty women!

As more males edited anthologies, more women seem to have been systematically excluded. Sylvestre C. Watkins's *Anthology of American Negro Literature* (1944), an extension of Calverton's, focused on authors who had "developed since 1929." Zora Neale Hurston was the sole female member of this developing group in the entire volume. Obviously Watkins suffered from male literary myopia.

Among all the anthologies of early black American literature, the woman who started it all, Lucy Terry, was not even mentioned until *The Poetry of the Negro 1746–1949* (1949) was collected by Langston Hughes and Arna Bontemps. The editors, however, seemed to have eyed her skeptically, for they warily noted, "Evidence of an earlier

Negro poet has been found in references to a Lucy Terry, to whom a verse account of an Indian raid on Deerfield in 1746 is credited." Black female anthologist Erlene Stetson did not equivocate in her *Black Sister: Poetry by Black American Women, 1746–1980* (1981); she straightforwardly stated, "The history of black women's poetry in the United States began when Lucy Terry (1730–1821) of Deerfield, Massachusetts, wrote 'Bars Fight, August 28, 1746.'"

The civil rights movement of the sixties and seventies with its resurgence of black identity spearheaded what is sometimes looked upon as a "second Renaissance" for black literature. Black writers were courted by mainstream publishers who now needed books to meet the demands of Afro-American studies courses. Again, as in the past, black literary foremothers were virtually ignored in the wave of anthologies edited by males.

Black and white collaborators James A. Emanuel and Theodore L. Gross coedited *Dark Symphony: Negro Literature in America* (1968) in which women were almost extinct. This is ludicrous since their preface read: "we have reached the moment in our history when it becomes possible, and indeed necessary, to designate which works by Negroes deserve to be a part of the heritage of American literature." Apparently black women writers did not "deserve" this honor, for none was included in the sections on "Early Literature," "The Negro Awakening," or "Major Authors." Four women were admitted to "Contemporary Literature," but where were the black women precursors? Not even Phillis Wheatley or Frances Ellen Watkins Harper was represented in this book.

A male and female team, Richard A. Long and Eugenia W. Collier, brought out the two-volume *Afro-American Writing: An Anthology of Prose and Poetry* (1972). "Part I: To the Civil War" included Wheatley and Harper; "Part II: World War I to World War II," which encompasses the Renaissance when black women writers flourished, reprinted only Zora Neale Hurston and Margaret Walker (the latter of the post-Renaissance period). A second one-volume edition retained the same two early writers, but added no one to the second section.

Women similarly were neglected in Richard Barksdale and Keneth Kinnamon's *Black Writers of America: A Comprehensive Anthology* (1972), which, in line with its title, purported to be "a comprehensive collection of Afro-American literature from the eighteenth-century beginnings to the present time." Wheatley and Harper made their usual appearance, and under the sexist heading "The Black Man in the Civil War: 1861–1865," excerpts from Charlotte Forten Grimké's *Journal* and Elizabeth Keckley's *Behind the Scenes* were presented. (Chapters from these books had been anthologized previously in *The Negro Caravan: Writings by American Negroes* (1943), edited by Sterling A. Brown, Arthur P. Davis, and Ulysses Lee, which also included only a very few early women writers.) Barksdale and Kinnamon did not name a single black foremother for "Reconstruction and Reaction: 1865–1915," and only four appeared in "Renaissance and Radicalism: 1915–1945"—Zora Neale Hurston, Angelina Grimké, Anne Spencer, and Margaret Walker.

Why—in the sixties and seventies when Afro-American women writers were coming into their own during the black and women's movements—were they still not given their rightful place in Afro-American literature anthologies? Louise Bernikow, a white anthologist, in her *The World Split Open: Four Centuries of Women Poets in England and America, 1552–1950* (1970), conjectured that literary history is made through a series of choices: "Which writers have survived their time and which have not depends upon who noticed them and chose to record the notice." This choice, she continues, revolves around a "process of selection" and depends heavily on who is doing the selecting. Those of the power structure behind the literary history making, she contends, are white males who are "clearly shaped by the attitudes, conscious or unconscious, of white men toward nonwhites and nonmales."

Bernikow's hypothesis is borne out by the attitudes of some white male literary historians of the past, whose heavy hand in the selection of black literary choices for distinction and extinction is indicated by their editorship of Afro-American literary anthologies. These men manifested sexism in their overwhelming preference for male writers and racism in their use of white traditional standards for selection.

Newman Ivey White's "Bibliographical and Critical Notes" for his *An Anthology of Verse by American Negroes* revealed his sexism, classism, and racism. White, a North Carolina Trinity College professor, neither understood nor was sympathetic to black history. He totally disregarded the influences of slavery, racism, illiteracy, and oppression on the writers' creativity, and criticized them according to white criteria. To him, Frances Ellen Watkins Harper's poems were "very

banal and commonplace," his white myopic literary eye overlooking
the pathos in her antislavery poems. There is little that is commonplace about the verses in which she deplores the bondage of mind
and spirit as in "Bury Me in a Free Land":

Make me a grave where'er you will,
In a lowly plain, or a lofty hill;
Make it among earth's humblest graves,
But not in a land where men are slaves.

White looked upon Georgia Douglas Johnson's works as having
"delicacy of feeling but no strength or originality." He failed to see
that the strength of her poetry came from her heart. As for originality,
could a white woman write a poem like "Cosmopolite": "Not wholly
this or that, / Of alien bloods am I"? Would he say the same of Sara
Teasdale to whom Johnson is frequently compared?

Priscilla Jane Thompson was criticized harshly by White for her
militant words against racism; he said her poetry was characterized by
"illiterate hatred." This is an excellent example of White utterly
failing to comprehend the plight of blacks under Reconstruction and
the systematic denial of educational opportunities for them. Why
shouldn't Thompson have struck out at efforts to destroy her life and
writing? Her rallying cry in "Ethiope Lays" urged her race to self-
attainment: "We need but conquer cow'ring self / And rise a man
with men." This, no doubt, was what annoyed White.

Another literary historian, V. F. Calverton, also used white judg-
mental criteria as the basis of his choices. His condescending introduction in *An Anthology of American Negro Literature* characterized the
poetry of Frances Ellen Watkins Harper, along with that of a few
black males, such as Albert A. Whitman, George Moses Horton, and
Joseph Seamon Cotter, as "hopeless, inept and sentimental." He
praised Countee Cullen, Langston Hughes, and Claude McKay as
being "distinguished by fine intelligence and advancing artistic vision." His own tunnel vision excluded Anne Spencer, Jessie Fauset,
Georgia Douglas Johnson, and Alice Dunbar-Nelson. Calverton credited himself with editing the first diversified black literature anthology. In his manner of doing so, however, he confirmed Bernikow's
theory of white male literary history makers.

Supporting the white literary power structure have been the black male editors of anthologies, who as scholars, critics, and writers select those whom they think should or should not be recognized. These men, too, are not without their own attitudes of sexism and personal or chauvinistic biases, all of which have helped obscure many black women writers.

Black scholar and anthologist Sterling A. Brown displayed both sexism and classism toward women writers in his study, *Negro Poetry and Drama* (1937), which was heavily biased toward males. He belittled Phillis Wheatley's poems, calling them "sentimental and pious" in comparison with Alexander Pope's, and said her place in American literature was no "greater than that of a curiosity." He thereby overlooked her distinction as writer of the first book of poems published by an Afro-American, as well as the circumstances under which she wrote. In the same manner, he minimized Ann Plato's work for being "without any literary value" beside the writings of "really educated Negroes like Daniel Payne, Charles Reason, and Elymas Rogers"— an unfair assessment, since these men were mature and recognized leaders in black church and educational circles. Brown, like his white counterparts, failed to take into account Plato's youth and minimal schooling.

A contemporary of Brown's, scholar and critic George Kent, communicated his male perception of black women writers to Roseann P. Bell in a black women's anthology, *Study Black Bridges: Visions of Black Women in Literature* (1979). Kent candidly expressed his opinion that black women writers do not explore their characters with real depth, the "problem" being they do not give a deep enough definition of their encounters with power and their responses to them. Kent's insight extended no further, for he did not realize that black women's literature is just that—their responses to power.

In her premier essay, "Toward a Black Feminist Criticism," Barbara Smith wrote: "the politics of sex as well as the politics of race and class are crucially interlocking factors in the works of Black women." It is the black women writers' reactions to encounters with power that form the marrow of the black feminist literary tradition. Women's responses to racism and sexism of both black and white males, and the struggle for self-identity typify the depth.

And as if these literary power brokers were not enough to bar the black women writers from the canon, black scholar Deborah E.

McDowell added a third factor, the white female scholar. In her "New Directions for Black Feminist Criticism," McDowell chastised white middle-class female scholars who adopted the very sins they deplored in white male scholars. These women, she said, "proceeded blindly to exclude the work of Black women writers from literary anthologies and critical studies."

Regardless of past inadequacies of the wielders of literary power, Afro-American women writers are now empowering themselves. Their inner strengthening can be attributed to various factors. In the beginning, the black and women's movements acted as strong catalysts for the reexamination and incorporation of neglected groups into the traditional white male scheme of history. White women writers like Virginia Woolf, Tillie Olsen, Margery Latimer, Charlotte Perkins Gilman, and Meridel LeSueur were assigned a new place in literary history. Coinciding with this, black women scholars and writers also began seeking out the roots not only of their black identity but of their self-identity as well; this involved locating and reevaluating the works of their literary foremothers. Ironically, women performed this task more than did male writers, whom black scholar Henry Louis Gates, Jr., observed "have ardently denied a connection to those who came before them," whereas "Hurston's daughters acknowledge her influence." To Gates, this influence is "a tradition within the tradition—voices that are black and women's."

The steady rise and the accomplishments of black women writers have provided an impetus that simply cannot be ignored. The climb sometimes has been slow and arduous, but constantly uphill. It was thirty-five years after Richard Wright became the first black to appear on the best-seller list for *Black Boy* before a black woman, Maya Angelou, achieved it in 1970 for *I Know Why the Caged Bird Sings*, both interestingly enough, autobiographies. Since then, Toni Morrison and Alice Walker have made the list. In 1950, Gwendolyn Brooks won the Pulitzer Prize for her volume of poems, *Annie Allen*, and thirty-four years later, Alice Walker was awarded a Pulitzer Prize for her novel, *The Color Purple*. Gloria Naylor's novel, *The Women of Brewster Place*, won an American Book Award in 1983, and playwright Lorraine Hansberry received the New York Drama Critics' Circle Award for the best American play of 1958–59. Hansberry's *A Raisin in the Sun* was the first Broadway play to be written by a black woman. Thus, as in the past, Afro-American women writers have continued their record of achievement.

Also highly instrumental in effecting the empowerment of Afro-American women writers has been the dramatic growth of young black women scholars and critics, who have successfully gained entrance into the power structure of literary history makers. These new Afro-American female literary historians are editing women's anthologies and writing critical studies. They are challenging the old guard of black and white males and white females by bringing new recognitions and feminist perspectives to Afro-American literary history, and by reassessing the significance of black women writers. Phillis Wheatley is no longer a "Pope imitator" but, in the words of scholar Gloria T. Hull, a writer "conscious of herself as a poet, a Black poet, a Black female poet" with "originality."

Among some of the critical works and anthologies edited by these women are *Sturdy Black Bridges: Visions of Black Women in Literature* (1979), edited by Roseann P. Bell, Bettye J. Parker, and Beverly Guy-Sheftall; *All the Women Are White, All the Blacks Are Men, But Some of Us Are Brave* (1982), edited by Gloria T. Hull, Patricia Bell-Scott, and Barbara Smith; *Conjuring: Black Women, Fiction, and Literary Tradition* (1985), edited by Marjorie Pryse and Hortense J. Spillers; *Black Feminist Criticism: Perspectives on Black Women Writers* (1985), by Barbara Christian; *Black Women Writers 1950–1980: A Critical Evaluation* (1983), edited by Mari Evans; and *Home Girls: A Black Feminist Anthology* (1983), edited by Barbara Smith.

This anthology represents a historical and literary documentation of women who were not only writers but leaders among their race, too. Many had little formal education, but because of race, sex, family, political, economic, and social pressures, they endeavored to create with courage, stamina, faith, wisdom, and joy. Some of the writings may seem unimaginative, but they must be read within the context of their times, bearing in mind the author's background, environment, and raison d'être for writing. The work should make Afro-American women literary precursors more visible and accord them their rightful place beside their male peers.

In the early twentieth century, poet Anne Spencer wrote: "I proudly love being a Negro woman—it's so involved and interesting. *We* are the PROBLEM—the great national game of TABOO."

Black women are no longer taboo, but as will be seen in these pages, they *were* involved and interesting, and problems only for those who made them oo. Readers should enjoy and admire these Negro, colored, black, Afro-American, or African-American women, as they may be called in time, and love them as they should be loved.

Ann Allen Shockley

Part 1
Colonial Period
to the Civil War
1746–1862

During the colonial period the first African women reached North American shores. On 20 August 1619, a Dutch man-of-war landed in Jamestown, Virginia, with a boatload of Africans captured from a Spanish frigate bound for the West Indies. The twenty Africans who had survived the perilous voyage were sold by the captain as indentured servants in exchange for food. During the passage, a shipboard romance developed between two of the captives, Antoney and Isabell, and by the latter part of 1623 or early 1624, they were married. Out of this union, a son, William, was born in Elizabeth City. This then uneventful birth brought into the New World the first black mother and child.

The value of the "black gold" human cargo was recognized by the close of the seventeenth century, and the slave trade persisted for four hundred years, bringing endless lines of ships to America. Women, men, and children, uprooted and torn from their homeland, family, history, and cultural ties, were transported under the most inhumane conditions at sea. No doubt, there were among the terrified

African women, estranged forever from their home, many muses whose words would never be heard, silenced forever by enforced illiteracy, the lash, and death.

Fortunately, two of these early stolen females, Lucy Terry and Phillis Wheatley, managed to speak and write, becoming the first black female poets and inaugurating Afro-American literature. Perhaps if fate or circumstances had decreed differently, others too might have emerged to be counted among the pioneer eighteenth- and nineteenth-century Afro-American women writers.

Lucy Terry and Phillis Wheatley, born twenty-three years apart, were products of the New England colonies. Both were spirited away from Africa at a young age and brought to Massachusetts. Landing there could be looked upon, under the circumstances, as a stroke of good fortune, for slavery in New England had a different texture from that in the other colonies. Lorenzo Johnston Greene, in his *The Negro in Colonial New England*, has pointed out that slavery in New England was comparatively more humane because of the Puritans' religious concept of bondage, which was based on the Old Testament and the Hebrew Mosaic law. Slaves were regarded as persons and part of the family "divinely committed to their stewardship." Under this "benign paternalism," slaves were converted to the Christian religion and given rudimentary instruction in learning and industrial training.

As slaves held by paternalistic masters, Lucy Terry and Phillis Wheatley were given the opportunity to learn and in turn, to unveil their talents. Thus, they, along with Jupiter Hammon, became the first black poets. Hammon, a Long Island slave, was the first black to publish a poem. His broadside, *An Evening Thought: Salvation by Christ with Penitential Cries*, appeared in 1760.

The early black female writers were influenced by religious teachings, personal experiences, historic events, and their surroundings. Puritan concepts of pious and moral living weighed heavily in the prose and poetry of Ann Plato, a third colonial New England writer. Plato's *Essays; Including Biographies and Miscellaneous Pieces in Prose and Poetry* (1841) was the second book authored by a black female in America, appearing sixty-eight years after Phillis Wheatley's first volume of verse, *Poems on Various Subjects, Religious and Moral* (1773).

Between 1830 and 1840, black autobiographies and biographies began to burgeon. Men and women wrote of their lives as slaves and as free persons. Some of the writings were the memoirs of female ministers with inner visions and God-given directives. Frances Smith Foster in her "Adding Color and Contour to Early American Self-Portraitures: Autobiographical Writings of Afro-American Women" termed them spiritual autobiographies flavored with traces of "Puritan and Quaker conversion narratives" when "reform literature" was at its peak.

The women Gospel bearers told of their conversions, religious pilgrimages at home and abroad, family difficulties, and confrontations with racism and sexism in black and white churches. Jarena Lee, an unordained but licensed minister of the African Methodist Episcopal Church, started writing autobiographical pamphlets as early as 1836, which she sold at camp meetings and on the streets. These reminiscences culminated in her book, *Religious Experiences and Journal of Jarena Lee, Giving an Account of Her Call to Preach the Gospel* (1849). A revealing aspect of her journal was her exposure to racism in the white church and sexism in the black. While worshiping at a white English church, she wrote, she had a pervading sense of "a wall between me and a communion with that people." Lee left the church only to face a second wall, that of sexism in the African Methodist Episcopal Church. There the Reverend Richard Allen informed her that his discipline "did not call for women preachers."

Zilpha Elaw, a lesser known antebellum minister of the Methodist Episcopal faith, also wrote of her life's religious work. Born free in Pennsylvania and reared by Quakers, her *Memoirs of the Life, Religious Experience, Ministerial Travels and Labours of Mrs. Zilpha Elaw, An American Female of Color; Together with Some Account of the Great Religious Revivals in America* (1846) was published in England. It is possible that she may have read or heard of Jarena Lee's earlier autobiographical pamphlets and they inspired her story. Both women published their own works—Lee, after the A. M. E. Church declined to do so, probably because of her feminist attitudes that amounted to heresy to the black male church establishment.

Lee and Elaw would not have thought of themselves as contributing to a black feminist literary tradition. Lee was self-taught and Elaw's education was meager. They did envision their works being read long after their deaths, however. What they left for posterity was a portrayal of two strong-willed antebellum church women imbued with enough egotism to write exactly what they wanted: a lasting account of their lives.

Personal experiences of female writers of the early nineteenth century are still being uncovered, Jean McMahon Humez has edited the writings of Rebecca Cox Jackson in *Gifts of Power: The Writings of Rebecca Jackson, Black Visionary, Shaker Eldress* (1981). Rebecca Cox Jackson was born free in Philadelphia in 1795 and died in 1871. Like Jarena Lee, disgruntled with the sexism of the A. M. E. Church of which she was a minister, she chose the Shaker theology whose views of feminism and celibacy coincided with her own. Rebecca went on to establish a black Shaker sisterhood in Philadelphia. Her writings cover the period 1830 to 1864.

The *Memoir of Old Elizabeth, a Colored Woman* (1863), an itinerant minister of the A. M. E. Church, was not written directly by her. The narrative was "taken mainly from her own lips in her 97th year" by the Quakers who relayed the account. Elizabeth was born in Maryland in 1766 of slave parents. She was freed around the age of thirty by a guilt-ridden Presbyterian minister and did not begin to preach until she was forty-two.

A different kind of autobiography by a black woman was presented in *A Narrative of the Life and Travels, of Mrs. Nancy Prince* (1850), an unprecedented travel narration of a woman who went abroad not as a religious courier but as the wife of a man employed in the czar of Russia's service. Although she was free, Mrs. Prince's account tells of sexism and racism, and of her fear of being captured and sold into slavery, a nightmare for many free black women. While teaching and engaging in humanitarian activities in Jamaica, she wrote a historic commentary on the plight of the newly freed Jamaicans.

The works of these Afro-American women living in the North merely skirted the evils of slavery. With the exception of Phillis Wheatley and Lucy Terry, all were born free. But the postrevolutionary period with its social, economic, and political upheavals ushered in a new black writing. The young nation, which had fought for independence to promote "certain unalienable Rights" of "Life, Liberty, and the pursuit of Happiness," looked into a mirror darkened by the image of slavery. What it saw caused attitudes to change about the enslavement of black people, and the North began gradually to free its slaves through legislation and court actions.

Free blacks, realizing they were only quasi-free, became more self-assertive in their quest for independence. Black churches, schools, newspapers, and benevolent organizations proliferated. The drive to abolish slavery intensified as anti-slavery societies increased the attack on the South's peculiar institution, and the Underground Railroad's intricate network helped innumerable slaves escape. All these forces were shaping a new black literature of protest.

The *Anglo-African*, a journal based in New York City and started by Thomas Hamilton in January 1859, served as a vehicle for black writers. It published female poet A. E. Chancellor, and the most popular black woman writer of the 1850s, Abolitionist Frances Ellen Watkins Harper, granddame of the Afro-American literary foremothers of the nineteenth century. Harper's poems on the horrors of slavery altered the passive tone of women writers. She also published the first Afro-American short story, "The Two Offers," in 1859.

Antislavery activities stimulated the genre of the slave narrative. These accounts continued to appear well into the twentieth century in response to the curiosity or genuine interest of readers. Only a few of these autobiographies were actually written by the ex-slaves themselves; most were told to or written by whites. Within the literature were a few stories of female slaves. Among these, the most widely known are those of two remarkable Abolitionists Sojourner Truth and Harriet Tubman.

The *Narrative of Sojourner Truth, Northern Slave, Emancipated from Bodily Servitude by the State of New York, in 1828*, was published in Boston in 1850. It was ghostwritten, for Sojourner could not read or write. The book was reprinted in 1855 with an introduction by Harriet Beecher Stowe. Harriet Tubman's narrative, *Scenes in the Life of Harriet Tubman* by white author Sarah Elizabeth Hopkins Bradford, first appeared after the Civil War in 1869. Biographies about both women were published in subsequent years.

A well-known narrative involving a female slave, *Running a Thousand Miles for Freedom; or, The Escape of William and Ellen Craft from Slavery* (1860), was published in London. Although the book was written by William Craft, Ellen is a crucial part of the story, which made the couple an international cause célèbre.

Female narratives of West Indian and American slaves were published both here and in London. *The History of Mary Prince, a West Indian Slave, Related by Herself, With a Supplement by the Editor, to Which Is Added the Narrative of Asa-Asa, A Captured African* (1831) came from London. In 1832, a "Lady of Boston" wrote a *Memoir of Mrs. Chloe Spear, a Native of Africa, Who Was Enslaved In Childhood, and Died in Boston, January 3, 1815*. More familiar is the *Autobiography of a Female Slave* (1857), which was challenged as a true history by black literary scholar Vernon Loggins. Loggins maintains it was written by a young white Kentucky woman, Mattie Griffiths, who later freed her slaves.

The female slave played several roles in the system of slavery. She was workhorse, concubine, breeder, and mother to her own children as well as to those of others, black and white, kin and no kin. Being a woman, black, and slave, she was in a more vulnerable position than her black male counterpart. She was exploited and oppressed maliciously by master, mistress, white and black males and females. Harriet Jacobs, a former slave, chronicled her dilemma in the narrative *Incidents in the Life of a Slave Girl* (1861). Writing under the pseudonym of Linda Brent, Jacobs exposed the sexual, physical, and mental abuses endured by female slaves, as well as the hazards of being a fugitive in the North. Now after closer study, Jacobs is receiving the attention she deserves as a literary foremother in the black feminist literary tradition. Jean Fagin Yellen, Jacob's biographer, in her illuminating essay, "Test and Contexts of Harriet Jacobs' Incidents in the Life of a Slave Girl: Written by Herself," called it "the first full length slave narrative by a woman published in this country."

Yellen established its value to feminist literary history by pointing out that it is "the only slave narrative that takes as its subject the sexual exploitation of female slaves—thus centering on sexual oppression as well as an oppression of race and condition." The book has been compared to the sentimental novels of the times, but Yellin found in it "new forms," "new language," "new characters," and above all, "new narrative voices" which added to the whole of nineteenth-century American literature.

The sexual oppression of slave women is vividly described in the book as Linda Brent attempts both to stave off the advances of her master, Dr. Flint, and to combat the physical and verbal abuse of what Minrose C. Gwin called the "Green-eyed Monster of the Slavocracy," the jealous mistress. Of her victimization, Jacobs wrote: "I would rather drudge out my life on a cotton plantation, til the grave opened to give me rest, than to live with an unprincipled master and a jealous mistress."

As ex-slaves were recounting their life histories, a young girl born free in a prosperous Philadelphia black family began to write of her life. Reticent Charlotte L. Forten started a diary as a Salem schoolgirl in 1854 and concluded it ten years later on St. Helena Island in South Carolina, where she went to teach the freedmen. A poet also, Forten wrote with a delicate sensitivity of the people around her, of herself, and of the natural beauty of the island. This journal, written by a talented intellectual women of color, who moved among some of the most prominent leaders of the day, was discovered in Howard University's Moorland-Spingarn Collection by Ray Allen Billington, who edited and published the manuscript as *The Journal of Charlotte L. Forten* (1953). Billington saw the diary as "a uniquely human document." Charlotte Forten's marriage into the distinguished Grimké family and her later writings added to her interesting life and craft.

Outside of Charlotte Forten's elitist existence were less fortunate free black women. Although they were free, they were enslaved by poverty, class, sexism, and prejudice. Harriet E. Wilson's *Our Nig; or, Sketches from the Life of a Free Black, In A Two-Story White House, North. Showing That Slavery's Shadows Fall Even There* (1859) attests to their problems in the story of Frado, which is categorized as an autobiographical novel. The book portrays the conflicts in the relationships between a black woman and white women, who, although they were not slave and mistresses, were nevertheless the powerless and the empowered. This time, the scene is in the North, where Frado, an indentured servant, is treated cruelly by Mrs. Bellmont, head of the house, and her daughter, Mary.

The book, like Jacobs's work, also includes Yellin's "new characters" and "new voices" besides illuminating "the taboo version of miscegenation, the marriage between a white woman and a black man," as Frances Smith Foster notes.

At this time in Canada a young black woman educator and writer was setting another precedent among Afro-American women writers. Mary Ann Shadd Cary (1823–93), as the "first colored newspaper woman on the North American continent," established in 1854 the first antislavery newspaper in Canada, the *Provincial Freeman*; thus she became the first black woman editor. Born in Wilmington, Delaware, and educated in Pennsylvania by Quakers, Mary Ann Shadd Cary went to Canada in the 1850s. An active Abolitionist, she lectured widely in the States and published a small pamphlet, *Notes on Canada West*, which told of opportunities for blacks there.

These eighteenth- to mid-nineteenth-century black women writers, although without models of their own, paved the way for the Afro-American literary tradition. They wrote at a time when the culture of a turbulent new country was not well established and when female writers were not encouraged. Most important, they wrote during the darkest time of black history, while they were suffering personal hardships and tragedies.

These women defied the constraints of their race, sex, and class, as well as the institution of slavery. As early as 1831, Maria Stewart, speaking and writing as a feminist, publicly urged her black sisters to cease burying "their minds and talents beneath a load of iron pots and kettles," "to Possess the spirit of independence," to capture "the spirit of men, bold and enterprising, fearless and undaunted," and to do "head-work." The women writers were heeding her call.

These women led diverse and productive lives. They were teachers, Abolitionists, humanitarians, lecturers, exhorters of the religious faith, domestic workers, and (unknowingly) early black feminists. They strove to keep their families together, to educate themselves, to free and help others of their color, and to survive in dignity. That they had the energy and initiative to also be creative is a marvel. By writing, they left us a part of themselves and the resolution to do and be what they were.

Chronology of Writings

1859   Harriet E. Wilson (Mrs. H. E. Wilson), *Our Nig; or, Sketches from the Life of a Free Black, In A Two-Story White House, North. Showing That Slavery's Shadows Fall Even There*

1861   Harriet Jacobs (Pseudonym, Linda Brent), *Incidents in the Life of a Slave Girl*

Lucy Terry Prince

1730–1821

Lucy Terry holds the distinction of being the first black American poet. She
was kidnapped as an infant in Africa and brought to Rhode Island. When
she was five, Ensign Ebenezer Wells of Deerfield, Massachusetts, bought
her to be his servant. Lucy was baptized on 15 June 1735, "on account of
her mistress," during the Great Awakening, or New Light Movement, which
sought to break the hold of Calvinism on New England. The movement was
characterized by a series of conversion revivals that brought blacks into the
church and Christianity. Lucy was received into the "fellowship of the
church" in 1744.

Her only known poem was inspired by an event of 28 August 1746,
when sixty Indians ambushed two families in the southwest corner of Deerfield, a section called "the Bars" (a colonial word for "meadows"). Moved
by the bloody massacre, the sixteen-year-old Lucy wrote a ballad on the
tragedy entitled "Bars Fight." This "first rhymed narration of an American
slave,"[1] recited and possibly sung by the poet, was described by Deerfield
historian George Sheldon as "the fullest contemporary account of that
bloody tragedy which has been preserved."[2] The original manuscript is not
in existence, but the poem was preserved by the oral historians of Deerfield.
In 1855, Josiah Gilbert Holland printed Lucy's poem for the first time in his

History of Western Massachusetts,[3] a documentation that contradicts those who have credited Sheldon with uncovering the poem in 1893.

Lucy married Abijah Prince, a former slave some twenty-four years her senior, in 1756. Abijah, a large landowner and one of the chartered founders of Sunderland, Vermont, bought his bride's freedom. They settled in Deerfield near a brook, which even today is called Bijah's Brook. Lucy was an entertaining raconteur, and her house was a favorite gathering place for young people who came to hear her talk. Holland, writing of her as "Luce Bijah," said she was "one of the most noteworthy characters in the early history of Deerfield."[4]

In 1760, the family moved to Guilford, Vermont, a thriving village where writers and poets lived and where Abijah had been left a one-hundred-acre lot by Deacon Samuel Field. Here Lucy's black-woman strength and courage was demonstrated in 1875 when she publicly confronted the governor's council, demanding protection against threats being made by her white neighbors, the Noyses. Because of this, the "selectmen of Guilford" were ordered to defend her home.

The mother of six children, Cesar, Festus, Drucilla, Tatnai, Durexa, and Abijah, Jr., Lucy wanted one of her sons to be educated at Williams College. In her effort to strike down the color barrier, she again imprinted her name in history as one of the first black women to fight openly against discrimination. Appearing before the trustees, she pressed her case for her son's admittance for three hours in a brilliant speech spliced heavily with the law and Gospel, but to no avail.

Her gift for oratory gained national prominence when she brought a suit against Colonel Eli Bronson, a neighbor in Sunderland, Vermont, for encroaching on her land. The suit reached the U.S. Supreme Court where she was represented by Isaac Ticknor, who was to become governor of Vermont. She became dissatisfied with his arguments, however, and pleaded her own case before the court. Presiding Justice Samuel Chase is said to have remarked that Lucy's plea surpassed that of any Vermont lawyer he had ever heard.[5]

Abijah died in 1794, and Lucy went to Sunderland to live. Throughout her later years, she continued to make an annual pilgrimage by horseback from Sunderland through the Green Mountains to Guilford, an eighteen-mile journey, to visit her husband's burial site. She died at the age of ninety-one, leaving a legacy of achievement and spirit that time cannot dim.

NOTES

1. Bernard Katz, "A Second Version of Lucy Terry's Early Ballad?" *Negro History Bulletin* 29 (Fall 1966):184.
2. George Sheldon, *History of Deerfield,* 2:899.

3. Kaplan, *Black Presence in the American Revolution*, p. 210
4. Ibid.
5. Greene, *Negro in Colonial New England*, p. 315.

SELECTED SOURCES

Secondary

Greene, Lorenzo Johnston. *The Negro in Colonial New England, 1620–1776*. New York: Columbia University Press, 1959.

Hughes, Langston, and Bontemps, Arna, eds. *The Poetry of the Negro, 1746–1949*. Garden City, N.Y.: Doubleday & Co., 1949.

Kaplan, Sidney. *The Black Presence in the Era of the American Revolution, 1770–1800*. New York: New York Graphic Society in association with the Smithsonian Institution Press, 1973.

Robinson, William H., Jr. *Early Black American Poets*. Dubuque, Iowa: Wm. C. Brown Publishers, 1969.

Sheldon, George. *History of Deerfield, Massachusetts, Vols. I, II*. Deerfield, Mass. 1895–1896.

————. "Negro Slavery in Old Deerfield." *New England Magazine*, 8 (March–August 1893):49–60.

Stetson, Erlene. *Black Sister: Poetry by Black American Women, 1746–1980*. Bloomington: Indiana University Press, 1981.

Bars Fight

August 'twas, the twenty-fifth,
Seventeen hundred forty-six,
The Indians did in ambush lay,
Some very valient men to slay,
The names of whom I'll not leave out:
Samuel Allen like a hero fout,
And though he was so brave and bold,
His face no more shall we behold;
Eleazer Hawks was killed outright,
Before he had time to fight,
Before he did the Indians see,
Was shot and killed immediately;
Oliver Amsden, he was slain,
Which caused his friends much grief and pain;

Simeon Amsden they found dead,
Not many rods off from his head,
Adonijah Gillet, we do hear,
Did lose his life, which was so dear;
John Saddler fled across the water,
And so escaped the dreadful slaughter;
Eunice Allen see the Indians comeing,
And hoped to save herself by running,
And had not her petticoats stopt her,
The awful creatures had not cotched her,
And tommyhawked her on the head,
And left her on the ground for dead;
Young Samuel Allen, oh! lack-a-day,
Was taken and carried to Canada.

Phillis Wheatley

1753?–1784

Phillis Wheatley, although a slave, was the first black and second woman, following Anne Bradstreet, to publish a volume of poetry in the United States. Brought to this country under the same horrendous circumstances as her predecessor Lucy Terry, she had been stolen from her African homeland by slave traders. Shipped with a cargo of seventy or eighty young girls on a boat from Senegal, Phillis arrived in the port of Boston in 1761 to be sold in the slave market.

Susannah Wheatley, a kind, gentlehearted Christian woman and wife of John Wheatley, a prosperous tailor, was in need of a young girl to train, for her servants were growing old. At the slave market, she was drawn to the frail child wrapped in a dirty carpet and purchased her for a pittance. Mrs. Wheatley determined the child's age to be around seven because she had no front teeth. She named the girl Phillis, and as was common during slavery, Phillis took the surname of her owner.

The Wheatley home on King Street was one of refinement and culture. This environment, no doubt, had an influence on the young, inquisitive, and intelligent Phillis. She began to try to write by making letters on the wall with chalk or charcoal very early. Impressed by her efforts, the Wheatley's eighteen-year-old daughter, Mary, began to tutor her.

Within sixteen months, Phillis's master wrote, she had learned the English language and was able to read the most difficult parts of the Bible. The special tutoring of the prodigy consisted of a "little astronomy, some ancient and modern geography, a little ancient history, a fair knowledge of the Bible, and a thoroughly appreciative acquaintance with the most important Latin classics, especially the works of Virgil and Ovid."[1]

This type of learning was indeed an achievement, not only for a slave, but for any female of her time, and distinguished Phillis "as one of the most highly educated young women in Boston."[2] Clearly a genius, she mastered the English language in four years and subsequently began to study Latin. Not long afterward, she translated one of Ovid's tales, which was eventually published. This was considered remarkable for an Afro-American consigned as less than human to slavery.

Gifted with creativity, Phillis showed an early talent for writing verse, and Alexander Pope became her model. At the age of fourteen in 1767, she wrote her first poem, "To the University of Cambridge," composed of thirty-two blank verses giving advice to college boys. The poet's second poem, "On the Death of Rev. Dr. Sewall," in 1769, was the first in a series of "occasion" poems written upon the births and deaths among Boston's gentry.

The Wheatleys soon discovered that "instead of obtaining a spirit born to serve, there had come among them a spirit born to create."[3] Encouraging their young slave poet, they provided Phillis with paper and pencil at her bedside for jotting down verse she might forget before morning. Because of her delicate health, she was assigned only light housework of dusting and polishing.

Phillis's first published poem in 1770, "On the Death of the Rev. Mr. George Whitefield," brought her international attention. The broadside was reprinted quickly in Boston, Newport, New York, Philadelphia, and England the following year. The *Massachusetts Spy* sensationally advertised the poem as *An Elegiac Poem, On the Death of that celebrated Divine . . . By Phillis, A Servant girl of 17 years of Age, Belonging to Mr. J. Wheatley . . . but 9 years in this country from Africa.*

Phillis became a kind of "poet laureate" in the social and literary circles of eighteenth-century Boston. Books were given to her, and eminent people praised her achievements. Dr. Benjamin Rush, the "Hippocrates of Pennsylvania" and prominent Abolitionist, in his *Address upon Slave-Keeping,* lauded the girl's genius and accomplishments which "not only do honor to her sex, but to human nature."

A lively conversationalist, Phillis was welcomed into the homes of scholars, clergymen, and merchants. Although they did not treat her as a slave, she was always conscious of her station and would decline to eat as a guest at their table, requesting a "side-table" apart. Her baptism in the Old

South Meeting House on 18 August 1771 was also unusual, for slaves were not baptized in the church.

She made no strong protests against slavery in her poetry, and because of this, she has been denigrated by some black contemporaries. Her sensitivity to enslavement, however, was expressed subtly. "Afric's muse," as she called herself in "An Hymn to Humanity," gave a small, muted cry in an early poem, the much-quoted "On Being Brought from Africa to America." The poem, dismissed by black scholar Benjamin Brawley as a "pathetic little juvenile poem," is coated with the missionary spirit; nevertheless, her pride in her "sable race" comes through. Reference to her African identity is made also in other poems. Phillis's "To the Right Honourable William, Earl of Darmouth, His Majesty's Secretary of State for North America, Etc.," believed to be her most unreserved polemic against slavery, combines a call for freedom with black patriotism. It was in her letters, however, that concern about slavery was strongest.

The poetry of Phillis Wheatley has been categorized by latter-day critics as smoothly crafted, but artificial and imitative of Pope and the neoclassicists. Others believe that when she veers away from the occasional poems, her originality and literary qualities shine through, as evident in her "An Hymn to Humanity" and the much anthologized "On Imagination."

The idea of collecting her poems in a book occurred to Phillis in the summer of 1772, and in November, John Wheatley sent the manuscript with a letter and biographical notes to Archibald Bell, a London bookseller. Bell showed the poems to the countess of Huntington, who was delighted with them but questioned that Phillis was real. To confirm her existence, eighteen eminent Bostonians testified to the authenticity of the young African poet.

Meanwhile, her poor health provoked concern among the Wheatleys, and the family physician suggested that sea air might help. Nathaniel Wheatley, Mary's twin, was to make a business trip to England, so it was decided that Phillis should go with him. Before sailing in May of 1773, Phillis wrote a poem, "A Farewell to America."

In England, she was introduced to society by the countess of Huntingdon, and the modest demure Phillis suddenly found herself a celebrity in London. "Thoughtful people praised her; titled people dined her, and the press extolled the name of Phillis Wheatley, the African poetess."[4]

While abroad, her first and only book, *Poems on Various Subjects, Religious and Moral*, was published in 1773. The small octavo of thirty-nine poems was dedicated to the countess of Huntingdon. Scipio Moorhead, a Boston slave artist and poet, drew the familiar portrait of her, depicting a pensive young black girl with quill in hand for the frontispiece. She composed a poem for him, "To S. M., a Young African Painter, on Seeing His Works."

Because of the illness of her beloved mistress, Phillis returned to America after four months away. Sailing for home, she left behind both accolades and a land unmarred by slavery.

The death of Mrs. Wheatley on March 3, 1774 left a deep void in her life. Her grief was revealed in a letter dated March 21, 1774 to her close black friend, Obour Tanner, of Newport, Rhode Island: "I have lately met with a great trial in the death of my mistress; let us imagine the loss of a parent, sister, or brother, the tenderness of all these were united in her."[5]

The reality of the Revolution now caught up with Phillis, and after the Battle of Bunker Hill, she left Cambridge, which was occupied by the British, to visit her friend Obour Tanner in Rhode Island. Upon learning that Washington had taken command of the American troops in Cambridge, she sent him a letter and poem in 1775. Washington liked the "elegant lines" and on 2 February 1776 responded by inviting her to Cambridge to be received by him and his officers.

On 12 March 1778 grief again descended on the Wheatley household when John Wheatley died at the age of seventy-two. Biographer G. Herbert Renfro believes that upon his death Phillis was set free by Mary Wheatley Lathrop, although Renfro adds, "the opinion prevails with many writers that she was emancipated in her twentieth year, the year of her mistress's decease."[6] Brawley claims, "Before she left America, Phillis was formally manumitted."[7]

A month after the death of John Wheatley, Phillis married John Peters, a "respectable" man of Boston who operated a grocery on Court Street and an acquaintance of Obour Tanner. A free and handsome black man who sported a cane and wig, Peters was said to have been engaged in various occupations at one time or another as merchant, lawyer, and physician. There are conflicting views about him, however; most agree that he was talented, but possessed a superior air and disagreeable mannerisms.

Her husband's personality and disdain for work in any occupation beneath his "fancied dignity" drove them into poverty. After her two oldest children—who like their mother had been in frail health—died, she supported herself and her youngest child through drudgery in a cheap boarding house. On 5 December 1784 in Boston, the "African poetess" at the age of thirty-one gave up her life and felt "the iron hand of pain no more." The death of her last child followed immediately, and the two were buried at the same time in an unknown location—a pathetic end to the life of a celebrated poet who had been honored on two continents.

Her last published poem in the *Boston Magazine*, September 1784, was on the death of an infant son. This poem was selected from a projected volume of poems to be published and dedicated to Benjamin Franklin. The manuscript was borrowed, however, and despite John Peters's solicitations for its return, it was never recovered.

NOTES

1. Brawley, *Negro in Literature and Art*, pp. 17–18.
2. Ibid., p. 18.
3. Renfro, *Life and Works of Phillis Wheatley*, p. 11.
4. Williams, *History of the Negro Race*, p. 198.
5. Renfro, *Life and Works of Phillis Wheatley*, p. 29.
6. Ibid., p. 21.
7. Brawley, *Early Negro American Writers*, p. 32.

SELECTED SOURCES

Primary

Wheatley, Phillis. *Poems on Various Subjects, Religious and Moral.* By Phillis Wheatley, Negro Servant to Mr. John Wheatley, of Boston, in New England. London: Printed for A. Bell, Bookseller, Aldgate; and sold by Messrs. Cox and Berry, King-Street, Boston, 1773.

Secondary

Brawley, Benjamin Griffith. *Early Negro American Writers: Selections with Biographical and Critical Introductions.* Chapel Hill: University of North Carolina Press, 1935.
————. *The Negro in Literature and Art in the United States.* Rev. ed. New York: Duffield & Co., 1921.
Heartman, Charles Frederick. *Phillis Wheatley (Phillis Peters): A Critical Attempt and a Bibliography of Her Writings.* New York: Charles F. Heartman, 1915.
Hull, Gloria T. "Black Women Poets from Wheatley to Walker." In *Sturdy Black Bridges: Visions of Black Women in Literature,* edited by Roseann P. Bell, Bettye J. Parker, and Beverly Guy-Sheftall. Garden City, N.Y.: Anchor Press/Doubleday, 1979.
Kaplan, Sidney. *The Black Presence in the Era of the American Revolution, 1770–1800.* New York: New York Graphic Society in association with the Smithsonian Institution Press, 1973.
Mason, Julian E. *The Poems of Phillis Wheatley.* Chapel Hill: University of North Carolina Press, 1966.
Porter, Dorothy B. *North American Negro Poets: A Bibliographical Checklist of Their Writings, 1760–1944.* Hattiesburg, Miss.: Book Farm, 1945.
Renfro, G. Herbert. *Life and Works of Phillis Wheatley, Containing Her Complete Poetical Works, Numerous Letters, and a Complete Biography of This Famous Poet of a Century and a Half Ago.* Also a sketch of the life of Mr. Renfro by Leila Amos Pendleton. Washington, D.C.: Robert L. Pendleton, 1916.
Richmond, Merle A. *Bid the Vassal Soar: Interpretive Essays on the Life and Poetry of Phillis Wheatley and George Moses Horton.* Washington, D.C.: Howard University Press, 1974.
Robinson, William H. *Phillis Wheatley: A Bio-Bibliography.* Boston: G. K. Hall & Co., 1981.

————. *Phillis Wheatley in the Black American Beginnings*, Broadside Critics Series, no. 5, edited by James A. Emanuel. Detroit: Broadside Press, 1975.

Schomburg, Arthur A. *A Bibliographical Checklist of American Negro Poetry*. New York: Charles F. Heartman, 1916.

Thatcher, B[enjamin] B[ussey]. *Memoir of Phillis Wheatley, a Native African and a Slave*. Boston: Geo. W. Light, 1834.

Williams, George W. *History of the Negro Race, 1619–1800*. New York: G. P. Putnam's Sons, 1883.

On Being Brought from Africa to America

Twas mercy brought me from my Pagan land,
Taught my benighted soul to understand
That there's a God, that there's a Saviour too.
Once I redemption neither sought nor knew.
Some view our sable race with scornful eye;
"Their colour is a diabolic dye."
Remember, Christians, Negroes, black as Cain,
May be refined, and join the angelic train.

To S. M., a Young African Painter, on Seeing His Works

To show the lab'ring bosom's deep intent,
And thought in living characters to paint.
When first thy pencil did those beauties give,
And breathing figures learnt from thee to live,
How did those prospects give my soul delight,
A new creation rushing on my sight?
Still, wond'rous youth! each noble path pursue,
On deathless glories fix thine ardent view:
Still may the painter's and the poet's fire
To aid thy pencil, and thy verse conspire!

And may the charms of each seraphic theme
Conduct thy footsteps to immortal fame!
High to the blissful wonders of the skies
Elate thy soul, and raise thy wishful eyes.
Thrice happy, when exalted to survey
That splendid city, crown'd with endless day,
Whose twice six gates on radiant hinges ring:
Celestial Salem blooms in endless spring.
   Calm and serene thy moments glide along,
And may the muse inspire each future song!
Still, with the sweets of contemplation bless'd,
May peace with balmy wings your soul invest!
But when these shades of time are chas'd away,
And darkness ends in everlasting day,
On what seraphic pinions shall we move,
And view the landscapes in the realms above?
There shall thy tongue in heav'nly murmurs flow,
And there my muse with heav'nly transport glow:
No more to tell of Damon's tender sighs,
Or rising radiance of Aurora's eyes,
For nobler themes demand a nobler strain,
And purer language on th' ethereal plain.
Cease, gentle muse! the solemn gloom of night
Now seals the fair creation from my sight.

On Imagination

Thy various works, imperial queen, we see,
How bright their forms! how deck'd with pomp by thee!
Thy wond'rous acts in beauteous order stand,
And all attest how potent is thine hand.
   From Helicon's refulgent heights attend
Ye sacred choir; and my attempts befriend:
To tell her glories with a faithful tongue,
Ye blooming graces, triumph in my song.
   Now here, now there; the roving Fancy flies,

'Till some lov'd object strikes her wand'ring eyes.
Whose silken fetters all the senses bind,
And soft captivity involves the mind.
    Imagination! who can sing thy force?
Or who describe the swiftness of thy course?
Soaring through air to find the bright abode,
Th' empyreal palace of the thund'ring God,
We on thy pinions can surpass the wind,
And leave the rolling universe behind:
From star to star the mental optics rove,
Measure the skies, and range the realms above.
There in one view we grasp the mighty whole,
Or with new worlds amaze th' unbounded soul.

    Though winter frowns to Fancy's raptur'd eyes
The fields may flourish, and gay scenes arise;
The frozen deeps may break their iron bands,
And bid their waters murmur o'er the sands.
Fair Flora may resume her fragrant reign,
And with her flow'ry riches deck the plain;
Sylvanus may diffuse his honors round,
And all the forest may with leaves be crown'd.
Show'rs may descend, and dews their gems disclose
And nectar sparkle on the blooming rose.
    Such is thy pow'r, nor are thine orders vain,
O thou the leader of the mental train:
In full perfection all thy works are wrought,
And thine the sceptre o'er the realms of thought.
Before thy throne the subject-passions bow,
Of subject-passions sov'reign ruler thou;
At thy command joy rushes on the heart,
And through the glowing veins the spirits dart.
Fancy might now her silken pinions try
To rise from earth, and sweep th' expanse on high;
From Tithon's bed now might Aurora rise,
Her cheeks all glowing with celestial dies,
While a pure stream of light o'erflows the skies,
The monarch of the day I might behold,
And all the mountains tipt with radiant gold.
But I reluctant leave the pleasing views,

Which Fancy dresses to delight the Muse;
Winter austere forbids me to aspire,
And northern tempests damp the rising fire;
They chill the tides of Fancy's flowing sea,
Cease then, my song, cease the unequal lay.

A Funeral Poem on the Death of C. E., an Infant of Twelve Months

Through airy roads he wings his infant flight
To purer regions of celestial light;
Enlarg'd he sees unnumber'd systems roll,
Beneath him sees the universal whole,
Planets on planets run their destin'd round,
And circling wonders fill the vast profound,
Th' ethereal now, and now th' empyreal skies
With growing splendors strike his wond'ring eyes:
The angels view him with delight unknown,
Press his soft hand, and seat him on his throne;
Then smiling thus: "To this divine abode,
"The seat of saints, of seraphs, and of God,
"Thrice welcome thou." The raptur'd babe replies,
"Thanks to my God, who snatch'd me to the skies;
"E'er vice triumphant had possess'd my heart,
"E'er yet the tempter had beguil'd my heart,
"E'er yet on sin's base actions I was bent,
"E'er yet I knew temptation's dire intent;
"E'er yet the lash for horrid crimes I felt,
"E'er vanity had led my way to guilt;
"But, soon arriv'd at my celestial goal
"Full glories rush on my expanding soul."
Joyful he spoke: Exulting cherubs round
Clapt their glad wings, the heav'nly vaults resound.
    Say, parents, why this unavailing moan?
Why heave your pensive bosoms with the groan?

Ann Plato

1820?–?

A young female schoolteacher, Ann Plato, born possibly in 1820 in Hartford, Connecticut, wrote the only book by a black between 1840 and 1865 "avowedly issued as a collection of essays."[1] The book, *Essays; Including Biographies and Miscellaneous Pieces in Prose and Poetry,* was printed in Hartford in 1841. It is considered also to be the second book published by a black American female. The 121-page volume contains sixteen short essays, four biographies, and twenty poems with themes on religion, morality, and death.

Information about the youthful author's life is sparse; what little is known comes from the introduction, "To the Reader," by her minister, the Reverend W. C. Pennington, pastor of the Colored Congregational Church of Hartford. The author's age is thought to have been around twenty years old, although some of the poems could have been composed when she was in her early teens. She may have had an Indian father, a speculation based on her poem, "The Natives of America," which laments Indian oppression.

The Reverend Pennington in his introduction continually refers to Ann Plato's youth and appeals for support for the young author, because "young writers are always in *peculiar need of patronage* [Pennington's italics] to enrich them to set out in a successful and useful career."[2] He speaks of her as "having a large heart full of chaste and pious affection for those of her own age and sex,"[3] and compares her to Phillis Wheatley in her fondness for reading, particularly the Holy Scriptures.

Ann Plato's writings reflect the moralistic and Christian fervor of her New England Puritan milieu. As a teacher in the black Zion Methodist Church School of Hartford, she was dedicated to the education of her students, who were not much younger than herself. She impressed upon them in her writings the importance of learning and leading a pious and industrious life.

The titles of her essays attest to her Puritan values on the subjects of "Education," "Religion," "Benevolence," and "Employment." They have been harshly judged as "self-righteous, routine essays . . . which, mercifully brief, have most value as species of essay compositions of the times."[4] Her poems have suffered similar criticism; they have been condemned as "absolutely jejune and devoid of intellectual and imaginative life [so] that their service to her race is doubtful."[5] She, like Phillis Wheatley before her, has also been accused of lacking originality. Only her romantic poem, "Forget Me Not," has been singled out over the others as "the most appealing."

The biographies in the book are eulogies to young female friends and acquaintances who died young. They are praised for their moral characters, good dispositions, and pious living. Noticeable are the spelling and grammatical errors in the work.

Ann Plato did not write of her race in bondage. The sole poem on enslavement is "To the First of August," which extolls Britain's abolishing slavery in the West Indies in 1838.

Despite the contemporary adverse literary criticism, however, her importance as a young black female seeking to express herself through literary endeavors during the colonial period of black bondage and female constraints is of great significance. The author's subjects were objects of her concern and were part of her daily life. Her philosophy was rooted in the preparation for death and a better life in eternity.

It is a pity that more about the girl Pennington called a "Platoess" is not known, and it is regrettable that we have only one book by her.

NOTES

1. Loggins, *Negro Author*, p. 248.
2. Plato, *Essays*, p. xix.
3. Ibid., p. xx.
4. Robinson, *Early Black American Poets*, p. 113.
5. White and Jackson, *Anthology of Verse*, p. 6.

SELECTED SOURCES

Primary

Plato, Ann. *Essays; Including Biographies and Miscellaneous Pieces in Prose and Poetry.* With an introduction by the Rev. James W. C. Pennington. Hartford, 1841.

Secondary

Loewenberg, Bert James, and Bogin, Ruth. *Black Women in Nineteenth-Century American Life: Their Words, Their Thoughts, Their Feelings.* University Park: Pennsylvania State University Press, 1976.

Loggins, Vernon. *The Negro Author: His Development in America.* New York: Columbia University Press, 1931.

Robinson, William H., Jr. *Early Black American Poets.* Dubuque, Iowa: Wm. C. Brown Publishers, 1969.

Sherman, Joan R. *Invisible Poets: Afro-Americans of the Nineteenth-Century.* Urbana: University of Illinois Press, 1974.

Stetson, Erlene. *Black Sister: Poetry by Black American Women, 1746–1980.* Bloomington: Indiana University Press, 1981.

White, Newman Ivey, and Jackson, Walter Clinton. *An Anthology of Verse by American Negroes.* Durham, N.C.: Trinity College Press, 1924.

To the First of August

Britannia's isles proclaim
    That freedom is their theme;
And we do view those honored lands
    With soul-delighting mien.

And unto those they held in gloom,
    Gave ev'ry one their right;
They did disdain fell slavery's shade,
    And trust in freedom's light.

Then unto ev'ry British blood,
    Their noble worth revere,
And think them ever noble men,
    And like them hence appear.

Advice to Young Ladies

Day after day I sit and write,
   And thus the moments spend—
The thought that occupies my mind,—
   Compose to please my friend.

And then I think I will compose,
   And thus myself engage—
To try to please young ladies minds,
   Which are about my age.

The greatest word that I can say,—
   I think to please, will be,
To try and get your learning young,
   And write it back to me.

But this is not the only thing
   That I can recommend;
Religion is most needful for
   To make in us a friend.

At thirteen years I found a hope,
   And did embrace the Lord;
And since, I've found a blessing great,
   Within his holy word.

Perchance that we may ne'er fulfill,
   The place of aged sires,
But may it with God's holy will,
   Be ever our desires.

Forget Me Not

When in the morning's misty hour,
When the sun beems gently o'er each flower;
When thou dost cease to smile benign,

And think each heart responds with thine,
When seeking rest among divine,
                    Forget me not.

When the last rays of twilight fall,
And thou art pacing yonder hall;
When mists are gathering on the hill,
Nor sound is heard save mountain rill,
When all around bids peace be still,
                    Forget me not.

When the first star with brilliance bright,
Gleams lonely o'er the arch of night;
When the bright moon dispels the gloom,
And various are the stars that bloom,
And brighten as the sun at noon,
                    Forget me not.

When solemn sighs the hollow wind,
And deepen'd thought enraps the mind;
If e'er thou doest in mournful tone,
E'er sigh because thou feel alone,
Or wrapt in melancholy prone,
                    Forget me not.

When bird does wait thy absence long,
Nor tend unto its morning song;
While thou art searching stoic page,
Or listening to an ancient sage,
Whose spirit curbs a mournful rage,
                    Forget me not.

Then when in silence thou doest walk,
Nor being round with whom to talk;
When thou art on the mighty deep,
And do in quiet action sleep;
If we no more on earth do meet,
                    Forget me not.

When brightness round thee long shall bloom,
And knelt remembering those in gloom;
And when in deep oblivion's shade,

This breathless, mouldering form is laid,
And thy terrestrial body staid,
        Forget me not.

Education

This appears to be the great source from which nations have become civilized, industrious, respectable and happy. A society or people are always considered as advancing, when they are found paying proper respect to education. The observer will find them erecting buildings for the establishment of schools, in various sections of their country, on different systems, where their children may at an early age commence learning, and having their habits fixed for higher attainments. Too much attention, then, can not be given to it by people, nation, society or individual. History tells us that the first settlers of our country soon made themselves conspicuous by establishing a character for the improvement, and diffusing of knowledge among them.

We hear of their inquiry, how shall our children be educated? and upon what terms or basis shall it be placed? We find their questions soon answered to that important part; and by attending to this in every stage of their advancement, with proper respect, we find them one of the most enlightened and happy nations on the globe.

It is, therefore, an unspeakable blessing to be born in those parts where wisdom and knowledge flourish; though it must be confessed there are even in these parts several poor, uninstructed persons who are but little above the late inhabitants of this country, who knew no modes of the civilized life, but wandered to and fro, over the parts of the then unknown world.

We are, some of us, very fond of knowledge, and apt to value ourselves upon any proficiency in the sciences; one science, however, there is, worth more than all the rest, and that is the science of living well—which shall remain "when tongues shall cease," and "knowledge shall vanish away."

It is owing to the preservation of books, that we are led to embrace their contents. Oral instructions can benefit but one age and one set of hearers; but these silent teachers address all ages and all nations. They may sleep for a while and be neglected; but whenever the desire of information springs up in the human breast, there they are with mild wisdom ready to instruct and please us.

Zilpha Elaw

?–?

Zilpha Elaw, a black female minister and teacher of the antebellum period, is virtually unknown. Parts of her life, however, can be pieced together through her autobiography, *Memoirs of the Life, Religious Experience, Ministerial Travels and Labours, of Mrs. Zilpha Elaw, an American Female of Colour; Together with Some Account of the Great Religious Revivals in America* (1846).[1] This rare personal narrative was written and published by the author in London while she was there preaching the Gospel. Before returning home to the States, she decided to present the kind people of England a "keepsake," her book, which she wrote in her dedication would be a "lively memento of my Christian esteem, and affectionate desires for your progressive prosperity and perfection in the Christian calling." Mrs. Elaw's 172-page memoir has no chapter divisions. Like the histories of other black female ministers that followed, it is suffused with religious visions, prophecies, dreams, and directives from God.

Zilpha Elaw was called to preach when sexism prevailed in the church and society. She was a sister in religious spirit to Jarena Lee, Old Elizabeth, Amanda Berry Smith, and the recently discovered Rebecca Cox Jackson. Her spiritual awakening was experienced at the age of fourteen, and in 1808, she joined the Methodist Episcopal Society, attended its classes for six months, and was baptized.

Two years later, she married Joseph Elaw, "a very respectable young man," but a church "backslider" who was fond of music and dancing. The couple moved to Burlington, New Jersey, and Zilpha became the mother of a daughter whose name is unknown. After a year of marriage, Joseph Elaw tried to persuade his wife to renounce her religion, but to no avail. Zilpha took seriously ill in 1816 and was not expected to live, but prayed over by a Quakeress preacher, she regained her strength. Believing her recovery to be an act of God, she began her "special calling" as a family or household minister for five years.

Despite her feeling that she was divinely inspired to preach, Zilpha nevertheless had misgivings. She became very ill again in 1819 and underwent an operation. While recuperating, she saw a supernatural figure by her bedside, who informed her that she would learn God's will at a camp meeting.

Fifteen months after the "angelic announcement," she heard of such a gathering to be held far from her home. Helped financially by the children of the Quaker family who had kept her, she was able to attend the meeting. There she was suddenly prompted to preach by "an invisible and heavenly personage sent from God." The listeners were so inspired by her words that the ministers and the Society sanctioned her to preach.

When Zilpha's husband became ill with consumption, she had to work hard to keep the family together. At his death in January 1823, she opened a school in Burlington to meet burial and living expenses. Assisted by the Quakers, she taught the "coloured children, whom the white people refused to admit into their seminaries, and who had been suffered formerly to run about the streets for want of a teacher."[2] Zilpha does not mention the extent of her own schooling, but observes that she was not prohibited from any school because of the color of her skin.

The communications from God urging her to preach persisted. Agonizing over the calling, she sought the advice of friends and ministers. Finally, she placed her daughter with a relative and set out with the help of friends on a religious trek to do the Lord's bidding. Her preaching took her up and down the eastern seaboard, and through the New England states, New York, and Rhode Island. She bravely ventured into the slave states of Virginia, Maryland, and Washington, D.C., where Satan worried her: she feared being arrested and sold as a slave. As a free black female minister preaching the Lord's words, she was an oddity, and wherever she went, she drew crowds of onlookers—black and white, men and women.

As a preacher to the slaves, she seemed more concerned with saving their souls than praying for their freedom, although fear of the South's retaliation may have restrained her. She did give voice in her book to her feelings about bondage at the death of a slave minister who had confided in her his fervent desire to be free. She wrote: "Oh, the abominations of slavery! . . . however lenient its inflictions, and mitigated its atrocities, indicates an oppressor, the oppressed, and the oppression."[3]

In 1837, she had a "remarkable vision" while visiting religious friends. Once again she heard a message from the Almighty instructing her to go upon the high seas. Three years later, in July 1840, she left for London, prior to Amanda Berry Smith's triumphant journey in 1878. Zilpha stayed in England for five years, preaching over a thousand sermons to the throngs who flocked to hear her. She made a host of friends and was treated to many courtesies. And here the story ends.

Zilpha Elaw wanted her "humble memoirs" to be read long after she ceased from her "earthly labours and existence." It took 137 years for the book to be revived. We should never lose it again.

NOTES

1. Zilpha Elaw was brought to my attention by Jualynne Dodson. The book is not noted in such reference sources as the *Dictionary Catalog of the Negro Collection of the Fisk University Library; Dictionary Catalog of the Arthur B. Spingarn Collection of Negro Authors* or the *Dictionary Catalog of the Jesse E. Moorland Collection of Negro Life and History of Howard University's Founders Library; Dictionary Catalog of the Schomburg Collection of Negro Literature and History, New York Public Library;* Monroe Work's *A Bibliography of the Negro in Africa and America;* or *Black American Writers, 1773–1949: A Bibliography and Union List* compiled by Geraldine O. Matthews and the African-American Materials Project Staff.
2. Elaw, *Memoirs*, p. 52.
3. Ibid., p. 73.

SOURCES

Primary

Elaw, Zilpha. *Memoirs of the Life, Religious Experience, Ministerial Travels and Labours, of Mrs. Zilpha Elaw, an American Female of Colour; Together with Some Account of the Great Religious Revivals in America.* London: Published by the author, 1846.

Secondary

Andrews, William L., ed. *Sisters of the Spirit: Three Black Women's Autobiographies of the Nineteenth-Century.* Bloomington: Indiana University Press, 1986.

Mrs. Elaw

I was born in the United States of America, in the State of Pennsylvania, and of religious parents. When about six years of age, my mother's parents, who resided on their own farm, far in the interior of America, at a distance of many hundred miles, came to visit us. My parents had three children then living; the eldest, a boy about twelve years of age, myself, and a younger sister. On his return, my grandfather took my brother with him, promising to bring him up to the business of his farm; and I saw him not again until more than thirty years afterwards.

At twelve years of age I was bereaved of my mother, who died in child-birth of her twenty-second child, all of whom, with the exception of three, died in infancy. My father, having placed my younger sister under the care of her aunt, then consigned me to the care of Pierson and Rebecca Mitchel, with whom I remained until I attained the age of eighteen. After I had been with the above-mentioned persons one year and six months, it pleased God to remove my dear father to the world of spirits; and, being thus bereft of my natural guardians, I had no other friends on earth to look to, but those kind benefactors under whom my dear father had placed me.

But that God whose mercy endureth for ever, still continued mindful of me; but oh, what a change did I experience in my new abode from that to which I had been accustomed. In my father's house, family devotion was regularly attended to morning and evening; prayer was offered up, and the praises of God were sung; but the persons with whom I now resided were Quakers, and their religious exercises, if they observed any, were performed in the secret silence of the mind; nor were religion and devotion referred to by them in my hearing, which rendered my transition from home the more strange; and, being very young, and no apparent religious restraint being laid upon me, I soon gave way to the evil propensities of an unregenerate heart, which is enmity against God, and heedlessly ran into the ways of sin, taking pleasure in the paths of folly. But that God, whose eyes are ever over all His handy works, suffered me not unchecked to pursue the courses of sin. My father's death frequently introduced very serious reflections into my mind; and often was I deeply affected, and constrained to weep before God, when no human eye beheld my emotion. But, notwithstanding these seasons of serious contrition, my associations with the juvenile members of the family were too generally marked by the accustomed gaities of a wanton heart. Our childish conversations sometimes turned upon the day of judgment, and our appearance in the presence of the great God on that portentous occasion, which originated in my breast the most solemn emotions whenever I was alone; for I felt myself to be so exceedingly sinful, that I was certain of meeting with condemnation at the bar of God. I knew not what to do; nor were there any persons to whom I durst open my mind upon the subject, and therefore remained ignorant of the great remedy disclosed by the plan of salvation afforded by the gospel, and incapable of religious progress. I was at times deeply affected with penitence, but could not rightly comprehend what it was that ailed me. Sometimes I resolutely shook off all my impressions, and became more thoughtless than before; one instance, in particular, is so rivetted on my memory, that I shall never forget it when ever I glance back upon my youthful life. On this occasion I was talking very foolishly, and even ventured to take the name of God in vain, in order to cater to the sinful tastes of my companions; it well pleased their carnal minds, and they laughed with delight at my profanity; but, whilst I was in the very act of swearing, I looked up, and imagined that I saw God looking down and frowning upon me: my tongue was instantly silenced; and I retired from my frolicsome companions to reflect upon what I had said and done. To the praise of divine mercy, that God who willeth not the death of a sinner, but rather that all should turn unto him and live, did not even now abandon me, but called me by an effectual call through the following dream. It was a prevailing notion in that part of the world with many, that whatever a person dreamed between the times of twilight and sunrise, was prophetically ominous, and would shortly come to pass; and, on that very night, after I had offended my heavenly Father by taking His name in vain, He aroused and alarmed my spirit, by presenting before me in a dream the awful terrors of the day of judgment, accompanied by its terrific thunders. I thought that the Angel Gabriel came and proclaimed that time should be no longer; and he said, "Jehovah was about to judge the world, and execute judgment on it." I then exclaimed in my dream, "Oh, Lord, what shall I do? I am unprepared to meet thee." I then meditated an escape, but could not effect it; and in this horrific dilemma I awoke: the day was just dawning; and the intense horror of my guilty mind was such as to defy description. I was now about fourteen years of age; and this dream proved an effectual call to my soul. I meditated deeply upon it, my spirits became greatly depressed, and I wept excessively. I was naturally of a very lively and active disposition, and the shock my feelings had sustained from this alarming dream, attracted the attention of my mistress, who inquired the reason of so great a change. I related my dream to her, and also stated my sentiments with respect to it: she used every endeavour to comfort me, saying that it was only a dream; that dreams have nothing ominous in them; and I ought not to give myself any more concern respecting it: but she failed in her attempt to tranquillize my mind, because the convictions of my sinfulness in the sight of God, and incompetency to meet my Judge, were immoveable and distressing. I now gave myself much to meditation, and lisped out of my simple and feeble prayers to God, as well as my limited apprehensions and youthful abilities admitted. About this time, the Methodists made their first appearance in that part of the country, and I was permitted to attend their meetings once a fortnight, on the Sabbath afternoons, from which I derived great satisfaction; but the divine work on my soul was a very gradual one, and my way was prepared as the dawning of the morning. I never experienced that terrific dread of hell by which some Christians appear to have been exercised; but I felt a godly sorrow for sin, in having grieved my God by a course of disobedience to His commands. I had been trained to attend the Quaker meetings; and, on their preaching occasions, I was pleased to be in attendance, and often found comfort from the word ministered by them; but I was, notwithstanding, usually very much cast down on account of my sins before God; and in this state I continued many months before I could attain sufficient confidence to say, "My Lord and my God." But as the darkness was gradually dispelled, the light dawned upon my mind, and I increased in knowledge daily; yet I possessed no assurance of my acceptance before God; though I enjoyed a greater peace of mind in waiting upon my heavenly father than at any previous time; my prayer was daily for the Lord to assure me of the forgiveness of my sins; and I at length proved the verification of the promise, "They that seek shall find"; for, one evening, whilst singing one of the songs of Zion, I distinctly saw the Lord Jesus approach me with open arms, and a most divine and heavenly smile upon his countenance. As He advanced towards me, I felt that his very looks spoke, and said, "Thy prayer is accepted, I own thy name." From that day to the present, I have never entertained a doubt of the manifestation of his love to my soul.

Yea, I may say further than this; because, at the time when this occurrence took place, I was milking in the cow stall; and the manifestation of his presence was so clearly apparent, that even the beast of the stall turned her head and bowed herself upon the ground. Oh, never, never shall I forget the scene. Some persons, perhaps, may be incredulous, and say, "How can these things be, and in what form did He appear?" Dear reader, whoever thou art, into whose hands this narrative may fall, I will try to gratify thee by endeavouring to describe his manifestation. It occurred as I was singing the following lines:—

"Oh, when shall I see Jesus,
　And dwell with him above;
And drink from flowing fountains,
　Of everlasting love.
When shall I be delivered
　From this vain world of sin;
And, with my blessed Jesus,
　Drink endless pleasures in?"

As I was milking the cow and singing, I turned my head, and saw a tall figure approaching, who came and stood by me. He had long hair, which parted in the front and came down on his shoulders; he wore a long white robe down to the feet; and, as he stood with open arms and smiled upon me, he disappeared. I might have tried to imagine, or persuade myself, perhaps, that it had been a vision presented merely to the eye of my mind; but, the beast of the stall gave forth her evidence to the reality of the heavenly appearance; for she turned her head and looked round as I did; and when she saw, she bowed her knees and cowered down upon the ground. I was overwhelmed with astonishment at the sight, but the thing was certain and beyond all doubt. I write as before God and Christ, and declare, as I shall give an account to my Judge at the great day, that every thing I have written in this little book, has been written with conscientious veracity and scrupulous adherence to truth.

After this wonderful manifestation of my condescending Saviour, the peace of God which passeth understanding was communicated to my heart; and joy in the Holy Ghost, to a degree, at the least, unutterable by my tongue and indescribable by my pen; it was beyond my comprehension; but, from that happy hour, my soul was set at glorious liberty; and, like the Ethiopic eunuch, I went on my way rejoicing in the blooming prospects of a better inheritance with the saints in light.

This, my dear reader, was the manner of my soul's conversion to God, told in language unvarnished by the graces of educated eloquence, nor transcending the capacity of a child to understand.

The love of God being now shed abroad in my heart by the Holy Spirit, and my soul transported with heavenly peace and joy in God, all the former hardships which pertained to my circumstances and situation vanished; the work and duties which had previously been hard and irksome were now become easy and pleasant; and the evil propensities of my disposition and temper were subdued beneath the softening and refining pressure of divine grace upon my heart.

Jarena Lee

1783–?

Jarena Lee felt imbued with a religious mission in life, and because of this, she bravely defied the conservative sex biases of the church to become, as she contended, the "first female preacher of the First African Methodist Episcopal Church." As an evangelist, Mrs. Lee sometimes traveled on foot to spread her religious message and would walk as far as 16 miles to preach. When over forty years old, the unordained minister logged 2,325 miles on the Gospel circuit. She preached up and down the Eastern Shore and traveled into sections of Illinois and Ohio, converting blacks and whites to the Christian faith.

Believed to have been born free in Cape May, New Jersey, 11 February 1783, to parents who were "wholly ignorant of the knowledge of God," she left home at the age of seven to work as a maid sixty miles away. Her first religious experience occurred relatively late in life—in 1804 when she was twenty-one. Listening to a local Protestant missionary who was holding services in a schoolroom, she became overwhelmed by the "weight of my sins." Afterward, she contemplated committing suicide and credited the "unseen arm of God" with preventing her.

After moving to Philadelphia, she was inspired by the preaching of the Reverend Richard Allen, founder of the African Methodist Episcopal Church, and became "gloriously" converted to God. Five years later, she experienced a religious sanctification of mind and spirit and was moved by a vision to preach. She went to see the Reverend Allen, who informed her that she could hold prayer meetings, but that his discipline did not call for women preachers. Later writing in her journal, she reflected on the decision, noting, "And why should it be thought impossible, heterodox, or improper for a woman to preach? seeing the Saviour died for the woman as well as for the man."[1]

In 1811, she married Joseph Lee, pastor of a congregation in Snow Hill, a town six miles from Philadelphia. Feeling that she did not fit into the community, she became discontented the first year and told her husband she wanted them to move. But because he felt that his obligation as a minister came first, he refused. Jarena Lee's passionate but stifled desire to preach caused her morbid suffering and ill health. Tragedy beleaguered the family, and five members died within six years, one of whom was her husband. Two children survived, a two-year-old and a six-month-old baby.

Her suppressed calling to preach was miraculously released in the church of Reverend Allen, where she went to hear the Reverend Richard Williams give a sermon. In the course of his preaching, she suddenly discerned that he had "lost the spirit." At that moment, she sprang to her feet and gave a stirring exhortation, writing in her journal later, "God made manifest his power in a manner sufficient to show the world that I was called to labor according to my ability."[2] Immediately following her sermon, the Reverend Allen, now bishop of the African Episcopal Methodist Church, rose to sanction her right to preach.

From that time on, Jarena Lee's life was dedicated to evangelizing, and as she did so, she challenged the prejudices against women as ministers of God. To tell others of her work, she had printed in Philadelphia a pamphlet of twenty-four pages entitled *The Life and Religious Experience of Jarena Lee, a Coloured Lady, Giving an Account of Her Call to Preach the Gospel* (1836). She kept a journal while traveling which she combined with her autobiography, and this expanded version appeared in 1849 as *Religious Experience and Journal of Mrs. Jarena Lee, Giving an Account of Her Call to Preach the Gospel*. She sold her book at church meetings to meet expenses. One source has categorized it as a "narrative of her pilgrimage with exhortations to the faithful and to those who might be falling away, designed, it appears, to make the story of her life an extension of her preaching."[3]

Mrs. Lee published the journal herself in Philadelphia after the A. M. E. Book Concern hesitated on the grounds it was "written in such a manner that it is impossible to decipher much of the meaning contained in it."[4] Since the book questioned sexism in the church, this could have influenced the all-male book committee's balking at publishing it, as well as their request that "Sister Lee . . . favor" the members with an explanation of portions they could not understand.

This enlightening autobiography of a black nineteenth-century female minister left a literary pattern for other women who followed her. I could not find a record of her death, but there is a questionable listing of another work by a Jarena Lee in Daniel Murray's *Preliminary List of Books and Pamphlets by Negro Authors, for Paris Exposition and Library of Congress* (1900). This entry indicates that Jarena Lee published a ninety-three-page work, *The Color of Solomon* (1895), in Philadelphia. At the age of 112?

NOTES

1. Lee, *Religious Experience*, p. 11.
2. Ibid., p. 17.
3. Mason and Green, *Journeys*, p. 74.
4. Payne, *History of the A. M. E. Church*, p. 190.

SELECTED SOURCES

Primary

Lee, Jarena. *Religious Experience and Journal of Mrs. Jarena Lee, Giving an Account of Her Call to Preach the Gospel.* Philadelphia, 1849.

Secondary

Andrews, William L., ed. *Sisters of the Spirit: Three Black Women's Autobiographies of the Nineteenth-Century.* Bloomington: Indiana University Press, 1986.
Foster, Frances Smith. "Adding Color and Contour to Early American Self-Portraitures: Autobiographical Writings of Afro-American Women." In *Conjuring: Black Women, Fiction, and Literary Tradition,* edited by Marjorie Pryse and Hortense J. Spillers. Bloomington: Indiana University Press, 1985.
Loewenberg, Bert James, and Bogin, Ruth. *Black Women in Nineteenth-Century American Life: Their Words, Their Thoughts, Their Feelings.* University Park: Pennsylvania State University Press, 1976.
McMahon, Jean, ed. *Gifts of Power: The Writings of Rebecca Jackson, Black Visionary, Shaker Eldress.* Amherst: University of Massachusetts Press, 1981.
Mason, Mary Grimley, and Green, Carol Hurd, eds. *Journeys: Autobiographical Writings by Women.* Boston: G. K. Hall & Co., 1979.
Payne, Daniel Alexander. *History of the African Methodist Episcopal Church.* Edited by C. S. Smith. Nashville: Publishing House of the A. M. E. Sunday School Union, 1891.

My Call to Preach the Gospel

Between four and five years after my sanctification, on a certain time, an impressive silence fell upon me, and I stood as if some one was about to speak to me, yet I had no such thought in my heart.—But to my utter surprise there seemed to sound a voice which I thought I distinctly heard, and most certainly understand, which said to me, "Go preach the Gospel!" I immediately replied aloud, "No one will believe me." Again I listened, and again the same voice seemed to say—"Preach the Gospel; I will put words in your mouth, and will turn your enemies to become your friends."

At first I supposed that Satan had spoken to me, for I had read that he could transform himself into an angel of light for the purpose of deception. Immediately I went into a secret place, and called upon the Lord to know if he had called me to preach, and whether I was deceived or not; when there appeared to my view the form and figure of a pulpit, with a Bible lying thereon, the back of which was presented to me as plainly as if it had been a literal fact.

In consequence of this, my mind became so exercised, that during the night following, I took a text and preached in my sleep. I thought there stood before me a great multitude, while I expounded to them the things of religion. So violent were my exertions and so loud were my exclamations, that I awoke from the sound of my own voice, which also awoke the family of the house where I resided. Two days after I went to see the preacher in charge of the African Society, who was the Rev. Richard Allen, the same before named in these pages, to tell him that I felt it my duty to preach the gospel. But as I drew near the street in which his house was, which was in the city of Philadelphia, my courage began to fail me; so terrible did the cross appear, it seemed that I should not be able to bear it. Previous to my setting out to go to see him, so agitated was my mind, that my appetite for my daily food failed me entirely. Several times on my way there, I turned back again; but as often I felt my strength again renewed, and I soon found that the nearer I approached to the house of the minister, the less was my fear. Accordingly, as soon as I came to the door, my fears subsided, the cross was removed, all things appeared pleasant—I was tranquil.

I now told him, that the Lord had revealed it to me, that must preach the gospel. He replied, by asking, in what sphere I wished to move in? I said, among the Methodists. He then replied, that a Mrs. Cook, a Methodist lady, had also some time before requested the same privilege; who, it was believed, had done much good in the way of exhortation, and holding prayer meetings; and who had been permitted to do so by the verbal license of the preacher in charge at the time. But as to women preaching, he said that our Discipline knew nothing at all about it—that it did not call for women preachers. This I was glad to hear, because it removed the fear of the cross—but no sooner did this feeling cross my mind, than I found that a love of souls had in a measure departed from me; that holy energy which burned within me, as a fire, began to be smothered. This I soon perceived.

O how careful ought we to be, lest through our by-laws of church government and discipline, we bring into disrepute even the word of life. For as unseemly as it may appear now-a-days for a woman to preach, it should be remembered that nothing is impossible with God. And why should it be thought impossible, heterodox, or improper for a woman to preach? seeing the Saviour died for the woman as well as for the man.

If the man may preach, because the Saviour died for him, why not the woman? seeing he died for her also. Is he not a whole Saviour, instead of a half one? as those who hold it wrong for a woman to preach, would seem to make it appear.

Did not Mary *first* preach the risen Saviour, and is not the doctrine of the resurrection the very climax of Christianity—hangs not all our hope on this, as argued by St. Paul? Then did not Mary, a woman, preach the gospel? for she preached the resurrection of the crucified Son of God.

But some will say that Mary did not expound the Scripture, therefore, she did not preach, in the proper sense of the term. To this I reply, it may be that the term *preach* in those primitive times, did not mean exactly what it is now *made* to mean; perhaps it was a great deal more simple then, than it is now—if it were not, the unlearned fishermen could not have preached the gospel at all, as they had no learning.

To this it may be replied, by those who are determined not to believe that it is right for a woman to preach, that the disciples, though they were fishermen and ignorant of letters too, were inspired so to do. To which I would reply, that though they were inspired, yet that inspiration did not save them from showing their ignorance of letters, and of man's wisdom; this the multitude soon found out, by listening to the remarks of the envious Jewish priests. If then, to preach the gospel, by the gift of heaven, comes by inspiration solely, is God straitened; must he take the man exclusively? May he not, did he not, and can he not inspire a female to preach the simple story of the birth, life, death, and resurrection of our Lord, and accompany it too with power to the sinner's heart. As for me, I am fully persuaded that the Lord called me to labor according to what I have received, in his vineyard. If he has not, how could he consistently bear testimony in favor of my poor labors, in awakening and converting sinners?

In my wanderings up and down among men, preaching according to my ability, I have frequently found families who told me that they had not for several years been to a meeting, and yet, while listening to hear what God would say by his poor female instrument, have believed with trembling tears rolling down their cheeks, the signs of contrition and repentance towards God. I firmly believe that I have sown seed, in the name of the Lord, which shall appear with its increase at the great day of accounts, when Christ shall come to make up his jewels.

At a certain time, I was beset with the idea, that soon or late I should fall from grace and lose my soul at last. I was frequently called to the throne of grace about this matter, but found no relief; the temptation pursued me still. Being more and more afflicted with it, till at a certain time, when the spirit strongly impressed it on my mind to enter into my closet and carry my case once more to the Lord; the Lord enabled me to draw nigh to him, and to his mercy seat, at this time, in an extraordinary manner; for while I wrestled with him for the victory over this disposition to doubt whether I should persevere, there appeared a form of fire, about the size of a man's hand, as I was on my knees; at the same moment there appeared to the eye of faith a man robed in a white garment, from the shoulders down to the feet; from him a voice proceeded, saying: "Thou shalt never return from the cross." Since that time I have never doubted, but believe that God will keep me until the day of redemption. Now I could adopt the very language of St. Paul, and say, that nothing could have separated me from the love of God, which is in Christ Jesus. Since that time, 1807, until the present, 1833, I have not even doubted the power and goodness of God to keep me from falling, through the sanctification of the spirit and belief of the truth.

Nancy Gardener Prince

1799–?

Nancy Gardener, who left home at the age of eight to become a domestic worker, changed the course of her life through her determination to become a teacher, author, and humanitarian. She was born in the seafaring commercial town of Newburyport in northeastern Massachusetts on 15 September 1799. Of mixed African and Indian ancestry, she had an Indian grandmother who was captured and made a slave by the English, and a slave grandfather, who fought in the Revolutionary War at the Battle of Bunker Hill.

Her father, Thomas Gardener,[1] was born in Nantucket and died in Newburyport when Nancy was only three months old. He left his wife a widow for the second time with two small children to support. Alone and without help, Nancy's mother returned to live in Gloucester with her father. She remarried and had six children by her third husband, who was unkind to Nancy and her sister. A seaman, he was pressed into service during the War of 1812 by a British privateer when his brig was captured. In 1813, he died of dropsy in the British dominions.

Alone anew with a six-week-old baby and several children, Nancy's young and inexperienced mother became distraught and was never the same again. Poverty-stricken, she had great difficulty taking care of her children, and three of the oldest were placed with various families. After being away from home, Nancy came back to help, but then had to leave again to find employment. At the age of fourteen, she went to Salem to work for a family of seven. Her labor was harsh and unremitting, and within three months, her health failed. She returned to Gloucester to recuperate, and after recovering, she and her eldest sister left once more to seek work in Salem. Nancy tried to keep watch over her scattered family and her wandering mother. At one time, she rescued her oldest sister from a house of ill-repute in Boston, where the girl had been lured to work unwittingly.

Finding what she called her "peace with God," Nancy was baptized on 9 May 1817. She became a deeply religious woman and dedicated her life and work to religious teachings.

At the age of twenty-three, when most women of that time resigned themselves to whatever their station was in life, Nancy said she wanted "to do something for herself." She decided to learn an unspecified "trade," which more than likely was sewing. But after seven years of "toil and anxiety," she made up her mind to leave the country.

On 1 September 1823, a Mr. Prince returned from a voyage to Russia. He had been a visitor in the home of Nancy's mother following a similar trip when Nancy was around twelve or thirteen years old. He had been born in Marlborough and had lived with several families in the city. After moving to Gloucester, he went into service with a sea captain, and on his last voyage in 1812 to Russia, he had remained to become a servant of a princess in the czar's court. On 15 February 1824, Nancy married Mr. Prince, and by 15 April, the newlyweds had sailed for Russia. Nancy was the sole female on board.

Mr. Prince's Christian name is never revealed by Nancy in her narrative. It could be that he was much older than she when they were married, and she addressed him by his last name out of respect, or perhaps she was imitating the manners of white wives for whom she had worked. She does not write of love for him, nor does she relate any intimacies between them. Mr. Prince's personality and physical appearance are never described, so that he remains a nebulous figure in the background of her narrative. Whether she married for love or as a way to leave the country is open to question.

Whatever the case, in Russia, Nancy Prince learned the language of the nobility in six months. It was, she said, a "modern Greek, French and English"; she also acquired some "proficiency in French." She began to board children, which led to her making baby linen and childrens' garments. So successful was this enterprise that she was able to hire a journeywoman and apprentices. Despite her modest education, except for the "kind counsel" of her religious grandfather and "pious teachers," Nancy Prince wrote perceptively of her years in Russia, colorfully describing the people, customs, and events during her stay.

The cold of Russia, however, did not agree with her lungs, and after nine and a half years she returned home. Mr. Prince, unable to leave at will the services of the czar, stayed two years longer and accumulated some property. They never saw each other again. Mr Prince died in Russia before he could follow her.

In Boston, Mrs. Prince found that having lived in another country gave her a different stature and a broader view of life. She met many interesting and prominent people, including Lucretia Mott, and became involved in antislavery and religious activities. Upon seeing black orphans shut out of asylums because of their color, she helped found a home for them as she had for the children of St. Petersburg.

With the emancipation of blacks in the West Indies in 1833, Nancy Prince envisioned "a field of usefulness spread out before me." Encouraged by friends in the ministry who were concerned about the moral status and conditions of the freed blacks, Nancy Prince sailed on 16 November 1840 for Jamaica. A year later, she published a slender fifteen-page pamphlet in Boston about her trip entitled *The West Indies: Being a Description of the Islands, Progress of Christianity, Education, and Liberty among the Colored Population Generally.* Later the pamphlet became part of a book entitled *A Narrative of the Life and Travels of Mrs. Nancy Prince,* published in 1850 by the author. In her book, Mrs. Prince tells of a return trip to Jamaica where she attempted to set up a Free Labor School for blacks. Unfortunately, because of insurrection and lawlessness on the island, she was forced to leave for her own safety.

Back in the States after a voyage dangerous for a free woman of color traveling alone, she was beset by adversity. Failing health, business setbacks, and the theft of her personal goods all made it necessary for friends to come to her rescue in 1848 and 1849.

Nancy Prince published a second edition of her book in 1853 and a third in 1856. In the preface of the third edition, from which the following selection is excerpted, she writes of having lost the power of her arms and hopes to obtain her necessities through the sale of her "little work."

When and how Nancy Prince died is not known. Only her book offers information about her, including a small hint at her appearance when she mentions a minister in Jamaica who showed much commiseration for her misfortune at being so black.

Her narrative was belittled in the 1930s by a black male critic as "a naive description of the impressions received by an American Negro woman during a sojourn of several years in Russia. . . . It contains also an account of a visit to Jamaica."[2] This summary ignores the impact of Mrs. Prince's West Indies experience and her witnessing of important historical events. For in the section on Jamaica, she exposes the exploitation of the newly emancipated blacks by their own people, by the church, and by whites, and gives us a good description of the deplorable conditions under which they lived.

And her book offers more: it is the account of a free black nineteenth-century woman who was determined to improve her own life as well as the lives of others. It gives the impressions of a woman of color living and traveling in other countries when most of her people were locked in slavery.

Nancy Prince wrote not as a writer but as a woman who wanted to share her experiences, observations, and life with others. This she did with compassion and humility.

NOTES

1. The name is spelled "Gardener" in the first edition of the narrative, and "Gardner" in subsequent editions.
2. Loggins, *Negro Author*, p. 229.

SELECTED SOURCES

Primary

Prince, Mrs. Nancy [Gardener]. *A Narrative of the Life and Travels, of Mrs. Nancy Prince.* Boston: Published by the author, 1850.
———. *A Narrative of the Life and Travels of Mrs. Nancy Prince.* 3d ed. Boston: Published by the author, 1856.
———. *The West Indies: Being a Description of the Islands, Progress of Christianity, Education, and Liberty among the Colored Population Generally.* Boston: Dow & Jackson Printers, 1841.

Secondary

Foster, Frances Smith. "Adding Color and Contour to Early American Self-Portraitures: Autobiographical Writings of Afro-American Women." In *Conjuring: Black Women, Fiction, and Literary Tradition,* edited by Marjorie Pryse and Hortense J. Spillers. Bloomington: Indiana University Press, 1985.
Loewenberg, Bert James, and Bogin, Ruth. *Black Women in Nineteenth-Century American Life: Their Words, Their Thoughts, Their Feelings.* University Park: Pennsylvania State University Press, 1976.
Loggins, Vernon. *The Negro Author: His Development in America.* New York: Columbia University Press, 1931.

Her Return Back to Jamaica, and the State of Things at That Time

As soon as I was able, I commenced my task of collecting funds for my Free Labor School in Jamaica. I collected in Boston and vicinity, in New York and Philadelphia, but not sufficient to make up the required sum, and I was obliged to take fifty dollars from my own purse, thinking that when I returned to Jamaica, they would refund the money to me. April 15th, embarked on board the brig Norma, of New York, for Jamaica. I arrived at Kingston May 6th, and found every thing different from what it was when I left; the people were in a state of agitation, several were hanged, and the insurrection was so great that it was found necessary to increase the army to quell it. Several had been hanged. On the very day I arrived a man was hanged for shooting a man as he passed through the street. Such was the state of things that it was not safe to be there.

A few young people met to celebrate their freedom on an open plain, where they hold their market; their former masters and mistresses, envious of their happiness, conspired against them, and thought to put them down by violence. This only served to increase their numbers; but the oppressors were powerful, and succeeded in accomplishing their revenge, although many of them were relations. There was a rule among the slave holders, to take care of the children they have by their slaves; they select them out and place them in asylums. Those who lived with their white fathers were allowed great power over their slave mothers and their slave children; my heart was often grieved to see their conduct to their poor old grandparents. Those over twenty-one were freed in 1834, all under twenty-one were to serve their masters till twenty-one. It is well known that at that time, the children, alike with others, received twenty-five dollars a head for their relatives. Were I to tell all my eyes have seen among that people, it would not be credited. It is well known that those that were freed, knowing their children were still in bondage, were not satisfied. In the year 1838, general freedom throughout the British Islands gave the death blow to the power of the master, and mothers received with joy their emancipated children; they no longer looked the picture of despair, fearing to see their mulatto son or daughter beating or abusing their younger brothers and sisters of a darker skin. On this occasion there was an outrage committed by those who were in power. What little the poor colored people had gathered during their four years of freedom, was destroyed by violence; their fences were broken down, and their horses and hogs taken from them. Most of the mulattoes and mustees are educated, many of them are very poor, some are very rich; the property is left to the oldest daughter, she divides it with her brothers and sisters; since slavery ended many of them have married; those who are poor, and mean to live in sin, make for New Orleans and other slave States; many of the planters left the island when slavery was abolished. In June, 1841, a number of people arrived from Sierra Leone at Jamaica; these were maroons who were banished from the island. They were some of the original natives who inhabited the mountains, and were determined to destroy the whites. These maroons would secrete themselves in trees, and arrest the whites as they passed along; they would pretend to guide them, when they would beat and abuse them as the whites did their slaves; the English, finding themselves defeated in all their plans to subdue them, proposed to take them by craft. They made a feast in a large tavern in Kingston, and invited them to come. After they had eaten, they were invited on board three ships of war that were all ready to set sail for Sierra Leone; many of them were infants in their mother's arms, they were well taken care of by the English and instructed; they were removed about the year 1796—they are bright and intelligent; I saw and conversed with them; when they heard of the abolition of slavery, they sent a petition to Queen Victoria that they might return to Jamaica, which was granted. Several of them were very old when they returned; they were men and women when they left the island, they had not forgot the injuries they had received from the hands of man, nor the mercies of God to them, nor his judgments to their enemies. Their numbers were few, but their power was great; they say the island, of right, belongs to them. Had there been a vessel in readiness, I should have come back immediately, it seemed useless to attempt to establish a Manual Labor School, as the government was so unsettled that I could not be protected. Some of my former friends were gone as teachers to Africa, and some to other parts of the island. I called on the American Consul to consult with him, he said that although such a school was much wanted, yet every thing seemed so unsettled that I had no courage to proceed. I told him there was so much excitement that I wished to leave the island as soon as he could find me a passage, it seemed useless to spend my time there. As soon as it was known that I intended to return, a movement was made to induce me to remain. I was persuaded to try the experiment for three months, not thinking their motive was bad. Before I left the United States, I got all that was needed, within fifty dollars. The fifty dollars I got from my own purse, expecting they would pay me. It cost me ten dollars for freight, and twenty-five for passage money; these people that I had hoped to serve, were much taken up with the things I had brought, they thought that I had money, and I was continually surrounded; the thought of color was no where exhibited, much notice was taken of me. I was invited to breakfast in one place, and to dine in another, &c. A society was organized; made up of men and women of authority. A constitution was drafted by my consent, by those who were appointed to meet at my rooms. Between the time of the adjournment they altered it to suit themselves. At the time appointed we came together with a spirit apparently becoming any body of Christians; most of them were members of Christian churches. The meeting was opened with reading the Scriptures and prayer. Then said the leader, since our dear sister has left her native land and her friends to come to us, we welcome her with our hearts and hands. She will dwell among us, and we will take care of her—Brethren, think of it! after which he sat down, and the Constitution was called for. The Preamble held out all the flattery that a fool could desire; after which they commenced the articles, supposing that they could do as they thought best. The fourth article unveiled their design. As we have designed to take care of our sister, *we the undersigned will take charge of all she has brought;* the vote was called, every person rose in a moment except myself; every eye was upon me; one asked me why I did not vote, I made no answer—they put the vote again and again, I remained seated. Well, said the President, we can do nothing without her vote; they remained some time silent, and then broke up the meeting. The next day the deacon called to see what the state of my mind was, and some of the women proposed that we should have another meeting. I told then no, I should do no more for them. As soon as they found they could not get the things in the way they intended, they started to plunder me; but I detected their design, and was on my guard. I disposed of the articles, and made ready to leave when an opportunity presented. A more skilful plan than this, Satan never designed, but the power of God was above it. It is not surprising that this people are full of deceit and lies, this is the fruit of slavery, it makes master and slaves knaves. It is the rule where slavery exists, o swell the churches with numbers, and hold out such doctrines as *obedience to tyrants* is a duty to God.

Frances Ellen Watkins Harper

1825–1911

Frances Ellen Watkins Harper's works as a poet, essayist, and novelist span a half century in Afro-American literature. Born an only child to free parents in Baltimore, Maryland, in 1825, she lost her mother before she was three years old. An aunt took her in, and she was educated in a school for free black children operated by her uncle, the Reverend William Watkins. At the school, "daily Bible readings, composition practice, and Watkins's zealous abolitionist teachings shaped her young mind."[1]

When she was almost thirteen, she was sent out to work and found a job as a housekeeper with a family who owned a bookstore. Frances was taught to sew, and during her spare time, she sought to educate herself further by reading the books surrounding her. Possessing "an ardent thirst for knowledge and a remarkable talent for composition,"[2] she wrote an article at the age of fourteen. Her early poetry and prose was published in Baltimore papers, and because they were unusually good for a person of her age, some readers questioned their originality.

Although she herself was free, Frances wanted to live in a state without slavery. In 1850, she went to teach at Union Seminary, an African Methodist Episcopal church school near Columbus, Ohio, which later became a part of Wilberforce University. A teacher of domestic science, she was the school's first black female instructor in vocational work.

About 1851, she had a small volume of prose, *Forest Leaves* (also called *Autumn Leaves*), privately printed in Baltimore. This work has been lost. The following year, she left for Little York, Pennsylvania, to teach. Here she was given a job of instructing and keeping in order what she called "fifty-three untrained little urchins" in her classroom. A delicate woman, she found the work overtaxing.

Adding to her unhappiness was the memory of the plight of her people under slavery in her homestead in Maryland. Their enslavement touched her, too, she thought, and she wrote that they were "homeless in the land of our birth and worse off than strangers in the home of our nativity." While in Little York, she heard distressing stories of the "poor, half-starved, flying fugitive" passing through the Underground Railroad, which added to her depression.

When in 1853 Maryland enacted a law that forbade free blacks from entering the state on pain of punishment by imprisonment or being remanded into slavery, she was deeply stirred by the story of a free man who defied the law and was sold into slavery in Georgia. The man had attempted to escape by hiding on a boat headed north, but was discovered. He died later in slavery from "exposure and suffering." Writing to a friend about the incident, Frances promised, "Upon that grave, I pledged myself to the anti-slavery cause."

In 1854, she went to Philadelphia and stayed at an Underground Railroad station, where she read antislavery documents and met runaway slaves. She wanted to work with the organization, but because of her youth, she was not asked. While there, she published the poem "Eliza Harris Crossing the River on Ice." Subsequent to her stay in Philadelphia, she visited antislavery offices in Boston and New Bedford where she was invited to give a lecture on "Education and the Elevation of the Colored Race" in August of 1854.

Frances Ellen Watkins became a permanent lecturer for the Maine Anti-Slavery Society that year and traveled throughout New England, Ohio, and New York. Her success and growing recognition led the Pennsylvania Anti-Slavery Society to hire her. "From 1854 to 1860, Miss Watkins took to the podium in more than eight states, usually daily but often two or three times a day, in the cause of emancipation."[3]

A small, dignified woman with penetrating black eyes and a handsome strong face, she had a "clear, plaintive melodious voice" and "musical speech." The "bronze muse," as she was called, was a spellbinding orator who combined poetry with her lectures on the degradation of slavery. When reading her poems and speaking without notes for the freedom of her people, she was reported to have kept large audiences enthralled.

A generous and sympathetic woman, she not only labored for Abolitionism but extended personal and financial assistance to people in need. To

Mrs. John Brown, she wrote sympathetic letters, referring to her as "the noble wife of the hero of the nineteenth century," For two weeks, Frances Ellen Watkins stayed with Mrs. Brown in the Philadelphia home of William Still, while Mrs. Brown awaited her husband's execution. William Still, who was Frances's close friend and a conductor on the Underground Railroad, wrote of her as being not only a "leading colored poet in the United States" but also "one of the most liberal contributors, as well as one of the ablest advocates of the Underground Rail Road and the slave."[4]

Her literary career was launched when her book *Poems on Miscellaneous Subjects* was published in 1854 while she was in Boston. The volume carried a preface by famed Abolitionist William Lloyd Garrison, who predicted a "poetic reputation" for her. The poems focused on slavery with an emphasis on the female's plight. Other themes dealt with temperance and Christianity. The latter part of the book contained discourses on "Christianity," "The Bible," and "The Colored People in America." Some of the Abolitionist poems have been characterized as showing the influence of Longfellow and Whittier. Clearly she was the most popular black poet of the fifties, and her book was reprinted in 1857, 1858, 1864, and 1871.

Five years following the initial publication of this book, Frances became the first Afro-American women to publish a short story, "The Two Offers." This story of a white woman who gives up an offer of marriage to devote her life to abolishing slavery has been referred to as probably being the American Negro's first attempt at the short-story form. It was published in the *Anglo-African* in September and October of 1859.

On 22 November 1860, Frances Ellen Watkins married Fenton Harper, a widower in Cincinnati, Ohio, and with the money from her lectures and the sales of her book, she bought a small farm near Columbus. She settled down now, and her public appearances diminished as she became a homemaker and mother of one child named Mary.

The next significant phase of her literary and public career began six years later after the end of the Civil War. This period in her life will be discussed in the next section.

NOTES

1. Sherman, *Invisible Poets*, p. 62.
2. Still, *The Underground Railroad*, p. 756.
3. Sherman, *Invisible Poets*, p. 63.
4. Still, *The Underground Railroad*, p. 755.

SELECTED SOURCES

Primary

Watkins, Frances Ellen. *Poems on Miscellaneous Subjects*. Boston: J. B. Yerrinton & Son, Printers, 1854.

Secondary

Brown, Hallie Quinn. *Homespun Heroines and Other Women of Distinction*. Xenia, Ohio: Aldine, 1926.

Dannett, Sylvia G. L. *Profiles of Negro Womanhood*. Vol. 1, *1619–1900*. Yonkers, N.Y.: Educational Heritage, 1964.

Gilbert, Sandra M., and Gubar, Susan. *The Norton Anthology of Literature by Women: The Tradition in English*. New York: W. W. Norton & Co., 1985.

Loewenberg, Bert James, and Bogin, Ruth. *Black Women in Nineteenth-Century American Life: Their Words, Their Thoughts, Their Feelings*. University Park: Pennsylvania State University Press, 1976.

Loggins, Vernon. *The Negro Author: His Development in America*. New York: Columbia University Press, 1931.

Majors, Monroe Alphus. *Noted Negro Women, Their Triumphs and Activities*. Chicago: Donohue & Henneberry, 1893.

Robinson, William H., Jr. *Early Black American Poets*. Dubuque, Iowa: Wm. C. Brown Publishers, 1969.

Sherman, Joan R. *Invisible Poets: Afro-Americans of the Nineteenth Century*. Urbana: University of Illinois Press, 1974.

Still, William. *The Underground Railroad*. Philadelphia: Porter & Coates, 1872.

The Slave Mother

Heard you that shriek? It rose
   So wildly on the air,
It seem'd as if a burden'd heart
   Was breaking in despair.

Saw you those hands so sadly clasped—
   The bowed and feeble head—
The shuddering of that fragile form—
   That look of grief and dread?

Saw you the sad, imploring eye?
  Its every glance was pain,
As if a storm of agony
  Were sweeping through the brain.

She is a mother pale with fear,
  Her boy clings to her side,
And in her kyrtle vainly tries
  His trembling form to hide.

He is not hers, although she bore
  For him a mother's pains;
He is not hers, although her blood
  Is coursing through his veins!

He is not hers, for cruel hands
  May rudely tear apart
The only wreath of household love
  That binds her breaking heart.

His love has been a joyous light
  That o'er her pathway smiled,
A fountain gushing ever new,
  Amid life's desert wild.

His lightest word has been a tone
  Of music round her heart,
Their lives a streamlet blent in one—
  Oh, Father! must they part?

They tear him from her circling arms,
  Her last and fond embrace:—
Oh! never more may her sad eyes
  Gaze on his mournful face.

No marvel, then, those bitter shrieks
  Disturb the listening air;
She is a mother, and her heart
  Is breaking in despair.

The Two Offers

"What is the matter with you, Laura, this morning? I have been watching you this hour, and in that time you have commenced a half-dozen letters and torn them all up. What matter of such grave moment is puzzling your dear little head, that you do not know how to decide?"

"Well, it is an important matter: I have two offers for marriage, and I do not know which to choose."

"I should accept neither, or to say the least, not at present."

"Why not?"

"Because I think a woman who is undecided between two offers has not love enough for either to make a choice; and in that very hesitation, indecision, she has a reason to pause and seriously reflect, lest her marriage, instead of being an affinity of souls or a union of hearts, should only be a mere matter of bargain and sale, or an affair of convenience and selfish interest."

"But I consider them both very good offers, just such as many a girl would gladly receive. But to tell you the truth, I do not think that I regard either as a woman should the man she chooses for her husband. But then if I refuse, there is the risk of being an old maid, and that is not to be thought of."

"Well, suppose there is? Is that the most dreadful fate that can befall a woman? Is there not more intense wretchedness in an ill-assorted marriage, more utter loneliness in a loveless home, than in the lot of the old maid who accepts her earthly mission as a gift from God and strives to walk the path of life with earnest and unfaltering steps?"

"Oh! what a little preacher you are. I really believe that you were cut out for an old maid—that when nature formed you she put in a double portion of intellect to make up for a deficiency of love; and yet you are kind and affectionate. But I do not think that you know anything of the grand, overmastering passion, or the deep necessity of woman's heart for loving."

"Do you think so?" resumed the first speaker, and bending over her work she quietly applied herself to the knitting that had lain neglected by her side during this brief conversation. But as she did so, a shadow flitted over her pale and intellectual brow, a mist gathered in her eyes, and a slight quivering of the lips revealed a depth of feeling to which her companion was a stranger.

But before I proceed with my story, let me give you a slight history of the speakers. They were cousins who had met life under different auspices. Laura Lagrange was the only daughter of rich and indulgent parents who had spared no pains to make her an accomplished lady. Her cousin, Janette Alston, was the child of parents rich only in goodness and affection. Her father had been unfortunate in business and, dying before he could retrieve his fortunes, left his business in an embarrassed state. His widow was unacquainted with his business affairs, and when the estate was settled, hungry creditors had brought their claims and the lawyers had received their fees, she found herself homeless and almost penniless, and she, who had been sheltered in the warm clasp of loving arms, found them too powerless to shield her from the pitiless pelting storms of adversity. Year after year she struggled with poverty and wrestled with want, till her toil-worn hands became too feeble to hold the shattered chords of existence, and her tear-dimmed eyes grew heavy with the slumber of death.

Her daughter had watched over her with untiring devotion, had closed her eyes in death and gone out into the busy, restless world, missing a precious tone from the voices of earth, a beloved step from the paths of life. Too self-reliant to depend on the charity of relations, she endeavored to support herself by her own exertions, and she had succeeded. Her path for a while was marked with struggle and trial, but instead of uselessly repining she met them bravely, and her life became not a thing of ease and indulgence, but of conquest, victory and accomplishments.

At the time when this conversation took place, the deep trials of her life had passed away. The achievements of her genius had won her a position in the literary world, where she shone as one of its bright particular stars. And with her fame came a competence of worldly means, which gave her leisure for improvement and the riper development of her rare talents. And she, that pale, intellectual woman, whose genius gave life and vivacity to the social circle and whose presence threw a halo of beauty and grace around the charmed atmosphere in which she moved, had at one period of her life known the mystic and solemn strength of an all-absorbing love. Years faded into the misty past had seen the kindling of her eye, the quick flushing of her cheek and the wild throbbing of her heart at tones of a voice long since hushed to the stillness of death. Deeply, wildly, passionately, she had loved. . . . This love quickened her talents, inspired her genius and threw over her life a tender and spiritual earnestness.

And then came a fearful shock, a mournful waking from that "dream of beauty and delight." A shadow fell around her path; it came between her and the object of her heart's worship. First a few cold words, estrangement, and then a painful separation: the old story of woman's pride. . . . And thus faded out from that young heart her bright, brief and saddened dream of life. Faint and spirit-broken, she turned from the scenes associated with the memory of the loved and lost. She tried to break the chain of sad associations that bound her to the mournful past; and so . . . her genius gathered strength from suffering, and wondrous power and brilliancy from the agony she hid within the desolate chambers of her soul . . . and turning, with an earnest and shattered spirit, to life's duties and trials, she found a calmness and strength that she had only imagined in her dreams of poetry and song.

We will now pass over a period of ten years, and the cousins have met again. In that calm and lovely woman, in whose eyes is a depth of tenderness tempering the flashes of her genius, whose looks and tones are full of sympathy and love, we recognize the once smitten and stricken Janette Alston. The bloom of her girlhood had given way to a higher type of spiritual beauty, as if some unseen hand had been polishing and refining the temple in which her lovely spirit found its habitation. . . .

Never in the early flush of womanhood, when an absorbing love had lit up her eyes and glowed in her life, had she appeared so interesting as when, with a countenance which seemed overshadowed with a spiritual light, she bent over the deathbed of a young woman just lingering at the shadowy gates of the unseen land.

"Has he come?" faintly but eagerly exclaimed the dying woman. "Oh! how I have longed for his coming, and even in death he forgets me."

"Oh, do not say so, dear Laura. Some accident may have detained him," said Janette to her cousin; for on that bed, from whence she will never rise, lies the once beautiful and lighthearted Laura Lagrange, the brightness of whose eyes had long since been dimmed with tears, and whose voice had become like a harp whose every chord is tuned to sadness—whose faintest thrill and loudest vibrations are but the variations of agony. A heavy hand was laid upon her once warm and bounding heart, and a voice came whispering through her soul that she must die. But to her the tidings was a message of deliverance—a voice hushing her wild sorrows to the calmness of resignation and hope.

Life had grown so weary upon her head—the future looked so hopeless—she had no wish to tread again the track where thorns had pierced her feet and clouds overcast her sky, and she hailed the coming of death's angel as the footsteps of a welcome friend. And yet, earth had one object so very dear to her weary heart. It was her absent and recreant husband; for, since that conversation [ten years earlier], she had accepted one of his offers and become a wife. But before she married she learned that great lesson of human experience and woman's life—to love the man who bowed at her shrine, a willing worshipper.

He had a pleasing address, raven hair, flashing eyes, a voice of thrilling sweetness and lips of persuasive eloquence; and being well versed in the ways of the world, he won his way to her heart and she became his bride, and he was proud of his prize. Vain and superficial in his character, he looked upon marriage not as a divine sacrament for the soul's development and human progression, but as the title deed that gave him possession of the woman he thought he loved. But alas for her, the laxity of his principles had rendered him unworthy of the deep and undying devotion of a pure-hearted woman. But, for a while, he hid from her his true character, and she blindly loved him, and for a short period was happy in the consciousness of being beloved. Though sometimes a vague unrest would fill her soul, when, overflowing with a sense of the good, the beautiful and the true, she would turn to him but find no response to the deep yearnings of her soul—no appreciation of life's highest realities, its solemn grandeur and significant importance. Their souls never met, and soon she found a void in her bosom that his earthborn love could not fill. He did not satisfy the wants of her mental and moral nature: between him and her there was no affinity of minds, no intercommunion of souls.

Talk as you will of woman's deep capacity for loving—of the strength of her affectional nature. I do not deny it. But will the mere possession of any human love fully satisfy all the demands of her whole being? You may paint her in poetry or fiction as a frail vine, clinging to her brother man for support and dying when deprived of it, and all this may sound well enough to please the imaginations of schoolgirls, or lovelorn maidens. But woman—the true woman—if you would render her happy, it needs more than the mere development of her affectional nature. Her conscience should be enlightened, her faith in the true and right established, and scope given to her heaven-endowed and God-given faculties. The true aim of female education should be, not a development of one or two, but all the faculties of the human soul, because no perfect womanhood is developed by imperfect culture. Intense love is often akin to intense suffering, and to trust the whole wealth of a woman's nature on the frail bark of human love may often be like trusting a cargo of gold and precious gems to a bark that has never battled with the storm or buffeted the waves. Is it any wonder, then, that so many life-barks . . . are stranded on the shoals of existence, mournful beacons and solemn warnings for the thoughtless, to whom marriage is a careless and hasty rushing together of the affections? Alas, than an institution so fraught with good for humanity should be so perverted, and [that] that state of life which should be filled with happiness [should] become so replete with misery. And this was the fate of Laura Lagrange.

For a brief period after her marriage her life seemed like a bright and beautiful dream, full of hope and radiant with joy. And then there came a change: he found other attractions that lay beyond the pale of home influences. The gambling saloon had power to win him from her side; he had lived in an element of unhealthy and unhallowed excitements, and the society of a loving wife, the pleasures of a well-regulated home, were enjoyments too tame for one who had vitiated his tastes by the pleasures of sin. There were charmed houses of vice, built upon dead men's loves, where, amid a flow of song, laughter, wine and careless mirth, he would spend hour after hour, forgetting the cheek that was paling through his neglect, heedless of the tear-dimmed eyes peering anxiously into the darkness, waiting or watching his return.

The influence of old associations was upon him. In early life, home had been to him a place of ceilings and walls, not a true home built upon goodness, love and truth. It was a place where velvet carpets hushed his tread, where images of loveliness and beauty, invoked into being by painter's art and sculptor's skill, pleased the eye and gratified the taste, where magnificence surrounded his way and costly clothing adorned his person; but it was not the place for the true culture and right development of his soul. His father had been too much engrossed in making money and his mother in spending it, in striving to maintain a fashionable position in society and shining in the eyes of the world, to give the proper direction to the character of their wayward and impulsive son. His mother put beautiful robes upon his body but left ugly scars upon his soul; she pampered his appetite but starved his spirit. . . .

That parental authority which should have been preserved as a string of precious pearls, unbroken and unscattered, was simply the administration of chance. At one time obedience was enforced by authority, at another time by flattery and promises, and just as often it was not enforced. . . . His early associations were formed as chance directed, and from his want of home training, his character received a bias, his life a shade, which ran through every avenue of his existence and darkened all his future hours. . . .

Before a year of his married life had waned, his young wife had learned to wait and mourn his frequent and uncalled-for absence. More than once had she seen him come home from his midnight haunts, the bright intelligence of his eye displaced by the drunkard's stare, and his manly gait changed to the inebriate's stagger; and she was beginning to know the bitter agony that is compressed in the mournful words "a drunkard's wife."

And then there came a bright but brief episode in her experience. The angel of life gave to her existence a deeper meaning and loftier significance: she sheltered in the warm clasp of her loving arms a dear babe, a precious child whose love filled every chamber of her heart. . . . How many lonely hours were beguiled by its winsome ways, its answering smiles and fond caresses! How exquisite and solemn was the feeling that thrilled her heart when she clasped the tiny hands together and taught her dear child to call God "Our Father!"

What a blessing was that child! The father paused in his headlong career, awed by the strange beauty and precocious intellect of his child; and the mother's life had a better expression through her ministrations of love. And then there came hours of bitter anguish, shading the sunlight of her home and hushing the music of her heart. The angel of death bent over the couch of her child and beckoned it away. Closer and closer the mother strained her child to her wildly heaving breast and struggled with the heavy hand that lay upon its heart. Love and agony contended with death. . . .

But death was stronger than love and mightier than agony, and won the child for the land of crystal founts and deathless flowers, and the poor stricken mother sat down beneath the shadow of her mighty grief, feeling as if a great light had gone out from her soul and that the sunshine had suddenly faded around her path. She turned in her deep anguish to the father of her child, the loved and cherished dead. For a while his words were kind and tender, his heart seemed subdued and his tenderness fell upon her worn and weary heart like rain on perishing flowers, or cooling waters to lips all parched with thirst and scorched with fever. But the change was evanescent; the influence of unhallowed associations and evil habits had vitiated and poisoned the springs of his existence. They had bound him in their meshes, and he lacked the moral strength to break his fetters and stand erect in all the strength and dignity of a true manhood, making life's highest excellence his ideal and striving to gain it.

And yet moments of deep contrition would sweep over him, when he would resolve to abandon the wine cup forever, when he was ready to forswear the handling of another card, and he would try to break away from the associations that he felt were working his ruin. But when the hour of temptation came his strength was weakness, his earnest purposes were cobwebs, his well-meant resolutions ropes of sand—and thus passed year after year of the married life of Laura Lagrange. She tried to hide her agony from the public gaze, to smile when her heart was almost breaking. But year after year her voice grew fainter and sadder, her once light and bounding step grew slower and faltering.

Year after year she wrestled with agony and strove with despair, till the quick eyes of her brother read, in the paling of her cheek and the dimming eye, the secret anguish of her worn and weary spirit. On that wan, sad face he saw the death tokens, and he knew the dark wing of the mystic angel swept coldly around her path.

"Laura," said her brother to her one day, "you are not well, and I think you need our mother's tender care and nursing. You are daily losing strength, and if you will go I will accompany you."

At first she hesitated; she shrank almost instinctively from presenting that pale, sad face to the loved ones at home. . . . But then a deep yearning for home sympathy woke within her a passionate longing for love's kind words, for tenderness and heart support, and she resolved to seek the home of her childhood and lay her weary head upon her mother's bosom, to be folded again in her loving arms, to lay that poor, bruised and aching heart where it might beat and throb closely to the loved ones at home.

A kind welcome awaited her. All that love and tenderness could devise was done to bring the bloom to her cheek and the light to her eye. But it was all in vain; hers was a disease that no medicine could cure, no earthly balm would heal. It was a slow wasting of the vital forces, the sickness of the soul. The unkindness and neglect of her husband lay like a leaden weight upon her heart. . . .

And where was he that had won her love and then cast it aside as a useless thing, who rifled her heart of its wealth and spread bitter ashes upon its broken altars? He was lingering away from her when the death damps were gathering on her brow, when his name was trembling on her lips! Lingering away! when she was watching his coming, though the death films were gathering before her eyes and earthly things were fading from her vision.

"I think I hear him now," said the dying woman, "surely that is his step," but the sound died away in the distance.

Again she started from an uneasy slumber: "That is his voice! I am so glad he has come."

Tears gathered in the eyes of the sad watchers by that dying bed, for they knew that she was deceived. He had not returned. For her sake they wished his coming. Slowly the hours waned away, and then came the sad, soul-sickening thought that she was forgotten, forgotten in the last hour of human need, forgotten when the spirit, about to be dissolved, paused for the last time on the threshold of existence, a weary watcher at the gates of death.

"He has forgotten me," again she faintly murmured, and the last tears she would ever shed on earth sprung to her mournful eyes, and . . . a few broken sentences issued from her pale and quivering lips. They were prayers for strength, and earnest pleading for him who had desolated her young life by turning its sunshine to shadows, it smiles to tears.

"He has forgotten me," she murmured again, "but I can bear it; the bitterness of death is passed, and soon I hope to exchange the shadows of death for the brightness of eternity, the rugged paths of life for the golden streets of glory, and the care and turmoils of earth for the peace and rest of heaven."

Her voice grew fainter and fainter; they saw the shadows that never deceive flit over her pale and faded face and knew that the death angel waited to soothe their weary one to rest, to calm the throbbing of her bosom and cool the fever of her brain. And amid the silent hush of their grief the freed spirit, refined through suffering and brought into divine harmony through the spirit of the living Christ, passed over the dark waters of death as on a bridge of light, over whose radiant arches hovering angels bent. They parted the dark locks from her marble brow, closed the waxen lids over the once bright and laughing eye and left her to the dreamless slumber of the grave.

Her cousin turned from that deathbed a sadder and wiser woman. She resolved more earnestly than ever to make the world better by her example, gladder by her presence, and to kindle the fires of her genius on the altars of universal love and truth. She had a higher and better object in all her writings than the mere acquisition of gold or acquirement of fame. She felt that she had a high and holy mission on the battlefield of existence—that life was not given her to be frittered away in nonsense or wasted away in trifling pursuits. She would willingly espouse an unpopular cause, but not an unrighteous one.

In her the downtrodden slave found an earnest advocate; the flying fugitive remembered her kindness as he stepped cautiously through our Republic to gain his freedom in a monarchial land, having broken the chains on which the rust of centuries had gathered. Little children learned to name her with affection; the poor called her blessed as she broke her bread to the pale lips of hunger.

Her life was like a beautiful story, only it was clothed with the dignity of reality and invested with the sublimity of truth. True, she was an old maid; no husband brightened her life with his love or shaded it with his neglect. No children nestling lovingly in her arms called her mother. No one appended Mrs. to her name.

She was indeed an old maid, not vainly striving to keep up an appearance of girlishness when "departed" was written on her youth, not vainly pining at her loneliness and her isolation. The world was full of warm, loving hearts, and her own beat in unison with them. Neither was she always sentimentally sighing for something to love; objects of affection were all around her, and the world was not so wealthy in love that it had no use for hers. In blessing others she made a life and benediction, and as old age descended peacefully and gently upon her, she had learned one of life's most precious lessons:

that true happiness consists not so much in the fruition of our wishes as in the regulation of desires and the full development and right culture of our whole natures.

Charlotte L. Forten Grimké
1837–1914

Charlotte L. Forten was more fortunate than most antebellum black women of her time. She was born free into a prosperous and leading black family of Philadelphia, Pennsylvania. Her grandfather, James Forten, served as a powder boy in the Revolutionary War, and went on to become an affluent sailmaker. By 1832, he was reputed to be one of the richest men in Philadelphia with a fortune valued at $100,000. A close friend and benefactor of famous Abolitionists, he contributed time and money to the antislavery movement.

A son, Robert Bridges Forten, also a sailmaker, was the father of Charlotte. Born on 17 August 1837 in the city she called "abominable Philadelphia" because of its racial segregation, she was reared in a cultural environment filled with an appreciation for art, music, and literature. A quiet, modest, delicate girl with finely chiseled features, she was imbued with her family's opposition to slavery. In her home, which was known as a "mecca for Abolitionists," she grew to despise the system that kept her people in bondage.

Charlotte's mother, Mary Wood Forten, died when she was in her teens, and the young girl's time was divided between her grandfather's house and that of her uncle, Robert B. Purvis, a wealthy Abolitionist and husband of her aunt, Harriet D. Forten. The Purvis family resided at Byberry, a suburb of Philadelphia, in an "elegant country home" called Saint's Rest by weary Abolitionists who frequented the residence.

Deploring the segregated schools of Philadelphia, Robert Forten had his daughter privately tutored. When she was sixteen, he sent her to study in Salem, Massachusetts, at the Higginson Grammar School for Girls, where she was the only Afro-American among 188 students.

In Salem, she continued to move in Abolitionist circles, living with Charles Lenox Remond, a friend of the family and agent for the Massachusetts Anti-Slavery Society. The young girl developed a warm friendship with thirty-nine-year-old Sarah Parker Remond, sister of Charles, the two sharing their dislike of slavery. At the Remonds' house and in Salem, Charlotte witnessed the visits of antislavery leaders and lecturers, meeting such people as William Lloyd Garrison, Wendell Phillips, William Wells Brown, and Lydia Marie Child. She formed a lasting affinity for John Greenleaf Whittier whom she revered.

Charlotte's talent for writing surfaced at the commencement exercises of the Higginson Grammar School in February 1855, when she wrote the prize-winning class poem "A Parting Hymn." From there, she went to the Salem Normal School, graduating in July 1856.

She began her teaching career at the white Epes Grammar School of Salem, where, oddly enough, she was "graciously received" in that conservative town, becoming the first black teacher of white children. When not teaching, she spent her time working for antislavery causes, attending cultural events, and reading and writing.

Owing to her ill health (which she called "lung disease"), she resigned her Salem post in 1858 and returned to Philadelphia. The *Salem Register* paid her a strong tribute, saying it was "happy to record" her success as a teacher in the public schools. For four years, she lived a quiet life recuperating at her home and Byberry. Occasionally she taught in Aunt Margaretta Forten's Philadelphia school, and again in Salem the winter of 1860 and summer of 1861.

With the outbreak of the Civil War, Charlotte, sensitive to the problems of her people, petitioned the Boston Educational Commission in August 1862 to be sent to teach the freed slaves at Port Royal, South Carolina. When she was rejected, she applied to the Philadelphia Port Royal Relief Association and was accepted. In October 1862, she sailed from New York to Port Royal and then to her home for two years on St. Helena Island. She was the first black teacher to participate in the experiment of educating ex-slaves.

Charlotte Forten's "bequest to humanity," her journal, was begun on 24 May 1854 when she first arrived as a girl in Salem. She wrote as her purpose for keeping the account: "A wish to record the passing events of my life, which, even if quite unimportant to others, naturally possess great interest to myself, and of which it will be pleasant to have some remembrance, has induced me to commence this journal."[1]

She kept the journal in "ordinary board-covered notebooks, writing in ink in a cultivated and legible hand."[2] Of historical importance, it captured the imagination, spirit, thoughts, and life of a highly intelligent, talented, and refined free black woman of the antebellum and Civil War periods. Her journal documents in detail the Port Royal experiment, which demonstrated that the ex-slaves could be educated and notes the bravery of the Negro troops. She is credited with being "among the first to appreciate and set down the hymns and shouts of the Sea Islanders,"[3] which helped preserve the black oral tradition.

The journal reveals her love for the beauty of nature, poetically captured in her prose describing the Sea Islands. She writes of her "inner turmoil" of self-doubts, loneliness, race oppression, and "her inhibitions which prohibited her involvement with a white man."[4] Two white men have been romantically linked with her. One was Dr. Seth Rogers, who treated her in Worcester with a water cure and whom she met again on St. Helena as a surgeon for the black First South Carolina Volunteers; the other was Col. Thomas Wentworth Higginson, dashing leader of the regiment. Her important journal was brought to light by Ray Allen Billington, who edited and published it in 1953 under the title *The Journal of Charlotte L. Forten.* Letters about her Port Royal experiences were published in the *Liberator* and the *Atlantic Monthly* through John Greenleaf Whittier.

Charlotte left Port Royal in June 1864 for Philadelphia. She served as assistant secretary of the teachers' committee of the Freedmen's Aid Society in the Boston area until it disbanded. After the Civil War, she spent her time writing and was published in the *Christian Register, Boston Commonwealth, Liberator,* and the *New England Magazine.* Her translation of M. M. Erckmann-Chartrain's *Madame Therese; or the Volunteers of '92* was issued by Charles Scribner's in 1869.

Upon moving to Washington, D.C., she met Francis James Grimké, prominent pastor of the Fifteenth Street Presbyterian Church and one of the illegitimate sons of Henry Grimké, a South Carolina planter and brother of Abolitionists Angelina and Sarah. They were married on 19 December 1878, and the following June, Francis Grimké graduated from the Princeton Theological Seminary. Charlotte was forty-one at the time of her marriage, thirteen years older than her husband. They had one daughter, Theodora Cornelia, who was born on 1 January 1880 and died six months later. The marriage lasted thirty-six years. Leading an "idyllic life" and sharing similar interests and tastes, they made their home a social and cultural center.

Charlotte Forten Grimké published fourteen poems between 1855 and the 1890s. Modest and filled with doubts about her writing, she once referred to her attempts at verse as "doggerel." But her poem "The Angel's Visit," which was written when she was on the "sunny side of twenty-five" and described a visit from her dead mother in a dream, was highly praised by William Wells Brown. Of the piece, Brown wrote, "for style and true poetical diction, [it] is not surpassed by anything in the English language."[5] Other comments on her verse pointed out its "charm and feeling," and she was said to have "sensitivity and creative skills beyond the ordinary." Perhaps it was as William Wells Brown noted: "Were she white, America would recognize her as one of its brightest gems."[6] Despite this praise, however, others have thought of her as only a minor poet, and she is remembered best for her journal.

In 1887, Charlotte Grimké became an invalid and never really recovered. She died on 23 July 1914. Beloved by her family, she was the subject of a poem by Angelina Weld Grimké, her husband's niece. Entitled "To Keep the Memory of Charlotte Forten Grimké," it ends "And to us here, ah / she remains / A lovely memory / Until Eternity."[7]

NOTES

1. Forten, *Journal*, p. 33.
2. Ibid., p. 31.
3. Sherman, *Invisible Poets*, p. 91.
4. Majors and Saunders, *Black Society*, p. 166.
5. Brown, *Rising Sun*, p. 475.
6. Brown, *Black Man*, p. 199.
7. Angelina W. Grimké, "To Keep the Memory of Charlotte Forten Grimké," in *Negro Poets and Their Poems*, by Robert T. Kerlin (Washington, D.C.: Associated Publishers, 1923), pp. 155–56.

SELECTED SOURCES

Primary

Forten, Charlotte L. *The Journal of Charlotte L. Forten*. Edited by Ray Allen Billington. New York: Dryden Press, 1953.

Secondary

Brown, William Wells. *The Black Man, His Genius, and His Achievements*. New York: Thomas Hamilton; Boston: R. F. Wallcut, 1863.
———. *The Rising Sun; or, The Antecedents and Advancement of the Colored Race*. Boston: A. G. Brown & Co., 1874.
Dannett, Sylvia G. L. *Profiles of Negro Womanhood*. Vol. 1, *1619–1900*. Yonkers, N.Y.: Educational Heritage, 1964.

Davis, Arthur P., and Redding, Saunders. *Cavalcade: Negro American Writing from 1760 to the Present.* Boston: Houghton Mifflin Co., 1971.

"The Forten Family." *Negro History Bulletin* 10 (January 1947):75–79, 95.

Majors, Gerri, and Saunders, Doris E. *Black Society.* Chicago: Johnson Publishing Co., 1976.

Majors, Monroe Alphus. *Noted Negro Women, Their Triumphs and Activities.* Chicago: Donohue & Hennesberry, 1893.

Sherman, Jean R. *Invisible Poets: Afro-Americans of the Nineteenth Century.* Urbana: University of Illinois Press, 1974.

Stetson, Erlene. *Black Sister: Poetry by Black American Women, 1746–1980.* Bloomington: Indiana University Press, 1981.

Wilson, Edmund. "Charlotte Forten and Colonel Higginson." *New Yorker* 30 (10 April 1954):132–47.

Emancipation Day on St. Helena Island

Thursday, New Year's Day, 1863. The most glorious day this nation has yet seen, *I* think. I rose early—an event here—and early we started, with an old borrowed carriage and a remarkably slow horse. Whither were we going? thou wilt ask, dearest A. To the ferry; thence to Camp Saxton, to the Celebration. From the Ferry to the camp the "Flora" took us.

How pleasant it was on board! A crowd of people, whites and blacks, and a band of music—to the great delight of the negroes. Met on board Dr. and Mrs. Peck and their daughters, who greeted me most kindly. Also Gen. S[axton]'s father whom I like much, and several other acquaintances whom I was glad to see. We stopped at Beaufort, and then proceeded to Camp Saxton, the camp of the 1st Reg[iment] S[outh] C[arolina] Vol[unteer]s. The "Flora" c[ou]ld not get up to the landing, so we were rowed ashore in a row boat.

Just as my foot touched the plank, on landing, a hand grasped mine and well known voice spoke my name. It was my dear and noble friend, Dr. Rogers. I cannot tell you, dear A., how delighted I was to see him; how *good* it was to see the face of a friend from the North, and *such* a friend. I think myself particularly blessed to have him for a friend. Walking on a little distance I found myself being presented to Col. Higginson, whereat I was so much overwhelmed, that I had no reply to make to the very kind and courteous little speech with which he met me. I believe I mumbled something, and grinned like a simpleton, that was all. Provoking, isn't it? that when one is most in need of sensible words, one finds them not.

I *cannot* give a regular chronicle of the day. It is impossible. I was in such a state of excitement. It all seemed, and seems still, like a brilliant dream. Dr. R[ogers] and I talked all the time, I know, while he showed me the camp and all the arrangements. They have a beautiful situation, on the grounds once occupied by a very old fort, "De La Ribanchine," built in 1629 or 30. Some of the walls are still standing. Dr. R[ogers] has made quite a good hospital out of an old gin house. I went over it. There are only a few invalids in it, at present. I saw everything; the kitchens, cooking arrangements, and all. Then we took seats on the platform.

The meeting was held in a beautiful grove, a live-oak grove, adjoining the camp. It is the largest one I have yet seen; but I don't think the moss pendants are quite as beautiful as they are on St. Helena. As I sat on the stand and looked around on the various groups, I thought I had never seen a sight so beautiful. There were the black soldiers, in their blue coats and scarlet pants, the officers of this and other regiments in their handsome uniforms, and crowds of lookers-on, men, women and children, grouped in various attitudes, under the trees. The faces of all wore a happy, eager, expectant look.

The exercises commenced by a prayer from Rev. Mr. Fowler, Chaplain of the reg[iment]. An ode written for the occasion by Prof. Zachos, originally a Greek, now Sup[erintendent] of Paris island— was read by himself, and then sung by the whites. Col. H[igginson] introduced Dr. Brisbane in a few elegant and graceful words. He (Dr. B.) read the President's [Emancipation] Proclamation, which was warmly cheered. Then the beautiful flags presented by Dr. Cheever's Church [in New York] were presented to Col. H[igginson] for the Reg[iment] in an excellent and enthusiastic speech, by Rev. Mr. [Mansfield] French. Immediately at the conclusion, some of the colored people—of their own accord sang "My Country Tis of Thee." It was a touching and beautiful incident, and Col. Higginson, in accepting the flags made it the occasion of some happy remarks. He said that *that* tribute was far more effective than any speech he c'ld make. He spoke for some time, and all that he said was grand, glorious. He seemed inspired. Nothing c'ld have been better, more perfect. And Dr. R[ogers] told me afterward that the Col. was much affected. That tears were in his eyes. He is as Whittier says, truly a "sure man." The men all admire and love him. There is a great deal of personal magnetism about him, and his kindness is proverbial. After he had done speaking he delivered the flags to the color-bearers with a few very impressive remarks to them. They each then, Sgt. Prince Rivers and [Cpl.] Robert Sutton, made very good speeches indeed, and were loudly cheered. Gen. Saxton and Mrs. Gage spoke very well. The good Gen. was received with great enthusiasm, and throughout the morning—every little while it seemed to me three cheers were given for him. A Hymn written I believe, by Mr. Judd, was sung, and then all the people united with the Reg[iment] in singing "John Brown." It was grand. During the exercises, it was announced that Fremont was appointed Commander-in chief of the Army, and this was received with enthusiastic and prolonged cheering. But as it is picket news, I greatly fear that it is not true.

We dined with good Dr. R[ogers] at the Col's [T. W. Higginson] table, though, greatly to my regret he, (the Col.) was not there. He partook of some of the oxen, (of which ten had been roasted) with his men. I like his doing that. We had quite a sumptuous dinner. Our party consisted of Dr. R[ogers], Adjutant D[ewhurst], Capt. R[ogers], Mr. and Miss Ware (Mrs. Winsor's brother and sister), Mr. Hall, their cousin, whom I like much, and Mr. and Miss H[unn] and me. We had a merry, delightful dinner. The only part that I did not enjoy was being obliged to read Whittier's Hymn aloud at the table. I wanted Dr. R[ogers] to do it. But he w'ld insist on my doing it. So of course it was murdered. I believe the older I grow the more averse I get to doing anything in public. I have no courage to do such things.

Col. H[igginson] invited us into his tent—a very nice, almost *homelike* one. I noticed a nice secretary, with writing utensils and "Les Miserables" on it. A *wreath* of beautiful oranges hung against the wall, fronting the door. I wanted to have a good look at this tent; but we were hardly seated when the Dr. and Col. were called away for a moment, and Lieut. Col. Billings coming in w'ld insist upon our going into his tent. I did not want to go at all, but he was so *persistent* we had to. I fear he is a somewhat vain person. His tent was very comfortable too, and I noticed quite a large piece of "Secesh" furniture, something between a secretary and a bureau, and quite a collection of photographs and daguerres. But I did not examine them, for my attention was occupied by Col. H[igginson] to whom I showed Whittier's poem, letter and photo. "He looks old," he said to me sadly, as he handed back the picture.

Dr. R[ogers] introduced me to Dr. H[awks] and his wife—pleasant people, and *good* anti-slavery. They mentioned having Liberators with my letters in them. I am sorry they have come down here.

Col. H[igginson] asked me to go out and hear the band play, which I very gladly did. But it stopped just as we stepped outside of the tent. Just then one of the soldiers came up to the Col. and said "Do Cunnel, do ask 'em to play Dixie, just for me, for my lone self." The Col. made the request, but the leader of the band said he feared they w'ld not be able to play the whole tune as they had not the necessary pieces. "Nebber mind," said the man "jus' half a tune will do." It was found impossible to play even that but the leader promised that the next time they came they would be fully prepared to play Dixie for him.

The Dress Parade—the first I had ever seen—delighted me. It was a brilliant sight—the long line of men in their brilliant uniform, with bayonets gleaming in the sunlight. The Col. looked splendid. The Dr. said the men went through with the drill remarkably well. It seemed to me nothing c'ld be more perfect. To me it was a grand triumph—that black regiment doing itself honor in the sight of the white officers, many of whom, doubtless "came to scoff." It was typical of what the race, so long down-trodden and degraded will yet achieve on this Continent.

After the Parade, we went to the Landing, intending to take a boat for Beaufort. But the boat was too crowded, and we decided to wait for another. It was the softest, loveliest moonlight. We sat down among the ruins of the old fort. Just [as soon] as the boat had reached a favorable distance from the shore the band in it commenced playing Home, sweet Home. It was exquisitely beautiful. The lovely moonlight on the water, the perfect stillness around seemed to give new beauty to that ever beautiful old song. And then as my dear friend, Dr. R[ogers] said, "It came *very near* to us all."

Finding the night air damp we went to the tent of Mr. Fowler, the chaplain, whom I like much better in private conversation than as an orator. He is a thoroughly good, earnest man. Thither came Col. H[igginson] and Dr. H[awks]. We sat around the nice fire—the tent has *chimney* and fire place, made by Mr. F[owler]'s own skilful hands.

Col. H[igginson] is a perfectly delightful person in private.—So genial, so witty, so kind. But I noticed when he was silent, a careworn almost sad expression on his earnest, noble face. My heart was full when I looked at him. I longed to say "I thank you, I thank you, for that noble glorious speech." And yet I *c'ld not*. It is always so. I do not know how to talk. Words always fail me when I want them most. The more I feel the more impossible it is for me to speak. It is very provoking. Among other things, Col. H[igginson] said how amusing it was to him—their plan of housekeeping down here. "This morning I was asked "Well, Colonel, how many oxen shall we roast today." And I said, just as calmly as I w'ld have ordered a pound or two of beef, at home.—well I think *ten* will do. And then to be consulted as to how many gallons of molasses, and of vinegar, and how many pounds of ginger w'ld be wanted seemed very odd." I wish I c'ld reproduce for you the dry humorous tones in which this was said. We had a pleasant chat, sitting there in the firelight, and I was most unwilling to go, for besides the happiness of being in the society of the Col. and the Dr. we wanted dreadfully to see the "shout" and grand jubilee which the soldiers were going to have that night. But it was already late, and hearing that the "Flora" was coming we had to hasten to the Landing. I was sorry to say good-bye to Dr. R[ogers]. What an *unspeakable* happiness it was to see him. But I fear for his health. I fear the exposure of a camp life. Am glad to see that he has warm robes and blankets, to keep him comfortable. I wish I c'ld do something for him. He has done so much for me.

Ah, what a grand, glorious day this has been. The dawn of freedom which it heralds may not break upon us at once; but it will surely come, and sooner, I believe, than we have ever dared hope before. My soul is glad with an exceeding great gladness. But before I close, dear A., I must bring our little party safe home to Oaklands. We had a good time on the Flora. L[izzie Hunn] and I promenaded the deck, and sang John Brown, and Whittier's Hymn and "My Country Tis of Thee." And the moon shone bright above us, and the waves beneath, smooth and clear, glistened in the soft moonlight. At Beaufort we took the row boat, and the boatmen sang as they rowed us across. Mr. Hall was with us, and seemed really to appreciate and enjoy everything. I like him. Arrived at St. Helena's we separated, he to go to "Coffin's Point" (a dreadful name, as Dr. R[ogers] says) and we to come hither [Oaklands]. Can't say that I enjoyed the homeward drive

very much. I was so intensely cold, yes *intensely*, for these regions. I
fear some of the hot enthusiasm with which my soul was filled got
chilled a little but it was only for a short time.

Old friend, my good and dear A. a very, very happy New Year to
you! Dear friends in both my Northern homes a happy, happy New
Year to you, too! And to us all a year of such freedom as we have
never yet known in this boasted but hitherto wicked land. The hymn,
or rather one of the hymns that those boat[men] sung [*sic*] is singing
itself to me now. The refrain "Religion so . . . sweet" was so sweet
and touching in its solemnity.

A Parting Hymn

When Winter's royal robes of white
    From hill and vale are gone,
And the glad voices of the spring
    Upon the air are borne,
Friends, who have met with us before,
Within these walls shall meet no more.

Forth to a noble work they go:
    O, may their hearts keep pure,
And hopeful zeal and strength be theirs
    To labor and endure,
That they an earnest faith may prove
By words of truth and deeds of love.

May those, whose holy task it is
    To guide impulsive youth,
Fail not to cherish in their souls
    A reverence for truth;
For teachings which the lips impart
Must have their source within the heart.

May all who suffer share their love—
    The poor and the oppressed;

So shall the blessing of our God
   Upon their labors rest.
And may we meet again where all
Are blest and freed from every thrall.

The Angel's Visit

'Twas on a glorious summer eve,—
   A lovely eve in June,—
Serenely from her home above
   Looked down the gentle moon;
And lovingly she smiled on me,
   And softly soothed the pain—
The aching, heavy pain that lay
   Upon my heart and brain.

And gently 'mid the murmuring leaves,
   Scarce by its light wings stirred,
Like spirit voices soft and clear,
   The night wind's song was heard;
In strains of music sweet and low
   It sang to me of peace;
It bade my weary, troubled soul
   Her sad complainings cease.

For bitter thoughts had filled my breast,
   And sad, and sick at heart,
I longed to lay me down and rest,
   From all the world apart.
"Outcast, oppressed on earth," I cried,
   "O Father, take me home;
O, take me to that peaceful land
   Beyond the moon-lit dome.

"On such a night as this," methought,
   "Angelic forms are near;
In beauty unrevealed to us
   They hover in the air.

O mother, loved and lost," I cried,
   "Methinks thou'rt near me now;
Methinks I feel thy cooling touch
   Upon my burning brow.

"O, guide and soothe thy sorrowing child;
   And if 'tis not His will
That thou shouldst take me home with thee,
   Protect and bless me still;
For dark and drear had been my life
   Without thy tender smile,
Without a mother's loving care,
   Each sorrow to beguile."

I ceased: then o'er my senses stole
   A soothing, dreamy spell,
And gently to my ear were borne
   The tones I loved so well;
A sudden flood of rosy light
   Filled all the dusky wood,
And, clad in shining robes of white,
   My angel mother stood.

She gently drew me to her side,
   She pressed her lips to mine,
And softly said, "Grieve not, my child;
   A mother's love is thine.
I know the cruel wrongs that crush
   The young and ardent heart;
But falter not; keep bravely on,
   And nobly bear thy part.

"For thee a brighter day's in store;
   And every earnest soul
That presses on, with purpose high,
   Shall gain the wished-for goal.
And thou, beloved, faint not beneath
   The weary weight of care;
Daily before our Father's throne
   I breathe for thee a prayer.

"I pray that pure and holy thoughts
  May bless and guard thy way;
A noble and unselfish life
  For thee, my child, I pray."
She paused, and fondly bent on me
  One lingering look of love,
Then softly said,—and passed away,—
  "Farewell! we'll meet above."

I woke, and still the silver moon
  In quiet beauty shone;
And still I heard amid the leaves
  The night wind's murmuring tone;
But from my heart the weary pain
  Forevermore had flown;
I knew a mother's prayer for me
  Was breathed before the throne.

Harriet E. Adams Wilson
Our Nig
1807?/1808?–1870

The discovery and close examination of Harriet E. Adams Wilson's *Our Nig; or, Sketches from the Life of a Free Black, In A Two-Story White House North. Showing That Slavery's Shadows Fall Even There* (1859) has altered the chronology of Afro-American writers as well as that of Afro-American literature. Hailed as a black literary landmark, the book has been identified as the first black novel published in the United States by a black man or woman. Further, the writer is said to be "one of the first two black women to publish a novel in any language."[1]

Previous novels by Afro-Americans had been published abroad. William Wells Brown, commonly referred to as the first Afro-American novelist, had his *Clotel; or, The President's Daughter: A Narrative of Slave Life in the United States* (1853) published in London. The Boston edition, with changes, came out in 1864 under a more acceptable title for white readers, *Clotelle: A Tale of the Southern States*. Frank J. Webb followed Brown with his novel *The Garies and Their Friends* (1857), also published in London.

Henry Louis Gates, a professor at Cornell University, has painstakingly ferreted out the submerged life of Harriet E. Adams Wilson, who used the self-derogatory nom de plume of "Our Nig" on the title page. In his introduction to the second edition of *Our Nig*, Gates set the probable birthplace of the writer at Fredericksburg, Virginia, in 1807 or 1808.[2] She married

Thomas Wilson in October 1851 at Milford, New Hampshire, and in late May or early June of 1852, gave birth to a son, George Mason, at Goffstown near Milford. The child was born at the county farm because Mrs. Wilson's husband had deserted her, and she was without funds.

Harriet E. Wilson had her book printed September 1858 in Boston where she was living alone, for her son was staying with a New Hampshire family until she could provide for him. She hoped to receive enough money from the publication of her book so that they could be reunited. But sadly this never happened, for George died of fever when almost eight years old in the county poorhouse in Milford, New Hampshire, on 15 February 1860, six months after the publication of his mother's book.

Mrs. Wilson's autobiographical account is written in the guise of fiction. She admits in her preface that she did not pretend to divulge every event in her life, for she did not want to provoke shame among her good antislavery friends at home. Shame would indeed have been aroused by the pathetic narrative, which was verified by three white acquaintances in the appendix. She spins a tragic Dickensian tale of social, racial, and economic dehumanization endured by an indentured servant and free mulatto woman in the antebellum North.

Our Nig is a girl, Alfrado ("Frado"), one of two children born from a marriage between a poor white woman, Mag Smith, and a black man. Prior to the mixed union, Mag has already been an outcast among her own because she has given birth to an illegitimate child who died. To escape this disgrace, she has moved away, only to discover the "publicity of her fall" has followed her. Living a wretched existence marked by poverty and loneliness, she accepts the offer of marriage by Jim, a "kind-hearted African" who pities her. Of this liaison, the author comments: "She [Mag] has descended another step down the ladder of infamy."[3]

The couple manages to live comfortably until Jim dies of consumption. Once more, Mag finds it difficult to make ends meet and marries another black man, Seth Shipley, Jim's business partner. Because of difficult times, they decide to give the children away and leave town.

Pretty, spirited Alfrado, at the age of six, is abandoned at the big white two-story house owned by the Bellmonts, a white family. There she grows up as an indentured servant, ruled over by the "she-devil" Mrs. Bellmont, who has an equally demonic daughter, Mary. Alfrado is overworked, constantly beaten, and deprived not only of clothing but of her beautiful curly black hair. From time to time, she is rescued from her maltreatment by the kindly Mr. Bellmont, his sister, Abby, and his son, James. The lives of the Bellmonts constitute a major part of the novel.

Upon reaching the age of eighteen, Alfrado is free to leave. She becomes a seamstress, but the long years of abuse and deprivation have taken their toll, and her health is fragile. She is shuffled back and forth to charity homes whenever she is sick and unable to care for herself. Finally, she marries a handsome black man named Samuel, who pretends to be a fugitive slave and gives lectures. When she becomes pregnant, Samuel abruptly leaves her to go to sea. Left alone, Alfrado has her baby in the county home. But as unexpectedly as he had left, Samuel returns to reclaim his wife and child. When he disappears once again, Alfrado hears that he has died from yellow fever in New Orleans.

Ill now and with no means of support, Alfrado writes her book to earn money to get her son back from the county farm. But her plea for a "worthy sale" to help her regain her son went unheeded. The book did not gain attention or a ready market—perhaps because she had brought that shame she had feared to the antislavery people of the North.

Gates speculates that Mrs. Wilson's book was obscure for over a century because of "the boldness of her themes." She wrote about marriage between a white woman and a black man, a decided departure for the times and an "unpopular subject." She told of the racism of the "white *petite bourgeoisie* of the North," and she portrayed a black man posing as an escaped slave for personal gain. Gates points too to her use of the "hated epithet, 'nigger,'" for title and authorship.

The book could also have been ignored or overlooked because of the misidentification of the author. Monroe N. Work, in his mammoth *A Bibliography of the Negro in Africa and America* (1928), a valuable reference source, lists Mrs. H. E. Wilson under the heading of "Novels by White Authors Relating to the Negro." (See Gates's discussion on this point.)

Aside from its firsts, the novel can be deemed important for other reasons. It attests to prejudice and a different kind of black bondage in the North at a time when Abolitionists were violently attacking slavery in the South. It exposes white women (themselves victimized by a nineteenth-century male-dominated society) who were committing the sins of the patriarchs, as well as those of southern slave mistresses, in their relationships with black women. In the portrayal of Mag Smith, it exhibits another kind of bias, that of white class consciousness. *Our Nig*'s family deserter, Samuel, is the first in a long line of abandoning black husbands in Afro-American fiction. And it is an early example of the tragic mulatto theme, although in this case it involves a white woman and black man instead of the more usual white man and black woman.

Mrs. Wilson, like other free black women of poor circumstances, obviously educated herself by reading, which not only gave her the inspiration to write but made it possible for her to do so. In *Our Nig*, while Alfrado is recuperating in the home of a benevolent white woman who has taken her in, she is introduced to books. Her new awareness changes her outlook and creates a "new impulse." As she observes: "She felt herself capable of elevation; she felt that this book information supplied an undefined dissatisfaction she had long felt, but could not express. Every leisure moment was carefully applied to self-improvement."[4] The fruits of Alfrado's and Harriet's reading are evidenced in the poetic quotes that begin each chapter.

By having faith in herself, Harriet E. Adams Wilson unknowingly set a precedent with her personal fictionalized memoir of a free—yet unfree—black northern woman of her time. She is believed to have died in Boston around 1870. The selection is from the 1859 edition.

NOTES

1. Wilson, *Our Nig*, 2d ed., p. xiii. Gates identifies Maria F. Dos Reis, author of the novel *Ursula* (Brazil, 1858), as the second woman.
2. Ibid., p. xiv.
3. Wilson, *Our Nig*, p. 13. The editor is quoting from the original text of *Our Nig* in the Fisk University Library.
4. Ibid., pp. 124–25.

SELECTED SOURCES

Primary

Wilson, Mrs. H. E. *Our Nig; or, Sketches from the Life of a Free Black, In A Two-Story White House, North. Showing That Slavery's Shadows Fall Even There.* By "Our Nig." Boston: Printed by Geo. Rand & Avery, 1859. Reprint. With introduction and notes by Henry Louis Gates, Jr. New York: Random House, Vintage Books, 1983.

Secondary

Foster, Frances Smith. "Adding Color and Contour to Early American Self-Portraitures: Autobiographical Writings of Afro-American Women." In *Conjuring: Black Women, Fiction, and Literary Tradition,* edited by Marjorie Pryse and Hortense J. Spillers. Bloomington: Indiana University Press, 1985.

Gilbert, Sandra M., and Gubar, Susan. *The Norton Anthology of Literature by Women: The Tradition in English.* New York and London: W. W. Norton & Co., 1985.

Loggins, Vernon. *The Negro Author: His Development in America.* New York: Columbia University Press, 1931.

Work, Monroe. *A Bibliography of the Negro in Africa and America.* 1928. Reprint. New York: Octagon Books, 1970.

A New Home for Me

Oh! did we but know of the shadows so nigh,
  The world would indeed be a prison of gloom;
All light would be quenched in youth's eloquent eye,
  And the prayer-lisping infant would ask for the tomb.

For if Hope be a star that may lead us astray,
  And "deceiveth the heart," as the aged ones preach;
Yet 'twas Mercy that gave it, to beacon our way,
  Though its halo illumes where it never can reach.

Eliza Cook

As the day closed and Mag did not appear, surmises were expressed by the family that she never intended to return. Mr. Bellmont was a kind, humane man, who would not grudge hospitality to the poorest wanderer, nor fail to sympathize with any sufferer, however humble. The child's desertion by her mother appealed to his sympathy, and he felt inclined to succor her. To do this in opposition to Mrs. Bellmont's wishes, would be like encountering a whirlwind charged with fire, daggers and spikes. She was not as susceptible of fine emotions as her spouse. Mag's opinion of her was not without foundation. She was self-willed, haughty, undisciplined, arbitrary and severe. In common parlance, she was a *scold*, a thorough one. Mr. B. remained silent during the consultation which follows, engaged in by mother, Mary and John, or Jack, as he was familiarly called.

"Send her to the County House," said Mary, in reply to the query what should be done with her, in a tone which indicated self-importance in the speaker. She was indeed the idol of her mother, and more nearly resembled her in disposition and manners than the others.

Jane, an invalid daughter, the eldest of those at home, was reclining on a sofa apparently uninterested.

"Keep her," said Jack. "She's real handsome and bright, and not very black, either."

"Yes," rejoined Mary; "that's just like you, Jack. She'll be of no use at all these three years, right under foot all the time."

"Poh! Miss Mary; if she should say, it wouldn't be two days before you would be telling the girls about *our* nig, *our* nig!" retorted Jack.

"I don't want a nigger 'round *me*, do you, mother?" asked Mary.

"I don't mind the nigger in the child. I should like a dozen better than one," replied her mother. "If I could make her do my work in a few years, I would keep her. I have so much trouble with girls I hire, I am almost persuaded if I have one to train up in my way from a child, I shall be able to keep them awhile. I am tired of changing every few months."

"Where could she sleep?" asked Mary. "I don't want her near me."

"In the L chamber," answered the mother.

"How'll she get there?" asked Jack. "She'll be afraid to go through that dark passage, and she can't climb the ladder safely."

"She'll have to go there; it's good enough for a nigger," was the reply.

Jack was sent on horseback to ascertain if Mag was at her home. He returned with the testimony of Pete Greene that they were fairly departed, and that the child was intentionally thrust upon their family.

The imposition was not at all relished by Mrs. B., or the pert, haughty Mary, who had just glided into her teens.

"Show the child to bed, Jack," said his mother. "You seem most pleased with the little nigger, so you may introduce her to her room."

He went to the kitchen, and, taking Frado gently by the hand, told her he would put her in bed now; perhaps her mother would come the next night after her.

It was not yet quite dark, so they ascended the stairs without any light, passing through nicely furnished rooms, which were a source of great amazement to the child. He opened the door which connected with her room by a dark, unfinished passage-way. "Don't bump your head," said Jack, and stepped before to open the door leading into her apartment,—an unfinished chamber over the kitchen, the roof slanting nearly to the floor, so that the bed could stand only in the middle of the room. A small half window furnished light and air. Jack returned to the sitting room with the remark that the child would soon outgrow those quarters.

"When she *does*, she'll outgrow the house," remarked the mother.

"What can she do to help you?" asked Mary. "She came just in the right time, didn't she? Just the very day after Bridget left," continued she.

"I'll see what she can do in the morning," was the answer.

While this conversation was passing below, Frado lay, revolving in her little mind whether she would remain or not until her mother's return. She was of wilful, determined nature, a stranger to fear, and would not hesitate to wander away should she decide to. She remembered the conversation of her mother with Seth, the words "given away" which she heard used in reference to herself; and though she did not know their full import, she thought she should, by remaining, be in some relation to white people she was never favored with before. So she resolved to tarry, with the hope that mother would come and get her some time. The hot sun had penetrated her room, and it was long before a cooling breeze reduced the temperature so that she could sleep.

Frado was called early in the morning by her new mistress. Her first work was to feed the hens. She was shown how it was *always* to be done, and in no other way; any departure from this rule to be punished by a whipping. She was then accompanied by Jack to drive the cows to pasture, so she might learn the way. Upon her return she was allowed to eat her breakfast, consisting of a bowl of skimmed milk, with brown bread crusts, which she was told to eat, standing, by the kitchen table, and must not be over ten minutes about it. Meanwhile the family were taking their morning meal in the dining-room. This over, she was placed on a cricket to wash the common dishes; she was to be in waiting always to bring wood and chips, to run hither and thither from room to room.

A large amount of dish-washing for small hands followed dinner. Then the same after tea and going after the cows finished her first day's work. It was a new discipline to the child. She found some attractions about the place, and she retired to rest at night more willing to remain. The same routine followed day after day, with slight variation; adding a little more work, and spicing the toil with "words that burn," and frequent blows on her head. These were great annoyances to Frado, and had she known where her mother was, she would have gone at once to her. She was often greatly wearied, and silently wept over her sad fate. At first she wept aloud, which Mrs. Bellmont noticed by applying a rawhide, always at hand in the kitchen. It was a symptom of discontent and complaining which must be "nipped in the bud," she said.

Thus passed a year. No intelligence of Mag. It was now certain Frado was to become a permanent member of the family. Her labors were multiplied; she was quite indispensable, although but seven years old. She had never learned to read, never heard of a school until her residence in the family.

Mrs. Bellmont was in doubt about the utility of attempting to educate people of color, who were incapable of elevation. This subject occasioned a lengthy discussion in the family. Mr. Bellmont, Jane and Jack arguing for Frado's education; Mary and her mother objecting. At last Mr. Bellmont declared decisively that she *should* go to school. He was a man who seldom decided controversies at home. The word once spoken admitted of no appeal; so, notwithstanding Mary's objection that she would have to attend the same school she did, the word became law.

It was to be a new scene to Frado, and Jack had many queries and conjectures to answer. He was himself too far advanced to attend the summer school, which Frado regretted, having had too many opportunities of witnessing Miss Mary's temper to feel safe in her company alone.

The opening day of school came. Frado sauntered on far in the rear of Mary, who was ashamed to be seen "walking with a nigger." As soon as she appeared, with scanty clothing and bared feet, the children assembled, noisily published her approach: "See that nigger," shouted one. "Look! look!" cried another. "I won't play with her," said one little girl. "Nor I neither," replied another.

Mary evidently relished these sharp attacks, and saw a fair prospect of lowering Nig where, according to her views, she belonged. Poor Frado, chagrined and grieved, felt that her anticipations of plea-

sure at such a place were far from being realized. She was just decid-
ing to return home, and never come there again, when the teacher
appeared, and observing the downcast looks of the child, took her by
the hand, and led her into the school-room. All followed, and, after
the bustle of securing seats was over, Miss Marsh inquired if the children knew "any cause for the sorrow of that little girl?" pointing to
Frado. It was soon all told. She then reminded them of their duties
to the poor and friendless; their cowardice in attacking a young innocent child; referred them to one who looks not on outward appearances, but on the heart. "She looks like a good girl; I think *I* shall
love her, so lay aside all prejudice, and vie with each other in shewing
kindness and good-will to one who seems different from you," were
the closing remarks of the kind lady. Those kind words! The most
agreeable sound which ever meets the ear of sorrowing, grieving
childhood.

Example rendered her words efficacious. Day by day there was
a manifest change of deportment towards "Nig." Her speeches often
drew merriment from the children; no one could do more to enliven
their favorite pastimes than Frado. Mary could not endure to see her
thus noticed, yet knew not how to prevent it. She could not influence
her schoolmates as she wished. She had not gained their affections by
winning ways and yielding points of controversy. On the contrary, she
was self-willed, domineering; every day reported "mad" by some of
her companions. She availed herself of the only alternative, abuse and
taunts, as they returned from school. This was not satisfactory; she
wanted to use physical force "to subdue her," to "keep her down."

There was, on their way home, a field intersected by a stream
over which a single plank was placed for a crossing. It occurred to
Mary that it would be a punishment to Nig to compel her to cross
over; so she dragged her to the edge, and told her authoritatively to
go over. Nig hesitated, resisted. Mary placed herself behind the
child, and, in the struggle to force her over, lost her footing and
plunged into the stream. Some of the larger scholars being in sight,
ran, and thus prevented Mary from drowning and Frado from falling.
Nig scampered home fast as possible, and Mary went to the nearest
house, dripping, to procure a change of garments. She came loitering
home, half crying, exclaiming, "Nig pushed me into the stream!" She
then related the particulars. Nig was called from the kitchen. Mary
stood with anger flashing in her eyes. Mr. Bellmont sat quietly read-

ing his paper. He had witnessed too many of Miss Mary's outbreaks to be startled. Mrs. Bellmont interrogated Nig.

"I didn't do it! I didn't do it!" answered Nig, passionately, and then related the occurrence truthfully.

The discrepancy greatly enraged Mrs. Bellmont. With loud accusations and angry gestures she approached the child. Turning to her husband, she asked,

"Will you sit still, there, and hear that black nigger call Mary a liar?"

"How do we know but she has told the truth? I shall not punish her," he replied, and left the house, as he usually did when a tempest threatened to envelop him. No sooner was he out of sight than Mrs. B. and Mary commenced beating her inhumanly; then propping her mouth open with a piece of wood, shut her up in a dark room, without any supper. For employment, while the tempest ranged within, Mr. Bellmont went for the cows, a task belonging to Frado, and thus unintentionally prolonged her pain. At dark Jack came in, and seeing Mary, accosted her with, "So you thought you'd vent your spite on Nig, did you? Why can't you let her alone? It was good enough for you to get a ducking, only you did not stay in half long enough."

"Stop!" said his mother. "You shall never talk so before me. You would have that little nigger trample on Mary, would you? She came home with a lie; it made Mary's story false."

"What was Mary's story?" asked Jack.

It was related.

"Now," said Jack, sallying into a chair, "the school-children happened to see it all, and they tell the same story Nig does. Which is most likely to be true, what a dozen agree they saw, or the contrary?"

"It is very strange you will believe what others say against your sister," retorted his mother, with flashing eye. "I think it is time your father subdued you."

"Father is a sensible man," argued Jack. "He would not wrong a dog. Where *is* Frado?" he continued.

"Mother gave her a good whipping and shut her up," replied Mary.

Just then Mr. Bellmont entered, and asked if Frado was "shut up yet."

The knowledge of her innocence, the perfidy of his sister, worked fearfully on Jack. He bounded from his chair, searched every room till he found the child; her mouth wedged apart, her face swollen, and full of pain.

How Jack pitied her! He relieved her jaws, brought her some supper, took her to her room, comforted her as well as he knew how, sat by her till she fell asleep, and then left for the sitting room. As he passed his mother, he remarked, "If that was the way Frado was to be treated, he hoped she would never wake again!" He then imparted her situation to his father, who seemed untouched, till a glance at Jack exposed a tearful eye. Jack went early to her next morning. She awoke sad, but refreshed. After breakfast Jack took her with him to the field, and kept her through the day. But it could not be so generally. She must return to school, to her household duties. He resolved to do what he could to protect her from Mary and his mother. He bought her a dog, which became a great favorite with both. The invalid, Jane, would gladly befriend her; but she had not the strength to brave the iron will of her mother. Kind words and affectionate glances were the only expressions of sympathy she could safely indulge in. The men employed on the farm were always glad to hear her prattle; she was a great favorite with them. Mrs. Bellmont allowed them the privilege of talking with her in the kitchen. She did not fear but she should have ample opportunity of subduing her when they were away. Three months of schooling, summer and winter, she enjoyed for three years. Her winter over-dress was a cast-off overcoat, once worn by Jack, and a sun-bonnet. It was a source of great merriment to the scholars, but Nig's retorts were so mirthful, and their satisfaction so evident in attributing the selection to "Old Granny Bellmont," that it was not painful to Nig or pleasurable to Mary. Her jollity was not to be quenched by whipping or scolding. In Mrs. Bellmont's presence she was under restraint; but in the kitchen, and among her schoolmates, the pent up fires burst forth. She was ever at some sly prank when unseen by her teacher, in school hours; not unfrequently some outburst of merriment, of which she was the original, was charged upon some innocent mate, and punishment inflicted which she merited. They enjoyed her antics so fully that any of them would suffer wrongfully to keep open the avenues of mirth. She would venture far beyond propriety, thus shielded and countenanced.

The teacher's desk was supplied with drawers, in which were stored his books and other *et ceteras* of the profession. The children observed Nig very busy there one morning before school, as they flitted in occasionally from their play outside. The master came; called the children to order; opened a drawer to take the book the occasion required; when out poured a volume of smoke. "Fire! fire!" screamed he, at the top of his voice. By this time he had become sufficiently acquainted with the peculiar odor, to know he was imposed upon. The scholars shouted with laughter to see the terror of the dupe, who, feeling abashed at the needless fright, made no very strict investigation, and Nig once more escaped punishment. She had provided herself with cigars, and puffing, puffing away at the crack of the drawer, had filled it with smoke, and then closed it tightly to deceive the teacher, and amuse the scholars. The interim of terms was filled up with a variety of duties new and peculiar. At home, no matter how powerful the heat when sent to rake hay or guard the grazing herd, she was never permitted to shield her skin from the sun. She was not many shades darker than Mary now; what a calamity it would be ever to hear the contrast spoken of. Mrs. Bellmont was determined the sun should have full power to darken the shade which nature had first bestowed upon her as best befitting.

Harriet Ann Jacobs
Linda Brent ✒
1813–1897

Harriet Ann Jacobs was one of the few ex-slaves who wrote her own slave narrative, a fact authenticated by her biographer, Jean Fagan Yellin, through correspondence between Jacobs and Amy Post, which "establishes Jacobs' authorship and clarifies the role of her editor [L. Maria Child]."[1] Post, an Abolitionist and feminist, was a white friend and confidante to Jacobs and encouraged her to pen her autobiography.

Under the pseudonym of Linda Brent, Jacobs published *Incidents in the Life of a Slave Girl*, a tragic account of a black woman's strong desire to free herself in mind and body from the dehumanization of slavery. "Jacobs spent years on the manuscript and when it was finished, more years trying to get it published in England and America."[2]

The author was born in 1813 at Edenton, North Carolina, where she was taught to read by a kind mistress. Recent factual details of her unwritten life have been revealed in Jean Fagan Yellin's edited work, *Incidents in the Life of a Slave Girl*.

Narrating her experiences as a slave for twenty-seven years, Linda Brent tells of being the daughter of a skillful carpenter who also has a son, William. (In actual life, her brother's name was John S.) Linda lives in comfortable circumstances as the slave of a mistress who permits her father to hire out at his trade with the condition that part of his earnings be paid to her. Linda does not know she is a slave until she is six years old and her mother dies. Even then, she does not understand the harsh reality of being in bondage until, when she is twelve (Yellin in her edited version says that she was eleven), her mistress dies and she is bequeathed to the five-year-old daughter (three, according to Yellin) of her deceased mistress's sister. Dr. Flint, a physician and husband of the sister, becomes master of Linda and her brother whom the family purchases. Dr. Flint is identified by Yellin as James Norcom, a prominent Edenton physician.

When Linda is fifteen, Flint begins to make advances to her. His unwelcome overtures become a recurring problem and provoke the jealousy of Flint's wife. Linda's life as a female slave then becomes unbearable: each day she is harassed and pursued by a master who is determined to make her succumb to his desires.

In need of solace, Linda is drawn to a Mr. Sands, actually Samuel Tredwell Sawyer, an unmarried young white man, who shows sympathy and compassion to her. (A letter of 21 June 1857 to Post by Jacobs states that Sands was a congressman.)[3] By the age of nineteen, Linda has had two children by him, a son, Benjamin, and daughter, Ellen. (In reality, they were Joseph and Louisa Matilda Jacobs.) Linda tries to hide her shame about their birth by justifying her relationship with Mr. Sands, comparing it to "something akin to freedom in having a lover who has no control over you, except that which he gains by kindness and attachments."[4]

Fearing that her children will be sold, Linda flees to the refuge of her freed grandmother, Molly Horniblow, characterized as Aunt Martha, who has been like a mother to her. Angered by her escape, Dr. Flint has her two children and her brother jailed. But through Mr. Sands's connivance with a slave dealer, the brother and children are purchased by him. The children are placed in the care of Linda's grandmother.

For seven years, Linda hides in a darkened garret of a small shed at her grandmother's house, squeezed in a tiny room with a leaky roof. Through a loophole, she can see her children, who are unaware of her presence, and hear Dr. Flint and a slave catcher discussing her.

With the help of her uncle and a trusted friend, she escapes in 1842 and boards a boat to the North. There again she is forced to hide, staying constantly ahead of those doggedly seeking her return. In the land of freedom, she learns of northerners who ape the South in their hostility toward her color. Finally she finds work in New York City as a housekeeper and nurse with a family who befriends her.

Yellin discloses Jacobs's protectors to have been Nathaniel P. Willis, author and editor of the weekly *Home Journal*, and his wife, Cornelia. It was Cornelia who bought Jacobs's freedom for three hundred dollars and a promise from those who controlled her children to give them up to the mother.

When the Willis family moved to Cornwall, New York, in the 1830s,

Jacobs began writing her story whenever she could "snatch an hour from household duties," which consisted of caring for an eighteen-room house and the Willis children. Although Willis was a literary man, he was also a pro-slaver and Jacobs did not inform him of her writing. Only her daughter, Louisa, and Amy Post were aware of what she was doing.

Jacobs says she was driven to write her autobiography not to "attract attention" or "to excite sympathy" but "to arouse the women of the North to a realizing sense of the condition of two millions of women at the South, still in bondage, suffering what I suffered, and most of them far worse."[5]

After she completed her book, Jacobs took a temporary leave from the service of the Willises to go to London where she unsuccessfully sought a publisher. Finally in 1860, according to Yellin, Lydia Maria Child, a leading white Abolitionist, arranged a contract with Boston publisher Thayer and Eldridge, to have the book brought out. Child, however, would have to commit her services to the project. The publishing concern went bankrupt before the book was released, but Jacobs managed to secure funds to buy the plates and have a Boston printer publish it for her.[6] It came out in 1861 and, a year later, was published in London with the title *The Deeper Wrong; or, Incidents in the Life of a Slave Girl*. Little money was derived from it by the author, who wanted to use it for antislavery causes.

Lydia Maria Child's name appears as editor, since she refined the manuscript at Jacobs's request. For those who would (and did) question an ex-slave's ability to write a book, Child's introduction sought to assure them that the revisions were "mainly for purposes of condensation and orderly arrangement," and with "trifling exceptions, both the ideas and the language are her [Jacobs's] own."[7]

When the Civil War broke out, Jacobs publicized her narrative for the cause of freedom. She severed her work with the Willises and went to Washington, D.C., where she nursed black troops and worked with homeless refugees. When the Emancipation Proclamation was issued, she rejoiced in a letter to Lydia Maria Child, on 1 January 1863: "I have lived to hear the Proclamation of Freedom for my suffering people. All my wrongs are forgiven. I am more than repaid for all I have endured. Glory to God in the highest!"[8]

Aside from one visit to the South and to Edenton, Jacobs spent the rest of her life in Washington, D.C., helping her people. She died there in 1897.

NOTES

1. Yellin, "Text and Contexts," p. 262.
2. Ibid., p. 266.
3. Sterling, *We Are Your Sisters*, p. 81.
4. Jacobs, *Incidents*, ed. Child, p. 85.

5. Ibid., p. 6.
6. Jacobs, *Incidents*, ed. Yellin, pp. xxiii–xxiv.
7. Jacobs, *Incidents*, p. 7.
8. Child, *Freedmen's Book*, p. 218.

SELECTED SOURCES

Primary

Jacobs, Harriet Ann [Linda Brent]. *Incidents in the Life of a Slave Girl, Written by Herself.* Edited by L. Maria Child. Boston, 1861.

———. *The Deeper Wrong; or, Incidents in the Life of a Slave Girl.* London: W. Tweedie, 1862.

———. *Incidents in the Life of a Slave Girl, Written by Herself.* Edited and with an introduction by Jean Fagan Yellin. Cambridge, Mass., and London, 1987.

Secondary

Child, Lydia Maria. *The Freedmen's Book.* Boston: Ticknor & Fields, 1865.

Gwin, Minrose C. *Black and White Women of the Old South: The Peculiar Sisterhood in American Literature.* Knoxville: University of Tennessee Press, 1985.

———. "Green-eyed Monsters of the Slavocracy: Jealous Mistresses in Two Slave Narratives." In *Conjuring: Black Women, Fiction, and Literary Tradition*, edited by Marjorie Pryse and Hortense Spillers. Bloomington: Indiana University Press, 1985.

Hooks, Bell. *Ain't I a Woman: Black Women and Feminism.* Boston: South End Press, 1981.

Loggins, Vernon. *The Negro Author: His Development in America.* New York: Columbia University Press, 1931.

Sterling, Dorothy, ed. *We Are Your Sisters: Black Women in the Nineteenth Century.* New York: W. W. Norton & Co., 1984.

White, Deborah Gray. *Ar'n't I a Woman? Female Slaves in the Plantation South.* New York: W. W. Norton & Co., 1985.

Yellin, Jean Fagan. "Text and Contexts of Harriet Jacobs' *Incidents in the Life of a Slave Girl: Written by Herself.*" In *The Slave's Narrative*, edited by Charles T. Davis and Henry Louis Gates, Jr. New York: Oxford University Press, 1985.

The Jealous Mistress

I would ten thousand times rather that my children should be the half-starved paupers of Ireland than to be the most pampered among the slaves of America. I would rather drudge out my life on a cotton plantation, till the grave opened to give me rest, than to live with an unprincipled master and a jealous mistress. The felon's home in a penitentiary is preferable. He may repent, and turn from the error of his ways, and so find peace; but it is not so with a favorite slave. She is not allowed to have any pride of character. It is deemed a crime in her to wish to be virtuous.

Mrs. Flint possessed the key to her husband's character before I was born. She might have used this knowledge to counsel and to screen the young and the innocent among her slaves; but for them she had no sympathy. They were the objects of her constant suspicion and malevolence. She watched her husband with unceasing vigilance; but he was well practised in means to evade it. What he could not find opportunity to say in words he manifested in signs. He invented more than were ever thought of in a deaf and dumb asylum. I let them pass, as if I did not understand what he meant; and many were the curses and threats bestowed on me for my stupidity. One day he caught me teaching myself to write. He frowned, as if he was not well pleased; but I suppose he came to the conclusion that such an accomplishment might help to advance his favorite scheme. Before long, notes were often slipped into my hand. I would return them, saying, "I can't read them, sir." "Can't you?" he replied; "then I must read them to you." He always finished the reading by asking, "Do you understand?" Sometimes he would complain of the heat of the tea room, and order his supper to be placed on a small table in the piazza. He would seat himself there with a well-satisfied smile, and tell me to stand by and brush away the flies. He would eat very slowly, pausing between the mouthfuls. These intervals were employed in describing the happiness I was so foolishly throwing away, and in threatening me with the penalty that finally awaited my stubborn disobedience. He boasted much of the forbearance he had exercised towards me, and reminded me that there was a limit to his patience. When I succeeded in avoiding opportunities for him to talk to me at home, I was ordered to come to his office, to do some errand. When there, I was obliged to stand and listen to such language as he saw fit to address to me. Sometimes I so openly expressed my contempt for him that he would become violently enraged, and I wondered why he did not strike me. Circumstanced as he was, he probably thought it was better policy to be forbearing. But the state of things grew worse and worse daily. In desperation I told him that I must and would apply to my grandmother for protection. He threatened me with death, and worse than death, if I made any complaint to her. Strange to say, I did not despair. I was naturally of a buoyant disposition, and always I had a hope of somehow getting out of his clutches. Like many a poor, simple slave before me, I trusted that some threads of joy would yet be woven into my dark destiny.

I had entered my sixteenth year, and every day it became more apparent that my presence was intolerable to Mrs. Flint. Angry words frequently passed between her and her husband. He had never punished me himself, and he would not allow any body else to punish me. In that respect, she was never satisfied; but, in her angry moods, no terms were too vile for her to bestow upon me. Yet I, whom she detested so bitterly, had far more pity for her than he had, whose duty it was to make her life happy. I never wronged her, or wished to wrong her; and one word of kindness from her would have brought me to her feet.

After repeated quarrels between the doctor and his wife, he announced his intention to take his youngest daughter, then four years old, to sleep in his apartment. It was necessary that a servant should sleep in the same room, to be on hand if the child stirred. I was selected for that office, and informed for what purpose that arrangement had been made. By managing to keep within sight of people, as much as possible, during the day time, I had hitherto succeeded in eluding my master, though a razor was often held to my throat to force me to change this line of policy. At night I slept by the side of my great aunt, where I felt safe. He was too prudent to come into her room. She was an old woman, and had been in the family many years. Moreover, as a married man, and a professional man, he deemed it necessary to save appearances in some degree. But he resolved to remove the obstacle in the way of his scheme; and he thought he had planned it so that he should evade suspicion. He was well aware how much I prized my refuge by the side of my old aunt, and he determined to dispossess me of it. The first night the doctor had the little child in his room alone. The next morning, I was ordered to take my station as nurse the following night. A kind Providence interposed in my favor. During the day Mrs. Flint heard of his new arrangement, and a storm followed. I rejoiced to hear it rage.

After a while my mistress sent for me to come to her room. Her first question was, "Did you know you were to sleep in the doctor's room?"

"Yes, ma'am."

"Who told you?"

"My master."

"Will you answer truly all the questions I ask?"

"Yes, ma'am."

"Tell me, then, as you hope to be forgiven, are you innocent of what I have accused you?"

"I am."

She handed me a Bible, and said, "Lay your hand on your heart, kiss this holy book, and swear before God that you tell me the truth."

I took the oath she required, and I did it with a clear conscience.

"You have taken God's holy word to testify your innocence," said she. "If you have deceived me, beware! Now take this stool, sit down, look me directly in the face, and tell me all that has passed between your master and you."

I did as she ordered. As I went on with my account her color changed frequently, she wept, and sometimes groaned. She spoke in tones so sad, that I was touched by her grief. The tears came to my eyes, but I was soon convinced that her emotions arose from anger and wounded pride. She felt that her marriage vows were desecrated, her dignity insulted; but she had no compassion for the poor victim of her husband's perfidy. She pitied herself as a martyr; but she was incapable of feeling for the condition of shame and misery in which her unfortunate, helpless slave was placed.

Yet perhaps she had some touch of feeling for me; for when the conference was ended, she spoke kindly, and promised to protect me. I should have been much comforted by this assurance if I could have had confidence in it; but my experiences in slavery had filled me with distrust. She was not a very refined woman, and had not much control over her passions. I was an object of her jealousy, and, consequently, of her hatred; and I knew I could not expect kindness or confidence from her under the circumstances in which I was placed. I could not blame her. Slaveholders' wives feel as other women would under similar circumstances. The fire of her temper kindled from small sparks, and now the flame became so intense that the doctor was obliged to give up his intended arrangement.

I knew I had ignited the torch, and I expected to suffer for it afterwards; but I felt too thankful to my mistress for the timely aid she rendered me to care much about that. She now took me to sleep in a room adjoining her own. There I was an object of her especial care, though not of her especial comfort, for she spent many a sleepless night to watch over me. Sometimes I woke up, and found her bending over me. At other times she whispered in my ear, as though it was her husband who was speaking to me, and listened to hear what I would answer. If she startled me, on such occasions, she would glide stealthily away; and the next morning she would tell me I had been talking in my sleep, and ask who I was talking to. At last, I began to be fearful for my life. It had been often threatened; and you can imagine, better than I can describe, what an unpleasant sensation it must produce to wake up in the dead of night and find a jealous woman bending over you. Terrible as this experience was, I had fears that it would give place to one more terrible.

My mistress grew weary of her vigils; they did not prove satisfactory. She changed her tactics. She now tried the trick of accusing my master of crime, in my presence, and gave my name as the author of the accusation. To my utter astonishment, he replied, "I don't believe it; but if she did acknowledge it, you tortured her into exposing me." Tortured into exposing him! Truly, Satan had no difficulty in distinguishing the color of his soul! I understood his object in making this false representation. It was to show me that I gained nothing by seeking the protection of my mistress; that the power was still all in his own hands. I pitied Mrs. Flint. She was a second wife, many years the junior of her husband; and the hoary-headed miscreant was enough to try the patience of a wiser and better woman. She was completely foiled, and knew not how to proceed. She would gladly have had me flogged for my supposed false oath; but, as I have already stated, the doctor never allowed any one to whip me. The old sinner was politic. The application of the lash might have led to remarks that would have exposed him in the eyes of his children and grandchildren. How often did I rejoice that I lived in a town where all the inhabitants knew each other! If I had been on a remote plantation, or lost among the multitude of a crowded city, I should not be a living woman at this day.

The secrets of slavery are concealed like those of the Inquisition. My master was, to my knowledge, the father of eleven slaves. But did the mothers dare to tell who was the father of their children? Did the other slaves dare to allude to it, except in whispers among themselves? No, indeed! They knew too well the terrible consequences.

My grandmother could not avoid seeing things which excited her suspicions. She was uneasy about me, and tried various ways to buy me; but the never-changing answer was always repeated: "Linda does not belong to *me*. She is my daughter's property, and I have no legal right to sell her." The conscientious man! He was too scrupulous to *sell* me; but he had no scruples whatever about committing a much greater wrong against the helpless young girl placed under his guardianship, as his daughter's property. Sometimes my persecutor would ask me whether I would like to be sold. I told him I would rather be sold to any body than to lead such a life as I did. On such occasions he would assume the air of a very injured individual, and reproach me for my ingratitude. "Did I not take you into the house, and make you the companion of my own children?" he would say. "Have I ever treated you like a negro? I have never allowed you to be punished, not even to please your mistress. And this is the recompense I get, you ungrateful girl!" I answered that he had reasons of his own for screening me from punishment, and that the course he pursued made my mistress hate me and persecute me. If I wept, he would say, "Poor child! Don't cry! don't cry! I will make peace for you with your mistress. Only let me arrange matters in my own way. Poor, foolish girl! you don't know what is for your own good. I would cherish you. I would make a lady of you. Now go, and think of all I have promised you."

I did think of it.

Reader, I draw no imaginary pictures of southern homes. I am telling you the plain truth. Yet when victims make their escape from this wild beast of Slavery, northerners consent to act the part of bloodhounds, and hunt the poor fugitive back into his den, "full of dead men's bones, and all uncleanness." Nay, more, they are not only willing, but proud, to give their daughters in marriage to slaveholders. The poor girls have romantic notions of a sunny clime, and of the flowering vines that all the year round shade a happy home. To what disappointments are they destined! The young wife soon learns that the husband in whose hands she has placed her happiness pays no regard to his marriage vows. Children of every shade of complexion play with her own fair babies, and too well she knows that they are born unto him of his own household. Jealousy and hatred enter the flowery home, and it is ravaged of its loveliness.

Southern women often marry a man knowing that he is the father of many little slaves. They do not trouble themselves about it. They regard such children as property, as marketable as the pigs on the plantation; and it is seldom that they do not make them aware of this by passing them into the slave-trader's hands as soon as possible, and thus getting them out of their sight. I am glad to say there are some honorable exceptions.

I have myself known two southern wives who exhorted their husbands to free those slaves towards whom they stood in a "parental relation"; and their request was granted. These husbands blushed before the superior nobleness of their wives' natures. Though they had only counselled them to do that which it was their duty to do, it commanded their respect, and rendered their conduct more exemplary. Concealment was at an end, and confidence took the place of distrust.

Though this bad institution deadens the moral sense, even in white women, to a fearful extent, it is not altogether extinct. I have heard southern ladies say of Mr. Such a one, "He not only thinks it no disgrace to be the father of those little niggers, but he is not ashamed to call himself their master. I declare, such things ought not to be tolerated in any decent society!"

Part 2

Reconstruction to the End of the Century
1868–1899

The significance of the period from Reconstruction to the century's end lies in the emergence of Afro-American women writers. Unrestrained by slavery and illiteracy, they began to evolve as novelists, poets, journalists, short-story writers, and essayists. Their work to better their race and improve the condition of women became the themes of their writing, as they tried to combat the rising tides of racism and sexism sweeping the country.

The aftermath of the Civil War brought on intersectional strife and political, economic, and social upheavals across the land. Newly freed slaves found themselves homeless, jobless, illiterate, and in poor health. Black women, inspired by their own intelligence and sense of humanity, were in the vanguard of those trying to alleviate the condition of their race. They started schools, self-help organizations, settlement houses, literary societies, and clubs. Novelist Victoria Earle Matthews, for example, founded the White Rose Mission in New York City to aid poor young working girls migrating from the South; poet and short-story writer Alice Ruth Moore Dunbar assisted as teacher.

When Federal troops were withdrawn from the South in 1877, embittered southerners regained home rule and the freedom of "whipping the Negro into submission." They passed laws that inaugurated the era of Jim Crow, disfranchisement, and white supremacy. To counteract this assault upon black freedom, black women writers fought with pen and voice. Frances Anne Rollin Whipper, who may well have been the first black woman editor in the United States, and the formidable Ida B. Wells, challenged discrimination in the courts after ugly experiences with racism in respect to public conveyances.

To enforce white supremacy in the South, terrorism against blacks rose to alarming heights with the Ku Klux Klan becoming ever more virulent. Unknown numbers of blacks were lynched without the perpetrators being brought to justice. Ida B. Wells, a young, militant Memphis editor, was the first person, male or female, to take up her pen and crusade against the lynchings, which produced the "strange fruit" hanging from southern trees. Wells wanted the world to know of "that degree of dehumanizing brutality which fixes upon America the blot of a national crime." Black historian John Hope Franklin credits her with writing the first "detailed history of the lynchings of Negroes" in her documentary, A Red Record: Tabulated Statistics and Alleged Causes of Lynchings in the United States, 1892–1893–1894 (1895).

Besides confronting racism, black women writers were also opposing sexism as "nineteenth-century [white] Americans democratized the concept of the lady," who stayed at home in her proper subordinate place. "Nineteenth century black women were more aware of sexist oppression than any other female group in American society," concluded Bell Hooks, black feminist critic, in Ain't I a Woman: Black Women and Feminism (1981).

Addressing this issue, educator, writer, and feminist Anna Julia Cooper published a landmark book of feminist essays, A Voice from the South: By a Black Woman of the South (1892), which Hooks praised as "one of the first feminist discussions of the social status of black women." While white women were being "ladies," Cooper was espousing "The Higher Education of Women" in her book. Education, to Cooper, would get women out of the home to develop as a "feminine force."

Frances Ellen Watkins Harper changed her theme of antislavery to sexism in such poems as "A Double Standard," "Died of Starvation," and "Vashti." She became a familiar face on the lecture circuit again, this time becoming "more outspoken on the subject of woman suffrage than any other black woman of her day."

Evangelist Amanda Berry Smith's *An Autobiography; the Story of the Lord's Dealings with Mrs. Amanda Smith* . . . (1893), told of sexism in the African Methodist Episcopal Church, like Jarena Lee and Rebecca Cox Jackson before her. She graphically related her experience with churchmen who tried to dissuade her from attending a General Conference in Nashville, Tennessee, for fear she wanted to be ordained.

In fiction, the new themes were not expressed so boldly. True, the works manifested the social, economic, and psychological pressures of being black, but they were written in a style reminiscent of the white Victorian novel. The women wrote what Carole McAlpine Watson regarded in *Prologue: The Novels of Black American Women, 1891–1965* (1985) as "romantic tales focused on black heroes and heroines of saintlike virtue." Lacking black literary models, the writers had little choice but to follow the pattern of the white sentimental novel that was in vogue.

The first two novels by Afro-American women of the post–Civil War period appeared as serials. Clarissa Minnie Thompson's romance, *Treading the Winepress; or, A Mountain of Misfortunes* (1885–86), which ran in the *Boston Advocate,* was filled with all the melodramatic perils that were features of nineteenth-century sentimental fiction. Seemingly endless chapters dealt with pâpier-maché characters suffering through unrequited loves, jealousies, seductions, alcoholism, hardships, death, family breakups, and reunions.

Propagandistic messages, another ingredient of nineteenth-century fiction, also burdened these works. Didactic speeches and arguments sustained their themes of Christian virtues, racism, or uplifting the race. Miss Garrison's serial, *A Ray of Light* (1889) in the *A. M. E. Church Review,* held forth on themes of Yankee racism and religious hypocrisy. Sophie, the protagonist, lectures her mother who desires to go to a white church: "it is very unpleasant, mother . . . to go among these so-called Christians, and be compelled to sit behind the lowest and meanest of them, when you know you are as good as the best."

Frances Ellen Watkins Harper's *Iola Leroy; or, Shadows Uplifted* (1892) was a propagandistic novel concerned with "morality, race loyalty, and uplift." Her heroine, Iola Leroy, was in the pattern of the "tragic mulatto," introduced in black fiction by William Wells Brown in *Clotel; or, The President's Daughter* (1853). Iola's tragedy begins when she learns from her mother that she has black blood, after having been reared as the cultured daughter of a plantation owner.

Mixed-blood characters continued to permeate black fiction throughout the nineteenth and early twentieth centuries. Clariss Minnie Thompson's Gertie Tremaine had "good" features and "fine, silken curly hair." Similarly, Miss Garrison's Sophie Leland possessed "black silken hair" and "exquisite features," and Frances Ellen Watkins Harper's Iola Leroy exhibited "Beautiful long hair," "purty blue eyes, an jis ez white ez anybody's."

Carole McAlpine Watson has suggested that black characters were designed to look white both to counteract stereotypes and so that white readers could identify with them. It was certainly a pathetic interval in literary history when black women writers were conditioned to think that white readers would not relate to lives unlike their own, and when they were writing of lives that did not reflect their own. Black negative stereotypes abound in white Reconstruction literature, a feature for which white historian Francis Butler Simkins holds white Mississippi writer Irwin Russell responsible: "Russell created a type that for generations would remain a conventional figure of American literature: the Negro as a superstitious, mercurial fellow, irresponsible and good-natured, shrewdly philosophical . . . with a fondness for the banjo and the 'possum.'"

Black characters were probably also fashioned to look white because blacks had few black literary models. Moreover, blacks as slaves had been denigrated for their African color, hair, and features. That black is beautiful was a concept still in the future, and beauty was gauged by white criteria.

Two black women who chose to write novels with what I discern as all white characters were Amelia Etta Hall Johnson and Emma Dunham Kelley-Hawkins. Johnson published the second novel in book form by a black woman, *Clarence and Corinne; or, God's Way* (1890), which was also the first Sunday school book by a black. The novel was published prior to Harper's *Iola Leroy*, which until recently was believed to be the first by a black woman. This ranking of Harper's book came from William Still, author of *The Underground Railroad* (1872) and a friend of the novelist's, who made the statement in the introduction to the first edition of her book. Whether Still was unaware of *Clarence and Corinne* or chose to ignore it because of its white characters and raceless theme is a matter for conjecture. Still certainly could not have been ignorant of the author's race, for Johnson said her reason for writing the book was "to help demonstrate the fact that the colored people have thoughts of their own."

Although Johnson published two other novels, *The Hazeley Family* (1894) and *Martina Meriden; or, What Is My Motive?* (1901), whose illustrations are clearly white, still she remained in the shadow of Harper. The reasons for this can be understood by knowing who Harper was and what she wrote about. She was already a well-known established writer. Her novel echoed what was uppermost in the minds of race leaders and herself—uplifting the race, the effects of slavery on families, miscegenation, and Christian living. Harper's was a protest novel that spoke of the "sins of slavery," whereas Johnson's Sunday school book invoked the "slavery of sin."

Emma Dunham Kelley's *Megda* (1891) ranks as a historical literary gem because it also predates *Iola Leroy*, but it is rarely alluded to. The author's almost lost second novel, *Four Girls at Cottage City*, appeared seven years later bearing the authorship of Emma D. Kelley-Hawkins. Her novels were moralistic romantic stories about young people for young people who were white. They sometimes bore faint messages on classism.

Marie Louise Burgess's *Ave Maria* (1895) also has white characters and a non-black story line about religious differences separating two lovers.

Regardless of the fact that these women decided to write not racially based books but contrived unrealistic novels about whites, they were nevertheless literary foremothers. As such, they should be recognized within the Afro-American black literary tradition, and they should not be looked down upon for writing such books. It was not easy for black women writers to get their works accepted by white publishers. These men were racists and sexists, and fearful of the white reading public's reactions. Black women fiction writers of the nineteenth century "had the choice of being silent completely or compromising their sense of reality if they were published," contended Barbara Christian in *Black Women Novelists: The Development of a Tradition, 1892–1976* (1980).

It is possible that Johnson and Kelley felt that they would have a better chance of publication and thus get their points across by writing about characters of the other race. Or in Johnson's case, she could have been pressured to do so by the white American Baptist Publication Society which brought out her works. Burgess may have merely wanted to write about the effects of religion on love and used white characters to simplify the story. In any case, of all the white publishers, James H. Earle of Boston seems to have published more books by blacks than did any other. Frances Ellen Watkins Harper's second and third editions of *Iola Leroy* bore the Earle imprint.

Frances Anne Rollin Whipper used the male pseudonym Frank A. Rollin to get her *Life and Public Services of Martin R. Delany* (1868) into print. To a lesser degree, some white women writers also found the road to publication a rocky one. This may have been a factor in white southern novelist Mary Noailles Murfree's use of various male pseudonyms. Nineteenth-century America had an abundance of women whom Sandra M. Gilbert and Susan Gubar called "madwomen in the attic," women frustrated by the stifling of their creative urges by the white patriarchy. For black women, the patriarchy was combined with racism.

Alice Ruth Moore Dunbar-Nelson was a fourth writer who utilized white characters. Her *The Goodness of St. Rocque and Other Stories* focused on white New Orleans. Her famous husband, Paul Laurence Dunbar, also wrote novels with white characters. Alice Dunbar's stories measured up to those of her white contemporaries. The pathetic story, "Tony's Wife," which concerns a bullying man who constantly humiliates the woman closest to him even unto his death bed, stands as a classic. Alice Dunbar's book appeared the same year as Charles Chesnutt's *The Conjure Woman and Other Stories*. Chesnutt achieved literary acclaim, but Dunbar, whose book was possibly the first collection of short stories by a black woman, remained in his shadow.

Autobiographies of female evangelists carried on their unique stories of conversion and their bold stance against the racism and sexism of the church. Mrs. Julia A. J. Foote's *A Brand Plucked from the Fire* was copyrighted by her in 1879, and finally printed nine years later by Lauer and Yost of Cleveland, Ohio. The now rediscovered memoir preceded that of the more well-known Amanda Berry Smith's *An Autobiography, the Story of the Lord's Dealing with Mrs. Amanda Smith, the Colored Evangelist . . .* (1893).

Foote was born in Schenectady, New York, in 1823. Her father bought his freedom, and that of his wife and first born. At the age of five, she drained a bottle of liquor found in the house, which made her deathly ill. Foote described her recovery "like a 'brand plucked from the burning.'" There followed other escapes from the devil's fire. Revelations of heavenly visitations similar to those of her sisters of the cloth before her, Jarena Lee and Zilpha Elaw, urged her to enter the ministry. Foote's narration is filled with religious preachments and conversions, combined with her life's experiences. She traveled the religious circuits of the Eastern states and Ohio, where she finally made her home in Cleveland.

Ex-slave narratives continued to be published during the post–Civil War period as more women penned their reminiscences. *The Life of Mrs. Edward Mix, Written by Herself in 1880* was a pamphlet-sized booklet presenting the memoir of a hard-working woman who managed to hold her family and herself together through her religious faith. Mrs. Mix (no other name is given for the author) was born in 1832 at Torrington, Connecticut. She died in 1884, the year her narrative appeared with an appendix by her husband. The autobiography, although a religious testament, should not be discounted as such, for so little is known from a personal perspective concerning the lives of antebellum free black women in the North.

Of the ex-slave narratives, Elizabeth Hobbs Keckley's *Behind the Scenes; or, Thirty Years a Slave, and Four Years in the White House* (1868) was the best known. It aroused the indignation of both whites and blacks, for it told of Mrs. Keckley's close friendship with Mrs. Abraham Lincoln. Keckley wrote the book out of altruistic motives, hoping to change the former first lady's financial state, as well as her controversial image. Instead, Mrs. Keckley was highly criticized for the memoir. Would this have been the case if she had been white, and not an ex-slave or a woman?

To help preserve female ex-slave narratives, Mrs. Octavia Rogers Albert, herself born of slave parents in Oglethorpe, Georgia, in 1853, collected narrations in Louisiana. Mrs. Albert, a schoolteacher and wife of a minister, first published the series in the *Southwestern Christian Advocate*. After her death, the reminiscences were published in a book by her husband and daughter under the title *The House of Bondage; or, Charlotte Brooks and Other Slaves* (1890).

A captivating female ex-slave narrative was issued by Lucy A. Delaney (Lucy Ann Berry Turner Delaney) entitled *From Darkness Cometh Light; or, Struggles for Freedom* (1892). In seven chapters, the author unfolds the story of her mother, Polly Crockett, who was kidnapped as a child in Illinois and taken to St. Louis, Missouri, where she was sold into slavery. Always remembering she was illegally held in bondage, Polly set in motion a lawsuit to regain her freedom and, in the same manner, freed her daughter, Lucy. The memoir bears witness to the plight of free antebellum black women who were always in jeopardy of being sold. But most of all, it is a heart-warming tale of a black mother determined to regain her freedom and that of her daughters. The story reveals her love for them and their love for each other. The book is very rare, for almost the entire edition was sold as waste paper shortly after its publication in St. Louis, Missouri, by J. T. Smith.

A Slave Girl's Story, Being an Autobiography of Kate Drumgoold, privately printed by the author in 1898, is another personal narrative, although its title is misleading. The account of a woman born on the brink of the Civil War, the story is not of enslavement but of postwar growth into womanhood. Filled with religious preachments and names of black and white benefactors, the book is repetitive and frequently digresses. Its importance lies in the detailing of the survival of a young illiterate black girl, who moves from what she terms a slave life "as free as any one could feel" to the life of a self-sufficient literate woman.

Aunt Lindy: A Story Founded on Real Life (1893) by Victoria Earle Matthews is another book with a deceptive title. It resembles an exslave narrative, but it is a short message tale of a woman who nurses her former cruel master back to health after he is injured in a fire. The author conveys the message that the white race should be forgiven for its past sins. Victoria Earle may have heard a similar story and decided to fictionalize it.

Since most of the authors, aside from the ex-slave narrators, lived in the North, perhaps a crucial part of black women's lives and experiences after the war was lost to fiction. The northern middle-class women writers could not know the demeaning economic life of black women domestics or ex-slaves locked in a tenant farm existence with their families, nor could they understand the brutalization of rapes, riots, and lynchings that were so much a part of southern life. As race leaders, there was an air of classism about them in their desire to uplift the black masses to the white level. Because of this, they failed to convey the stark realism in the black existence that would have revolutionized their fiction and humanized their characters.

Frances Ellen Watkins Harper went to live for a short time

among the freedmen, and Victoria Earle Matthews visited Tuskegee, Alabama, but neither remained. If they or others had stayed, it is possible that the literary works of nineteenth-century women might have had more depth, meaning, and true drama in their pictures of black life. It was in the South that folklore, the oral tradition, and the African heritage were to be found, a discovery made by white author Joel Chandler Harris.

Poetry appears to have been a favorite genre among Afro-American women writers. They contributed verses to magazines, journals, and newspapers, although the poets encountered the same obstacles to book publishing as did the prose writers.

Poetry anthologist Erlene Stetson suggests in *Black Sister* that publishers were loath to produce poetry books by black women, owing to their "social biases." Stetson added the factor of classism, since "black women did not have control of the institutions that enable writers to get their thoughts and visions into print."

Frances Ellen Watkins Harper was one, however, who was able to get her poetry published. *Moses: A Story of the Nile* appeared in 1869, *Poems* in 1871, and *Sketches of Southern Life* in 1872. The latter introduced a new ingredient of witticism combined with protest in the narrative dialect poems of Aunt Chloe or Uncle Jacob, a forerunner of Paul Laurence Dunbar's dialect poems.

Harper's poetry books were the only ones to be published between Phillis Wheatley's time and 1890 when Josephine D. Henderson Heard brought forth a volume, *Morning Glories*, which may have been privately published. This was followed five years later by Eloise Bibb Thompson's *Poems*, and Frances Ellen Watkins Harper's *Atlanta Offerings: Poems*.

Mary Weston Fordham's *Magnolia Leaves* (1897) was enhanced with an introduction by Booker T. Washington. Vernon Loggins referred to the book as "containing a number of old-fashioned Puritan elegies and verses on a variety of subjects." Something of the author's background can be discerned from the section "In Memoriam" where the poems are dedicated to family members. Olivia Ward Bush made her publishing debut the last year of the century with *Original Poems* (1899), which launched a writing career that lasted well into the next century.

Much of nineteenth-century black women's poetry was Victorian. They wrote eulogies, lyrical verses, and poems with themes of romance, family, religion, and nature. The women muses had not benefited from what Stetson saw as "a self-conscious tradition," writing "in isolation without the inspiration of earlier sister poets or the help of contemporaries." Too often they wrote of things far removed from their own black lives, like Mary Weston Fordham in "Song to Erin":

> Oh! Erin my country, my ancestor's home!
> Impelled by my wants, I, from these, had to roam;
> And now my heart yearneth, sore longeth for thee
> My dear native Ireland, my "gem of the sea."

Mary Eliza Perine Tucker (Lambert?) has been mistakenly identified in Joan R. Sherman's *Invisible Poets* and an essay in *But Some of Us Are Brave* as a black poet. An autobiographical chapter in *Female Writers of the South* (1872) by Mrs. Mary E. Tucker (who does not have the last name of Lambert even in the *National Union Catalog*) identifies herself as white and a "rebel" born in Alabama. Her writings do not speak to or of blackness.

The black writer, Mrs. M. E. Lambert, was born in Toronto, Canada, and lived in Detroit, Michigan. She was a poet, news correspondent, and editor of the *St. Matthews Lyceum Journal*, published by the St. Matthews Episcopal Church. She is mentioned in Mossell's *The Work of the Afro-American Woman*, Penn's *The Afro-American Press and Its Editors*, Schomburg's *A Biographical Checklist of American Poetry* (1916), and Major's *Noted Negro Women*. From her essay, "A Bunch of Pansies," in the *A. M. E. Church Review*, it can be discerned that she was a teacher. Two of her poems, "Hymn to the New Year" and "My Dreams," were published in the *Review*. She did not write the book of poems cited by Sherman.

In the field of journalism, I. Garland Penn's historic compilation *The Afro-American Press and Its Editors* listed nineteen black female journalists. The first black women's newspaper, the *Women's Era*, was begun in Boston in 1894 by the New Era Club of black women, adding its president, Josephine St. Pierre Ruffin, to the roster of trend-setting women editors. Mrs. N. R. Mossell (Gertrude E. H. Bustill Mossell) counted the "corps of lady writers employed on most of the popular magazines and papers just as large as the male contingent and often more popular if not as scholarly."

Mrs. Mossell was an outstanding journalist who issued a call for black women to consider her field as a career over "domestic work, teaching, or dressmaking." Her notable book contribution, *The Work of the Afro-American Woman* (c. 1894, 1908), gave evidence of the various levels of attainments of black women at that time in all spheres of endeavor.

The growth of the black church gave rise to religious publications that provided an outlet for women writers. In church-related newspapers and magazines, they published poems, short stories, essays, and articles. The *A. M. E. Church Review*, founded in 1841, and believed to be the first black magazine, introduced Miss Garrison's serialized novel. Other writers who utilized the pages of the *Review* were Frances Ellen Watkins Harper, Victoria Earle Matthews, Josephine Turpin Washington, Lillian Lewis, N. F. Mossell, and Alice Dunbar-Nelson as an associate editor.

The Baptist-sponsored *Our Women and Children* magazine, originating in 1888 at Louisville, Kentucky, afforded a special market for women writers. Ione E. Wood, when twenty years old, served as editor of the Temperance Department; Mrs. Mary V. Cook, as editor of the Educational Department; Ida B. Wells, as editor of the Home Department; and Mrs. C. C. Strumm, as correspondent and business manager.

Some women writers branched out on their own with publications. Mrs. Amelia E. Johnson began a journal for black women, the *Joy* in 1887, and the *Ivy* in 1888 for black children. Ida B. Wells, the "Princess of the Press," was editor and co-owner of the *Free Speech*, a newspaper based in Memphis, Tennessee. Miss A. L. Tilghman, a musician and educator, published the *Musical Messenger* for women musicians.

The postwar nineteenth century, then, saw a galaxy of literary firsts by Afro-American women writers and was looked upon by Mrs. N. F. Mossell as the "women's century." In their dual roles as race leaders and women of letters, Afro-American women writers created models for others to follow. It is unfortunate that for a few, parts of their lives are still to be uncovered or have been lost forever.

Chronology of Writings

1868   Frances Anne Rollin Whipper (Pseudonym, Frank A. Rollin), *Life and Public Services of Martin R. Delany*

Elizabeth Hobbs Keckley, *Behind the Scenes; or, Thirty Years a Slave, and Four Years in the White House*

1869   Frances Ellen Watkins Harper, *Moses: A Story of the Nile*

1871   Frances Ellen Watkins Harper, *Poems*

1872   Frances Ellen Watkins Harper, *Sketches of Southern Life*

1884   Mrs. Edward Mix, *The Life of Mrs. Edward Mix, Written by Herself in 1880*

1885–86   Clarissa Minnie Thompson, *Treading the Winepress; or, a Mountain of Misfortune*

1886   Julia A. J. Foote, *A Brand Plucked from the Fire*

1889–90   Miss Garrison, *A Ray of Light*

1890   Amelia Etta Hall Johnson (Mrs. A. E. Johnson), *Clarence and Corinne; or, God's Way*

Josephine Delphine (Henderson) Heard, *Morning Glories*

Octavia Victoria Rogers Albert, *The House of Bondage; or, Charlotte Brooks and Other Slaves*

1891 Emma Dunham Kelley ("Forget-me-Not"), *Megda*

1892 Lucy A. Delaney, *From the Darkness Cometh the Light; or, Struggles for Freedom*

Anna Julia Cooper, *A Voice from the South: By a Black Woman of the South*

Frances Ellen Watkins Harper, *Iola Leroy; or Shadows Uplifted*

1893 Victoria Earle Matthews, *Aunt Lindy: A Story Founded on Real Life*

Amanda Berry Smith, *An Autobiography; the Story of the Lord's Dealings With Mrs. Amanda Smith, the Colored Evangelist; Containing an Account of Her Life Work of Faith, and Her Travels in America, England, Ireland, Scotland, India and Africa, as an Independent Missionary*

H. Cordelia Ray (Henrietta Cordelia Ray), *Sonnets*

1894 Amelia Etta Hall Johnson (Mrs. A. E. Johnson), *The Hazeley Family*

Mrs. N. F. Mossell (Gertrude E. H. Bustill Mossell), *The Work of the Afro-American Woman*

1895 Eloise Bibb (Eloise Bibb Thompson), *Poems*

Marie Louise Burgess (M. L. Burgess), *Ave Maria*

Frances Ellen Watkins Harper, *Atlanta Offerings: Poems*

Ida B. Wells (Ida Bell Wells-Barnett), *A Red Record: Tabulated Statistics and Alleged Causes of Lynchings in the United States, 1892–1893–1894*

Alice Ruth Moore (Alice Ruth Moore Dunbar-Nelson), *Violets and Other Tales*

1897 Mary Weston Fordham, *Magnolia Leaves*

1898 Kate Drumgoold, *A Slave Girl's Story; Being an Autobiography of Kate Drumgoold*

Emma D. Kelley-Hawkins, *Four Girls at Cottage City*

1899 Alice Dunbar (Alice Ruth Moore Dunbar-Nelson), *The Goodness of St. Rocque*

Olivia Ward Bush, *Original Poems*

Frances Anne Rollin Whipper
Frank A. Rollin

1845?/1847?–1901

Frances Anne Rollin was one of four daughters of a Frenchman and mulatto mother from Santo Domingo. She was born free in Charleston, South Carolina, where some of the "choicest society of the Old South," black and white, reigned. The Beaufort, South Carolina, census for 12 June 1900 records her birth date as November 1845. A family account gives it as 19 November 1847.[1]

All the Rollin girls were not only strikingly beautiful, but possessed brains, talent, and a strong feminist outlook. The family was part of the free educated and affluent black society of Charleston. "Strictly top-drawer," they lived in a "well-situated and graciously furnished home on a good street in Charleston."[2]

While the family was visiting in Philadelphia, the Civil War broke out, and they were forced to remain until its end. To continue her education, Frances was enrolled in the Institute for Colored Youth, a school run by Quakers. After the war, she applied to the American Missionary Association for her first teaching position and was hired by Thomas W. Cardoza on 1 May 1865 to teach in the freedmen school in Charleston.

In July 1865, she challenged a racist white boat captain, W. F. McNelty, of the inter-island steamer, *Pilot Boy*, who refused to sell her a first-class ticket between Charleston and Beaufort. When she filed a complaint against him at army headquarters, she met Maj. Martin R. Delany, a black army officer who assisted her with the charge. Captain McNelty was found guilty of discrimination against Frances A. Rollin and was fined $250. The decision was reputed to have set a "precedent for the country, coming before the 14th Amendment had been ratified and eight years before Congress itself in the Civil Rights Act of 1875, applied."[3]

Becoming friendly with Delany, Frances told him of her interest in writing, and the two planned a book about his life. All during the summer and fall of 1867, they worked on the biography with Frances interviewing him and studying his personal papers. The task was not an easy one, for Martin R. Delany was an extraordinary man. Born free of African parents at Charleston, Virginia, in 1812, he did not receive formal schooling until he was ten years old and his parents moved to Chambersburgh, Pennsylvania. Eventually they settled in Pittsburgh, where he grew up and started a newspaper, the *Mystery*, in 1843. When the paper ceased publication in 1847, he joined Abolitionist Frederick Douglass in publishing the *North Star*.

Delany was a journalist, scientist, explorer, medical doctor, and author. His novel, *Blake, or, the Huts of America: A Tale of the Mississippi Valley, the Southern United States and Cuba,* which dealt with life in the slave quarters, was serialized in the *Anglo-African* in January–July 1859. After receiving his medical training at Harvard, Delany practiced in Pittsburgh and Canada. As an explorer, he led a group of prospective colonizers into the Niger Valley of Africa. He published books on his travels, as well as scientific studies. Delany is popularly recognized today as the Father of Black Nationalism. He favored the emigration of black people to Central and South America and expounded on the concept of black power. An interview with President Lincoln led to his appointment as the first black army officer.

With so many accomplishments behind him, it is little wonder that young impressionable Frances Rollin became his ardent admirer. She went to Boston in 1867 to write her book and find a publisher. There she kept a diary, and her entry of 3 January 1868, reads: "Writing as hard as ever, I know not with what success I shall meet, but I feel there is a strength in the endeavor which will be of service to me hereafter."[4] Staying at the home of family friends who were connected with Harvard, she wrote in the mornings and read the classics in the afternoon. At night, she attended cultural events and meetings of the Anti-Slavery League.

The time was not without difficulties. Frances became ill, and money problems were pressing. Her parents were unable to help her, for they had not received restitution for their property sacked by the Union forces. Delany sent money from time to time, but a dispute with the government over pay caused him to fall behind with his promise of support.

After completing the book, Frances encountered racist and sexist publishers. Her "manuscript was flatly rejected by several companies who were not interested in a book written by a black woman on any subject."[5] Finally she decided to use the male pseudonym of Frank A. Rollin. (Frank was a nickname given her by her parents.) The book, *Life and Public Services of Martin R. Delany*, was brought out in 1868 by Boston publishers Lee and Shepard. With the publication of the work, Frances A. Rollin, like her black female predecessors, had added another significant precedent to Afro-American literature: she had written the first biography of a free-born black man. A review in the *Christian Record* called it "decidedly the best book of its kind that has emanated from a colored author in this country."[6] The biography, which was reissued in 1883, enjoyed a "moderate success in its day and became a valuable reference for later historians."[7]

Soon after returning to Charleston, Frances Rollin married widower William J. Whipper, son of an Underground Railroad conductor, moralist, and lumber merchant William Whipper of Pennsylvania. Whipper opened the "first black law firm in the United States," Whipper, Elliott, and Allen, in Charleston in 1868.[8] Upon entering the newspaper business, he started the *Beaufort Times*, which Frances edited.

A prominent political figure in the Republican party, Whipper was a member of the Reconstructionist Congress and an advocate for women's suffrage. He and Frances had five children, two of whom died at an early age. The three surviving children grew up to make names for themselves. Ionia, after ten years of teaching in Washington, D. C., entered Howard University's medical school over the objections of her friends. She graduated in 1903 and later founded the Ionia Whipper Home for Unwed Mothers, still in operation. Winifred became a dedicated teacher in the public school system of Washington, D.C., and son Leigh gave up a law career to become an outstanding actor.

Being a wife and mother did not prevent Frances Rollin Whipper from participating, along with her three sisters, in the radical politics of the day. The sisters in Columbia, South Carolina, were known as the "social arbiters of Negro and Radical Society in the city."[9] Louisa spoke before the House of Representatives in 1869 for "sexless suffrage," and in 1871, Lottie led the drive in the capital for female suffrage with brother-in-law William J. Whipper as a spokesman. Frances's deep regard for Delany could also have been based on his nonsexist outlook. Delany took a stand for the equality of women, professing that "men would not be elevated without women's elevation."

Frances and Whipper encountered problems in their marriage over the years, and she left him in 1881, saying "she could no longer tolerate her husband's drinking and gambling."[10] She moved with her three children to Washington, D.C., where she obtained employment as a court transcriber. By this means, she educated her son and daughters.

Writing of his adopted mother, Demps Whipper Powell observed that "there was something refreshing and stimulating, something more than ordinary. Yes, something worthy of remembrance and emulation."[11] Truly, Frances Rollin Whipper was an extraordinary woman who broke the white male publishing barrier to produce an important work. Her great-granddaughter Carole Bovoso is writing a book about her foremothers' lives, which should shed additional light on Frances's career. She died 17 October 1901 in Beaufort, South Carolina.

NOTES

1. Demps Whipper Powell, "A Providential Revelation; Relationship with the Whipper Family," Leigh Whipper Papers, Moorland-Spingarn Research Center, Howard University, Washington, D.C., p. 5.
2. Majors and Saunders, *Black Society*, p. 178.
3. Ullman, *Delany*, p. 410.
4. Carole Bovoso, "Discovering My Foremothers," *Ms.* 6 (September 1977:56–59.
5. Ibid.
6. Sterling, *Afro-American*, p. 280.
7. Ibid.
8. Majors and Saunders, *Black Society*, p. 178
9. Williamson, *After Slavery*, p. 176.
10. Bovoso, "Discovering," p. 57.
11. Powell, "Providential Revelation," p. 5.

SELECTED SOURCES

Primary

Rollin, Frances A. [Frank A. Rollin]. *Life and Public Service of Martin R. Delany.* Boston: Lee & Shepard, 1868.

Secondary

Loggins, Vernon. *The Negro Author: His Development in America.* New York: Columbia University Press, 1931.
Majors, Gerri, and Saunders, Doris E. *Black Society.* Chicago: Johnson Publishing Co., 1976.
Sterling, Dorothy. *The Making of an Afro-American: Martin Robison Delany, 1812–1885.* New York: Doubleday & Co., 1971.
Ullman, Victor. *Martin R. Delany: The Beginning of Black Nationalism.* Boston: Beacon Press, 1971.
Williamson, Joel. *After Slavery: The Negro in South Carolina During Reconstruction, 1861–1877.* Chapel Hill: University of North Carolina Press, 1965.

The Council-Chamber—President Lincoln

We give in Major Delany's own language his interview with President Lincoln.

He tells us, "On entering the executive chamber, and being introduced to his excellency, a generous grasp and shake of the hand brought me to a seat in front of him. No one could mistake the fact that an able and master spirit was before me. Serious without sadness, and pleasant withal, he was soon seated, placing himself at ease, the better to give me a patient audience. He opened the conversation first.

"'What can I do for you, sir?' he inquired.

"'Nothing, Mr. President,' I replied; 'but I've come to propose something to you, which I think will be beneficial to the nation in this critical hour of her peril.' I shall never forget the expression of his countenance and the inquiring look which he gave me when I answered him.

"'Go on, sir,' he said, as I paused through deference to him. I continued the conversation by reminding him of the full realization of arming the blacks of the South, and the ability of the blacks of the North to defeat it by complicity with those at the South, through the medium of the *Underground Railroad*—a measure known only to themselves.

"I next called his attention to the fact of the heartless and almost relentless prejudice exhibited towards the blacks by the Union army, and that something ought to be done to check this growing feeling against the slave, else nothing that we could do would avail. And if such were not expedited, all might be lost. That the blacks, in every capacity in which they had been called to act, had done their part faithfully and well. To this Mr. Lincoln readily assented. I continued: 'I would call your attention to another fact of great consideration; that is, the position of confidence in which they have been placed, when your officers have been under obligations to them, and in many instances even the army in their power. As pickets, scouts, and guides, you have trusted them, and found them faithful to the duties assigned; and it follows that if you can find them of higher qualifications, they may, with equal credit, fill higher and more important trusts.'

"'*Certainly*,' replied the president, in his most emphatic manner. 'And what do you propose to do?' he inquired.

"I responded, 'I propose this, sir; but first permit me to say that, whatever I may desire for black men in the army, I know that there exists too much prejudice among the whites for the soldiers to serve under a black commander, or the officers to be willing to associate with him. These are facts which must be admitted, and, under the circumstances, must be regarded, as they cannot be ignored. And I propose, as a most effective remedy to prevent enrolment of the blacks in the rebel service, and induce them to run to, instead of from, the Union forces—the commissioning and promotion of black men now in the army, according to merit.'

"Looking at me for a moment, earnestly yet anxiously, he demanded, 'How will you remedy the great difficulty you have just now so justly described, about the objections of white soldiers to colored commanders, and officers to colored associates?'

"I replied, 'I have the remedy, Mr. President, which has not yet been stated; and it is the most important suggestion of my visit to you. And I think it is just what is required to complete the prestige of the Union army. I propose, sir, an army of blacks, commanded entirely by black officers, except such whites as may volunteer to serve; this army to penetrate through the heart of the South, and make conquests, with the banner of Emancipation unfurled, proclaiming freedom as they go, sustaining and protecting it by arming the emancipated, taking them as fresh troops, and leaving a few veterans among the new freedmen, when occasion requires, keeping this banner unfurled until every slave is free, according to the letter of your proclamation. I would also take from those already in the service all that are competent for commission officers, and establish at once in the South a camp of instructions. By this we could have in about three months an army of forty thousand blacks in motion, the presence of which anywhere would itself be a power irresistible. You should have an army of blacks, President Lincoln, commanded entirely by blacks, the sight of which is required to give confidence to the slaves, and retain them to the Union, stop foreign intervention, and speedily bring the war to a close.'

"'This,' replied the president, 'is the very thing I have been looking and hoping for; but nobody offered it. I have thought it over and over again. I have talked about it; I hoped and prayed for it; but till now it never has been proposed. White men couldn't do this, because they are doing all in that direction now that they can; but we find, for various reasons, it does not meet the case under consideration. The blacks should go to the interior, and the whites be kept on the frontiers.'

"'Yes, sir,' I interposed; 'they would require but little, as they could subsist on the country as they went along.'

"'Certainly,' continued he; 'a few light artillery, with the cavalry, would comprise your principal advance, because all the siege work would be on the frontiers and waters, done by the white division of the army. Won't this be a grand thing?' he exclaimed, joyfully. He continued, 'When I issued my Emancipation Proclamation, I had this thing in contemplation. I then gave them a chance by prohibiting any interference on the part of the army; but they did not embrace it,' said he, rather sadly, accompanying the word with an emphatic gesture.

"'But, Mr. President,' said I, 'these poor people could not read your proclamation, nor could they know anything about it, only, when they did hear, to know that they were free.'

"'But you of the North I expected to take advantage of it,' he replied.

"'Our policy, sir,' I answered, 'was directly opposite, supposing that it met your approbation. To this end I published a letter against embarrassing or compromising the government in any manner whatever; for us to remain passive, except in case of foreign intervention, then immediately to raise the slaves to insurrection.'

"'Ah, I remember the letter,' he said, 'and thought at the time that you mistook my designs. But the effect will be better as it is, by giving character to the blacks, both North and South, as a peaceable, inoffensive people.' Suddenly turning, he said, 'Will you take command?'

"'If there be none better qualified than I am, sir, by that time I will. While it is my desire to serve, as black men we shall have to prepare ourselves, as we have had no opportunities of experience and practice in the service as officers.'

"'That matters but little, comparatively,' he replied; 'as some of the finest officers we have never studied the tactics till they entered the army as subordinates. And again,' said he, 'the tactics are easily learned, especially among your people. It is the head that we now require most—men of plans and executive ability.'

"'I thank you, Mr. President,' said I, 'for the—'

"'No—not at all,' he interrupted.

"'I will show you some letters of introduction, sir,' said I, putting my hand in my pocket to get them.

"'Not now,' he interposed; 'I know all about you. I see nothing now to be done but to give you a line of introduction to the secretary of war.'

"Just as he began writing, the cannon commenced booming.

"'Stanton is firing! listen! he is in his glory! noble man!' he exclaimed.

"'What is it, Mr. President?' I asked.

"'The firing!'

"'What is it about, sir,' I reiterated, ignorant of the cause.

"'Why, don't you know? Haven't you heard the news? Charleston is ours!' he answered, straightening up from the table on which he was writing for an instant, and then resuming it. He soon handed me a card, on which was written,—

'February 8, 1865.

'Hon. E. M. Stanton, *Secretary of War.*

'Do not fail to have an interview with this most extraordinary and intelligent black man.

'A. Lincoln.'

"This card showed he perfectly understood my views and feelings; hence he was not content that my color should make its own impression, but he expressed it with emphasis, as though a point was gained. The thing desired presented itself; not simply a man that was *black*, because these had previously presented themselves, in many delegations and committees,—men of the highest intelligence,—for various objects; but that which he had wished and hoped for, their own proposed measures matured in the council-chamber had never been fully presented to them in the person of a black man."

This, then, was what was desired to complete the plans of the president and his splendid minister, the secretary of war. The "ponderous beam," being removed, to use his figurative expression, his passport was clear to every part of the mansion. He entered the war department for the purpose of seeing the minister. As he entered, a glance revealed to him the presiding genius of the situation, surrounded by his assistants. In the room was a pressing crowd of both sexes, representing nearly every condition of life, each in turn endeavoring to reach the centre of the room, where, at an elevated desk, stood one of the greatest men of the times, and the able director of the war department.

After he had sent forward his card, he was requested by the secretary in person, to whom he was not previously unknown, to call at the department again.

He had gained the interview with the president that he wished, and the indications were brighter than his most sanguine expectations had promised. The war minister's influence alone could effect the balance.

He sought Dr. William Elder, the distinguished biographer of Dr. Kane, of Arctic memory, who was then chief of the bureau of statistics, and gave him an account of his mission to the president.

After explaining everything to the doctor, his face assuming an expression peculiar to himself, of a whole-souled satisfaction, he exclaimed, "I'll be hanged if I haven't got the thing! just the thing! Will you give me that in writing?" he asked; "I mean the points touched upon, that may be written in a letter to me."

On receiving it, in the afternoon of the same day, after he had read it, he turned to the future major, and said, "*You shall* have what you want," in like manner as he replied to a speech of Louis Kossuth, when he told him if he went to war with Austria, *he shouldn't die.*

When Delany left Dr. Elder, he was thoroughly convinced, that if the secretary of war could be influenced by any man, in regard to his mission, in none abler could he depend than upon this true and earnest advocate of his race.

The next call at the war department was made the following Monday, the 12th inst. His reception there, being equally as cordial as the first, seemed already to indicate success to his measures.

"What do you propose to do, doctor?" asked the secretary, as Dr. Delany began to explain to him as he did to the president. "I understand the whole thing, and fully comprehend your design; I have frequently gone over the whole ground, in council with the president. What do you wish? What position?" He replied,—

"In any position or place whatever, in which I may be instrumental in promoting the measures proposed, and be of service to the country, so that I am not subject and subordinate to every man who holds a commission, and, with such, chooses to assume authority."

"Will you take the field?" asked the secretary.

"I should like to do so as soon as possible, but not until I have had sufficient discipline and practice in a camp of instruction, and a sufficient number of black officers to command each regiment," was the answer given.

"Of course," said the secretary, "you must establish your camp of instruction; and as you have a general knowledge of the qualified colored men of the country, I propose to commission you at once, and send you South to commence raising troops, to be commanded by black officers, on the principles you proposed, of which I most highly approve, to prevent all clashing or jealousy,—because of no contact to arouse prejudices. It is none of white men's business what rank a black man holds over his own people. I shall assign you to Charleston, with advices and instructions to Major General Saxton. Do you know him?" he asked. Being answered, he continued, "He is an unflinching friend of your race. You will impart to him, in detail, that which will not be written. The letter giving special instructions will be given to you—all further instructions to be obtained at the department."

Assistant Adjutant General of Volunteers Colonel C. W. Foster, at this juncture having been sent for, was instructed by the secretary of war to take him to his department, and make the necessary examination; there being no rejection, to prepare and fill out a parchment, with commission of *Major of Infantry*, the *regiment* to be left blank, to be filled by order of Major General Saxton, according to instructions to be given, and to report the next morning at eleven o'clock.

After the examination by the adjutant general, he remarked, "This is certainly an important and interesting feature of the war. And the secretary must expect much to be done by you, for he certainly holds you in high esteem."

"I hope, colonel," he replied, "that neither the honorable secretary of war nor the government will expect too much from an individual like myself. My only hope is, that I may be able to do my duty well and satisfactorily."

"I have no fears for your success," returned the colonel; "you have qualifications and ability, and must succeed, when your chances are such as they will now be. This is a great thing for you," he continued, "and you have now an opportunity of making yourself *anything that you please,* and doing for your race all that may be required at the hands of the government." He, attempting to thank the colonel for the encouraging as well as complimentary remarks, was stopped by him, saying, "I speak as I think and feel about it. The secretary has great confidence in you, and I simply wish to indorse it for your encouragement. There is nothing now to be done," he continued, "but to call tomorrow, and go with me to the war department to report finally to the secretary of war, and receive your commission from his hands." All arrangements being completed in the adjutant's department, he withdrew.

Elizabeth Hobbs Keckley

1824/5?–1907

In writing of her life, Elizabeth Hobbs Keckley, respectfully referred to as Madame Keckley by President Lincoln, became the first black to write an intimate exposé, or what she called "the secret history" of the White House. Her book, *Behind the Scenes; or, Thirty Years a Slave, and Four Years in the White House* (1868) was written when she was over forty. The narrative is now considered a classic in Lincolniana, particularly for its perceptive insights into the life of Mary Todd Lincoln.

As with Phillis Wheatley and Harriet Jacobs, the question has arisen as to whether Mrs. Keckley actually wrote the book. She admitted having received constructive grammatical assistance from her publishers, G. W. Carleton, but that was all. Her writing has been praised as being of "a high and elegant style, in the best novelistic diction of the times."[1] When the work was reissued in 1931, the matter of its true authorship came up again, causing the Reverend Francis Grimké, her minister and longtime friend, together with other prominent blacks, to come to her defense.

Agnes Hobbs, a mulatto slave of Col. A. Burwell, gave birth to Elizabeth at Dinwiddie Court-House, Virginia. The exact birth date varies with the sources. John E. Washington, a Lincoln scholar, placed the date at "about 1818" in his *They Knew Lincoln*. Some anthologists have suggested 1825, and the Library of Congress records it as 1824. Elizabeth assumed at first that George Pleasant, a slave on another plantation, was her father. She saw him twice a year, at Christmas and Easter, when he was allowed to visit her mother. The occasional visits ceased when he was sold away. In the twilight of her life she disclosed to a friend that her mother once told her that her real father was her master.[2]

Elizabeth's life as a slave was similar to her black sisters in bondage, the burden usually hard but sometimes light, depending on the whims and hearts of the owners. At the age of four, when most children are still being cared for, Elizabeth was removed from the slave cabin to attend to her master's newborn child, not realizing, of course, that she was her half sister, also named Elizabeth. When she was fourteen, Elizabeth was loaned out to work for her master's eldest son, a Presbyterian minister of poor circumstances. The minister moved his family to Hillsboro, North Carolina, where he took charge of a church. Although she did the work of three servants, Elizabeth was disliked and mistreated by her mistress. Apparently jealous of the fair-skinned slave girl with "Grecian" features and long black hair, the woman had a sadistic schoolteacher try to beat her into submissiveness. Savage beatings by the teacher, as well as her clergyman master, failed to subdue Elizabeth's "proud, rebellious spirit."

When she reached eighteen years of age, she was given by her master to a friend, Alexander Kirkland, who had had designs on her since she was fifteen years old. She was compelled to be his mistress for four years, a time that later in her life she preferred to forget. She bore him a child whom she named George, perhaps after the George who had been her only father image. Her son never knew his white father, however, for Kirkland died when the child was eighteen months old.

Elizabeth returned to Virginia to live with a new master, a Mr. Garland, who had married one of her old master's daughters. The family followed him to St. Louis, where he had a difficult time making ends meet. Rather than having her master place her aging mother out for hire, Elizabeth offered her services as a seamstress. By this work, she kept bread in the mouths of seventeen persons for two years and five months. The strain of the task, however, told on her health. During this time, James Keckley, a close friend from Virginia, came to St. Louis. He proposed to her and they were married in her master's parlor. The marriage was a disappointment: Keckley was not the free man he had claimed to be, and he led a life of dissipation.

Bent on purchasing freedom for herself and her son, Elizabeth saved whatever she could from her labors. When her mistress, Anne P. Garland, promised her her freedom for twelve hundred dollars, a patron, Mrs. LeBourgois, solicited money from her friends to lend her. With this, Elizabeth bought her freedom in 1855 after thirty years as a slave.

The turning point in Elizabeth Keckley's life came in 1860, when she left her husband and went to Baltimore. In that city, she attempted to set up sewing classes for "young, colored women," but she was unsuccessful and after six weeks, she continued on to Washington, D.C. Because she was a skillful seamstress, her business increased through word of mouth, and she became a modiste for Washington society. She made dresses for the wives of Jefferson Davis, Stephen A. Douglas, and E. M. Stanton. As Washington's "most famous seamstress," she hired twenty girls in her establishment.

Mrs. Lincoln's accidental spilling of coffee on a dress she had planned to wear at an inaugural reception brought Elizabeth Keckley and Mary Todd Lincoln together. Mrs. McClean, daughter of General Sumner, recommended Lizzie Keckley to the president's wife to make another dress, and after Mrs. Lincoln interviewed several seamstresses, Mrs. Keckley was chosen. She made a rose-colored moiré-antique, which was warmly admired by the president.

As Mrs. Lincoln's modiste during her years in the White House, "Lizabeth," as she was affectionately called by the first lady, became her intimate friend and confidante. Some considered this quite an accomplishment, in view of Mrs. Lincoln's temper and volatile disposition. According to John E. Washington, it was said that Mrs. Lincoln would yield to Mrs. Keckley when her husband could not get her to budge. When the first lady suffered from her frequent headaches, she wanted Lizabeth to be with her, and the night of the assassination, it was Lizabeth she wanted more than anyone by her side.

Early in the war, Mrs. Keckley's son was killed at the Battle of Lexington, Missouri (Wilson Creek), on 10 August 1861. A former student at Wilberforce University, he had enlisted in the Union army as "white."[3] In 1863, with the aid of Mrs. Lincoln, Elizabeth began to receive a small pension as a result of his death, which helped support her in her later years.

Upon seeing freedmen from Virginia and Maryland crowding the capitol in 1862, she was appalled by their predicament and assisted in founding the Contraband Relief Association. She succeeded in getting money from prominent blacks, philanthropists, and the Lincolns. She was reelected president of the association in 1863 and held that office until the war ended.

Mrs. Keckley's devotion and loyalty to Mrs. Lincoln was more than proven after the president's death. At the request of the first lady, she went to live with her in Chicago, when Mrs. Lincoln had to leave the White House. During this trying period of transition, Mrs. Lincoln told her, "Lizabeth, you are my best and kindest friend, and I love you as my best friend."[4]

Mrs. Lincoln was financially unable to retain Mrs. Keckley, who returned to Washington to reopen her shop. In 1867, Mrs. Lincoln wrote to her, asking her to come and help her sell her wardrobe, for she could not meet expenses. Mrs. Lincoln was known for her extravagant and expensive tastes—the inaugural gown alone had cost two thousand dollars. The most haunting and controversial section of *Behind the Scenes* deals with Mrs. Lincoln's attempt to sell her clothes, for which little was realized.

Mrs. Keckley was harshly criticized for writing the book. A racist mockery of it entitled *Behind the Scenes; by a Nigger Woman who Took in Work from Mrs. Lincoln and Mrs. Davis* was published in New York, also in 1868. The preface was signed "Betsey (x) Kickley (Nigger)."[5] Even Robert Todd Lincoln became incensed because his mother's letters to Mrs. Keckley were published, and he tried to have the book suppressed. Although Mrs. Keckley tried to explain that the letters were included without her permission, he remained hostile toward her. Blacks in domestic service felt the book jeopardized their positions. As a result of the animosity toward the publication of the book, Mrs. Keckley's trade fell off.

She apparently had anticipated some criticism, judging from her preface: "It may be charged that I have written too freely on some questions, especially in regard to Mrs. Lincoln. I do not think so; at least I have been prompted by the purest motive."[6] Throughout the preface, Mrs. Keckley maintains that the writing of the book was to help Mrs. Lincoln: "If I have betrayed confidence in anything I have published, it has been to place Mrs. Lincoln in a better light before the world."[7]

After giving up her trade, Mrs. Keckley went to Wilberforce University in 1892 and became a teacher in domestic art for two years. The tall, stately, always well-groomed woman with scars from slavery on her back was well loved by all her students.

The last days of her life were spent at the Home for Destitute Women and Children, which she had helped establish in Washington, D.C. There, alone, she passed away her hours in a dingy basement room she rented. It was said that she suffered greatly from headaches and crying spells nearly all the time, but no one knew why she grieved so. "All day long she looked at Mrs. Lincoln's picture above the dresser, and seldom left her room for meals."[7] Elizabeth Keckley died in her sleep from a paralytic stroke on 20 May 1907. It was an unheralded passing of "One who, through love, carried throughout life a condemnation undeserved, just because she loved her friend, Mrs. Lincoln with a love that never died."[9]

This friendship between two women of different races and background—one black, a former slave, and the other white, of old-line Kentucky stock and the first lady of the land—is unparalleled and makes a captivating story of women bonding despite their differences.

NOTES

1. Barksdale and Kinnamon, *Black Writers*, p. 306.
2. Washington, *They Knew Lincoln*, p. 205.
3. Ibid., p. 208.

4. Keckley, *Behind the Scenes*, p. 210.
5. Davis and Redding, *Cavalcade*, p. 132.
6. Keckley, *Behind the Scenes*, p. xiii.
7. Ibid., p. xiv.
8. Washington, *They Knew Lincoln*, p. 241.
9. Ibid., p. 223.

SELECTED SOURCES

Primary

Keckley, Elizabeth. *Behind the Scenes; or, Thirty Years a Slave, and Four Years in the White House.* New York: G. W. Carleton, 1868.

Secondary

Barksdale, Richard, and Kinnamon, Keneth. *Black Writers of America: A Comprehensive Anthology.* New York: Macmillan Co., 1972.

Brown, Hallie Quinn. *Homespun Heroines and Other Women of Distinction.* Xenia, Ohio: Aldine, 1926.

Brown, Sterling Allen; Davis, Arthur P.; and Lee, Ulysses, eds. *The Negro Caravan: Writings by American Negroes.* New York: Dryden Press, 1941.

Dannett, Sylvia G. L. *Profiles of Negro Womanhood.* Vol. 1, *1619–1900.* Yonkers, N.Y.: Educational Heritage, 1964.

Davis, Arthur P., and Redding, Saunders. *Cavalcade: Negro American Writing from 1760 to the Present.* Boston: Houghton Mifflin Co., 1971.

Gwin, Minrose C. *Black and White Women of the Old South: The Peculiar Sisterhood in American Literature.* Knoxville: University of Tennessee Press, 1985.

———. "Green-eyed Monsters of the Slavocracy: Jealous Mistresses in Two Slave Narratives." In *Conjuring: Black Women, Fiction, and Literary Tradition,* edited by Marjorie Pryse and Hortense J. Spillers. Bloomington: Indiana University Press, 1985.

Loggins, Vernon. *The Negro Author: His Development in America.* New York: Columbia University Press, 1931.

Majors, Monroe Alphus. *Noted Black Women, Their Triumphs and Activities.* Chicago: Donohue & Hennesberry, 1893.

Washington, John E. *They Knew Lincoln.* New York: E. P. Dutton & Co., 1942.

The Secret History of Mrs. Lincoln's Wardrobe in New York

In March, 1867, Mrs. Lincoln wrote to me from Chicago that, as her income was insufficient to meet her expenses, she would be obliged to give up her house in the city, and return to boarding. She said that she had struggled long enough to keep up appearances, and that the mask must be thrown aside. "I have not the means," she wrote, "to meet the expenses of even a first-class boarding-house, and must sell out and secure cheap rooms at some place in the country. It will not be startling news to you, my dear Lizzie, to learn that I must sell a portion of my wardrobe to add to my resources, so as to enable me to live decently, for you remember what I told you in Washington, as well as what you understood before you left me here in Chicago. I cannot live on $1,700 a year, and as I have many costly things which I shall never wear, I might as well turn them into money, and thus add to my income, and make my circumstances easier. It is humiliating to be placed in such a position, but, as I am in the position, I must extricate myself as best I can. Now, Lizzie, I want to ask a favor of you. It is imperative that I should do something for my relief, and I want you to meet me in New York, between the 30th of August and the 5th of September next, to assist me in disposing of a portion of my wardrobe."

I knew that Mrs. Lincoln's income was small, and also knew that she had many valuable dresses, which could be of no value to her, packed away in boxes and trunks. I was confident that she would never wear the dresses again, and thought that, since her need was urgent, it would be well enough to dispose of them quietly, and believed that New York was the best place to transact a delicate business of the kind. She was the wife of Abraham Lincoln, the man who had done so much for my race, and I could refuse to do nothing for her, calculated to advance her interests. I consented to render Mrs. Lincoln all the assistance in my power, and many letters passed between us in regard to the best way to proceed. It was finally arranged that I should meet her in New York about the middle of September. While thinking over this question, I remembered an incident of the White

House. When we were packing up to leave Washington for Chicago, she said to me, one morning:

"Lizzie, I may see the day when I shall be obliged to sell a portion of my wardrobe. If Congress does not do something for me, then my dresses some day may have to go to bring food into my mouth, and the mouths of my children."

I also remembered of Mrs. L. having said to me at different times, in the years of 1863 and '4, that her expensive dresses might prove of great assistance to her some day.

"In what way, Mrs. Lincoln? I do not understand," I ejaculated, the first time she made the remark to me.

"Very simple to understand. Mr. Lincoln is so generous that he will not save anything from his salary, and I expect that we will leave the White House poorer than when we came into it; and should such be the case, I will have no further need for an expensive wardrobe, and it will be policy to sell it off."

I thought at the time that Mrs. Lincoln was borrowing trouble from the future, and little dreamed that the event which she so dimly foreshadowed would ever come to pass.

I closed my business about the 10th of September, and made every arrangement to leave Washington on the mission proposed. On the 15th of September I received a letter from Mrs. Lincoln, postmarked Chicago, saying that she should leave the city so as to reach New York on the night of the 17th, and directing me to precede her to the metropolis, and secure rooms for her at the St. Denis Hotel in the name of Mrs. Clarke, as her visit was to be *incog.* The contents of the letter were startling to me. I had never heard of the St. Denis, and therefore presumed that it could not be a first-class house. And I could not understand why Mrs. Lincoln should travel, without protection, under an assumed name. I knew that it would be impossible for me to engage rooms at a strange hotel for a person whom the proprietors knew nothing about. I could not write to Mrs. Lincoln, since she would be on the road to New York before a letter could possibly reach Chicago. I could not telegraph her, for the business was of too delicate a character to be trusted to the wires that would whisper the secret to every curious operator along the line. In my embarrassment, I caught at a slender thread of hope, and tried to derive consolation from it. I knew Mrs. Lincoln to be indecisive about some things, and I hoped that she might change her mind in regard to the strange programme proposed, and at the last moment despatch me to this effect. The 16th, and then the 17th of September passed, and no despatch reached me, so on the 18th I made all haste to take the train for New York. After an anxious ride, I reached the city in the evening, and when I stood alone in the streets of the great metropolis, my heart sank within me. . . .

It is not necessary for me to dwell upon the public history of Mrs. Lincoln's unfortunate venture. The question has been discussed in all the newspapers of the land, and these discussions are so recent that it would be useless to introduce them in these pages, even if I had an inclination to do so. The following, from the New York *Evening Express*, briefly tells the story:

"The attraction for ladies, and the curious and speculative of the other sex in this city, just now, is the grand exposition of Lincoln dresses at the office of Mr. Brady, on Broadway, a few doors south of Houston street. The publicity given to the articles on exhibition and for sale has excited the public curiosity, and hundreds of people, principally women with considerable leisure moments at disposal, daily throng the rooms of Mr. Brady, and give himself and his shop-woman more to do than either bargained for, when a lady, with face concealed with a veil, called and arranged for the sale of the superabundant clothing of a distinguished and titled, but nameless lady. Twenty-five dresses, folded or tossed about by frequent examinations, lie exposed upon a closed piano, and upon a lounge; shawls rich and rare are displayed upon the backs of chairs, but the more exacting obtain a better view and closer inspection by the lady attendant throwing them occasionally upon her shoulders, just to oblige, so that their appearance on promenade might be seen and admired. Furs, laces, and jewelry are in a glass case, but the 'four thousand dollars in gold' point outfit is kept in a paste-board box, and only shown on special request.

"The feeling of the majority of visitors is adverse to the course Mrs. Lincoln has thought proper to pursue, and the criticisms are as severe as the cavillings are persistent at the quality of some of the dresses. These latter are labelled at Mrs. Lincoln's own estimate, and prices range from $25 to $75—about 50 per cent less than cost. Some of them, if not worn long, have been worn much; they are jagged under the arms and at the bottom of the skirt, stains are on the lining, and other objections present themselves to those who oscillate between the dresses and dollars, 'notwithstanding they have been worn by Madam Lincoln,' as a lady who looked from behind a pair of gold spectacles remarked. Other dresses, however, have scarcely been worn—one, perhaps, while Mrs. Lincoln sat for her picture, and from one the basting threads had not yet been removed. The general testimony is that the wearing apparel is high-priced, and some of the examiners say that the cost-figures must have been put on by the dress-makers; or, if such was not the case, that gold was 250 when they were purchased, and is now but 140—so that a dress for which $150 was paid at the rate of high figures cannot be called cheap at half that sum, after it has been worn considerable, and perhaps passed out of fashion. The peculiarity of the dresses is that most of them are cut low-necked—a taste which some ladies attribute to Mrs. Lincoln's appreciation of her own bust.

"On Saturday last an offer was made for all the dresses. The figure named was less than the aggregate estimate placed on them. Mr. Brady, however, having no discretionary power, he declined to close the bargain, but notified Mrs. Lincoln by mail. Of course, as yet, no reply has been received. Mrs. L. desires that the auction should be deferred till the 31st of the present month, and efforts made to dispose of the articles at private sale up to that time.

"A Mrs. C—— called on Mr. Brady this morning, and examined minutely each shawl. Before leaving the lady said that, at the time when there was a hesitancy about the President issuing the Emancipation Proclamation, she sent to Mrs. Lincoln an ashes-of-rose shawl, which was manufactured in China, forwarded to France, and thence to Mrs. C——, in New York. The shawl, the lady remarked, was a very handsome one, and should it come into the hands of Mr. Brady to be sold, would like to be made aware of the fact, so as to obtain possession again. Mr. Brady promised to acquaint the ashes-of-rose donor, if the prized article should be among the two trunks of goods now on the way from Chicago."

So many erroneous reports were circulated, that I made a correct statement to one of the editors of the New York *Evening News*. The article based upon the memoranda furnished by me appeared in the *News* of Oct. 12, 1867. I reproduce a portion of it in this connection:

"Mrs. Lincoln feels sorely aggrieved at many of the harsh criticisms that have been passed upon her for travelling incognito. She claims that she adopted this course from motives of delicacy, desiring to avoid publicity. While here, she spoke to but two former acquaintances, and these two gentlemen whom she met on Broadway. Hundreds passed her who had courted her good graces when she reigned supreme at the White House, but their was no recognition.

It was not because she had changed much in personal appearance, but was merely owing to the heavy crape veil that hid her features from view.

"She seeks to defend her course while in this city—and with much force, too. Adverting to the fact that the Empress of France frequently disposes of her cast-off wardrobe, and publicly too, without being subjected to any unkind remarks regarding its propriety, she claims the same immunity here as is accorded in Paris to Eugenie. As regards her obscurity while in this city, she says that foreigners of note and position frequently come to our stores, and under assumed names travel from point to point throughout our vast domain, to avoid recognition and the inconveniences resulting from being known, though it even be in the form of honors. For herself she regards quiet preferable to ostentatious show, which would have cost her much indirectly, if not directly; and this she felt herself unable to bear, according to the measure of her present state of finances.

"In a recent letter to her bosom friend, Mrs. Elizabeth Keckley, Mrs. Lincoln pathetically remarks, 'Elizabeth, if evil come from this, pray for my deliverance, as I did it for the best.' This referred to her action in placing her personal effects before the public for sale, and to the harsh remarks that have been made thereon by some whom she had formerly regarded as her friends."

Clarissa Minnie Thompson

?–?

If the serialized novel *Treading the Winepress; or, A Mountain of Misfortune* by Clarissa Minnie Thompson had been published in book form, the author would have been remembered as the second black woman to publish a novel.[1] As it is, she has been remembered hardly at all. Her very long serial was published in forty-one front-page weekly chapters in the *Boston Advocate*, a black newspaper, from 1885 through 1886.

Like the characters in her story, Clarissa Minnie Thompson was born of mixed ancestry in Columbia, South Carolina. Her father, Samuel Benjamin Thompson, could trace his lineage to a Frenchman, who was one of the South Carolina Huguenots; his own father was of Indian extraction. Samuel E. Thompson became a recognized leader of his race. He was a delegate in 1865 to the South Carolina Constitutional Convention, a member of the state legislature for six years, and a justice of the peace for eight. He married a woman who enhanced his position in the community, Eliza Henrietta Montgomery. They had nine children, of whom Clarissa was the oldest.

Clarissa went to the Howard School, and on to South Carolina's State Normal School, located on the campus of South Carolina University. There, some of the best educators in the country taught and lectured to the students.

After completing her courses, Clarissa returned to the Howard School as first assistant. From there, she went to head the Poplar Grove School in Abbeville. At the request of Bishop William F. Dickerson of the African Methodist Episcopal Church, Miss Thompson was invited to teach at the Methodist-supported Allen University in Columbia. She taught a variety of courses—Latin, algebra, physical geography, and ancient and modern history. The young teacher left Allen after fifteen months in September 1886 to teach in the public school of Jefferson, Texas. Spending three years there, she resigned to accept a position as the first assistant in the Fort Worth City School System.

The seeds of her literary efforts were sown early as a schoolgirl when she wrote for the press. Her essays were published in the *Christian Recorder*, organ of the African Methodist Episcopal Church. The first three chapters of her novel were also published in the *Recorder*, but the work was withdrawn because "the plot and development of the story would scarcely become an ecclesiastical paper."[2]

Treading the Winepress is filled with what its subtitle connotes, *A Mountain of Misfortune.* The long drawn out episodes spill over with unrequited love, murder, insanity, and death, and preachments on morality, respect for people within and outside the race, and the virtues of womanhood. Two black aristocratic families, the Tremaines and DeVernes, live in the city of Capitolia (actually Columbia, South Carolina), where their lives become entwined. Gertie Tremaine, the protagonist, is secretly in love with a brilliant doctor, Will DeVerne. He, in turn, is in love with her sister, Lenore "Gypsy" Tremaine.

Gypsy disappears after a ball, as does Will Tremaine, so that all are convinced the two went away together. When Will returns alone, however, it is discovered that Gypsy is not with him. When she does come home after an extended absence, she hints of having been "deceived" by a man. She suffers and dies. Some time later, Will DeVerne is found shot to death. Two pistols belonging to Gertie's brother, Walter Tremaine, a priest, are beside him. Walter is accused, a long trial ensues, and he is convicted; nevertheless, the reader is left with doubts about his guilt. It is in chapter 35 that Gertie bemoans her "mountain of misfortunes" which make her "tread the winepress." Successive tragedies occur within both families throughout the story. In the end, Gertie devotes her life to being the town's do-gooder and helping others.

According to the author, she never expected her serial to be published in book form. Minnie Clarissa Thompson diffidently looked upon her work as merely a "girlish protest against what seemed to be serious dangers threatening her race. Her object was not to gain 'name and fame' but to call the attention of thinking people to these blots in our social Firmament."[3]

Clarissa also wrote poetry. One poem, "A Glass of Wine," expressed her intolerance for alcohol, and was printed in the Texas *Blade*. Sometimes under the nom de plume of "Minnie Myrtle," she wrote letters and poems for black newspapers. A novelette, *Only a Flirtation*, was published in the *Dallas Enterprise*. She was also an essayist, and her "Humane Education," which was read before a teachers' convention in Forth Worth in 1892, appeared in part in the *Afro-American Encyclopaedia*.

But Miss Thompson was first of all a dedicated educator, who felt the uplifting of her race depended on the "character of the work in the school room." Her classroom occupation was the top priority in her life.

NOTES

1. Grateful acknowledgment is extended to Tamara Ann Shockley who aided in rescuing Clarissa Minnie Thompson.
2. Majors, *Noted Negro Women*, p. 68.
3. Ibid., p. 69.

SELECTED SOURCES

Primary

Thompson, Clarissa Minnie. *Treading the Winepress; or, A Mountain of Misfortune*, *Boston Advocate* 1, 2 (1885–86).

Secondary

Haley, James T. *Afro-American Encyclopaedia; or, Thoughts, Doings, and Sayings of the Race*. Nashville: Haley & Florida, 1895.
Majors, Monroe Alphus. *Noted Negro Women, Their Triumphs and Activities*. Chicago: Donohue & Henneberry Printers, 1893.

De Verne or Herbert—Which?

She dashed the note on the carpet, looked round wildly, for a second or two, then motioning to Lorraine to pick it up, she leaned forward on the table and groaned aloud. Lorraine read it through from beginning to end, re-read it, examined it as if he was weighing every syllable, and said, finally, "What do you make of this, Miss Tremaine?"

Gertie raised her eyes, which now gleamed like stars, and gave him a glance he never forgot. Yet she spoke very calmly.

"She has eloped, Mr. Tracy. Gypsy, Gypsy, poor, dear, misguided girl, while you had a mother and a brother and a sister who would have shed their lifeblood to shield you from harm, could you not have confided in them and made the wretch, whoever he is, marry you from your home?"

Lorraine started as if he had been shot.

"By all the saints," he exclaimed, bringing down his hand on the table with such force as to knock off several pieces of bric-a-brac it supported, "I see—I see! I can see the whole thing from beginning to end. I understand now why he was so determined to make that trip and so willing that I should stay behind. Oh, Will, I should never have thought it of you!"

Gertie looked at him, and said quietly, "And so you think it was Will DeVerne who has persuaded my poor sister to elope?"

"I did not say so, Miss Tremaine, in so many words, but really, putting things together, it looks that way."

"Mr. Tracy, I love my sister devotedly, and, as she says, I have heretofore had implicit confidence in her and have it still. In spite of this rash, long-to-be-regretted step she has taken, I believe that she was persuaded to it by a stronger mind than hers—for Gypsy is just the kind of woman who will yield up everything—save honor, for she comes of a pure, virtuous stock—to the man she loves. Some one has won her love, and then, knowing her susceptible, passionate, impulsive disposition, has induced her to run away with him. What his object is, God only knows, for had he intended to do the fair and honorable thing by her, he would have married her here, from among her friends and relatives, and not advised her to do an act which she will regret to the end of her days. Only a villain would have urged her to such a step—only a deep-dyed, black-hearted villain. A real gentleman would die before permitting the woman he intended making his wife to do anything that would compromise her fair fame in the eyes of the world."

"You make a heavy charge against my friend, Miss Tremaine. Though things point that way, I should be indeed shocked should he turn out to be the guilty party."

"I have made no charge against your friend, Mr. Tracy, if by your *friend* you mean Dr. DeVerne."

"Pardon, me, I thought your words referred to him. Knowing of his attentions to her for such a long time and putting together the fact of her disappearance and his sudden trip, both occurring about the same time, and then reading this note, is it strange to you that even I, for a moment, should believe that my old friend had allowed his love to run away with his reason and eloped with the girl he professed to love and who appeared to return his affection?"

"Will DeVerne is not the man guilty of this sin, Mr. Tracy. An angel from Heaven could not convince me that he is. The only thing that would convince me would be his own words—and even then I should know that it was not the Will DeVerne I knew but a crazed thing wearing his image."

"I trust that you may be right, Miss Tremaine. For her sake, I could wish that her companion would turn out to be DeVerne."

"Will DeVerne wanted my sister, Mr. Tracy—the whole town knows that—but, had she accepted him, he would have been only too proud to have made her his in the face of the whole world. No, whoever the villain is, it is not Will DeVerne."

"You have indeed an exalted opinion of him, Miss Tremaine. I could wish, for your sake, that the town could be brought over to your opinion, though you must pardon me if I sincerely hope, for Miss Lenore's sake that the *finale* may prove you to be the one laboring under a mistaken idea."

"I am weary and cannot discuss this further to-night. To-morrow morning I shall see my brother and quietly set to work to solve this mystery. May I request you to keep silent about this affair a few days, sir, and also ask Mrs. Livingstone to do the same? I thank you from the bottom of my heart for your kindness this evening. Pardon me— I am worn out and must bid you good night."

The next morning very early, as Gertie was preparing to go down to seek her brother, one of Mrs. Livingstone's servants appeared with a note from that lady, saying, "I have searched in every nook and corner and have been able to find only this one page, which I came across in Gypsy's *escritoire*—which she must have overlooked, in her haste, for every other scrap of writing has been destroyed. I trust that it may furnish a clue to your sister's whereabouts, Miss Tremaine. If either Claude or I can be of any assistance to you, let me know, for, as you know, however dear our poor girl may be to you, no one living can love her any more deeply than I."

It was only one page, and ran thus:

"Dear Gypsy: I have loved you so long and so fervently! For your sake I have tried to be a better man. I know that I am not as influential as Dr. DeVerne, nor as fascinating in the eyes of your sex; but, dear, neither am I as arrogant nor as conceited. I will make you a good husband, my angel—far better than Will DeVerne, with his French airs and egotism could ever make. You say your family do not fancy me; are you going to marry to please your family, or please yourself? I know your peace-loving disposition—I know how you hate to disagree with them concerning this most important step of your life; I know it, and I appreciate it. Now, love, let me show you a way out of this dilemma. You can, for 'perfect love casteth out fear.' Now, suppose you let me come back and marry you at a moment's notice, and then take you off immediately; or (what I should infinitely prefer), suppose you come out to me here and be married from my mother's house? You know she loves you and would be proud to welcome you as a daughter—and then we can spend our honeymoon among the springs, or at Harper's Ferry—which you know you have so long been anxious to visit? After we are man and wife, your family will see that opposition is both foolish and useless, and ——"

Here the paper gave out, and what followed on the next page could only be conjectured.

Of course, it was impossible to keep the flight of one so prominent in the social world as Gypsy, a secret. Before many days, in spite of her brother and sister's efforts, the whole affair leaked out, and, as a consequence, her name suffered greatly.

Some people love scandal, and are prone to believe evil of one rather than good; and though some of the romantic declared that she had eloped with Dr. DeVerne, and others with the same fibre held, with equal tenacity, the opinion that she had gone to Baltimore to wed Herbert, while the majority of those who had once professed themselves to be her steadfast friends whispered dark things about her inexplicable behaviour.

Tracy, who claimed to have business in Washington, offered to run up to Baltimore to clear up the mystery, but Gertie, whose old distrust of him had returned, declined with thanks, and told him that her brother had resolved to leave Capitolia, after he could get no reply to his telegrams, and attend to the matter himself.

Walter did go to Baltimore on this errand, but not a word could he hear of Gypsy. Herbert and his friends avowed so solemnly that he had not left the city since his arrival and that Gypsy had not been seen there, that he was constrained to believe them. He returned to the city, fully convinced, in spite of his skepticism, that DeVerne was his sister's companion. Gertie, with that faith characteristic of devoted womanhood, still held to her belief, and so matters stood, until the return of Dr. DeVerne a few days later—with no Gypsy.

Miss Garrison

?–?

In July 1889, the novel *A Ray of Light* began to appear in the *A. M. E. Church Review*, concluding with chapter 14 in April 1890. Little is known of the author, Miss Garrison, whose story is probably the second serialized novel by an Afro-American woman, following Clarissa Minnie Thompson's *Treading the Winepress*.

When L. J. Coppin, editor of the *Review*, launched the story in an editorial, "One Year in Journalism," he announced: "With this we introduce a new class of literature . . . by a writer hitherto unknown to the readers of the *Review*."[1]

The only other information to be found about Miss Garrison is in her own brief preface to her novel:

The writer of this little volume when quite young was passionately fond of reading stories, and thought it so strange that colored persons, if mentioned at all in them, were always spoken of as "an old Negro," an old slave or servant, as if they were fitted for nothing else. As she grew older and reflected more, she often asked this question, Does people's color prevent them from being ladies and gentlemen? When answered in the negative, it seemed almost incredible.

As time passed on, and the writer became more experienced in the ways of the world, she resolved to write a story in which these persecuted people should take a prominent part, knowing that they were in every way capable, if rights and privileges were equally bestowed. It was during the progress of the war that this story was leisurely commenced, and finished at about its close.

Without making any alterations, and by the advice of friends, it is presented to you, reader, with all its faults.[2]

The serial starts prior to the Civil War and revolves around the black Leland family, who live a comfortable existence in a New England town. Upon the unexpected death of Mr. Leland (no first names are given for the father and mother), his widow is left alone with two children. The fourteen-year-old son, Harwood, called Hardie, is in delicate health because of a spinal disease, and his sister, Sophie, a beautiful girl of seventeen, becomes a seamstress to help her ailing mother sustain the family.

In leaving the shelter of her home to sew for white families, Sophie learns firsthand about white northern prejudices and discrimination against those of her color. There are involved subplots concerning the white Chapin and Carleton families and their intrigues of love, avarice, and bigotry.

The story's title is derived from the outbreak of the Civil War—"when slavery died, a 'Ray of Light' commenced to dawn!" The "Ray of Light" grows brighter for the Lelands after the Carletons, absentee North Carolina plantation owners, are stripped of their slave property because of the war. Destitute, they are forced to sell their New England farm estate, Oakland, and leave town.

Oakland is purchased by a tall, handsome, newly arrived young black man, Frederic Ashley, who wants to have a home while visiting the country of his birth. Born a slave, Frederic's mother escaped with him as a baby to Canada. There she died, and Frederic was adopted by a visiting English noblewoman, Lady Ashley. Frederic is reared and educated in England amidst wealth, aristocracy, and culture. The "boy meets girl" motif ensues when Frederic and Sophie marry in grand style and go to England to live.

Miss Garrison obviously lived in the New England of which she writes. She delivers chapter after chapter of messages and speeches about Yankee superiority, northern disdain for blacks, the unequal treatment of blacks because of their color, and the hypocrisy of "Yankee religion."

As can be discerned from the brief description of herself, the author must have been an educated woman of some means to have had the leisure to write. The name, Miss Garrison, may have been a pseudonym, or perhaps the author withheld her first name owing to trepidations about the merits of her writing. This she implies when she modestly presents her work "with all its faults." Given the importance of the serial to the lineage of nineteenth-century Afro-American women writers, one wishes we knew the identity of Miss Garrison.

NOTES

1. L. J. Coppin, "Editorial: One Year in Journalism," *A. M. E. Church Review* 6 (July 1889):110–11.
2. Miss Garrison, *A Ray of Light*, A. M. E. *Church Review* 6 (July 1889):74.

SOURCE

Primary

Miss Garrison. *A Ray of Light*, A. M. E. *Church Review* 6 (July 1889–90):74–489.

Churches and Religion

Sweet Sabbath! day of rest when all nature seems to lay aside her wonted activity, and seek a repose from her labor of the week, and with reverential silence seems to praise Him who has said "Six days shalt thou labor, and do all thy work." The little birds, as they hop from branch to branch, pour forth sweet notes of praise, as a morning song to Him who has kept them from harm during the long winter.

The sounds of life are hushed in nearly every household. The bustle and activity of the week gave place to order and quietness, which reign supreme.

How beautiful the bells sound on the air, as they call people to the house of God, where they ought to praise, and give Him thanks.

"I feel as if I would like to hear a sermon preached to-day," said Mrs. Leland, seating herself at the breakfast table. "Wouldn't you like to attend Pilgrim Church this morning, Sophie? We've plenty of time."

"It is very unpleasant, mother," replied Sophie, "to go among these so-called Christians, and be compelled to sit behind the lowest and meanest of them, when you know you are as good as the best, and have them shun you, as if you were the vilest reptile on earth, I never take any comfort or enjoy the services in the least."

"Such things are very trying and enough to make an infidel of any one," said Mrs. Leland. "Prejudice grows stronger and stronger in the churches, I think."

"Certainly, it does," said Hardie; "these churches are hot beds of prejudice. In the theatre they are not ashamed nor afraid to sit near you; but in the Christian Church they will stand, or even leave the house before they will do it. How they dare say they love Christ, and follow His examples, when they hate their brother because his color is not like their own, is more than I can comprehend."

"The members of the Pilgrim Church," continued Sophie, "are a proud set of idolaters; they assemble Sabbath after Sabbath to worship their money and color, and to see who owns the finest carriage, and wears the most expensive clothes. But, mother, I am willing to go this morning, if you think they'll not turn us out."

"I do not see how they can do that," was the reply; "they pretend to call their church a place of public worship."

"Perhaps they have no pigsty reserved there for your accommodation," said Hardie. "If you expect an insult, I should advise you not to go. Christian," he added, curling his lips disdainfully, as he arose from the table; "hypocrite is the best name"; and, turning on his heel, he left the room.

Church time found Mrs. Leland and Sophie wending their way toward Pilgrim Church. On entering the vestibule they beheld a group of the boasted American gentlemen conversing in low tones. They took no notice of Mrs. Leland or her daughter excepting a bold stare, and then resumed their conversation.

They remained standing a long time, when two other women entered. Mr. Leslie left the group, and immediately stepped forward, hat in hand, and asked politely, "Will you have seats, ladies?" and escorted them in.

At that moment the sexton appeared with a pitcher of water.

"Can we have seats here this morning?" inquired Mrs. Leland, stepping forward.

"I will see," he replied; and approaching the gentlemen he asked "Can these persons be accommodated here with seats this morning?"

"No," answered Mr. Leslie, who had just returned to the vestibule; "the seats here are all sold."

The reader must imagine their feelings, as they left the church and proceeded homeward.

"I am sorry you went there this morning," said Hardie, when they had completed the story of their wrongs.

"I am not exactly sorry, Hardie," was his mother's reply; "for now I know just how they feel, and can tell it for truth."

"I suppose we ought to expect nothing more of such a church," remarked Hardie, after a long pause, "controlled as it is by a gambling slaveholder."

"They are all slaveholders at heart," said Sophie. "I hope Mr. Leslie will remember in his prayers to-day the orphans whom he once robbed."

"I hope so, too," replied Mrs. Leland. "It seems dreadful to have such people control a church."

"The Church, like society, mother, has become very corrupt. The meanest beggar can, after a while, be admitted into aristocratic society, if he gains wealth, no matter how he gets it; while gamblers, robbers and even murderers can find their way into polished society without any trouble if by their crime they secure a large amount of wealth," continued Sophie. "The right complexion, of course, is of the greatest importance."

"How long we will be compelled to bear this cruel injustice for the crime of color," said Mrs. Leland, "I know not."

"The greatest injustice ever known," said Hardie, indignantly. "They have taken away our rights and our liberties. The doors of their churches, their Sabbath-schools, their machine shops, their banks and their counting rooms are closed against us; they compel us to be menials, and then say we are degraded and inferior; we have no mechanical abilities and no talent for business! What they think we are I should like to know."

"They consider us a trifle higher than the brutes, fitted only for their servants," answered Sophie, and they want us to think so too. The only reason people dislike our family is because we have some independence, and consider ourselves human beings. The lower you stoop, the better you please them. Show the least independence, and you are proud, and feel above your station."

"I have taken their insults from childhood," said Mrs. Leland, "but my feelings were severely hurt at their unprincipled injustice this morning. I wonder they never think of the Golden Rule."

"Oh! dear!" groaned Hardie, throwing himself on the sofa, "these things are enough to drive one distracted!"

"We will say no more about it, at present," said his mother, looking greatly alarmed. "Compose yourself, Hardie; you are not as well as usual to-day. Come, Sophie, we will remove our things and try to spend the remainder of the Sabbath the best we can."

"I've heard some news to-day," said Hardie, entering the house the next evening.

"What is it?" asked Sophie and her mother at the same time.

"I walked home from school with Charlie Leslie this evening," said he; "he says that, when the corner-stone of Pilgrim Church was laid, among the other documents put in was one which said that 'No person of African descent should be allowed a seat within its sacred walls.' This document was gotten up by Mr. Carleton, approved of by the leading men, and, of course, is considered a law of the Church. Your appearance there yesterday greatly annoyed the gentlemen present. The seats were not all sold, but his father said this, in order to have you leave as speedily and quietly as possible, and not trouble them with your presence again."

"I don't wonder Mr. Leslie told a falsehood rather than bring to light such an infamous law as that," said Mrs. Leland. "But if they consider that law just and right, why did they refrain from having it published in the papers at the time the others were? Where there are such laws, there cannot be much Christianity?"

"Leslie said," continued Hardie, "that last Christmas they had a minstrel performance in the chapel for the amusement and instruction of the Sabbath-school children; but the performers were not genuine black men, but men painted black."

"Intolerable ignorance!" exclaimed Sophie; "as if a black man would disgrace them or their Church, more than one painted black. This nation has yet to learn the superiority of the black race."

"I gave Leslie my opinion of their Church and minstrel performance pretty freely," said Hardie; "I hope he will tell his father every word of it."

"I don't consider their Church any too good for minstrels to perform in," returned Mrs. Leland with considerable spirit. "They are imposters every one knows, and those that patronize them are no better. If I was wealthy, I would have a seat in that church, law or no law. They have the power now, but may not always have it."

One pleasant afternoon a week or two after the above conversation a lady called at the door of Mrs. Leland's dwelling, and asked if she could see the lady of the house.

"Certainly," replied Sophie, and invited her in. "Here is Mrs. Leland," said she.

The lady looked surprised, and turning to Sophie said, "You misunderstood me; it was the mistress I wished to see."

"I am the mistress here," said Mrs. Leland promptly.

"Indeed!" replied the lady, seating herself, and smiling pleasantly as she looked around. "How comfortable you look here. Do you occupy all this house?"

"Certainly," was the reply.

"I am visiting every family in this vicinity, distributing religious reading among them, and making inquiries concerning their spiritual welfare. How large a family have you?" she asked.

"There are only three of us," replied Mrs. Leland. "This is my daughter, and my son is at school."

"Here is some good reading for you," said the lady, handing her a tract and a last year's Child's Paper. "I presume your daughter can read, if you can't."

Mrs. Leland smiled faintly, as she took them and thanked her.

"Where do you attend church?" inquired the lady.

"We don't attend church," was the prompt reply.

The lady looked distressed. "This is the third time during my two weeks' mission that I have received that reply," said she; "and you have no idea what a shock it is to my feelings. But in both instances they promised to come to our new church as soon as we provided necessaries for them. Our church is large, and its accommodations are ample for all. Perhaps I can persuade you to go to some church. Living as you do in this Christian neighborhood, with models of piety all around you, it seems dreadful to stay at home on the Sabbath, when there are so many places of public worship in the city."

"The places of worship are public to one class of people, while another class is excluded," returned Mrs. Leland. "It wouldn't do for you to persuade me to go to your new church, as that would be against the law."

"How so?" asked the lady. "I do not understand you."

"I will soon explain," said Mrs. Leland. "Two weeks ago on Sunday I felt a strong desire to go to church and hear a sermon. I persuaded my daughter to accompany me to Pilgrim Church, it was so neai, and we had never been there. When we entered no one noticed us, and I finally inquired of the sexton if we could have seats, and were told that the seats were all sold, and there was no room for us. I afterward learned that the seats were not all sold, but a law of the Church excludes all persons of African descent, so I find that Mr. Leslie told a falsehood, for fear we should come there again."

"Mr. Leslie," repeated the lady, in surprise; "why he is one of our best men, and I think you judge him too severely. The objection was made entirely by Mr. Carleton. He has a great deal of influence there, and we all feel under great obligations to him for his liberality. If a man builds a church, I suppose he has a right to control it. He seems to be governed by that peculiar prejudice so common among Southern gentlemen, caused no doubt by the system of slavery. I feel thankful that I have no such feelings. My father generally employed colored servants, and used to call them into prayers the same as any of us. We had a girl who lived with us a number of years, and she seemed almost like one of the family. She used to sit in the same room with us when we were alone. She often went to the same church, sat in the back pew, and no one ever objected that we knew of."

Mrs. Leland and her daughter looked greatly annoyed.

"Did you ever read of an instance, madame," asked Mrs. Leland, "where back pews were reserved for one class of people when Christ and His disciples or the apostles preached on earth?"

"Why—I—no—well, I have never read of anything of that kind," stammered the lady. "But I think that this feeling between the races must have existed."

"Where's your proof of that?" inquired Mrs. Leland sharply. "The only instance I ever read was when Miriam and her brother Aaron spoke against Moses because he married an Ethiopian woman. The Lord was angry, and cursed Miriam with leprosy, and she became white as snow. She probably possessed that feeling you speak of. This is the only place I have been able to find where the idolized white complexion is mentioned. The Ethiopians were a great nation, but were finally subdued by the Egyptians under Moses, who was brought up in Egypt, and taught in all the wisdom of the Egyptians. All the arts and learning of Egypt were taken from Ethiopia. Most of the eminent men in ancient days were African."

"But not Negroes," said the lady.

"Who are the Negroes?" asked Mrs. Leland and Sophie at the same time.

"I do not know—as—I can—tell you that," she replied, looking both surprised and confused. "You know the colored people are always called Negroes; it seems to be a popular word. I will ask Mr. Shirley about it."

"Mr. Shirley or any other minister would be unable to inform you, madame, on the subject correctly," returned Mrs. Leland, "for all they make such elaborate use of the word. There is no such nation as Negroes——"

"Oh! you are mistaken," interrupted the lady. "The word is used by our best people; our tract societies and our Bible societies always use it."

"Their using it will never convince me," was Mrs. Leland's firm reply. "The editor of that Negro sheet, the Evening Times, would fail to do it, although he loves the word dearly, and uses it so freely. If the Egyptian, the Moor, the Tunisian or the Ethiopian come to this country, they are forthwith termed Negroes; but when their greatness is spoken of, they are not Negroes. The truth is, these Americans cherish that word tenderly to insult respectable people with."

The lady made no reply, evidently thinking Mrs. Leland a full match for her.

"Couldn't I persuade you to go to the Spring Street Church?" she asked at length. "There is an interesting Sabbath-school connected with it. Mr. Shirley has been there, and addressed the school. I should think you would enjoy it, and feel more at home by yourselves."

"That is another absurd idea some people have," returned Mrs. Leland, "in believing that it is impossible for colored persons to find any comfort or enjoyment unless by themselves. It is a great mistake. If the Spirit of Christ dwelt in these churches, as it should, and all were treated with Christian kindness, there would be no need of so much separation. Neither am I a Methodist," continued she. "When quite young I united with a band of Christians who held their meetings in a hall. The members subscribed monthly what they could afford to pay expenses; the seats were free to all, and we were a prosperous band. Their numbers increased, and they rented a vacant church for a number of years. Here I noticed a change in the members; they appeared less familiar than formerly, and wished to crowd me back, I maintained my place, however, and continued to enjoy the meetings. But when the fine new church on Seventh Street was completed, they passed me by unnoticed. My health has not been good for a number of years, and my attendance at church has been very irregular. During the great revival there last winter my daughter and I attended most of the meetings. The pastor would say, 'The meetings are free to all; come and bring your friends; we will do our best to find seats for you.' But if the back seats were filled, no one was particular about seating us; they seemed to think we would stand or leave. I sometimes thought it was more a revival of pride than religion."

"I don't know much about that church," said the lady, "but I thought the members and congregation were mostly mechanics and the lower class of people."

"They are," was the reply, "but they have the same pride and follow the example of the rich in despising the oppressed."

"That class of people always make themselves ridiculous I think," said the lady, "trying to imitate their superiors. But go on with your recital."

"One Sabbath morning, during that revival of pride, we went to church early, and it was astonishing to see how soon that large church was filled, and still they came pouring in. The pews there will seat four, but they crowded five and six into every one. They brought in benches and stools; still all were not supplied with seats. We were the only occupants of a back pew, but they passed and repassed, preferring to stand rather than sit with us. We were so disgusted with their Christian conduct that we rose and left the house, when instantly the vacant pew was filled. I shall make application to the committee to rent a pew before I go there again. Such things are a shame to New England, with its boasted religious liberty."

"Well," said the lady, after a long pause, "there is no distinction in Heaven; you will occupy as good a place there as any one."

"How can that be?" asked Mrs. Leland. "If we cannot dwell together here in love, we cannot hereafter. For John says, in his epistle, 'Whoever says he loves God and not his brother is a liar; if he cannot love his brother, whom he hath seen, how can he love God, whom he hath not seen? For therefore do we know that we have passed from death unto life, because we love the brethren.'"

"I am certainly obliged to you for the instruction you have given me this afternoon," said the lady, suddenly rising; "I shall not forget you"; and after inviting them to call and see her, at her residence on Madison Avenue, she remarked, "My name is Miner. I am a sister of Mr. Shirley."

Mrs. Leland thanked her, and Mrs. Miner took her leave.

Amelia Etta Hall Johnson
Mrs. A. E. Johnson🖋

1858–1922

Amelia Etta Hall Johnson, novelist, editor, and poet, wrote the second novel to be published in book form by an Afro-American woman. The book, *Clarence and Corinne; or, God's Way,* was issued in 1890 by the American Baptist Publication Society. Mrs. Johnson was not only one of the society's first women authors but the first black to be published by the organization. The novel also has the historic distinction of being the first Sunday school book written by a black writer.

Clarence and Corinne; or, God's Way has been overlooked or dismissed by some scholars, possibly because it has no black characters and its moralistic story line is aimed at youth. Unlike Frances Ellen Watkins Harper's more familiar novel, *Iola Leroy; or, Shadows Uplifted* (1892), which has been cited erroneously as the first novel written by a black woman, the book is not well known and existing copies are rare.

Born in Toronto, Canada, in 1858 of parents who were natives of Maryland, Amelia Etta Hall was educated in Montreal; she moved to Baltimore in 1874. Three years later, she married a leading Baltimore minister, the Reverend Harvey Johnson, on 17 April 1877. Dr. Johnson, a Virginian, was an early civil rights leader, successful pastor of the Union Baptist Church, and author of a book and several religious pamphlets.

Amelia became interested in writing poetry at an early age, but it was not until after her marriage that she began to write and publish in earnest. Instilled with a concern for young people, she felt there should be a journal in which black women could publish short stories, poetry, and articles for them. Thus, in 1887, she began an eight-page monthly paper, the *Joy*. A year later, to encourage reading among black children, she started a second publication, the *Ivy*, which focused on black history.

Mrs. Johnson wrote children's stories for Philadelphia's the *National Baptist* and poems for the *Joy*. She originated "The Children's Corner" column for the *Sower and Reaper* of Baltimore, for which she contributed "The Animal Convention" and "The Mignonette's Mission." Additional writings appeared in the *Baptist Messenger, Our Women and Children Magazine,* and the *American Baptist.*

The publication of *Clarence and Corinne; or, God's Way* established her reputation as an author. She was widely acclaimed for this book, particularly by the white presses. Although the book had no identifiable black characters, Mrs. Johnson was purported to have written it out of "affection for the race, and loyalty to it, the author desiring to help demonstrate the fact that the colored people have thoughts of their own, and only need suitable opportunities to give them utterance."[1]

The novel is a poignant little story suffused with religious teachings sustained by a thin layer of plot and suspense. Clarence, twelve, and his sister, Corinne, nine, are the woeful children of Jim Burton, a wife-beating drunkard. Mrs. Burton, an un-Christian woman, is resigned to her misery and the family's poverty. When she dies of a heart attack, the father walks off, leaving the burial of his wife and his children's fate to the townspeople.

After their mother's funeral, brother and sister are separated. Clarence goes to work for a doctor, but soon leaves town to try his fortune elsewhere, hence becoming lost to his sister. Corinne is taken in by Rachel Penrose, a miserly seamstress, who overworks and hardly feeds her. Helen Gray, a schoolteacher, pities Corinne, and asks permission for the child to come to her house on Sundays to be given Sunday school lessons by her invalid sister. On a visit, Corinne suddenly becomes ill and stays with the Grays to be nursed back to health. When Miss Gray has to move her sister away for health reasons, she secures a new home for Corinne with her aunt, Anna Stone, and her husband at Sweetbriar Farm in a town named Brierton.

Corinne finds happiness living with the Stones. She is sent to Sunday school and makes friends with the minister's children, Bebe and Charley Reade. Meanwhile, Clarence has had his ups and downs and by chance arrives in Brierton. There he is reunited with his sister and is given a home also with the Stones. Clarence grows up to be a doctor and Corinne a schoolteacher; they marry their childhood friends, Bebe and Charley, and go on to lead productive Christian lives. All their misfortunes, which nevertheless end happily for Clarence and Corinne, are attributed to "God's way," or God's plan for the best.

Mrs. A. E. Johnson's second novel, *The Hazeley Family* (1894), followed four years later. It was another Sunday school book dealing with the evils of drink and family separations, but in which people reunite in the end.

The Hazeley children are Flora, and her brothers, Harry and Alec. The father works on a railroad and is frequently away from home, leaving daughter and sons in the care of, yes, an un-Christian mother who neglects the management of the household. Flora, at the age of five, is sent to live with a well-to-do sympathetic aunt, Bertha Graham. Also living with her is a sister, Sarah Martin, who is cold and stern. Aunt Bertha teaches Flora how to be a good homemaker and the rewards of living a Christian life. When Aunt Bertha dies, Flora, now eleven, is returned to her mother by Aunt Sarah.

Back home, Flora, through diligence and a sense of responsibility, creates a better home for her family. She becomes a Sunday school teacher and makes a Christian out of her mother. When the father is killed at work, Harry shoulders the burden of the family. Alcohol and misleading friends, however, cause him to leave home and travel a wayward path. But after he has learned his lesson, he returns home to enter the ministry. Flora goes on to change the rigid attitudes of her Aunt Sarah, reunites a neighbor, Ruth, with her unknown grandparents, and promotes a marriage between her good friend, Lottie, and brother, Alec.

The third novel, *Martina Meriden; or, What Is My Motive?* (1901) features a similar family group of a girl, Martina ("Tina"), and her two brothers, Billy and Joe. The book—again for Sunday school shelves—is plodding, uneventful, and not as readable as the other two. Didactic lessons are given through speech and action on truth, obedience, right and wrong, and love for the Heavenly Father. The theme concerns the importance of having a high Christian motive for life in order to be happy and helpful.

Like her fictional families, Amelia Johnson had a daughter, Mrs. N. A. M. Shaw, and two sons, Prentiss and Harvey, Jr. She died in Baltimore on 29 March 1922 after a two-day illness at the age of sixty-four. She was remembered more as the wife of Dr. Harvey Johnson, whose prominence may have overshadowed her literary accomplishments. Her obituary in the *Afro-American* newspaper on 7 April noted nothing of her writings, only of her union with Dr. Johnson, which was "happy" and "ideal." Amelia E. Johnson's literary pursuits suffered when she, like many women of her day, placed them second to her husband's career and their home.

NOTE

1. Penn, *Afro-American Press*, pp. 425–26.

SELECTED SOURCES

Primary

Johnson, Amelia E. *Clarence and Corinne; or, God's Way*. Philadelphia: American Baptist Publication Society, 1890.

———. *The Hazeley Family*. Philadelphia: American Baptist Publication Society, 1894.

———. *Martina Meriden; or, What Is My Motive?* Philadelphia: American Baptist Publication Society, 1901.

Secondary

Majors, Monroe Alphus. *Noted Negro Women, Their Triumphs and Activities*. Chicago: Donohue & Henneberry, 1893.

Pegues, A. W. *Our Baptist Ministers and Schools*. Springfield, Mass.: Willey & Co., 1892.

Penn, I. Garland. *The Afro-American Press and Its Editors*. 1891. Reprint. New York: Arno Press and The New York Times Co., 1969.

The Reunion

"Brierton! Brierton!" was at length called, as the train rolled up to the little station; and Clarence was soon standing upon the very spot where, but a short time before, his sister Corinne had stood.

Unlike her, he had no home in view. He struck out for the wood which was close by, and whose cool shade offered him at least a place to think what next to do.

He really enjoyed rambling along under the trees; it had been so long since he had been in the country. Coming to a brook, he followed its course for a while, partly to see where it would lead him, and partly because it furnished him something to divert his mind from its perplexities.

Suddenly he was startled to hear a voice call "Halloo!" and, looking up, his eyes fell upon our friend, Charley Reade, who was perched upon a rock by the brook, rod in hand, waiting for the fish to bite.

"Halloo!" answered Clarence, sitting down beside him. "Having good luck?"

"Not yet," was the reply. "I haven't caught a single fish. But there! Be quiet. I believe I've got one!"

Sure enough he had. And when the line was pulled in, it brought with it a fine trout.

The day proved to be a good one for fishing. Charley was delighted; for soon there lay a goodly number of flapping, panting victims at his feet.

Having fished until he was satisfied, he turned his attention to his companion, whom he catechised pretty freely. "Well, I don't know," he said, reflectively, in answer to the query whether he knew where Clarence could find work: "My aunt might give you something to do. Anyway, we can go and see, and you can get something to eat. Hungry?"

"Guess I am," answered Clarence. "You'd be hungry too, if you hadn't had anything to eat since early this morning."

And so the two boys started off together in the direction of Charley's home.

They found Aunt Patty willing to give the wanderer some food, for which he was to pay afterward by sawing wood. As to whether he might remain all night, was left for Mr. Reade to decide; and Charley, as we know, was gone in quest of his father, in order to learn his decision.

"Clarence," said Bebe, after a short silence, "have you a father and mother?"

"My mother is dead," said he, evasively.

"Have you any sisters or brothers?" persisted Bebe.

"I've a sister," said the boy, in a tone that plainly said he wished she would not ask him any more questions. But Bebe was too intent on making herself acquainted with the past history of the "tramp" to heed his tone.

"Where is your sister?" she demanded.

"I don't know," said Clarence, sawing away desperately, hoping by this means to put an end to the dialogue.

It was interrupted in another way, however; for just then Charley made his appearance on the scene. And throwing himself down upon the ground, he began to pick up handfuls of chips and throw them vigorously, this way and that.

"What are you doing, Charley Reade?" cried Bebe, as one of the handfuls flew over her. "I think you are very rude."

"Oh, I beg your pardon, Miss Reade," exclaimed the mischievous boy, springing to his feet and making a very low bow; "but really I couldn't help doing something to relieve my feelings."

"Well, please don't relieve your feelings on me, next time," said Bebe, severely. "But what are you so excited about?"

"Why, you see, I've got some good news for my tramp," said Charley, resuming his seat.

Clarence laughed. He did not object to being called a "tramp" one bit, at least by Charley.

"I asked papa," continued the boy, "if he wouldn't let Clarence stay here; but he said 'No, he didn't need another boy."

"Well," said Bebe, ruefully, "I don't call that good news."

"Oh, but you see you don't wait until I can finish."

"Because you are so provokingly long about telling," retorted his sister.

"And you are so provokingly impatient," returned Charley. But seeing that Bebe began to look a little ruffled, he pitched into the middle of his news, very much after the fashion in which he would have vaulted into a pile of hay.

"We're to take him to Auntie Stone's in the morning. Mr. Stone told papa that he wanted a boy to help about the place."

"But maybe he won't take Clarence; what then?" suggested Bebe. The boy, with his honest face, had thoroughly enlisted her sympathy, and she was as much interested in seeing him provided for as if he had been a relative.

"Oh, I'm pretty sure he'll take him," answered Charley, confidently. "Papa says he is too, especially as I recommend him." And Charley walked off whistling, while Bebe, in obedience to a call from Aunt Patty, went into the house.

Clarence finished the wood by nightfall, had his supper, and was given a bed in the attic. The next morning, after breakfast, Charley, Clarence, and Bebe started off together for Sweetbrier Farm.

It was a long walk. But they did not mind this, since they could take their time, and rest as often as they pleased.

When they reached the house, they saw Corinne sitting on the doorstep, paring apples. At least, this had been her occupation; but she had stopped, and was now bending over a torn newspaper. So interested was she in what it contained, that she did not notice the young people.

"Heigho, what's the news?" called the irrepressible Charley. "Anything strange?" The sound of his voice startled the little girl; but when her eyes fell upon the three visitors she sprang up, scattering the contents of her lap in every direction, and, rushing toward Clarence, threw her arms about his neck, passionately exclaiming, "Oh, Clarence!"

"If it isn't my own dear little sister!" cried he, returning her embrace with a will. For a while they all acted as though they had lost their wits. Charley hopped about on one leg; Corinne cried, and so did Bebe, for company; while Clarence did not know whether to laugh or cry. He felt like doing both at once; but compromised the matter by doing a little of each in turn.

In the midst of the confusion "Auntie Stone" came upon the scene; and seeing her little adopted daughter clinging to a strange lad, and noting the general excitement, demanded, in perplexed tones, the cause of it all. She also asked: "Who is that you have there, Corrie?"

"Oh, Aunt Anna, it's Clarence, my brother, whom I thought I would never see again!"

"Well! well! well! Who'd have thought it? How did it all come about?" And Auntie Stone looked inquiringly at Bebe, who said: "Tell her about it, Charley."

Nothing loth, in graphic style Master Charley told the whole story, beginning from where he met his "tramp" by the brook. During his recital, one more listener was added to the group, in the person of Mr. Stone. When Charley was through, he turned to Clarence and asked him if what he had heard was true—if he really had come to Brierton to get work.

"Yes, sir, it's so," answered the boy.

"And where have you been all this time, that your sister has not heard from you?" asked Mr. Stone, looking at him a little suspiciously.

Then Clarence told the tale of his wanderings, haps and mishaps; and his hearers were both interested and moved.

Auntie Stone could say nothing but "Well! well! well!" and wipe her glasses on the corner of her apron.

"Just see how God works! His hand is in all this," said Mr. Stone, gravely.

"Yes, indeed," said his wife, beginning to regain her composure.

"Anna," continued the good man, "I believe that God means

that we shall rear these two children; else why should they be led right here to our door so miraculously?"

"Why, indeed?" said Auntie Stone.

"Well, what do you say, Anna?"

"I say what you say, Nathan."

"Then I say they shall both stay with us, and be to us as our own flesh and blood."

"I say so too," rejoined his wife, delightedly. It was just what she wished; but not knowing how her husband would regard the idea, she had said nothing about it.

"Now, Clarence," said Mr. Stone, turning to our young friend, who was so astonished that he could scarcely speak, "now, Clarence, what have you to say to staying here with us?"

"Say!" exclaimed Clarence, his voice trembling with emotion; "I don't know how to thank you enough; but I give you my word that I will prove my gratitude to you, by faithfully serving you in every way I can."

"All right, my boy, all right; I believe you will." And Mr. Stone left the group.

Auntie Stone, too, knowing that the long separated brother and sister would like to be alone for a while, called Charley and Bebe to come with her and see old Polly, the cat, and her new family of six kittens.

When Clarence and Corinne were left to themselves, such a talk as they had!

Corinne told all about her long illness and her kind friends and their care. "And, oh, Clarence," she cried, as her eyes fell upon the old newspaper which had fallen from her hand when she saw her brother, "see!" And she pointed to a certain paragraph. This was what Clarence read:

"Yesterday, about ten o'clock, A.M., a man, while crossing K— — Street, was knocked down and run over by a runaway horse and wagon. He was fatally injured, and was carried to the hospital, where he died after suffering a great deal. Before he died, the man told a sad story of a debauched life. He stated that his name was James Burton, and that he had two children, a boy and a girl, whom he had deserted at the death of their mother, because he did not wish to be burdened with them. He expressed sorrow for his misspent life, but laid all the blame on whisky."

The name of the paper and its date were torn off; but Clarence and Corinne had no doubt that the poor unfortunate was none other than their father. And their hearts softened as they thought of his sad end.

But their quiet was now at an end. For Charley and Bebe came running toward them, exclaiming: "Why, what a time you have been talking! Here it's time for us to go home!"

Auntie Stone insisted on giving them all a lunch before they separated; and then the children took leave of each other, and Charley and Bebe set out for home alone.

Mr. Reade and Aunt Patty were delighted when they heard of the result of the visit to Sweetbriar Farm.

In time, Clarence and Corinne were considered a part of Brierton. They attended the same school that Charley and Bebe attended, and were regularly at Sunday school, the two girls being in the same class.

Charley and Clarence were inseparable companions; and the steady, manly course of the latter exerted such a good influence upon the impetuous Charley, that Mr. Reade determined that the two boys should be educated together. So when the time came for Charley to leave home and the Brierton school, he persuaded Mr. Stone to let Clarence go too. The boy had endeared himself to both Mr. Stone and his wife, and had rendered himself a necessity to Sweetbrier Farm—so much so that they were loth to let him leave, even for a time. But "Uncle Nathan" was sure that there was "something in that boy that ought to be brought out," and so it was settled that he should go. Corinne and Bebe too were so much attached to each other, that Auntie Stone said it would be a pity to separate them. So they were sent away together to boarding school.

Josephine Delphine Henderson Heard

1861–1921

As a child, Josephine ("Josie") Delphine Henderson displayed literary and musical talents. When five years old, she was able to read and play musical instruments. The daughter of slave parents, Lafayette and Annie M. Henderson, she was born on 11 October 1861, in Salisbury, North Carolina. Permitted to hire themselves out, her father and mother lived and worked in Charlotte, North Carolina.

When Josie finished the Charlotte schools, she went to Scotia Seminary at Concord, North Carolina, and Bethany Institute in New York. She embarked on a teaching career in South Carolina, first at Maysville and then at Orangeburg. Leaving there, she taught at Covington, Tennessee.

When a schoolgirl, Josie wrote poetry for religious periodicals. She gave no serious attention to her writing until her marriage in 1882 to the Reverend William Henry Heard, who became a bishop of the African Methodist Episcopal Church. An author also, Bishop Heard wrote admiringly in his autobiography of his wife's attributes, describing her as being "scholarly and poetic" with "her use of the English language," and saying that she had done much to assist him as a minister.[1]

As the second wife of Bishop Heard, Josie's horizons were broadened by travel to Europe and Africa. When he was appointed United States minlster resident and consul general to Liberia by President Grover Cleveland in 1895, Bishop Heard helped establish the first African Methodist Episcopal Church in Monrovia. While in England, Josie met and dined with the lord mayor and lady mayoress of London, as well as Sir Walter Wilkins and Lady Wilkins. Through them, she was presented to Queen Victoria in 1896.

Bishop Heard, along with Bishop Benjamin Tucker Tanner and other friends, persuaded Josie to devote more time to her writing. Encouraged by them, she published *Morning Glories* (1890), a collection of poems with an introduction by Bishop Tanner, who praised her "brightness of imagination" and "delicateness of touch." The fact that Bishop Tanner wrote the introduction was a compliment, for he had been a moving force in black literary circles since 1868. Josie's husband sketched her life for the book, manifesting his husbandly pride.

William H. Robinson, Jr., felt the salient features of the book were the letters of commendation, which showed "something of the social and political contacts made by some of these early Negro poets."[2] There are letters from John Greenleaf Whittier concerning her dedicatory poem, "To Whittier," and her reply to him, as well as one from Robert Todd Lincoln thanking the author for her poem, "Solace," on the death of his son, Abraham. A second edition with new poems was published in 1901.

Among present-day critics, one has said that Josie's poems were "uninspired verse,"[3] whereas another said the "special merit" of her poems was that "they all have a SUBJECT."[4] These subjects were nature, love, religion, race, and death; other poems were dedicated to prominent individuals.

In her preface, Mrs. Heard invited readers to "accept a Bunch of 'MORNING GLORIES,' freshly plucked . . . coming as they do, from a heart that desires to encourage and inspire the youth of the Race."[5] That was her motivation.

NOTES

1. W. H. Heard, *From Slavery to the Bishopric*, p. 94.
2. Robinson, *Early Black Poets*, p. 261.
3. Ibid.
4. Sherman, *Invisible Poets*, p. 209.
5. Josephine Heard, *Morning Glories*, p. iii.

SELECTED SOURCES

Primary

Heard, Josephine D. (Henderson). *Morning Glories*. Philadelphia: Published by the author, 1890.

Secondary

Heard, William Henry. *From Slavery to the Bishopric in the A. M. E. Church: An Autobiography*. Philadelphia: A. M. E. Book Concern, 1924.

Majors, Monroe Alphus. *Noted Negro Women, Their Triumphs and Activities*. Chicago: Donohue & Henneberry, 1893.

Robinson, William H., Jr. *Early Black American Poets*. Dubuque, Iowa: Wm. C. Brown Publishers, 1969.

Sherman, Joan R. *Invisible Poets: Afro-Americans of the Nineteenth Century*. Urbana: University of Illinois Press, 1974.

To Whittier

In childhood's sunny day my heart was taught to love
Thy name, all other poet's names above,
And when to womanhood at last I came,
Behold the spark was fanned into a flame,
Nor did I dare presume that I should live,
And to the honored, white-haired poet give
My sentiment in rude constructed rhyme;
O, wondrous change wrought by the hand of time!

When he who came the slaves among to dwell,
From frigid Idaho (we loved him well),
Athirst for knowledge I stood at his side,
With quickening thought and eyes astonished, wide.
He nightly read, and held me on his knee,
From Whittier's "Snowbound" filling me with glee.
The seed sown by his hand in infant heart,
Has lived and grown, and cannot now depart.

Now to the sunset thou hast set thy face,
And silvery crown thy head doth grace;
The mind of fertile thought doth not decline
Preserved yet from the ravages of time
Since I can never hope my first desire,
To shake thy hand, which would my soul inspire,
Now e're yet "the cord is loosed or pitcher broken,"

Grant me with thine own hand this little token:
Ere yet that hand by feebleness grows lame,
With condescension write for me thy name.

The Black Sampson

There's a Sampson lying, sleeping in the land,
He shall soon awake, and with avenging hand,
In an all unlooked for hour,
He will rise in mighty power;
　　What dastard can his righteous rage withstand?

E'er since the chains were riven at a stroke,
E'er since the dawn of Freedom's morning broke,
He has groaned, but scarcely uttered,
While his patient tongue ne'r muttered,
　　Though in agony he bore the galling yoke.

O, what cruelty and torture has he felt?
Could his tears, the heart of his oppressor melt?
In his gore they bathed their hands,
Organized and lawless bands—
　　And the innocent was left in blood to welt.

The mighty God of Nations doth not sleep,
His piercing eye its faithful watch doth keep,
And well nigh His mercy's spent,
To the ungodly lent:
　　"They have sowed the wind, the whirlwind they shall
　　　　reap."

From His nostrils issues now the angry smoke,
And asunder bursts the all-oppressive yoke;
When the prejudicial heel
Shall be lifted, we shall feel,
　　That the hellish spell surrounding us is broke.

The mills are grinding slowly, slowly on,
And till the very chaff itself is gone;

Our cries for justice louder,
'Till oppression's ground to powder—
  God speed the day of retribution on!

Fair Columbia's filmy garments all are stained;
In her courts is blinded justice rudely chained;
The black Sampson is awaking,
And his fetters fiercely breaking;
  By his mighty arm his rights shall be obtained!

Emma Dunham Kelley-Hawkins
Forget-me-Not✒

?–?

Emma Dunham Kelley's novel, *Megda*, appeared in 1891, a year after Amelia E. Johnson's *Clarence and Corinne; or, God's Way*, making it the third published by a black woman. A second edition appeared in 1892. Unlike Amelia E. Johnson whose life is documented, Emma Dunham Kelley remains in the shadows.

She may possibly have been a schoolteacher or attended school in New England, and we do know she was married to a man named Hawkins. A little about the author's family life can be discerned from her dedication of *Megda* to her widowed mother, where she effusively acknowledges: "With deepest joy and thankfulness . . . to my widowed mother to whose patient love and unwearied devotion during years of hard struggle and self-sacrifice I owe all that I am and all that hope holds before me in the future."[1]

Under the sentimental pen name of "Forget-me-not," Emma Dunham Kelley contrives a story about Megda ("Meg") Randal and her little circle of school friends. Their lives are followed from graduation through marriages, births, and adversities. Meg has a sister, Elsie, a brother, Hal, and a widowed mother whose desire is for her daughters to "grow to be good, pure, noble-minded women."

As with Amelia E. Johnson's novels, the characters are white, possibly with the exception of Ruth Dean who, judging from innuendoes, could be black. Ruth, daughter of a seamstress (a popular occupation for black women at the time), is the poor one of Meg's friends. On the fringe of the clique, she is taken in under Meg's charitable wings. She is described as a "small, slight, dark-faced girl," and oddly enough, as the only one whose "face had no beauty in it except in the beauty of expression." Other hints of blackness are the author's mentions of Ruth's "rich color that was always in her dark cheek," and of Meg's "white hand" being taken by Ruth's "dark, work-worn one."

The novel should have carried the subtitle of the conversion of Megda and her friends. Megda, however, is the last to profess the faith, for she is spirited, lighthearted, and fun-loving, and does not wish to give up her pleasure of dancing, cardplaying, and the theater—cardinal sins in her day. But Meg's close friend, wealthy Ethel Lawton, is devoutly religious. In her patient way, Ethel tries to steer Megda in the direction of joining the church which Megda faithfully attends. A romantic note is sounded when Ethel becomes engaged to the twenty-six-year-old minister, Arthur Stanley, who is secretly admired also by Megda.

Overwhelmed by the Reverend Stanley's Easter sermon, Megda finally succumbs and follows her friends in becoming a member of the church. Ethel contracts an unnamed malady and dies on her wedding day. Five years later, Meg becomes the wife of the Reverend Stanley. Together with him, "her life was filled up with work—noble work—in her home and in the world outside."

Four years after *Megda*, a second novel, *Four Girls at Cottage City* by Emma Dunham Kelley-Hawkins, was published by the Continental Printing Company of Providence, Rhode Island. This work was issued by James H. Earle in 1898, who was the Boston publisher of *Megda*. The book is dedicated to the author's "Dear Aunt Lottie," who was like a "'Second Mother.'"

The novel is a plotless Christian moralizing story stretched through twenty-six unexciting chapters with white characters. Four young high school girls—two sisters, Jessie Isabel and Garnet "Net" Dare, and their two friends, Allie Hunt and Vera Earle—go on a three-week vacation trip to Cottage City, a resort on Cape Cod. En route, they meet two young men, Fred Travers, cousin of the Dares, and his friend, Erford Merlin Richards, who also are going to Cottage City.

The girls stay at the cottage of an elderly married couple, "Mother" and "Grandpa" Atherton. They remember it as being the same place where their fictional heroine Megda stayed. They meet a poor widow, Charlotte Hood, and her crippled son, Robin. A considerable part of the book is taken up by Mrs. Hood relating to the young people the story of her life's sad trials and tribulations when she was growing up on the "bleak Cape Cod."

The novel ends five years later with the group paying a Boston physician for an operation for Robin so that he may walk again, and the doctor's finding Mrs. Hood work as a seamstress. Fred and Vera are now the parents of a two-year-old girl, Marjorie, and Erford and Jessie have become man and wife.

The book mentions that a sequel to *Megda* was in the making, but this apparently did not materialize. The picture of Emma Dunham Kelley in *Megda* is of an attractive serious-looking young woman. It would be interesting to know why she chose the nom de plume of "Forget-me-not" for the first book but not for the second.

NOTE

1. Kelley, *Megda*, p. iv.

SELECTED SOURCES

Primary

Kelley, Emma Dunham. *Megda*. Boston: James H. Earle, 1891.
Kelley-Hawkins, Emma D. *Four Girls at Cottage City*. Boston: James H. Earle, Publisher, 1898.

Joy and Sorrow

"The ordinance of baptism will be administered on the morning of Sunday next—Easter—at nine o'clock."

Such was the announcement made from the pulpit, by the Rev. A. N. Stanley; and as Meg heard it, a thrill of happiness passed over her, and from her heart arose the glad cry, "Praise the Lord, oh, my soul, and all that is within me, praise and bless His holy name."

Thursday evening found the vestry of the church nearly filled. There were fifty-two testimonies given. By every one the Spirit of the Lord was felt. It was a joyful meeting; there was such a blessed feeling of relationship, as if each one realized that they were all brothers and sisters in Christ—children of the same loving, all-merciful Father.

When at the last, Meg rose to give her "experience," it was very quiet. At first the beautiful voice trembled a little, then, as she forgot all else but her one great happiness, it grew strong and firm. She said:

"I think my experience can be given in a very few words. Last

April I became convinced that the life I was leading was not the right one. I was happy—at least, I thought I was—but I was not satisfied. There was a longing for something that I did not have; a feeling of unrest that I could not explain. I listened to a sermon preached in this place on Easter Sunday morning, and that sermon was just what I needed. It explained the feeling of longing and unrest. I knew then that it was the Saviour I wanted. He had said, 'Come unto me, and I will give you rest.' 'Though your sins be as scarlet, I will make them like wool.' I went to Him, and He did give me rest. I asked Him to forgive me my sins, and He has forgiven them. The love I have for Him in my heart for His great mercy, is unspeakable. If I were to devote all the years of my life to His service, I could not begin to pay Him the debt I owe. It is impossible for me to express the great happiness I feel—to know that all my sins have been forgiven, washed away by the blood of the Lamb. I have never felt ready to unite with any church until now. I wanted to be sure of myself, I am sure of myself now. I want to be baptized. I feel sure that it is not only my duty to do so, but that I shall not be perfectly happy until I am. Then I shall feel as if I am, in reality, one of His children."

Easter Sunday was one of the most beautiful days that ever dawned. The morning was perfect. It seemed as if it could not have been pleasanter. The sky was of the loveliest, most delicate shade of blue; not a cloud was to be seen. The sun shone brightly, the air was clear and warm. As Meg was driven through the quiet streets that led to the river, not a sound disturbed the Sabbath stillness, but the singing of the birds in the trees, until the carriage entered the great gate that opened into the beautiful grove; then the low hum of voices was heard from the crowd of people congregated under the trees, and on the banks of the river.

The place of baptism was the most beautiful spot in that section of the country. The river lay between two groves. On one side nothing was to be seen but green banks and giant trees; on the other, the land rose higher, and among the trees, down near the water's edge, were several huge rocks. At one end the river wound itself around shelving banks, and between small, bush-covered islands, as far as the eye could reach; at the other it disappeared under an old, gray, moss-grown arch of stone, which helped to form what was called the "stone-bridge." People stood on both banks of the river, and on the bridge. Some stood in groups, others stood by themselves, or leaned carelessly against the trunk of a tree, while others sat on the rocks.

There was not one thing to mar the beauty of the scene, and all observed perfect order.

The choir, consisting of "our girls," with Will, Ed, Bert and Melvin, were already in their places when the carriage containing Meg, Mrs. Randal, Hal and Mr. Stanley, entered the grove. They took their places at the water's edge, and then a solemn stillness settled over everything. Meg was not dressed in white; she wore one of the baptismal robes. The deep black made her face look like marble. People looked at her anxiously, and asked each other if she were going to faint.

Meg could hardly realize that "our young sister," who was the burden of Mr. Stanley's prayer as he stood at the water's edge, was really herself; it seemed too good to be true. The first hymn that Meg had chosen was, "Just as I am, without one plea." Oh, how they sung it! At first Meg stood with her eyes cast down, but before the second line was finished, she lifted her face to the blue sky, and sang with them out of the very fullness of her heart. At the words, "O, Lamb of God, I come," she threw aside the long cloak that covered her robe, and stepped down to where Mr. Stanley was waiting for her, hardly feeling the strong clasp of Hal's hand on hers as he led her down.

It was the supreme hour of Meg's life. Never could she forget the feeling of joy and happiness, rest and peace, that she realized as she was led out, firmly and tenderly, to a spot underneath an overhanging branch of a huge oak.

"Just as I am, and waiting not,
To rid myself of one dark blot."

For months and years afterward, whenever Meg heard that hymn, she seemed to feel again the baptismal waters close over her; the deep, blessed feeling of rest and peace, joy and happiness. She said once, "If I were ever tempted to go astray, and I should hear that hymn—either played or sung—it would save me."

Not for all the wealth of the world, would she have parted with the memory of that hour. It was, verily, "a foretaste of heaven below" to her. The choir of youthful voices seemed to her like the angelic choir of heaven. Oh, no; she would part with anything else, but never with that blessed memory, for she knew then, what was meant by "true happiness."

Victoria Earle
Mrs. W. E. Matthews

1861–1907

Victoria Earle Matthews was an unusual woman who combined a successful journalistic and writing career with that of a leading social worker and pioneer women's organizer. She was born at Fort Valley, Georgia, 27 May 1861, to slave parents, William and Caroline Smith. Her mother had a cruel master, and she attempted to escape numerous times. Finally, she succeeded in making her way to New York, leaving her children behind in the care of an old nurse. For eight years, she worked hard to save enough money to return to the South for her family. When she went back, she found only Victoria and three other of her children alive. Although she encountered legal difficulties in claiming them, she eventually won custody and took them with her to live in New York.

For the first time, the fair-skinned, "tall, lank, straight haired girl, with large soulful eyes,"[1] had the opportunity to attend school. She was a bright, diligent student, who was especially fond of reading. Owing to her poor family circumstances, however, she had to leave school and go to work.

She found a job in service at a home with a rich library. One day when her employer discovered her engrossed in a book, he was so impressed that he gave her permission to use the library when time allowed. By reading, meeting learned people, going to lectures and special studies, she undertook to educate herself further.

Victoria's journalistic career began when she became a "sub" for reporters on several large-city daily papers. She filled in at the *Times, Herald, Mail and Express, Sunday Mercury,* the *Earth,* and the *Phonographic World.* In addition, she acted as a correspondent for the *National Leader, Detroit Plaindealer,* and the *Southern Christian.* She entered the news field with enthusiasm, joining the Women's National Press Association. "No other Afro-American woman was so eagerly sought after for stories and articles of a general news character, by the magazines and papers of the whites, than Victoria Earle."[2] She also wrote prolifically for black newspapers, such as the *Boston Advocate, Washington Bee, Richmond Planet, Cleveland Gazette, New York Age,* and the *New York Globe.* She contributed to the noted black literary journal, the *A. M. E. Church Review.*

Another aspect of her full life evolved when she became a social reformer and women's organizer. As a member of a group of women who sponsored a fund-raising rally for antilynching crusader Ida B. Wells in 1892, she met Mrs. Josephine St. Pierre Ruffin of Boston and Dr. Susan McKinney of Brooklyn. This occasion prompted the formation of the first two black women's clubs in the country, one in Washington, D.C., and the second in New York City. Victoria Earle was elected president of a New York and Brooklyn women's club, the Women's Loyal Union. Always ready to share her energy and labor, she worked also with the National Association of Colored Women, serving as chairperson of its executive board in 1896 and as a national organizer.

At the age of eighteen, she married William E. Matthews. They had one son, who died at the age of sixteen. His death had a strong impact on Victoria Earle, "and immediately her heart went out to other people's boys and girls too."[3] She visited Tuskegee Institute and similar places in the South with the idea of remaining to help her people. A New York minister, however, persuaded her to return home where much work needed to be done, too.

On visiting homes in the city, she was appalled by the ignorance and lack of skills among blacks. As a result, she set up training classes for young women in domestic science and classes for children ranging in age from three to fifteen. One of the kindergarten teachers was Alice Ruth Moore, recently arrived from the South, who was a writer and later, wife of the poet Paul Laurence Dunbar.

Grieved by the fate of some innocent black girls when they left the rural South to go north, she founded the White Rose Mission Industrial Association, which established a "home for Colored Working Girls" at 217 East Eighty-Sixth Street. The women were housed, fed, and clothed for a modest sum while seeking employment. To keep the girls arriving on boats from becoming victimized by unscrupulous persons, Victoria Earle organized a chain of protective women to meet them at the New York and Norfolk piers. She called the women "White Roses," which to her signified "purity, goodness, and virtue."

The home gradually became a settlement house, offering classes in cooking, sewing, recreation, and literary activities. It contained a rare collection of books by and about blacks in America, which was reputed to be "one of the most unique special libraries in New York," predating the Schomburg Center for Research in Black Culture collection. Victoria used her books to teach classes in race history.

An admirer of Booker T. Washington, she selected and arranged some of his speeches, addresses, and talks to students in a small volume entitled *Black-Belt Diamonds* (1898). Her literary gift was revealed, also, by her contributions to the *Waverly Magazine* and the *Family Story Paper* where she published children's stories. Her most memorable one, *Aunt Lindy: A Story Founded on Real Life,* appeared as a sixteen-page book in 1893. It is listed in some sources as a novel. The story's theme, "don't return evil for evil," illustrates the author's belief in the patient and forgiving nature of her people.

Victoria Earle died on 10 March 1907 at the home of her sister in New York. She had been ill for four years with tuberculosis, which it was believed, she contracted at the wharves where she performed her mission work as a White Rose.

NOTES

1. Brown, *Homespun Heroines*, p. 208.
2. Penn, *Afro-American Press*, p. 376.
3. Brown, *Homespun Heroines*, p. 211.

SELECTED SOURCES

Primary

Earle, Victoria. *Aunt Lindy: A Story Founded on Real Life.* New York: J. J. Little & Co., 1893.

Secondary

Brown, Hallie Quinn. *Homespun Heroines and Other Women of Distinction.* Xenia, Ohio: Aldine, 1926.
Davis, Elizabeth Lindsay. *Lifting as They Climb.* Chicago, 1933.
Majors, Monroe Alphus. *Noted Negro Women, Their Thoughts and Activities.* Chicago: Donohue & Henneberry, 1893.

Mussell, N. F. *The Work of the Afro-American Woman*. 2d ed. Philadelphia: Geo. S. Ferguson Co., 1908.

Penn, I. Garland. *The Afro-American Press and Its Editors*. 1891. Reprint. New York: Arno Press and The New York Times Co., 1969.

Robinson, William H., Jr. *Early Black American Prose*. Dubuque, Iowa: Wm. C. Brown Co., 1971.

Aunt Lindy:
A Story Founded on Real Life

In the annals of Fort Valley, Georgia, few events will last longer in the minds of her slow, easy-going dwellers than the memory of a great conflagration that left more than half the town a complete waste. 'Twas generally conceded to be the most disastrous fire that even her oldest residents had ever witnessed. It was caused, as far as could be ascertained, by some one who, while passing through the sampling room of the Cotton Exchange, had thoughtlessly tossed aside a burning match; this, embedding itself in the soft fleecy cotton, burned its way silently, without smoke, through the heart of a great bale to the flooring beneath, before it was discovered.

Although the watchman made his regular rounds an hour or so after the building closed for the night, yet he saw nothing to indicate the treacherous flame which was then, like a serpent, stealing its way through the soft snowy cotton. But now a red glare, a terrified cry of "Fire! Fire!" echoing on the still night air, had aroused the unconscious sleepers, and summoned quickly, strong, brave-hearted men from every direction, who, as though with one accord, fell to fighting the fire-fiend (modern invention was unknown in this out-of-the-way settlement); even the women flocked to the scene, not knowing how soon a helping hand would be needed.

Great volumes of black smoke arose from the fated building, blinding and choking the stout fellows who had arranged themselves in small squads on the roofs of adjacent dwellings to check, if possible, the progress of the fire, while others in line passed water to them.

As the night wore on, a rising wind fanned the fiery tongue into a fateful blaze; and, as higher rose the wind, fiercer grew the flame;

from every window and doorway poured great tongues of fire, casting a lurid glare all over the valley, with its shuddering groups of mute, frightened white faces, and its shrieking, prayerful, terror-stricken negroes, whose religion, being of a highly emotional character, was easily rendered devotional by any unusual excitement: their agonized "'Mi'ty Gawd! he'p us pore sinners," chanted in doleful tones, as only the emotional Southern negro can chant or moan, but added to the weird, wild scene. Men and women with blanched faces looked anxiously at each other; piercing screams rent the air, as some child, relative, or loved one was missed, for, like a curse, the consuming fire passed from house to house, leaving nothing in its track but the blackened and charred remains of what had been, but a few short hours before, "home."

All through the night the fire raged, wasting its force as the early morning light gradually penetrated the smoky haze, revealing to the wellnigh frantic people a sad, sad scene of desolation. When home has been devastated, hearts only may feel and know the extent of the void; no pen or phrase can estimate it.

As the day advanced, sickening details of the night's horror were brought to light. Magruder's Tavern, the only hotel the quaint little town could boast of, served as a death trap; several perished in the flames; many were hurt by falling beams; some jumped from windows and lay maimed for life; others stood in shuddering groups, homeless, but thankful withal that their lives had been spared: as the distressed were found, neighbors who had escaped the scourge threw wide their doors and bestirred themselves to give relief to the sufferers, and temporary shelter to those who had lost all. Ah! let unbelievers cavil and contend, yet such a time as this proves that there is a mystic vein running through humanity that is not deduced from the mechanical laws of nature.

A silver-haired man, a stranger in the town, had been taken to a humble cot where many children in innocent forgetfulness passed noisily to and fro, unconscious that quiet meant life to the aged sufferer. Old Dr. Bronson, with his great heart and gentle, childlike manner, stood doubly thoughtful as he numbered the throbbing pulse. "His brain won't—can't bear it unless he's nursed and has perfect quiet," he murmured as he quitted the house. Acting upon a sudden thought, he sprang into his buggy and quickly drove through the shady lanes, by the redolent orchards, to a lone cabin on the outskirts of the town, situated at the entrance to the great sighing pine-woods.

Seeing a man weeding a small garden plot, he called, without alighting, "Hi there, Joel: where's Aunt Lindy?"

"Right dar, in de cabin, doctor; jes wait a minnit," as he disappeared through the doorway.

"Good day, Aunt Lindy," as a tall, ancient-looking negro dame hurried from the cabin to the gate. Well accustomed was she to these sudden calls of Dr. Bronson, for her fame as a nurse was known far beyond the limits of Fort Valley.

"Mawning, doctor; Miss Martha and de chil'en was not teched by de fi'er?" she inquired anxiously.

"Oh, no; the fire was not our way. Lindy, I have a bad case, and nowhere to take him. Mrs. Bronson has her hands full of distressed, suffering children. No one to nurse him, so I want to bring him here— a victim of the great fire."

"De Lawd, doctor, yo kin, yo kno' yo kin; de cabin is pore, but Joel ner me ain't heathins; fetch him right along, my han's ain't afeered of wuk when trubble comes."

Tenderly they lifted him, and bore him from the cottage resounding with childish prattle and glee, to the quiet, cleanly cabin of the lonely couple, Lindy and Joel, who years before had seen babes torn from their breasts and sold—powerless to utter a complaint or appeal, whipped for the tears they shed, knowing their children would return to them not again till the graves gave up their dead. But in the busy life that freedom gave them, oft, when work was done and the night of life threw its waning shadows around them, their tears would fall for the scattered voices—they would mourn o'er their past oppression. Yet they hid their grief from an unsympathizing generation, and the memory of their oppressors awoke but to the call of fitful retrospection.

"Joel, does yo 'member what de 'scriptur' ses about de stranger widin dy gates?" asked Aunt Lindy, as she hurriedly made ready for the "victim of the great fire."

"Ole 'oman, I gits mo' forgitful each day I lib, but it 'pears to me dat it says su'thin 'bout 'Heal de sick an' lead the blind,'" the old man said, as he stood with a look of deep concern settling on his aged face; "yes, ole 'oman," brightening up, "yes, dat's hit, kase I 'member de words de bressed Marster say to dem lis'ning souls geddered 'roun him, 'If yo hab dun it to de least ob dese my brudderin, yo hab dun it onto me.'"

"Yas, yas, I 'members now," Aunt Lindy murmured, as she moved the bed that the stranger was to rest upon out in the middle of the small room, the headboard near the window almost covered with climbing honeysuckle, all in sweet bloom.

"It am won'erful," she continued, meditatively, "how de Marster 'ranges t'ings to suit His work and will. I'se kep dis bed fixed fur yeahs, 'maginin' dat somehow, in de prov'dence ob Gawd, one ob de chil'en mou't chance dis away wid no place to lay his hed—de law me! Joel, mak' hast' an' fetch in dat shuck bed, de sun hab made it as sweet as de flowers, 'fore de dew falls offen dem, an' reckolec I wants a hole passel of mullen leaves; dey's powerful good fur laying fever, an' as yo's gwine dat way yo mou't jes as well get er han'ful ob mounting mint, sweet balsam—an' cam'ile," she called after him, "ef yo pass enny."

About candle-light Dr. Bronson arrived with his patient, while his two assistants placed him on the bed prepared for him; the doctor explained the critical condition of the sick man to the trusty old nurse, and directed as to the medicine. "Do not disturb him for an hour at least, Aunt Lindy; let him sleep, for he needs all the strength he can rally—he has but one slim chance out of ten."

"Pore sole, I'll look arter him same's ef he war my own chile."

"I know that, Aunt Lindy; I will stop in on my way back from the ridge in about a couple of hours."

"All rite, sah."

Uncle Joel, with the desired herbs, returned shortly afterward. "Is he cum yit, ole 'oman?"

"Shsh! sure nuff," she whispered, with a warning motion of her head toward the partitioned room where the sick man lay. Heeding the warning, Uncle Joel whispered back:

"If dar's nuffin I kin do jes now to he'p yo, I'll jes step ober to Brer An'erson's; I heah dere's a new brudder who's gwine to lead de meetin', as Brer Wilson is ailin'."

"Go 'long, Joel, dere's nuffin yo kin do jes now."

"Well den, s'long, ole 'oman," the old man said, as he stepped noiselessly out into the sweet perfume-laden air.

For a long time Aunt Lindy sat dozing by the smothered fire; so lightly, though, that almost the rustling of the wind through the leaves would have awakened her.

The moonlight streamed in the doorway; now and then sounds issuing from the "pra'r meetin'," a few doors away, could be heard on the still evening air. After a while the nurse rose, lighted a candle, and went to make sure the sick man was comfortable. Entering softly, she stepped to the bedside and looked at the face of the sleeper; suddenly she grew dizzy, breathless, amazed, as though her eyes had deceived her; she placed the candle close by his face and peered wildly at this bruised, bandaged, silver-haired stranger in a fascinated sort of way, as though she were powerless to speak. At last:

"Great Gawd! it's Marse Jeems!"

The quick, vengeful flame leaped in her eyes, as her mind, made keen by years of secret suffering and toil, travelled through time and space; she saw wrongs which no tongue can enumerate; demoniac gleams of exultation and bitter hatred settled upon her now grim features; a pitiless smile wreathed her set lips, as she gazed with glaring eyeballs at this helpless, homeless "victim of the great fire," as though surrounded by demons; a dozen wicked impulses rushed through her mind—a life for a life—no mortal eye was near, an intercepted breath, a gasp, and——

"Lindy, Lindy, don't tell Miss Cynthia," the sick man weakly murmured: in the confused state of his brain it required but this familiar black face to conduct his disordered thoughts to the palmiest period of his existence. He again revelled in opulence, saw again the cotton fields—a waving tract of bursting snowballs—the magnolia, the oleander——

"Whar's my chil'en?" Nurse Lindy fairly shrieked in his face. "To de fo' win's ob de ear'fh, yo ole debbil, yo." He heard her not now, for white and unconscious he lay, while the long pent-up passion found vent. Her blood was afire, her tall form swayed, her long, bony hands trembled like an animal at bay; she stepped back as if to spring upon him, with clutching fingers extended; breathless she paused; the shouts of the worshippers broke upon the evening air—the olden-time melody seemed to pervade the cabin; she listened, turned, and fled—out through the open doorway,—out into the white moonlight, down the shadowed lane, as if impelled by unseen force. She unconsciously approached the prayer-meeting door. "Vengeance is mine, ses de Lawd," came from within; her anger died away; quickly her steps she retraced. "Mi'ty Gawd, stren'fin my arm, an pur'fy my heart," was all she said.

Soon from the portals of death she brought him, for untiringly she labored, unceasingly she prayed in her poor broken way; nor was it in vain, for before the frost fell the crisis passed, the light of reason beamed upon the silver-haired stranger, and revealed in mystic characters the service rendered by a former slave—Aunt Lindy. He marvelled at the patient faithfulness of these people. He saw but the gold—did not dream of the dross burned away by the great Refiner's fire. From that time Aunt Lindy and Uncle Joel never knew a sorrow, secret or otherwise; for not only was the roof above their heads secured to them, but the new "brudder" who came to "lead de meetin' in Brer Wilson's place," was proved beyond a doubt, through the efforts of the silver-haired stranger, to be their first-born. The rest were "sleeping until the morning," and not to the 'fo' win's ob de ear'fh,'" as was so greatly feared by Aunt Lindy.

Frances Ellen Watkins Harper

1825–1911

With the death of her husband on 23 May 1866, Frances Ellen Watkins Harper emerged publicly again to embark on a new phase of her life as a social and moral reformer, lecturer, and author.

From 1867 to 1871, she began a grueling daily lecture tour through thirteen southern states at her own expense, buttressed by meager audience collections and sales of her poetry. She addressed black and white assemblages on morality, industry, building strong families and homes, education, temperance, and women's rights. She spoke on such topics as "The Demands of the Colored Race in the Work of Reconstruction," "Enlightened Motherhood," and "Racial Literature." Her lectures extended into Sunday schools, churches, schools, town meetings, and homes. Sometimes she spoke two, three, and four times a day.

Although in ill health, she not only talked constantly but conversed and listened to those who had something to say to her. There were occasions when she became discouraged by the callous indifference of the freedmen, but as she wrote in a letter from Greenville, Georgia: "After all, whether they encourage or discourage me, I belong to this race, and when it is down I belong to a down race; when it is up I belong to a risen race."[1]

During her pilgrimage, she stayed in the lowly cabins of the former slaves. At Montgomery in 1870, she described a home as "one of those southern shells through which both light and cold enter at the same time."[2]

Believing the needs of women were "far more pressing than any other class," she gave private lectures without charge to freedwomen. An ardent advocate of women's rights, she penned in a letter: "Now is the time for our women to begin to try to lift up their heads and plant the roots of progress under the hearthstone."[3]

With the rise of the women's movement and clubs, Frances Harper was frequently called upon as a speaker. In 1888, she addressed the International Council of Women in Washington. Before the Columbian Exposition in Chicago, she spoke on "Woman's Political Future."

One of her most eloquent lectures on women was presented to the National Council of Women, 23 February 1891, on "Duty to Dependent Races." In this, she strongly declared: "If the fifteenth century discovered America to the Old World, the nineteenth is discovering woman to herself."[4]

She was a staunch temperance supporter and played a leading role in the Women's Christian Temperance Union (WCTU). From 1875 to 1882, she was superintendent of the Philadelphia and Pennsylvania chapters of the national WCTU's colored branch, and she headed the northern United States WCTU from 1883 to 1890. Her work was posthumously honored in 1922, when the world WCTU placed her name on their Red Letter Calendar.

Her concern about the evils of alcohol had long been expressed in her poetry. "The Drunkard's Child" (1854), "Signing the Pledge" (1888), "Nothing and Something" (1888), and "The Ragged Stocking" (1889)—all depicted her feelings about the ill effects of alcohol on family life. And her interest in women's rights appeared in such poems as "A Double Standard," and "Died of Starvation." By utilizing universal themes of religion, morality, and social issues, she established herself as a black writer who did not restrict herself to racial subjects.

Despite her involvement in other endeavors, Frances Ellen Watkins Harper continued to produce her literary works. In 1869, she published *Moses: A Story of the Nile*, which has been called her "notable artistic success." This long narrative poem in blank verse was inspired by Emancipation and the death of Lincoln. A second edition was issued by the author in 1889. *Sketches of Southern Life*, published in 1872, contained poems of "wit and irony" emanating from the sagacious mouth of Aunt Chloe. An ex-slave, Aunt Chloe dispenses wry discourses on the Civil War and Reconstruction in colloquial language. It was published again in 1888. Three pamphlets, *Light Beyond the Darkness*, *The Sparrow's Fall and Other Poems*, and *The Martyr of Alabama* were issued and subsequently included in *Atlanta Offering* (1895).

Frances Harper's most memorable literary effort during her later years was the publication of her only novel when she was sixty-seven, *Iola Leroy;*

or, Shadows Uplifted 1892, which appeared in three editions in Philadelphia and Boston. The novel is filled with moralistic messages, which the author acknowledges in a note at the back of the book. She professes her motivation for writing the novel was "to awaken in the hearts of our countrymen a stronger sense of justice and a more Christlike humanity."[5] Her lifelong friend, William Still, wrote the introduction to *Iola Leroy*. Reflecting on her work as a moralizer, he said, "Doubtless the thousands of colored Sunday-Schools in the South, in casting about for an interesting, moral story-book, full of practical lessons, will not be content to be without 'IOLA LEROY, OR SHADOWS UPLIFTED.'"[6]

The work has been called a transitional novel for it spans the antebellum and Reconstruction periods. The plot centers around a very fair-skinned family of a mixed marriage. Iola Leroy is one of three children born to Eugene Leroy, a wealthy southern Creole painter, and Marie, a beautiful mulatto whom he has educated and freed. Unaware of their black blood, the children are brought up on the plantation, insulated by their wealth and comfort. They are waited on by slaves, who do not divulge the secret, and they are sent north to school.

When the father dies of yellow fever, a conniving and greedy cousin, Lorraine, who knows of Marie's former bondage, schemes to inherit the plantation. To do this, he finds a flaw in the legality of Eugene's marriage. The children are told of their true identity, and Iola and her mother are sold into slavery. Gracie, the second daughter, dies of the fever shortly after her father. Harry, a son, away in school, joins the Union army as a black. When freed, Iola Leroy becomes a nurse in the Union army and meets her mother's brother. After the war, the family is reunited in North Carolina, and the "shadows [are] lifted from all their lives."

Obviously propagandistic like many of her other works, the book has been cited as having "helped to establish the precedent of developing well-mannered, educated colored characters to offset the stock figures of the plantation tradition."[7] It has been claimed, however, that the book lacks realism and objectivity.

Mrs. Harper continued to write into the twentieth century, publishing *Poems* in 1900 and *Idylls of the Bible* in 1901. Having made her home in Philadelphia since 1871, she died there of a heart ailment on February 22, 1911 at the age of eighty-seven. Her daughter, Mary, a lecturer, Sunday school teacher, and volunteer social worker who had remained single, died two years before her mother. *Iola Leroy* is "Lovingly Dedicated" to Mary E. Harper.

Frances Ellen Watkins Harper's rich and varied career as an Abolitionist, orator, suffragist, social reformer, poet, and author bridged half a century. The most popular and well-known black poet prior to Paul Laurence Dunbar, she stands majestically as a testament to the literary talents of Afro-American women.

NOTES

1. Still, *Underground Railroad*, p. 773.
2. Ibid.
3. Ibid., p. 772.
4. Loewenberg and Bogin, *Black Women*, p. 244.
5. Harper, *Iola Leroy*, p. 282.
6. Ibid., p. 3.
7. Gloster, *Negro Voices*, p. 31.

SELECTED SOURCES

Primary

Harper, Frances E. W. *Atlanta Offerings: Poems*. Philadelphia, 1895.
———. *Iola Leroy; or, Shadows Uplifted*. 3d ed. Boston: James H. Earle, 1895.

Secondary

Christian, Barbara. *Black Women Novelists: The Development of a Tradition, 1892–1976*. Westport, Conn.: Greenwood Press, 1980.
Gloster, Hugh M. *Negro Voices in American Fiction*. New York: Russell & Russell, 1965; Chapel Hill: University of North Carolina Press, 1948.
Loewenberg, Bert James, and Bogin, Ruth. *Black Women in Nineteenth-Century American Life: Their Words, Their Thoughts, Their Feelings*. University Park: Pennsylvania State University Press, 1976.
Sherman, Joan R. *Invisible Poets: Afro-Americans of the Nineteenth Century*. Urbana: University of Illinois Press, 1974.
Still, William. *The Underground Railroad*. Philadelphia: Porter & Coates, 1872.
Watson, Carole McAlpine. *Prologue: The Novels of Black American Women, 1891–1965*. Westport, Conn.: Greenwood Press, 1985.

School-girl Notions

During Iola's stay in the North she found a strong tide of opposition against slavery. Arguments against the institution had entered the Church and made legislative halls the arenas of fierce debate. The subject had become part of the social converse of the fireside, and had enlisted the best brain and heart of the country. Anti-slavery discussions were pervading the strongest literature and claiming a place on the most popular platforms.

Iola, being a Southern girl and a slave-holder's daughter, always defended slavery when it was under discussion.

"Slavery can't be wrong," she would say, "for my father is a slave-holder, and my mother is as good to our servants as she can be. My father often tells her that she spoils them, and lets them run over her. I never saw my father strike one of them. I love my mammy as much as I do my own mother, and I believe she loves us just as if we were her own children. When we are sick I am sure that she could not do anything more for us than she does."

"But, Iola," responded one of her school friends, "after all, they are not free. Would you be satisfied to have the most beautiful home, the costliest jewels, or the most elegant wardrobe if you were a slave?"

"Oh, the cases are not parallel. Our slaves do not want their freedom. They would not take it if we gave it to them."

"That is not the case with them all. My father has seen men who have encountered almost incredible hardships to get their freedom. Iola, did you ever attend an anti-slavery meeting?"

"No; I don't think these Abolitionists have any right to meddle in our affairs. I believe they are prejudiced against us, and want to get our property. I read about them in the papers when I was at home. I don't want to hear my part of the country run down. My father says the slaves would be very well contented if no one put wrong notions in their heads."

"I don't know," was the response of her friend, "but I do not think that that slave mother who took her four children, crossed the Ohio River on the ice, killed one of the children and attempted the lives of the other two, was a contented slave. And that other one, who, running away and finding herself pursued, threw herself over the Long Bridge into the Potomac, was evidently not satisfied. I do not think the numbers who are coming North on the Underground Railroad can be very contented. It is not natural for people to run away from happiness, and if they are so happy and contented, why did Congress pass the Fugitive Slave Bill?"

"Well, I don't think," answered Iola, "any of our slaves would run away. I know mamma don't like slavery very much. I have often heard her say that she hoped the time would come when there would not be a slave in the land. My father does not think as she does. He thinks slavery is not wrong if you treat them well and don't sell them from their families. I intend, after I have graduated, to persuade pa to buy a house in New Orleans, and spend the winter there. You know this will be my first season out, and I hope that you will come and spend the winter with me. We will have such gay times, and you will so fall in love with our sunny South that you will never want to come back to shiver amid the snows and cold of the North. I think one winter in the South would cure you of your Abolitionism."

"Have you seen her yet?"

This question was asked by Louis Bastine, an attorney who had come North in the interests of Lorraine. The scene was the New England village where Mr. Galen's academy was located, and which Iola was attending. This question was addressed to Camille Lecroix, Bastine's intimate friend, who had lately come North. He was the son of a planter who lived near Leroy's plantation, and was familiar with Iola's family history. Since his arrival North, Bastine had met him and communicated to him his intentions.

"Yes; just caught a glimpse of her this morning as she was going down the street," was Camille's reply.

"She is a most beautiful creature," said Louis Bastine. " She has the proud poise of Leroy, the most splendid eyes I ever saw in a woman's head, lovely complexion, and a glorious wealth of hair. She would bring $2000 any day in a New Orleans market."

"I always feel sorry," said Camille, "when I see one of those Creole girls brought to the auction block. I have known fathers who were deeply devoted to their daughters, but who through some reverse of fortune were forced to part with them, and I always think the blow has been equally terrible on both sides. I had a friend who had two beautiful daughters whom he had educated in the North. They were cultured, and really belles in society. They were entirely ignorant of their lineage, but when their father died it was discovered that their mother had been a slave. It was a fearful blow. They would have faced poverty, but the knowledge of their tainted blood was more than they could bear."

"What became of them?"

"They both died, poor girls. I believe they were as much killed by the blow as if they had been shot. To tell you the truth, Bastine,

I feel sorry for this girl. I don't believe she has the least idea of her negro blood."

"No, Leroy has been careful to conceal it from her," replied Bastine.

"Is that so?" queried Camille. "Then he has made a great mistake."

"I can't help that," said Bastine; "business is business."

"How can you get her away?" asked Camille. "You will have to be very cautious, because if these pesky Abolitionists get an inkling of what you're doing they will balk your game double quick. And when you come to look at it, isn't it a shame to attempt to reduce that girl to slavery? She is just as white as we are, as good as any girl in the land, and better educated than thousands of white girls. A girl with her apparent refinement and magnificent beauty, were it not for the cross in her blood, I would be proud to introduce to our set. She would be the sensation of the season. I believe to-day it would be easier for me to go to the slums and take a young girl from there, and have her introduced as my wife, than to have society condone the offense if I married that lovely girl. There is not a social circle in the South that would not take it as a gross insult to have her introduced into it."

"Well," said Bastine, "my plan is settled. Leroy has never allowed her to spend her vacations at home. I understand she is now very anxious to get home, and, as Lorraine's attorney, I have come on his account to take her home."

"How will you do it?"

"I shall tell her her father is dangerously ill, and desires her to come as quickly as possible."

"And what then?"

"Have her inventoried with the rest of the property."

"Don't she know that her father is dead?"

"I think not," said Bastine. "She is not in mourning, but appeared very light-hearted this morning, laughing and talking with two other girls. I was struck with her great beauty, and asked a gentleman who she was. He said, 'Miss Leroy, of Mississippi.' I think Lorraine has managed the affair so as to keep her in perfect ignorance of her father's death. I don't like the job, but I never let sentiment interfere with my work."

Poor Iola! When she said slavery was not a bad thing, little did she think that she was destined to drink to its bitter dregs the cup she was so ready to press to the lips of others.

"How do you think she will take to her situation?" asked Camille.

"O, I guess," said Bastine, "she will sulk and take it pretty hard at first; but if she is managed right she will soon get over it. Give her plenty of jewelry, fine clothes, and an easy time."

"All this business must be conducted with the utmost secrecy and speed. Her mother could not have written to her, for she has been suffering with brain fever and nervous prostration since Leroy's death. Lorraine knows her market value too well, and is too shrewd to let so much property pass out of his hands without making an effort to retain it."

"Has she any brothers or sisters?"

"Yes, a brother," replied Bastine; "but he is at another school, and I have no orders from Lorraine in reference to him. If I can get the girl I am willing to let well enough alone. I dread the interview with the principal more than anything else. I am afraid he will hem and haw, and have his doubts. Perhaps when he sees my letters and hears my story, I can pull the wool over his eyes."

"But, Louis, this is a pitiful piece of business. I should hate to be engaged in it."

A deep flush of shame overspread for a moment the face of Lorraine's attorney, as he replied: "I don't like the job, but I have undertaken it, and must go through with it."

"I see no 'must' about it. Were I in your place I would wash my hands of the whole business."

"I can't afford it," was Bastine's hard, business-like reply. On the next morning after this conversation between these two young men, Louis Bastine presented himself to the principal of the academy, with the request that Iola be permitted to leave immediately to attend the sick-bed of her father, who was dangerously ill. The principal hesitated, but while he was deliberating, a telegram, purporting to come from Iola's mother, summoned Iola to her father's bedside without delay. The principal, set at rest in regard to the truthfulness of the dispatch, not only permitted but expedited her departure.

Iola and Bastine took the earliest train, and traveled without pausing until they reached a large hotel in a Southern city. There they were obliged to wait a few hours until they could resume their journey, the train having failed to make connection, Iola sat in a large, lonely parlor, waiting for the servant to show her to a private room. She had never known a great sorrow. Never before had the shadows of death mingled with the sunshine of her life.

Anxious, travel-worn, and heavy-hearted, she sat in an easy chair, with nothing to divert her from the grief and anxiety which rendered every delay a source of painful anxiety.

"Oh, I hope that he will be alive and growing better!" was the thought which kept constantly revolving in her mind, until she fell asleep. In her dreams she was at home, encircled in the warm clasp of her father's arms, feeling her mother's kisses lingering on her lips, and hearing the joyous greetings of the servants and Mammy Liza's glad welcome as she folded her to her heart. From this dream of bliss she was awakened by a burning kiss pressed on her lips, and a strong arm encircling her. Gazing around and taking in the whole situation, she sprang from her seat, her eyes flashing with rage and scorn, her face flushed to the roots of her hair, her voice shaken with excitement, and every nerve trembling with angry emotion.

"How dare you do such a thing! Don't you know if my father were here he would crush you to the earth?"

"Not so fast, my lovely tigress," said Bastine, "your father knew what he was doing when he placed you in my charge."

"My father made a grave mistake, if he thought he had put me in charge of a gentleman."

"I am your guardian for the present," replied Bastine. "I am to see you safe home, and then my commission ends."

"I wish it were ended now," she exclaimed, trembling with anger and mortification. Her voice was choked by emotion, and broken by smothered sobs. Louis Bastine thought to himself, "she is a real spitfire, but beautiful even in her wrath."

During the rest of her journey Iola preserved a most freezing reserve towards Bastine. At length the journey was ended. Pale and anxious she rode up the avenue which led to her home.

A strange silence pervaded the place. The servants moved sadly from place to place, and spoke in subdued tones. The windows were heavily draped with crape, and a funeral air pervaded the house.

Mammy Liza met her at the door, and, with streaming eyes and convulsive sobs, folded her to her heart, as Iola exclaimed, in tones of hopeless anguish:—

"Oh, papa's dead!"

"Oh, my pore baby!" said mammy, "ain't you hearn tell 'bout it? Yore par's dead, an' your mar's bin drefful sick. She's better now."

Mam Liza stepped lightly into Mrs. Leroy's room, and gently apprised her of Iola's arrival. In a darkened room lay the stricken mother, almost distracted by her late bereavement.

"Oh, Iola," she exclaimed, as her daughter entered, "is this you? I am so sorry you came."

Then, burying her head in Iola's bosom, she wept convulsively. "Much as I love you," she continued, between her sobs, "and much as I longed to see you, I am sorry you came."

"Why, mother," replied Iola, astonished, "I received your telegram last Wednesday, and I took the earliest train I could get."

"My dear child, I never sent you a telegram. It was a trick to bring you down South and reduce you to slavery."

Iola eyed her mother curiously. What did she mean? Had grief dethroned her reason? Yet her eye was clear, her manner perfectly rational.

Marie saw the astounded look on Iola's face, and nerving herself to the task, said: "Iola, I must tell you what your father always enjoined me to be silent about. I did not think it was the wisest thing, but I yielded to his desires. I have negro blood in my veins. I was your father's slave before I married him. His relatives have set aside his will. The courts have declared our marriage null and void and my manumission illegal, and we are all to be remanded to slavery."

An expression of horror and anguish swept over Iola's face, and, turning deathly pale, she exclaimed, "Oh, mother, it can't be so! you must be dreaming!"

"No, my child; it is a terrible reality."

Almost wild with agony, Iola paced the floor, as the fearful truth broke in crushing anguish upon her mind. Then bursting into a paroxysm of tears succeeded by peals of hysterical laughter, said:—

"I used to say that slavery is right. I didn't know what I was talking about." Then growing calmer, she said, "Mother, who is at the bottom of this downright robbery?"

"Alfred Lorraine. I have always dreaded that man, and what I feared has come to pass. Your father had faith in him; I never have."

"But, mother, could we not contest his claim. You have your marriage certificate and papa's will."

"Yes, my dear child, but Judge Starkins has decided that we have no standing in the court, and no testimony according to law."

"Oh, mother, what can I do?"

"Nothing, my child, unless you can escape to the North."

"And leave you?"

"Yes."

"Mother, I will never desert you in your hour of trial. But can nothing be done? Had father no friends who would assist us?"

"None that I know of. I do not think he had an acquaintance who approved of our marriage. The neighboring planters have stood so aloof from me that I do not know where to turn for either help or sympathy. I believe it was Lorraine who sent the telegram. I wrote to you as soon as I could after your father's death, but fainted just as I finished directing the letter. I do not think he knows where your brother is, and, if possible, he must not know. If you can by any means, *do* send a letter to Harry and warn him not to attempt to come home. I don't know how you will succeed, for Lorraine has us all under surveillance. But it is according to law."

"What law, mother?"

"The law of the strong against the weak."

"Oh, mother, it seems like a dreadful dream, a fearful nightmare! But I cannot shake it off. Where is Gracie?"

"The dear child has been running down ever since her papa's death. She clung to me night and day while I had the brain fever, and could not be persuaded to leave me. She hardly ate anything for more than a week. She has been dangerously ill for several days, and the doctor says she cannot live. The fever has exhausted all her rallying power, and yet, dear as she is to me, I would rather consign her to the deepest grave than see her forced to be a slave."

"So would I. I wish I could die myself."

"Oh, Iola, do not talk so. Strive to be a Christian, to have faith in the darkest hour. Were it not for my hope of heaven I couldn't stand all this trouble."

"Mother, are these people Christians who made these laws which are robbing us of our inheritance and reducing us to slavery? If this is Christianity I hate and despise it. Would the most cruel heathen do worse?"

"My dear child, I have not learned my Christianity from them. I have learned it at the foot of the cross, and from this book," she said, placing a New Testament in Iola's hands. "Some of the most beautiful lessons of faith and trust I have ever learned were from among our lowly people in their humble cabins."

"Mamma!" called a faint voice from the adjoining room. Marie immediately arose and went to the bedside of her sick child, where Mammy Liza was holding her faithful vigils. The child had just awakened from a fitful sleep.

"I thought," she said, "that I heard Iola's voice. Has she come?"

"Yes, darling; do you want to see her?"

"Oh, yes," she said, as a bright smile broke over her dying features.

Iola passed quickly into the room. Gracie reached out her thin, bloodless, hand, clasped Iola's palm in hers, and said: "I am so glad you have come. Dear Iola, stand by mother. You and Harry are all she has. It is not hard to die. You and mother and Harry must meet me in heaven."

Swiftly the tidings went through the house that Gracie was dying. The servants gathered around her with tearful eyes, as she bade them all good-bye. When she had finished, and Mammy had lowered the pillow, an unwonted radiance lit up her eye, and an expression of ineffable gladness overspread her face, as she murmured: "It is beautiful, so beautiful!" Fainter and fainter grew her voice, until, without a struggle or sigh, she passed away beyond the power of oppression and prejudice.

A Double Standard

Do you blame me that I loved him?
　If when standing all alone
I cried for bread a careless world
　Pressed to my lips a stone.

Do you blame me that I loved him,
　That my heart beat glad and free,
When he told me in the sweetest tones
　He loved but only me?

Can you blame me that I did not see
　Beneath his burning kiss
The serpent's wiles, nor even hear
　The deadly adder hiss?

Can you blame me that my heart grew cold
    That the tempted, tempter turned;
When he was feted and caressed
    And I was coldly spurned?

Would you blame him, when you draw from me
    Your dainty robes aside,
If he with gilded baits should claim
    Your fairest as his bride?

Would you blame the world if it should press
    On him a civic crown;
And see me struggling in the depth
    Then harshly press me down?

Crime has no sex and yet to-day
    I wear the brand of shame;
Whilst he amid the gay and proud
    Still bears an honored name.

Can you blame me if I've learned to think
    Your hate of vice a sham,
When you so coldly crushed me down
    And then excused the man?

Would you blame me if to-morrow
    The coroner should say,
A wretched girl, outcast, forlorn,
    Has thrown her life away?

Yes, blame me for my downward course,
    But oh! remember well,
Within your homes you press the hand
    That led me down to hell.

I'm glad God's ways are not our ways,
    He does not see as man;
Within His love I know there's room
    For those whom others ban.

I think before His great white throne,
    His throne of spotless light,
That whited sepulchres shall wear
    The hue of endless night.

That I who fell, and he who sinned,
   Shall reap as we have sown;
That each the burden of his loss
   Must bear and bear alone.

No golden weights can turn the scale
   Of justice in His sight;
And what is wrong in woman's life
   In man's cannot be right.

Anna Julia Haywood Cooper

1859–1964

The life story of Anna Julia Haywood Cooper adds to the history of Afro-American women writers another impressive chronicle of a woman moving from slavery to leadership. This unusual woman—"feminist, human rights advocate, educational reformer—was also a teacher, lecturer, scholar, and the author of essays, vignettes, and poems."[1]

Her slave mother, Hannah Stanley Haywood, gave birth to Anna in Raleigh, North Carolina on 10 August 1859. As in the case of many slave women whose bondage made them victims, her father was presumed to have been her mother's master, George Washington Haywood, about whom she was "always too modest and shamefaced ever to mention."[2] Two brothers, Andrew J. and Rufus Haywood, completed the family.

Ahead of her peers as a child, nine-year-old Anna was singled out in 1868 for a scholarship at the newly opened St. Augustine Normal School and Collegiate Institute. The school was founded by the executive committee of the Board of Missions of the Episcopal church to educate teachers for the vast number of illiterate freedmen, as well as to prepare candidates for the ministry.

She attended St. Augustine for fourteen years, serving also as a tutor for other students. An early confrontation with sexism occurred when she sought to enroll in the school's first Greek class, which was designed for male theology students. After forcefully pushing her claim, she was finally permitted to take the course. The class was taught by a thirty-year-old theology student, George A. C. Cooper, who had been a tailor in his native Nassau, British West Indies. A romance developed between Anna and her teacher, and the two were married on 21 June 1877 in St. Augustine's chapel.

The second black to be ordained in the Episcopal church in North Carolina, Cooper and his eighteen-year-old bride pledged themselves, as minister and teacher, to serving their race. The marriage was short-lived, however, for Cooper died on 27 September 1879, his premature death attributed by his widow to "hard work and exposure suffered while serving his parish."

Realizing she needed a solid educational background to train her people more effectively, Anna Julia Cooper left St. Augustine in 1881 to pursue additional studies at Oberlin College. The historic town of Oberlin, Ohio, had been a bastion of Abolitionists and the Underground Railroad. The college in 1833 was the first to accept women, and it admitted blacks the following year. More mature than the other students, Anna studied hard, tutored her white classmates in advanced algebra, and made a marked impression on her teachers.

She graduated in 1884, along with two other black women who like herself rose to fame, Mary Eliza Church and Ida A. Gibbs. Another black woman, Mary Jane Patterson, came before them in the class of 1862. The "three women were among the first Afro-American women to earn B.A. degrees from an American college. (Mary Jane Patterson is believed to have been the first.)"[3]

Returning to St. Augustine to teach, she again faced sexism when the position offered her was that of instructing girls. Instead, she went to head the Department of Modern Languages at Wilberforce in Xenia, Ohio, in September 1884. Concern about her mother, however, induced her to leave after a year and return to St. Augustine to teach mathematics, Greek, and Latin.

In 1887, Oberlin awarded her a M.A. degree in mathematics "on the strength of Anna Cooper's three years of teaching experience on the college level."[4] That year was a turning point in her career, for she accepted a position to teach mathematics and science at the sole black high school in the District of Columbia, the Washington Colored High School, popularly called the M Street School.

Living up to her credo of "education for service," Anna J. Cooper advanced to principal of the school from 1901 to 1906. Backed by an outstanding faculty, she strengthened the curriculum, and the school became accredited for the first time. Graduates of the M Street School, which later became Dunbar High School, were admitted to such institutions as Harvard, Yale, Brown, Amherst, and Radcliffe. When conflict developed over lowering the curriculum standards of the "colored school," Anna J. Cooper stood her ground on upholding its high standards. The controversy gained widespread publicity in the Washington papers with prominent black leaders supporting Mrs. Cooper, "who refused to compromise her convictions and principles." On 30 June 1906, the Board of Education did not reappoint her.

Adhering to her belief that "strong-minded women could be, when they thought it worth their while, quite endurable,"[5] she taught languages on a college level at Lincoln Institute in Missouri. Meanwhile, "she instituted a claim for reinstatement to her position and back salary."[6]

Not only was Cooper a fighter for equal education for all regardless of sex and race, but she was a pacesetter in the black women's movement of the latter part of the nineteenth century. She assisted in organizing the Colored Women's League in Washington, D.C. (1894), whose program was aimed at uplifting the race through social services and training programs. Out of this evolved the first Colored Social Settlement House in Washington, which she helped found; she served as supervisor in 1906–7. Eventually, the Colored Women's League merged with Boston's New Era Club and the Federation of Afro-American Women's League to become the National Association of Colored Women's Clubs.

An ardent feminist, Anna J. Cooper lectured widely on the equality of women, advocating their freedom to develop as individuals without the "ridicule and censure of males." Her classic and most important work, *A Voice from the South: By a Black Woman of the South* (1892), "showed her well ahead of her time in arguing for women's rights and the importance of a role for the black woman."[7] Calling herself a "black woman" at the time "Negro" was in vogue, Anna J. Cooper gave her raison d'être for writing the work: "not many can more sensibly realize and more accurately tell the weight and the fret of the 'long dull pain' than the open-eyed but hitherto voiceless Black Woman of America."[8] She wanted the black woman to speak for herself, something neither the black man nor others could adequately do for her.

The eight essays on women and race addressed such topics as "Womanhood a Vital Element in the Regeneration and Progress of a Race" and "The Status of Women in America." The best-known essay, "The Higher Education of Women," was read before the American Conference of Educators in March 1890.

The book, which sold for $1.25, was highly praised in newspapers. The *Public Opinion* said, "This volume possesses a fresh attraction, because it comes from the eager heart and mind of a 'Black Woman of the South.'"[9] The *Detroit Plaindealer* told its readers, "There has been no book on the race question that has been more cogently and forcibly written by either white or black authors. The book is not only a credit to the genius of the race, but to woman whose place and sphere in life men have so long dictated."[10] The

Iowa Times (Kingsley) compared Cooper's mind to that of "Susan B. Anthony, a George Eliot, or Frances Willard." And writer Albion W. Tourgee observed that few women writers had demonstrated "a daintier wit, and few works give promise of a purer literary art."[11]

As women's editor of the *Southland* magazine in 1890, she wrote on the issues of sex and race, views she took to the lecture platform, along with writers Frances Ellen Watkins Harper and Alice Ruth Moore Dunbar. At the Women's Congress in 1893, held at the same time in Chicago as the World's Columbian Exposition, she spoke on "The Needs and Status of Black Women."

She was active in organizations founded to advance the race. In 1900, she shared the rostrum of the historic Pan-African Conference in London with W. E. B. Du Bois. As a member of the Bethel Literary Society, she participated in a cultural exchange visit with black Canadian teachers. Recognized for her intellect, she was the lone female to be elected to the American Negro Academy, which "only invited and selected the best minds and scholars into its membership."[12]

Always seeking to better her educational background, Anna J. Cooper began doctoral studies at Columbia University in July 1914. Three years later, she had completed her course work and needed only to meet a one-year residency requirement. But the loss in 1915 of the wife of her brother's adopted son, John R. Haywood, who had five children ranging in age from six months to twelve years, had caused her to give up her residency plans. "At about the age of fifty-five, then, Anna Cooper was called upon to make a decision that would necessitate further adjustments in her lifestyle and resources."[13] To rear the children, she bought a spacious home owned by former congressman Benjamin Le Fevre in a section once barred to blacks at 201 T Street, N.W.

Still determined to get her Ph.D., however, she transferred credits to the University of France. To keep her mind and language skills fresh, she published a college text, *Le Pèlerinage de Charlemagne* (1925), in Paris, with an introduction by Abbé Klein of the Catholic Institute of Paris. At the amazing age of sixty-five, Anna Julia Cooper was awarded the Ph.D. degree from the Sorbonne, which made her the fourth black woman to receive a doctorate. Interestingly, all four women had been associated with the M Street School.

When she retired in 1930, Anna Cooper accepted a position as the second president of Frelinghuysen University in Washington, D.C., for employed blacks. The university was planned "to provide social services, religious training, and educational programs for the people who needed them the most."[14] It was a university without a campus, and classes were held in homes, offices, apartments, and educational centers throughout the city. Even the home of Mrs. Cooper was a part of the network. Students were those "persons who had had no opportunity for intellectual training in their earlier days." To this concept, Anna J. Cooper directed her remaining years, energy, spirit, and educational acumen.

On 27 February 1964, at the age of 105, this extraordinary woman, who had received congratulatory messages from President and Mrs. Dwight D. Eisenhower on her 100th birthday, died in her home on T Street and was buried in Raleigh, North Carolina.

NOTES

1. Hutchinson, *Anna J. Cooper*, p. 3.
2. Ibid.
3. Ibid., p. 36.
4. Ibid., p. 43.
5. Cooper, *A Voice from the South*, p. 72.
6. Hutchinson, *Anna J. Cooper*, p. 83.
7. Ibid., p. xiv.
8. Cooper, *A Voice from the South*, p. ii.
9. Majors, *Noted Negro Women*, p. 285.
10. Ibid., p. 286.
11. Ibid., p. 287.
12. Hutchinson, *Anna J. Cooper*, p. 110.
13. Ibid., p. 132.
14. Ibid., p. 157.

SELECTED SOURCES

Primary

Cooper, Anna J. *The Third Step*, N.p., n.d.
———. *A Voice from the South: By a Black Woman of the South*. Xenia, Ohio: Aldine Printing House, 1892. Reprint. New York: Negro University Press, 1969.

Secondary

Dannett, Sylvia G. L. *Profiles of Negro Womanhood*. Vol 1, *1619–1900*. Yonkers, N.Y.: Educational Heritage, 1964.
Giddings, Paula. *When and Where I Enter: The Impact of Black Women on Race and Sex in America*. New York: William Morrow & Co., 1984.
Harley, Sharon. "Anna J. Cooper: A Voice for Black Women." In *The Afro-American Woman: Struggles and Images*, edited by Sharon Harley and Rosalyn Terborg-Penn. New York: Kennikat Press, 1978.
Hutchinson, Louise Daniel. *Anna J. Cooper: A Voice from the South*. Washington, D.C.: Published by the Anacostia Neighborhood Museum of the Smithsonian Institution by the Smithsonian Institution Press, 1981.

Loewenberg, Bert James, and Bogin, Ruth. *Black Women in Nineteenth-Century American Life: Their Words, Their Thoughts, Their Feelings.* University Park: Pennsylvania State University Press, 1976.

Majors, Monroe Alphus. *Noted Negro Women, Their Triumphs and Activities.* Chicago: Donohue & Henneberry, 1893.

Scruggs, Lawson Andrew. *Women of Distinction: Remarkable Works and Invincible Character.* Raleigh: L. A. Scruggs, 1893.

The Higher Education of Women

In the very first year of our century, the year 1801, there appeared in Paris a book by Silvain Marechal, entitled "Shall Woman Learn the Alphabet." The book proposes a law prohibiting the alphabet to women, and quotes authorities weighty and various, to prove that the woman who knows the alphabet has already lost part of her womanliness. The author declares that woman can use the alphabet only as Moliere predicted they would, in spelling out the verb *amo*; that they have no occasion to persue Ovid's *Ars Amoris*, since that is already the ground and limit of their intuitive furnishing; that Madame Guion would have been far more adorable had she remained a beautiful ignoramus as nature made her; that Ruth, Naomi, the Spartan woman, the Amazons, Penelope, Andromache, Lucretia, Joan of Arc, Petrarch's Laura, the daughters of Charlemagne, could not spell their names; while Sappho, Aspasia, Madame de Maintenon, and Madame de Stael could read altogether too well for their good; finally, that if women were once permitted to read Sophocles and work with logarithms, or to nibble at any side of the apple of knowledge, there would be an end forever to their sewing on buttons and embroidering slippers.

Please remember this book was published at the *beginning* of the Nineteenth Century. At the end of its first third, (in the year 1833) one solitary college in America decided to admit women within its sacred precincts, and organized what was called a "Ladies' Course" as well as the regular B. A. or Gentlemen's course.

It was felt to be an experiment—a rather dangerous experiment—and was adopted with fear and trembling by the good fathers, who looked as if they had been caught secretly mixing explosive compounds and were guiltily expecting every moment to see the foundations under them shaken and rent and their fall superstructure shattered into fragments.

But the girls came, and there was no upheaval. They performed their tasks modestly and intelligently. Once in a while one or two were found choosing the gentlemen's course. Still no collapse; and the dear, careful, scrupulous, frightened old professors were just getting their hearts out of their throats and preparing to draw one good free breath, when they found they would have to change the names of those courses; for there were as many ladies in the gentlemen's course as in the ladies', and a distinctively Ladies' Course, inferior in scope and aim to the regular classical course, did not and could not exist.

Other colleges gradually fell into line, and to-day there are one hundred and ninety-eight colleges for women, and two hundred and seven coeducational colleges and universities in the United States alone offering the degree of B. A. to women, and sending out yearly into the arteries of this nation a warm, rich flood of strong, brave, active, energetic, well-equipped, thoughtful women —women quick to see and eager to help the needs of this needy world—women who can think as well as feel, and who feel none the less because they think—women who are none the less tender and true for the parchment scroll they bear in their hands—women who have given a deeper, richer, nobler and grander meaning to the word "womanly" than any one-sided masculine definition could ever have suggested or inspired—women whom the world has long waited for in pain and anguish till there should be at last added to its forces and allowed to permeate its thought the complement of that masculine influence which has dominated it for fourteen centuries.

Since the idea of order and subordination succumbed to barbarian brawn and brutality in the fifth century, the civilized world has been like a child brought up by his father. It has needed the great mother heart to teach it to be pitiful, to love mercy, to succor the weak and care for the lowly.

Whence came this apotheosis of greed and cruelty? Whence this sneaking admiration we all have for bullies and prize-fighters? Whence the self-congratulation of "dominant" races, as if "dominant" meant "righteous" and carried with it a title to inherit the earth? Whence the scorn of so-called weak or unwarlike races and individuals, and the very comfortable assurance that it is their manifest destiny to be wiped out as vermin before this advancing civilization? As if the possession of the Christian graces of meekness, non-resistance and forgiveness, were incompatible with a civilization professedly based on Christianity, the religion of love! Just listen to this little bit of Barbarian brag:

"As for Far Orientals, they are not of those who will survive. Artistic attractive people that they are, their civilization is like their own tree flowers, beautiful blossoms destined never to bear fruit. If these people continue in their old course, their earthly career is closed. Just as surely as morning passes into afternoon, so surely are these races of the Far East, if unchanged, destined to disappear before the advancing nations of the West. Vanish, they will, off the face of the earth, and leave our planet the eventual possession of the dwellers where the day declines. Unless their newly imported ideas really take root, it is from this whole world that Japanese and Koreans, as well as Chinese, will inevitably be excluded. Their Nirvana is already being realized; already, it has wrapped Far Eastern Asia in its winding sheet."—*Soul of the Far East—P. Lowell.*

Delightful reflection for "the dwellers where day declines." A spectacle to make the gods laugh, truly, to see the scion of an upstart race by one sweep of his generalizing pen consigning to annihilation one-third the inhabitants of the globe—a people whose civilization was hoary headed before the parent elements that begot his race had advanced beyond nebulosity.

How like Longfellow's Iagoo, we Westerners are, to be sure! In the few hundred years, we have had to strut across our allotted territory and bask in the afternoon sun, we imagine we have exhausted the possibilities of humanity. Verily, we are the people, and after us there is none other. Our God is power; strength, our standard of excellence, inherited from barbarian ancestors through a long line of male progenitors, the Law Salic permitting no feminine modifications.

Says one, "The Chinaman is not popular with us, and we do not like the Negro. It is not that the eyes of the one are set bias, and the other is dark-skinned; but the Chinaman, the Negro is weak—*and Anglo Saxons don't like weakness.*"

The world of thought under the predominant man-influence, unmollified and unrestrained by its complementary force, would become like Daniel's fourth beast: "dreadful and terrible, and *strong* exceedingly"; "it had great iron teeth; it devoured and brake in pieces, and stamped the residue with the feet of it"; and the most independent of us find ourselves ready at times to fall down and worship this incarnation of power.

Mrs. Mary A. Livermore, a woman whom I can mention only to admire, came near shaking my faith a few weeks ago in my theory of the thinking woman's mission to put in the tender and sympathetic chord in nature's grand symphony, and counteract, or better, harmonize the diapason of mere strength and might.

She was dwelling on the Anglo-Saxon genius for power and his contempt for weakness, and described a scene in San Francisco which she had witnessed.

The incorrigible animal known as the American small-boy, had pounced upon a simple, unoffending Chinaman, who was taking home his work, and had emptied the beautifully laundried contents of his basket into the ditch. "And," said she, "when that great man stood there and blubbered before that crowd of lawless urchins, to any one of whom he might have taught a lesson with his two fists, *I didn't much care.*"

This is said like a man! It grates harshly. It smacks of the worship of the beast. It is contempt for weakness, and taken out of its setting it seems to contradict my theory. It either shows that one of the highest exponents of the Higher Education can be at times untrue to the instincts I have ascribed to the thinking woman and to the contribution she is to add to the civilized world, or else the influence she wields upon our civilization may be potent without being necessarily and always direct and conscious. The latter is the case. Her voice may strike a false note, but her whole being is musical with the vibrations of human suffering. Her tongue may parrot over the cold conceits that some man has taught her, but her heart is aglow with sympathy and loving kindness, and she cannot be true to her real self without giving out these elements into the forces of the world.

No one is in any danger of imagining Mark Antony "a plain blunt man," nor Cassius a sincere one—whatever the speeches they may make.

As individuals, we are constantly and inevitably, whether we are conscious of it or not, giving out our real selves into our several little worlds, inexorably adding our own true ray to the flood of starlight, quite independently of our professions and our masquerading; and so in the world of thought, the influence of thinking woman far transcends her feeble declamation and may seem at times even opposed to it.

A visitor in Oberlin once said to the lady principal, "Have you no rabble in Oberlin? How is it I see no police here, and yet the streets are as quiet and orderly as if there were an officer of the law standing on every corner."

Mrs. Johnston replied, "Oh, yes; there are vicious persons in Oberlin just as in other towns—*but our girls are our police.*"

With from five to ten hundred pure-minded young women threading the streets of the village every evening unattended, vice must slink away, like frost before the rising sun: and yet I venture to say there was not one in a hundred of those girls who would not have run from a street brawl as she would from a mouse, and who would not have declared she could never stand the sight of blood and pistols.

There is, then, a real and special influence of woman. An influence subtle and often involuntary, an influence so intimately interwoven in, so intricately interpenetrated by the masculine influence of the time that it is often difficult to extricate the delicate meshes and analyze and identify the closely clinging fibers. And yet, without this influence—so long as woman sat with bandaged eyes and manacled hands, fast bound in the clamps of ignorance and inaction, the world of thought moved in its orbit like the revolutions of the moon; with one face (the man's face) always out, so that the spectator could not distinguish whether it was disc or sphere.

Now I claim that it is the prevalence of the Higher Education among women, the making it a common everyday affair for women to reason and think and express their thought, the training and stimulus which enable and encourage women to administer to the world the bread it needs as well as the sugar it cries for; in short it is the transmitting the potential forces of her soul into dynamic factors that has given symmetry and completeness to the world's agencies. So only could it be consummated that Mercy, the lesson she teaches, and Truth, the task man has set himself, should meet together: that righteousness, or *rightness*, man's ideal,—and *peace*, its necessary 'other half,' should kiss each other.

We must thank the general enlightenment and independence of woman (which we may now regard as a *fait accompli*) that both these forces are now at work in the world, and it is fair to demand from them for the twentieth century a higher type of civilization than any attained in the nineteenth. Religion, science, art, economics, have all needed the feminine flavor; and literature, the expression of what is permanent and best in all of these, may be gauged at any time to measure the strength of the feminine ingredient. You will not find theology consigning infants to lakes of unquenchable fire long after women have had a chance to grasp, master, and wield its dogmas. You will not find science annihilating personality from the government of the Universe and making of God an ungovernable, unintelligible, blind, often destructive physical force; you will not find jurisprudence formulating as an axiom the absurdity that man and wife are one, and that one the man—that the married woman may not hold or bequeath her own property save as subject to her husband's direction; you will not find political economists declaring that the only possible adjustment between laborers and capitalists is that of selfishness and rapacity—that each must get all he can and keep all that he gets, while the world cries *laissez faire* and the lawyers explain, "it is the beautiful working of the law of supply and demand"; in fine, you will not find the law of love shut out from the affairs of men after the feminine half of the world's truth is completed.

Nay, put your ear now close to the pulse of the time. What is the key-note of the literature of these days? What is the banner cry of all the activities of the last half decade? What is the dominant seventh which is to add richness and tone to the final cadences of this century and lead by a grand modulation into the triumphant harmonies of the next? Is it not compassion for the poor and unfortunate, and, as Bellamy has expressed it, "indignant outcry against the failure of the social machinery as it is, to ameliorate the miseries of men!" Even Christianity is being brought to the bar of humanity and tried by the standard of its ability to alleviate the world's suffering and lighten and brighten its woe. What else can be the meaning of Matthew Arnold's saddening protest, "We cannot do without Christianity," cried he, "and we cannot endure it as it is."

When went there by an age, when so much time and thought, so much money and labor were given to God's poor and God's invalids, the lowly and unlovely, the sinning as well as the suffering—homes for inebriates and homes for lunatics, shelter for the aged and shelter for babes, hospitals for the sick, props and braces for the falling, reformatory prisons and prison reformatories, all show that a "mothering" influence from some source is leavening the nation.

Now please understand me. I do not ask you to admit that these benefactions and virtues are the exclusive possession of women, or even that women are their chief and only advocates. It may be a man who formulates and makes them vocal. It may be, and often is, a man who weeps over the wrongs and struggles for the amelioration; but that man has imbibed those impulses from a mother rather than from a father and is simply materializing and giving back to the world in tangible form the ideal love and tenderness, devotion and care that have cherished and nourished the helpless period of his own existence.

All I claim is that there is a feminine as well as a masculine side to truth; that these are related not as inferior and superior, not as better and worse, not as weaker and stronger, but as complements—complements in one necessary and symmetric whole. That as the man is more noble in reason, so the woman is more quick in sympathy. That as he is indefatigable in pursuit of abstract truth, so is she in caring for the interests by the way—striving tenderly and lovingly that not one of the least of these "little ones" should perish. That while we not unfrequently see women who reason, we say, with the coolness and precision of a man, and men as considerate of helplessness as a woman, still there is a general consensus of mankind that the one trait is essentially masculine and the other as peculiarly feminine. That both are needed to be worked into the training of children, in order that our boys may supplement their virility by tenderness and sensibility, and our girls may round out their gentleness by strength and self-reliance. That, as both are alike necessary in giving symmetry to the individual, so a nation or a race will degenerate into mere emotionalism on the one hand, or bullyism on the other, if dominated by either exclusively; lastly, and most emphatically, that the feminine factor can have its proper effect only through woman's development and education so that she may fitly and intelligently stamp her force on the forces of her day, and add her modicum to the riches of the world's thought.

"For woman's cause is man's: they rise or sink
Together, dwarfed or godlike, bond or free:
For she that out of Lethe scales with man
The shining steps of nature, shares with man
His nights, his days, moves with him to one goal.
If she be small, slight-natured, miserable,

How shall men grow?
* * * Let her make herself her own
To give or keep, to live and learn and be
All that not harms distinctive womanhood.
For woman is not undeveloped man
But diverse; could we make her as the man
Sweet love were slain; his dearest bond is this,
Not like to like, but like in difference.
Yet in the long years liker must they grow;
The man be more of woman, she of man;
He gain in sweetness and in moral height,
Nor lose the wrestling thews that throw the world;
She mental breadth, nor fail in childward care,
Nor lose the childlike in the larger mind;
Till at the last she set herself to man,
Like perfect music unto noble words."

Now you will argue, perhaps, and rightly, that higher education for women is not a modern idea, and that, if that is the means of setting free and invigorating the long desired feminine force in the world, it has already had a trial and should, in the past, have produced some of these glowing effects. Sappho, the bright, sweet singer of Lesbos, "the violet-crowned, pure, sweetly smiling Sappho" as Alcaeus calls her, chanted her lyrics and poured forth her soul nearly six centuries before Christ, in notes as full and free, as passionate and eloquent as did ever Archilochus or Anacreon.

Aspasia, that earliest queen of the drawing-room, a century later ministered to the intellectual entertainment of Socrates and the leading wits and philosophers of her time. Indeed, to her is attributed, by the best critics, the authorship of one of the most noted speeches ever delivered by Pericles.

Later on, during the Renaissance period, women were professors in mathematics, physics, metaphysics, and the classic languages in Bologna, Pavia, Padua, and Brescia. Olympia Fulvia Morata, of Ferrara, a most interesting character, whose magnificent library was destroyed in 1553 in the invasion of Schweinfurt by Albert of Brandenburg, had acquired a most extensive education. It is said that this wonderful girl gave lectures on classical subjects in her sixteenth year, and had even before that written several very remarkable Greek and Latin poems, and what is also to the point, she married a professor at Heidelberg, and became a *help-meet for him*.

It is true then that the higher education for women—in fact, the highest that the world has ever witnessed—belongs to the past; but we must remember that it was possible, down to the middle of our own century, only to a select few; and that the fashions and traditions of the times were before that all against it. There were not only no stimuli to encourage women to make the most of their powers and to welcome their development as a helpful agency in the progress of civilization, but their little aspirations, when they had any, were chilled and snubbed in embryo, and any attempt at thought was received as a monstrous usurpation of man's prerogative.

Lessing declared that "the woman who thinks is like the man who puts on rouge—ridiculous"; and Voltaire in his coarse, flippant way used to say, "Ideas are like beards—women and boys have none." Dr. Maginn remarked, "We like to hear a few words of sense from a woman sometimes, as we do from a parrot—they are so unexpected!" and even the pious Fenelon taught that virgin delicacy is almost as incompatible with learning as with vice.

That the average woman retired before these shafts of wit and ridicule and even gloried in her ignorance is not surprising. The Abbe Choisi, it is said, praised the Duchesse de Fontanges as being pretty as an angel and silly as a goose, and all the young ladies of the court strove to make up in folly what they lacked in charms. The ideal of the day was that "women must be pretty, dress prettily, flirt prettily, and not be too well informed"; that it was the *summum bonum* of her earthly hopes to have, as Thackeray puts it, "all the fellows battling to dance with her"; that she had no God-given destiny, no soul with unquenchable longings and inexhaustible possibilities—no work of her own to do and give to the world—no absolute and inherent value, no duty to self, transcending all pleasure-giving that may be demanded of a mere toy; but that her value was purely a relative one and to be estimated as are the fine arts—by the pleasure they give. "Woman, wine and song," as "the world's best gifts to man," were linked together in praise with as little thought of the first saying, "What doest thou," as that the wine and the song should declare, "We must be about our Father's business."

Men believed, or pretended to believe, that the great law of self development was obligatory on their half of the human family only;

that while it was the chief end of man to glorify God and put his five talents to the exchangers, gaining thereby other five, it was, or ought to be, the sole end of woman to glorify man and wrap her one decently away in a napkin, retiring into "Hezekiah Smith's lady during her natural life and Hezekiah Smith's relict on her tombstone"; that higher education was incompatible with the shape of the female cerebrum, and that even if it could be acquired it must inevitably unsex woman destroying the lisping, clinging, tenderly helpless, and beautifully dependent creatures whom men would so heroically think for and so gallantly fight for, and giving in their stead a formidable race of blue stockings with corkscrew ringlets and other spinster propensities.

But these are eighteenth century ideas.

We have seen how the pendulum has swung across our present century. The men of our time have asked with Emerson, "that woman only show us how she can best be served"; and woman has replied: the chance of the seedling and of the animalcule is all I ask— the chance for growth and self development, the permission to be true to the aspirations of my soul without incurring the blight of your censure and ridicule.

"Audetque viris concurrere virgo."

In soul-culture woman at last dares to contend with men, and we may cite Grant Allen (who certainly cannot be suspected of advocating the unsexing of woman) as an example of the broadening effect of this content on the ideas at least of the men of the day. He says in his *Plain Words on the Woman Question,* recently published:

"The position of woman was not [in the past] a position which could bear the test of nineteenth-century scrutiny. Their education was inadequate, their social status was humiliating, their political power was nil, their practical and personal grievances were innumerable; above all, their relations to the family—to their husbands, their children, their friends, their property—was simply insupportable."

And again: "As a body we 'Advanced men' are, I think, prepared to reconsider, and to reconsider fundamentally, without prejudice or misconception, the entire question of the relation betwen the sexes. We are ready to make any modifications in those relations which will satisfy the woman's just aspiration for personal independence, for intellectual and moral development, for physical culture, for political activity, and for a voice in the arrangement of her own affairs, both domestic and national."

Now this is magnanimous enough, surely; and quite a step from eighteenth century preaching, is it not? The higher education of Woman has certainly developed the men;—let us see what it has done for the women.

Matthew Arnold during his last visit to America in '82 or '83, lectured before a certain co-educational college in the West. After the lecture he remarked, with some surprise, to a lady professor, that the young women in his audience, he noticed, paid as close attention as the men, *all the way through*." This led, of course, to a spirited discussion of the higher education for women, during which he said to his enthusiastic interlocutor, eyeing her philosophically through his English eyeglass: "But—eh—don't you think it—eh—spoils their *chawnces*, you know!"

Now, as to the result to women, this is the most serious argument ever used against the higher education. If it interferes with marriage, classical training has a grave objection to weigh and answer.

For I agree with Mr. Allen at least on this one point, that there must be marrying and giving in marriage even till the end of time.

I grant you that intellectual development, with the self-reliance and capacity for earning a livelihood which it gives, renders woman less dependent on the marriage relation for physical support (which, by the way, does not always accompany it). Neither is she compelled to look to sexual love as the one sensation capable of giving tone and relish, movement and vim to the life she leads. Her horizon is extended. Her sympathies are broadened and deepened and multiplied. She is in closer touch with nature. Not a bud that opens, not a dew drop, not a ray of light, not a cloud-burst or a thunderbolt, but adds to the expansiveness and zest of her soul. And if the sun of an absorbing passion be gone down, still 'tis night that brings the stars. She has remaining the mellow, less obtrusive, but none the less enchanting and inspiring light of friendship, and into its charmed circle she may gather the best the world has known. She can commune with Socrates about the *daimon* he knew and to which she too can bear witness; she can revel in the majesty of Dante, the sweetness of Virgil, the simplicity of Homer, the strength of Milton. She can listen to the pulsing heart throbs of passionate Sappho's encaged soul, as she beats her bruised wings against her prison bars and struggles to flutter out into Heaven's æther, and the fires of her own soul cry back as she listens. "Yea; Sappho, I know it all; I know it all." Here, at last, can be communion without suspicion; friendship without misunderstanding; love without jealousy.

We must admit then that Byron's picture, whether a thing of beauty or not, has faded from the canvas of to-day.

> "Man's love," he wrote, "is of man's life a thing apart,
> 'Tis woman's whole existence.
> Man may range the court, camp, church, the vessel and
> the mart,
> Sword, gown, gain, glory offer in exchange.
> Pride, fame, ambition, to fill up his heart—
> And few there are whom these cannot estrange.
> Men have all these resources, we *but one*—
> *To love again and be again undone.*"

This may have been true when written. *It is not true to-day.* The old, subjective, stagnant, indolent and wretched life for woman has gone. She has as many resources as men, as many activities beckon her on. As large possibilities swell and inspire her heart.

Now, then, does it destroy or diminish her capacity for loving?

Her standards have undoubtedly gone up. The necessity of speculating in "chawnces" has probably shifted. The question is not now with the woman "How shall I so cramp, stunt, simplify and nullify myself as to make me eligible to the honor of being swallowed up into some little man?" but the problem, I trow, now rests with the man as to how he can so develop his God-given powers as to reach the ideal of a generation of women who demand the noblest, grandest and best achievements of which he is capable; and this surely is the only fair and natural adjustment of the chances. Nature never meant that the ideals and standards of the world should be dwarfing and minimizing ones, and the men should thank us for requiring of them the richest fruits which they can grow. If it makes them work, all the better for them.

As to the adaptability of the educated woman to the marriage relation, I shall simply quote from that excellent symposium of learned women that appeared recently under Mrs. Armstrong's signature in answer to the "Plain Words" of Mr. Allen, already referred to. "Admitting no longer any question as to their intellectual equality with the men whom they meet, with the simplicity of conscious strength, they take their place beside the men who challenge them, and fearlessly face the result of their actions. They deny that their education in any way unfits them for the duty of wifehood and maternity or primarily renders these conditions any less attractive to them than to the domestic type of woman. On the contrary, they hold that their knowledge of physiology makes them better mothers and housekeepers; their knowledge of chemistry makes them better cooks; while from their training in other natural sciences and in mathematics, they obtain an accuracy and fair-mindedness which is of great value to them in dealing with their children or employees."

So much for their willingness. Now the apple may be good for food and pleasant to the eyes, and a fruit to be desired to make one wise. Nay, it may even assure you that it has no aversion whatever to being tasted. Still, if you do not like the flavor all these recommendations are nothing. Is the intellectual woman *desirable* in the matrimonial market?

This I cannot answer. I confess my ignorance. I am no judge of such things. I have been told that strong-minded women could be, when they thought it worth their while, quite endurable, and, judging from the number of female names I find in college catalogues among the alumnae with double patronymics, I surmise that quite a number of men are willing to put up with them.

Now I would that my task ended here. Having shown that a great want of the world in the past has been a feminine force; that that force can have its full effect only through the untrammelled development of woman; that such development, while it gives her to the world and to civilization, does not necessarily remove her from the home and fireside; finally, that while past centuries have witnessed sporadic instances of this higher growth, still it was reserved for the latter half of the nineteenth century to render it common and general enough to be effective; I might close with a glowing prediction of what the twentieth century may expect from this heritage of twin forces—the masculine battered and toil-worn as a grim veteran after centuries of warfare, but still strong, active, and vigorous, ready to help with his hard-won experience the young recruit rejoicing in her newly found freedom, who so confidently places her hand in his with mutual pledges to redeem the ages.

"And so the twain upon the skirts of Time,
Sit side by side, full-summed in all their powers,
Dispensing harvest, sowing the To-be,
Self-reverent each and reverencing each."

Fain would I follow them, but duty is nearer home. The high ground of generalities is alluring but my pen is devoted to a special cause: and with a view to further enlightenment on the achievements of the century for THE HIGHER EDUCATION OF COLORED WOMEN, I wrote a few days ago to the colleges which admit women and asked how many colored women had completed the B. A. course in each during its entire history. These are the figures returned: Fisk leads the way with twelve; Oberlin next with five; Wilberforce, four; Ann Arbor and Wellesley three each, Livingstone two, Atlanta one, Howard, as yet, none.

I then asked the principal of the Washington High School how many out of a large number of female graduates from his school had chosen to go forward and take a collegiate course. He replied that but one had ever done so, and she was then in Cornell.*

Others ask questions too, sometimes, and I was asked a few years ago by a white friend, "How is it that the men of your race seem to outstrip the women in mental attainment?" "Oh," I said, "so far as it is true, the men, I suppose, from the life they lead, gain more by contact; and so far as it is only apparent, I think the women are more quiet. They don't feel called to mount a barrel and harangue by the hour every time they imagine they have produced an idea."

But I am sure there is another reason which I did not at that time see fit to give. The atmosphere, the standards, the requirements of our little world do not afford any special stimulus to female development.

It seems hardly a gracious thing to say, but it strikes me as true, that while our men seem thoroughly abreast of the times on almost every other subject, when they strike the woman question they drop back into sixteenth century logic. They leave nothing to be desired generally in regard to gallantry and chivalry, but they actually do not seem sometimes to have outgrown that old contemporary of chivalry—the idea that women may stand on pedestals or live in doll

---

*Graduated from Scientific Course, June, 1890, the first colored woman to graduate from Cornell.

houses, (if they happen to have them) but they must not furrow their brows with thought or attempt to help men tug at the great questions of the world. I fear the majority of colored men do not yet think it worth while that women aspire to higher education. Not many will subscribe to the "advanced" ideas of Grant Allen already quoted. The three R's, a little music and a good deal of dancing, a first rate dressmaker and a bottle of magnolia balm, are quite enough generally to render charming any woman possessed of tact and the capacity for worshipping masculinity.

My readers will pardon my illustrating my point and also giving a reason for the fear that is in me, by a little bit of personal experience. When a child I was put into a school near home that professed to be normal and collegiate, i.e. to prepare teachers for colored youth, furnish candidates for the ministry, and offer collegiate training for those who should be ready for it. Well, I found after a while that I had a good deal of time on my hands. I had devoured what was put before me, and, like Oliver Twist, was looking around to ask for more. I constantly felt (as I suppose many an ambitious girl has felt) a thumping from within unanswered by any beckoning from without. Class after class was organized for these ministerial candidates (many of them men who had been preaching before I was born). Into every one of these classes I was expected to go, with the sole intent, I thought at the time, of enabling the dear old principal, as he looked from the vacant countenances of his sleepy old class over to where I sat, to get off his solitary pun—his never-failing pleasantry, especially in hot weather—which was, as he called out "Any one!" to the effect that "*any* one" then meant "*Annie* one."

Finally a Greek class was to be formed. My inspiring preceptor informed me that Greek had never been taught in the school, but that he was going to form a class *for the candidates for the ministry*, and if I liked I might join it. I replied—humbly I hope, as became a female of the human species—that I would like very much to study Greek, and that I was thankful for the opportunity, and so it went on. A boy, however meager his equipment and shallow his pretensions, had only to declare a floating intention to study theology and he could get all the support, encouragement and stimulus he needed, be absolved from work and invested beforehand with the dignity of his far away office. While a self-supporting girl had to struggle on by teaching in the summer and working after school hours to keep up with her board bills, and actually to fight her way against positive discouragements to the higher education; till one such girl one day flared out and told the principal "the only mission opening before a girl in his school was to marry one of those candidates." He said he didn't know but it was. And when at last that same girl announced her desire and intention to go to college it was received with about the same incredulity and dismay as if a brass button on one of those candidate's coats had propounded a new method for squaring the circle or trisecting the arc.

Now this is not fancy. It is a simple unvarnished photograph, and what I believe was not in those days exceptional in colored schools, and I ask the men and women who are teachers and co-workers for the highest interests of the race, that they give the girls a chance! We might as well expect to grow trees from leaves as hope to build up a civilization or a manhood without taking into consideration our women and the home life made by them, which must be the root and ground of the whole matter. Let us insist then on special encouragement for the education of our women and special care in their training. Let our girls feel that we expected something more of them than that they merely look pretty and appear well in society. Teach them that there is a race with special needs which they and only they can help; that the world needs and is already asking for their trained, efficient forces. Finally, if there is an ambitious girl with pluck and brain to take the higher education, encourage her to make the most of it. Let there be the same flourish of trumpets and clapping of hands as when a boy announces his determination to enter the lists; and then, as you know that she is physically the weaker of the two, don't stand from under and leave her to buffet the waves alone. Let her know that your heart is following her, that you hand, though she sees it not, is ready to support her. To be plain, I mean let money be raised and scholarships be founded in our colleges and universities for self-supporting, worthy young women, to offset and balance the aid that can always be found for boys who will take theology.

The earnest well trained Christian young woman, as a teacher, as a home-maker, as wife, mother, or silent influence even, is as potent a missionary agency among our people as is the theologian; and I claim that at the present stage of our development in the South she is even more important and necessary.

Let us then, here and now, recognize this force and resolve to make the most of it—not the boys less, but the girls more.

Amanda Berry Smith

1837–1915

Forty-four years after evangelist Jarena Lee published her journal, another unordained female minister, Amanda Berry Smith, ascended to national and international fame. An account of her life's work, which touched various ethnic groups and religious creeds, was given in her book, *An Autobiography; the Story of the Lord's Dealings with Mrs. Amanda Smith, the Colored Evangelist.* . . . (1893).

Amanda Berry was born a slave in Long Green, Maryland, on 23 January 1837. She was fortunate to have had two parents who were literate and who had decent masters. Her father, Samuel Berry, lived on a plantation adjoining that of his wife, Mariam. To earn money, he was permitted to work for himself at nights and on holidays. By doing this, he was able to buy freedom for himself, his wife, and their five children. (The family subsequently grew to thirteen.)

The Berrys moved to Pennsylvania where Amanda grew up, witnessing as a child her father's harboring and helping runaway slaves. Amanda's schooling was almost nil, although her parents taught her what they knew. On Sundays her father read the Bible to them, and Amanda, anxious to learn, would cut out letters from newspapers so her mother could make words for her to read.

She started attending a private school at the age of eight in a house across the street from where her mother lived. The school was open only in the summer, and she attended for six weeks. She did not go again until she was thirteen, when she and her brother had to walk over five miles to and from another school. There the white children had their full lessons first, and what little time remained was devoted to the few blacks. During her lifetime, then, Amanda had only three months of formal schooling.

Her first marriage was to C. Devine in September of 1854 when she was seventeen. Devine "talked" religion, but had a weakness for drink. Two children were born, but only one, Mazie, survived. When the Civil War began, her husband joined the army and never returned. She met her second husband, James Smith, when she moved to Philadelphia to do domestic work. Smith was a local preacher and an ordained deacon in the African Methodist Episcopal Church. But her dream of having a good Christian marriage was frustrated again, for she had been deceived by the character of her second husband, too. Living in New York with him, she had to take in laundry to make ends meet for the family. James Smith died in 1869.

It was in Columbia, Pennsylvania, on 17 March 1856 that Amanda was converted after praying alone in the cellar of the house where she worked. She received the blessing of sanctification in 1868 when, as the sole black in a white church, she heard a Presbyterian minister, Reverend John Inskip, preach. There, also, she lost her fear of white people, which was actually awe of them. Years later, it was John Inskip who encouraged her to write of her experiences.

Amanda was spiritually directed to preach for the first time at Salem, New Jersey, in November 1869. She had inherited her mother's rich singing voice, which helped her deliver her initial sermons. She sang at camp meetings and churches and was called the "Singing Pilgrim." She joined the Fisk University Jubilee Singers at Music Hall in Boston when the singers were on tour to raise money for the school. The performance was repeated in Nashville while she attended the fourteenth and first delegated General Conference of the A. M. E. Church in May 1872. Although Amanda Berry Smith was much in demand as an evangelist, she went nowhere without first praying for guidance to her Lord. As a minister, the strong-faced, handsome woman was easily recognized by her plain Quaker garb, a bonnet with strings, and a cross around her neck.

As a black female minister setting out to spread the Gospel, she defied taboos and prejudices against women preaching and participating publicly in religious services. When she was abroad, especially in India, a discussion would always arise concerning a woman's right to preach. The question was soon settled, however, when challengers heard her stirring sermons.

When her health declined from overwork, one of her white friends invited her to England for a rest. In the beginning, she hesitated, thinking of the humbleness of her background and how she would fare because of it. A second invitation came from Mrs. Eli Johnson, a Brooklyn Quaker, who persuaded her to attend the Keswick Conference in England for the promotion of a higher life, with expenses to be paid by Mrs. Johnson. Following her customary prayers for counsel, she sailed for Great Britain in 1878 and spent a year preaching throughout England, Scotland, and Ireland.

In the summer of 1879, she was invited by Reverend W. P. Osborne to travel to India, and on 12 November, she arrived in Bombay, where she stayed until 1 January 1880. Bishop J. M. Thoburn of Calcutta, who had been impressed by hearing her speak at a camp meeting outside Cincinnati, asked her to join him. Her stay was a novelty for "it was something entirely new in India for a woman to mount the pulpit . . . added the fact that she was a colored woman, once a slave, come from America."[1]

A woman of "vision" and great "spiritual power," she attracted throngs of churchgoers and nonchurchgoers wherever she went. In describing her trip, Bishop Thoburn wrote in the introduction to her book: "*During the seventeen years that I have lived in Calcutta, I have known many famous strangers to visit the city, some of whom attracted large audiences, but I have never known anyone who could draw and hold so large an audience as Mrs. Smith*" (Thoburn's italics).[2] She continued her travels to Africa, following a second trip to England in 1881. She remained in Africa for eight years as a missionary on the west coast. On her departure, her coworker, Bishop William Taylor, "often remarked that Amanda Smith had done more for the cause of missions and temperance in Africa than the combined efforts of all the missionaries before her."[3]

While attending a WCTU convention in London in 1894, the thought occurred to the evangelist to do something for her people. Having lost five of her children and with only her daughter, Mazie, living, she decided to start a home for colored children.

Having been urged by friends all over the world to write about her life, she prayed as usual for spiritual guidance. Now in declining health, she had the time, but doubted her ability to do so because of her "deficiency in education." When opening her Bible while seeking the Lord's advice, her eyes fell on the passage "Now, therefore, perform the doing of it." That settled the matter.

The autobiography is simply written with touches of humor, and is enlivened by a three-way dialogue between Satan, the Lord and Amanda. Her foreign travel segments are incorporated with entries from the diary she kept on her trips. The book is a personal literary account of a black woman who had the courage and will to follow her calling despite the prevailing sexist and religious odds. Profits from the book went to purchase a twelve-room brick house for her orphanage outside of Chicago. For herself, friends provided a comfortable cottage in Seabright, Florida, so that she might rest with her ever-present thoughts of the Lord.

NOTES

1. Brown, *Homespun Heroines*, p. 130.
2. Smith, *An Autobiography*, p. vi.
3. Brown, *Homespun Heroines*, pp. 131–32.

SELECTED SOURCES

Primary

Smith, Amanda Berry. *An Autobiography; the Story of the Lord's Dealings with Mrs. Amanda Smith, the Colored Evangelist; Containing an Account of Her Life Work of Faith, and Her Travels in America, England, Ireland, Scotland, India and Africa, as an Independent Missionary.* Chicago: Meyer & Brother, 1893.

Secondary

Brown, Hallie Quinn. *Homespun Heroines and Other Women of Distinction.* Xenia, Ohio: Aldine, 1926.
Dennett, Sylvia G. L. *Profiles of Negro Womanhood.* Vol. 1, *1619–1900.* Yonkers, N.Y.: Educational Heritage, 1964.
Loewenberg, Bert James, and Bogin, Ruth. *Black Women in Nineteenth Century American Life: Their Words, Their Thoughts, Their Feelings.* University Park: Pennsylvania State University Press, 1976.

The General Conference at Nashville . . .

In May, '70 or '71, ['72] the General Conference of the A. M. E. Church was held at Nashville, Tenn. It was the first time they ever held a General Conference south of Mason and Dixon's line. I had been laboring in Salem, where the Lord first sent me, and blessed me in winning souls; the people were not rich; they gave me a home, and something to eat; but very little money. So, before I could get back to New York, my home, I took a service place, at Mrs. Mater's, in Philadelphia, corner of Coach and Brown streets, while her servant, Mary, went to Wilmington to see her child; she was to be gone a month, but she stayed five weeks; and now the Annual Conference was in session, at the A. M. E. Union Church, near by where I was, so I had a chance to attend.

The election of delegates to the General Conference the next year was a very prominent feature of the Conference; of course every minister wanted, or hoped to be elected as a delegate. As I listened, my heart throbbed. This was the first time in all these years that this religious body of black men, with a black church from beginning to end, was to be assembled south of Mason and Dixon's line.

But the great battle had been fought, and the victory won: slavery had been abolished; we were really free. There were enthusiastic speeches made on these points. Oh, how I wished I could go; and a deep desire took possession of me; but then, who was I? I had no money, no prominence at that time, except being a plain Christian woman, heard of and known by a few of the brethren, as a woman preacher, which was to be dreaded by the majority, especially the upper ten. Fortunately I had a good friend in Bishop Campbell, knowing him so well years before he was elected to this office. Also Bishop Wayman, Bishop Brown, and Bishop Quinn, were friends of mine. I believe I always had their sympathy and friendship. But there was no opportunity for me to speak to them personally. So I ventured to ask one of the brethren, who had been elected delegate, to tell me how much it would cost to go to Nashville; I would like to go if it did not cost too much.

He looked at me in surprise, mingled with half disgust; the very idea of one looking like me to want to go to General Conference; they cut their eye at my big poke Quaker bonnet, with not a flower, not a feather. He said, "I tell you, Sister, it will cost money to go down there; and if you ain't got plenty of it, it's no use to go"; and turned away and smiled; another said:

"What does she want to go for?"

"Woman preacher; they want to be ordained," was the reply.

"I mean to fight that thing," said the other. "Yes, indeed, so will I," said another.

Then a slight look to see if I took it in. I did; but in spite of it all I believed God would have me go. He knew that the thought of ordination had never once entered my mind, for I had received my ordination from Him, Who said, "Ye have not chosen Me, but I have chosen you, and ordained you, that you might go and bring forth fruit, and that your fruit might remain."

I spoke to some of the good sisters who were expecting to go; they said they did not know what it would cost. So I went home, and prayed, and asked the Lord to help me; and the conviction that I was to go deepened, and yet it seemed so impossible. Just before the Conference closed I ventured to ask another good brother, who had been elected delegate, and whom I knew very well, and he was so nice, I thought he would tell me. "Brother S.," I said, "how much do you think it will cost?" This was the uppermost thought then— the cost to go to Nashville. "Oh, my sister," he replied, "I don't know; it will take all of a hundred dollars"; and with a significant toss of the head shot through the door, and I saw him no more till I met him next year at Nashville; and that was a surprise, but he managed to speak to me, as we both stopped at the Sumner House, and sat at the same table.

I was quite a curiosity to most of the visitors, especially the Southern brethren, in my very plain Quaker dress; I was eyed with critical suspicion as being there to agitate the question of the ordination of women. All about, in the little groups that would be gathered talking, could be heard, "Who is she?"

"Preacher woman."

"What does she want here?"

"I mean to fight that thing."

"I wonder what day it will come up?"

Of course, I was a rank stranger to most of them; the bishops, and all those whom I did know, had all got there before me, and were settled, and I was not going to trouble them for anything. Then those of the ladies whom I knew, wives of ministers or bishops, were dressed to the height of their ability; I could not rank with them; so I was all alone; "And His brethren did not believe in Him." "The servant is not above his Lord."

No one but God knows what I passed through the first three days. God, in answer to prayer, had marvelously opened my way to go; through the kindness of my dear friend, Mrs. Kibbey, of Albany, N. Y., who is now in Heaven, I had my outfit; a pretty tan dress, with a drab shawl and bonnet to match. I thought I was fine; but bless you, I found I did not shine in that land, worth a nickel; for my people, as a rule, like fine show.

Before I left New York for Nashville, I had heard that the bishops were to have a certain number of tickets at reduced rates; so I wrote

Bishop Campbell and asked him if he would get me a ticket. About two weeks after, he was passing through New York, and called to see me, and explained the matter. How very kind he was. God bless his memory. I gave him the money—thirty some dollars—and in a day or two he sent me the ticket. Now I thought I was all right, and so thanked the Lord. He had answered prayer up to this time in all that I had asked.

I was expecting when I got to Philadelphia to find several ladies who had told me they were expecting to go without fail; but when I got there, there was but one lady—Sister Burley—and her husband; there were about twenty or thirty preachers, and just two ladies.

Poor Sister Burley was glad I was going, as she was alone; and I was glad she was going, as I was alone. She and I kept together as much as her husband would allow her; Brother Burley was a remarkably selfish man, and stout accordingly; if he dropped his handkerchief his wife must be by him to catch it before it touched the ground, or pick it up immediately, or get him a clean one.

Of course, I was only a visitor. We arrived three days before the opening of the Conference. This was to give all the delegates time to get in. I thought I would have no difficulty in getting a place to stop, and, perhaps, it would not have been so bad if I had been more stylish looking.

We arrived, I think, about two P.M. Friday; we were driven to a large church where tickets were given with the name and address where each one was to stop. Now, there were five or six ladies, but none whom I knew; they seemed to eye me sharply, but took no further notice; by and by, plans were settled, and two or three of these ladies, and six or eight ministers got in a 'bus and were taken to their places. I inquired of those who had charge, but they said they only had the names of those who were delegates. Poor me; I almost cried, and was tempted to wish I had not come. . . .

If ever the Lord did help me, He helped me that day. And the Spirit of the Lord seemed to fall on all the people. The preachers got happy. They wept and shouted "Amen." "Praise the Lord!" At the close a number of them came to me and shook hands, and said, "God bless you, sister. Where did you come from? I would like to have you come on my charge." Another would say, "Look here, sister, when are you going home? God bless you. I would like to have you come to my place." And so it went. So that after that many of my brethren believed in me, especially as the question of ordination of women never was mooted in the Conference.

But how they have advanced since then. Most of them believe in the ordination of women, and I believe some have been ordained. But I am satisfied with the ordination that the Lord has given me. Praise His name!

I had no trouble after I had Prof. White's and Prof. Spence's kind recognition, and I had the pleasure of spending a week or more at the University with those good people. And as I would talk at several of the meetings, the Lord blessed the dear teachers and students. I also spent a week at Dr. Braden's. They were very kind, and the Lord gave us blessing in some meetings. They have done, and are doing, a grand work among my people. May God bless them all.

I give this little story in detail, to show that even with my own people, in this country, I have not always met with the pleasantest things. But still I have not backslidden, nor felt led to leave the church. His grace has ever been sufficient. And all we need to-day is to trust Him.

"Simply trusting every day,
Trusting through the stormy way,
Even when my faith is small,
Trusting Jesus, that is all."

Eloise Bibb Thompson

1878–1928

On 29 June 1878 in the picturesque city of New Orleans, Eloise Alberta Veronica Bibb was born three years after the birth in the same city of a friend and future writer, Alice Ruth Moore Dunbar-Nelson. Like Alice, Eloise became a poet, short-story writer, journalist, and playwright. She was the product of middle-class parents, Charles H. and Catherine Adele Bibb; her father was a U.S. Customs inspector.

Eloise Bibb went to Oberlin College's Preparatory Academy from 1899 to 1901 and taught for two years in New Orleans. Further education was pursued at Howard University, where she graduated from its Teachers' College. She held a position as head resident of the Social Settlement House at Howard University from 1908 until 1911.

On 4 August 1911, she married Noah Davis Thompson in Chicago, Illinois. A thirty-three-year-old widower, Thompson had been employed in the money department of the United States Express Company in Chicago and was affiliated with Tuskegee Institute from 1909 to 1911. A native Baltimorean, Thompson's first wife was Lillian B. Murphy, daughter of John H. Murphy, owner of the Baltimore *Afro-American* newspaper. The first Mrs. Thompson died in 1905, leaving one son, Noah Murphy.

Eloise and Noah were considered to be a well-matched couple, for they shared mutual interests. When they moved to Los Angeles, the two became very prominent in social, religious, and literary circles. Although Noah was engaged in the real estate business, he was also on the editorial staff of the *Evening Express* and *Morning Tribune*, where he wrote feature stories on race. At the same time, he was associate editor of the *Liberator* from 1912 to 1913. Eloise, too, as a rising journalist, was making her mark by writing for the *Los Angeles Tribune* and the *Morning Sun* on "Negro leaders and happenings in the colored world." Additionally, she contributed to the widely circulated magazines *Out West* and the *Tidings*.

Eloise, like her husband, was a devout Catholic. She gave a speech about her race to the Catholic Women's Clubs of Los Angeles, which newspapers praised "in the highest terms." One of her "notable contributions" to the *Tidings*, an organ of the Diocese of Monterey and Los Angeles, was her article, "The Church and the Negro."[1]

Eloise Bibb Thompson made her writing debut at a young age. She was seventeen when her book *Poems* (1895) was published by the Monthly Review Press, which also published Alice Dunbar-Nelson's first book. One of the poems in the book was a tribute to her friend: "To the Sweet Bard of the Woman's Club, Miss Alice Ruth Moore." The book is dedicated to Mrs. S. F. Williams, president of the Phillis Wheatley Club of New Orleans. In her dedication, Eloise affectionately wrote: "Through all the censure, I shall be content if I have but pleased you." Sylvanie F. Williams was a moving force behind the aspiring women writers of the Phillis Wheatley Club, and she wrote the perceptive preface to Alice Ruth Moore Dunbar-Nelson's maiden writing venture, *Violets and Other Tales* (1895). Eloise's poetry has not received high grades. One male critic viewed it as simply "neat and prim" ignoring her youth at the time of writing. Joan Sherman categorized it as "romantic narratives of star-crossed lovers and agonized heroes."[2]

Eloise had two short stories, "Mademoiselle 'Tasie—A Story" and "Masks," published in *Opportunity* magazine. The stories are of New Orleans Creoles, sharing the same colorful background, language, and romance found in Alice Dunbar-Nelson's short fiction. Eloise Bibb Thompson also tried her hand as a dramatist and had three of her plays produced. *Caught* was performed in 1920 at the Gamut Club by the Playcrafters. Two years later, *Africans* was given at the Grand Theatre in Los Angeles, a play that J. Rosamond Johnson called "an excellent piece of work." On 15 October 1924, her play about Creole life, *Cooped Up*, was produced at the LaFayette Theatre in New York City. It was lauded as an "amazingly realistic play" that told a "remarkable story."[3]

The Thompsons moved to New York City in January 1927, where Noah became the business manager for *Opportunity* magazine. The Los Angeles black community lamented the departure of the couple with a front-page article in the *California Eagle* saying, "Mr. Thompson and his talented wife were most highly appreciated at their home in this city and will be sorely missed."[4]

The following year, however, the life of Eloise Bibb Thompson, "with all the rich promise of a career in letters only half fulfilled,"[5] abruptly ended when she died on 8 January 1928.[6]

NOTES

1. Beasley, *Negro Trail Blazers*, p. 254.
2. Sherman, *Invisible Poets*, p. 205. Sherman gives an analysis of Eloise Bibb Thompson's poetry.
3. For an account of her playwriting activities, see *Opportunity* 3 (February 1925): 63–64.
4. *California Eagle*, 4 February 1927.
5. "Eloise Bibb Thompson," *Opportunity* 2 (February 1928):37.
6. Contrary to Sherman's date of 1927, the year 1928 is verified in *Negro Catholic Writers*, a biographical sketch of Noah D. Thompson in *Who's Who in Colored America* (1929), her obituary in *Opportunity* (1928), and a death notice in the *Oakland Western Outlook*, 21 January 1928.

SELECTED SOURCES

Primary

Bibb, Eloise. *Poems*. Boston: Monthly Review Press, 1895.
Thompson, Eloise Bibb. "Mademoiselle 'Tasie—A Story." *Opportunity* 3 (September 1925):272–76.
———. "Masks." *Opportunity* 5 (October 1927):300–302.

Secondary

Abajian, James de T. *Blacks in Selected Newspapers, Censuses and Subjects*. Boston: G. K. Hall & Co., 1977.
Beasley, Delilah L. *The Negro Trail Blazers of California, 1919*. Reprint. New York: Negro Universities Press, 1969.
Loggins, Vernon. *The Negro Author: His Development in America*. New York: Columbia University Press, 1931.
Scally, Anthony Sister. *Negro Catholic Writers, 1900–1943: A Bio-Bibliography*. Grosse Point, Mich.: Walter Romig, 1945.
Sherman, Joan R. *Invisible Poets: Afro-Americans of the Nineteenth Century*. Urbana: University of Illinois Press, 1974.

Gerarda

The day is o'er and twilight's shade,
Is darkening forest, glen and glade;
It steals within the old church door,
And casts its shadows on the floor;
It throws its gloom upon the bride,
And on her partner by her side:
But ah! it has no power to screen
The loveliest form that e'er was seen.

Sweet tones as from the angels' lyre,
Came pealing from the ancient choir;
They rouse the brain with magic power,
And fill with light that twilight hour.
Some artist's soul one easily sees,
Inspires the hands that touch the keys;
A genius sits and wakes the soul,
With sounds that o'er the passions roll.

"Till death we part," repeats the bride.
She shuddered visibly and sighed;
And as she leaves the altar rail,
She's startled, and her features pale,
For in the ancient choir above,
The man who sits and plays of love,
Has held her heart for many a year.
Alas! her life is sad and drear.

He never dreamed he roused a thrill,
Within that heart that seemed so still;
He never knew the hours of pain,
That racked that tired and troubled brain.
He could not see that bleeding heart,
From which his face would not depart;
He never could have known her grief,
From which, alas! there's no relief.

At last she thought the fire had cooled,
And love's strong guardian she had ruled;

'Twas then she vowed to be the bride
Of him who stands at her side.
Ill-fated hour! she sees too late,
This man she cannot help but hate;
He, whom she promised to obey,
Until from earth she's called away.

This life is sometimes dark and drear,
No lights within the gloom appear.
Gerarda smiled and danced that night,
As though her life had been all bright;
And no one knew a battle waged,
Within that heart so closely caged.
The few who've never felt love's dart,
Know not the depth of woman's heart.

II.

Gerarda sat one summer day,
With easel, brush, and forms of clay,
Within her much-loved studio,
Where all that makes the senses glow
Were placed with great artistic skill;
Content, perhaps, she seems, and still,
She'd give this luxury and more,
To ease that heart so bruised and sore.

Her paintings hang upon the wall,
The power of genius stamps them all;
On this material soil she breathes,
But in her spiritual word she leaves
Her mind, her thoughts, her soul, her brain,
And wakes from fancy's spell with pain.
And thus her pictures plainly show,
Not nature's self but ideal glow.

And now to-day o'er canvas bent,
She strives to place these visions sent
From that bright world she loves so well,
But fancy fails to cast her spell,
And sick at heart, Gerarda sighs,

And wonders why her muse denies
The inspiration given before,
When oft in heaven her soul would soar.

But now her ear has caught a sound,
That causes heart and brain to bound,
With rapture wild, intense, sincere,
For, list! those strains are coming near;
She grasps the brush, her muse awoke,
Within those notes her genius spoke;
An Angelo might e'en be proud,
Of forms that o'er her vision crowd.

What power is this that swells that touch,
And sends it throbbing with a rush,
That renders all its hearers dumb!
If he be man, whence did he come?
Lo! 'tis the same who played with power
The wedding march that twilight hour;
The strains seem caught from souls above,
It is the very food of love.

And yet, he's neither old nor bent,
A comeliness to youth is lent;
A radiant eye, a natural grace,
An eager, noble, passionate face,—
All these are his, with genius spark,
That guides him safely through the dark,
To hearts that throb and souls that feel,
At every grand and solemn peal.

Triumphant Wagner's soul he reads,
And then with Mozart gently pleads,
And begs the weary cease to mope,
But rise and live in dreams of hope.
The sounds have ceased,—how drear life seems!
He wakes from out his land of dreams,
And finds Gerarda rapt, amazed,
In speechless ecstasy she gazed.

"Neville! thou king of heroes great,
A tale of love thou dost relate,

In tones that rend my heart in twain,
With intense agony and pain,
Forgive whate'er I say to-day,
Thy touch has ta'en my sense away;
O man that dreams, thou can'st not see,
That I, alas! doth worship thee!

"Behold! thou Orpheus, I kneel
And beg thee, if thou e'er canst feel,
Or sympathize with my unrest,
To thrust this dagger in my breast.
Shrink not! I can no longer live
Content in agony to writhe;
And death win thy hand given to me,
Will be one blissful ecstasy."

He starts, and lifts her from her knees,
Her features pale, and soon he sees
That tired heart so sick and sore
Can bear its grief and woe no more.
She swoons—her pulse has ceased to beat,
A holy calm, divine and sweet,
Has settled on the saintly face,
Lit up with beauty, youth and grace.

Neville amazed, in rapture stands,
Admiring hair, and face, and hands.
Forgetful then of hour and place,
He stoops to kiss the beauteous face,
And at the touch the fire of love,
So pure as to come from above,
Consumes his heart and racks his brain,
With longing fear and infinite pain.

The kiss, as with a magic spell,
Has roused Gerarda,—it seems to tell,
'Tis time to bid her conscience wake,
And off her soul this burden shake.
"Neville, forgive,'" with downcast eyes,
Gerarda sorrowfully cries:
"I've told thee of my love and woe,—
The things I meant thou should'st not know."

239

"Gerarda thou hast woke the heart,
That ne'er before felt passion's smart:
Oh! is it true thou'rt lost to me,
My love, my heart knows none but thee!"
"Enough! Neville, we must forget,
That in this hour our souls have met.
Farewell! we ne'er must meet in life,
For I'm, alas! a wedded wife."

III.

Why ring those bells? what was that cry?
The night winds bear it as they sigh;
What is this crushing, maddening scene?
What do those flames of fire mean?
They surge above Gerarda's home,
Through attic, cellar, halls, they roam,
Like some terrific ghost of night,
Who longs from earth to take his flight.

Gerarda stands amid the fire,
That leaps above with mad desire,
And rings her hands in silent grief,
She fears for her there's no relief.
But now she hears a joyous shout,
A breathless silence from without,
That tells her God has heard her prayer,
And sent a noble hero there.

And here he comes, this gallant knight,
Her heart rejoices at the sight,
For 'tis Neville, with aspect grave.
Who risked his life, his love to save.
And all have perished now but she,
Her husband and her family.
Mid tears and sobs she breathes a prayer,
For loved ones who are buried there.

Neville has brushed her tears away,
Together silently they pray

And bless the Lord with thankful prayer
For all his watchfulness and care.
"Gerarda, love," he whispers now,
Implanting kisses on her brow,
"This earth will be a heaven to me,
For all my life, I'll share with thee."

Tribute

(To the sweet bard of The Woman's Club, Miss Alice Ruth Moore.)

I peer adown a shining group,
　　Where sages grace the throng,
And see the bard of Wheatley Club
　　Proclaimed the Queen of Song.

I see her reach the portico,
　　Where muses smiling now.
Adorn with the green laurel wreath,
　　Her broad and thoughtful brow.

Fair Alice! shed thy radiance more,
　　And charm us with thy verse;
So dulcet, so harmonious,
　　So graceful, sweet, and terse.

Marie Louise Burgess
M. L. Burgess

?–?

Marie Louise Burgess joins the shadowy band of nineteenth-century black women writers of whom we know only their names. She may have been a Bostonian, for her thirty-three-page novel, *Ave Maria* (1895), was published by Boston's Press of the Monthly Review. Her book photograph portrays a nice-looking young woman with a melancholy face and pensive eyes. She is unmarried, for there is the distinguishing "Miss" before her name.

Ave Maria is a typical nineteenth-century romantic novel. In it, Miss Burgess weaves a tragic love story with white characters. Judging from her depiction of Roman Catholicism, that may have been her religion. Protagonist Marguerite Earle has "blue eyes" and "brown ringlets." She and Ronald Ives have been in love since childhood, but Marguerite is Catholic and Ronald is Presbyterian. Both are sole caretakers of families, Ronald of his mother, and Marguerite of young "children" (a number is not given). Marguerite will not give up Catholicism to marry Ronald, and he will not leave his church to become a Catholic, for it would "hasten" his mother's "end."

Ronald sets forth the novel's message when he mourns: "Remember the depth of the chasm between Catholicism and the other religions. Were it any other church we would have no need of all this unhappiness. It is one God we serve; I wish it were through only one church."[1]

There is nothing of black people or their concerns in the book. It is a story for white readers to identify with and black ones to fantasize over. Even when Marguerite becomes a nurse, a saintly Florence Nightingale who goes into the slums to treat the sick, it is not to minister to blacks but to care for Italians and Russians.

After years of nursing, Marguerite returns home to rest. She is called upon to care for a child, Theresa, who turns out to be the daughter of Ronald. Marguerite baptizes the little girl before she dies. Then all ends well as Ronald's wife persuades him to be baptized, and Marguerite witnesses this on Palm Sunday "happier than she had been for years" (suggestive of Amelia Johnson's conversions).

Although plotless and sentimental, the little-known work helps fill in the gaps of lost nineteenth-century black women writers.

NOTE

1. Burgess, *Ave Maria*, p. 14.

SOURCE

Primary

Burgess, Marie Louise. *Ave Maria*. Boston: Press of the Monthly Review, 1895.

Marguerite Earle

Rugged strength and radiant beauty—
　　These were one in nature's plan:
Humble toil and heavenward duty—
　　These will make the perfect man."
MRS. HALL.

The bells of St. Cecelia's Church rang at the close of vespers one joyous Lenten evening; the priest had pronounced his blessing and all had departed in peace. The old organist was playing the sweet strains of Ave Maria, Dolorosa, as he sat at the organ which was built in the right side of the chancel.

The strains soft and sweet fell on the still air, filling the church with an air of Heaven. One could not listen to Ave Maria without a feeling akin to sadness, stealing over him.

Just outside the chancel railing, knelt a beautiful girl with the bloom of youth stamped on her rosy cheeks. A girl over whom, perhaps, twenty-one years had rolled, with large, dreamy, blue eyes, which had a glad light of their own in them. On this particular evening the bright eyes were filled with tears; her heart was full of sorrow. Hers was not an unhappy face; a shadow apparently had fallen over her young life. As we find her, her attitude bespeaks a keen sorrow,— she kneels with head bowed and hands uplifted.

"O Father," she prayed as she knelt, "help me to bear my burden, help me to do the right. What would it profit me to gain the desire of my heart? yet, how can I yield! No, come what may I must bear my burden. Holy Mother, help me to do the right"; thus she prayed.

Again the sweet strains of Ave Maria swelled on the still air, fainter and fainter became each note till at last they died away. Silently the organist withdrew, and Marguerite Earle was left alone. We picture her just as the twilight deepens. The sun had long since sunk to rest, and only a faint light was visible. The windows of the Cathedral which were beautiful by daylight were more so in the twilight. One indeed must have a hard heart who could pass these pictures without a feeling of adoration for the Saviour stealing over him. The beautiful head was still bowed and the brown ringlets fell unconsciously around her face. Thus she knelt struggling against fate.

Every brick in this church was sacred to Marguerite. It was within these sacred walls that she was brought when only a few days old to receive her name, and when twelve years of age to receive the Rite of Confirmation and make her First Communion. Year after year she had knelt before the altar, and as she grew in years, and strength of mind and body, her love for this church grew stronger. She had watched her brothers grow up in this church, and they knew no other. Now with a weight of sorrow she knelt once more before the altar. How long she knelt there she knew not. She remembered nothing until a hand was laid gently on her bowed head, and when she looked up she saw Sister Dorothea looking earnestly at her.

"My child," she asked with gentleness, "what has caused thy sorrow? Leave all your grief here and go forth as one anew, your Heavenly Father does not intend such anguish."

Slowly Marguerite lifted her tear-stained face, and looking at the sister, said, "I cannot, my heart will break."

She told the sweet sister the cause of her grief; the sister smiled as she said; "Such grief seldom kills, do your duty and God will bless you."

The girl arose and with the hand of the sister gently clasped in hers, went towards the door. Smiling through her tears, she said to her: "Good-night, dear sister; thank you for your kindness."

Her heart seemed lighter as homeward she turned. No mother came forth to share her sorrow, no one in whom she might confide. The children were asleep. She stole quietly into the room where little Jamie lay, sleeping that peaceful sleep of a child who knows no sorrow. Jamie was only about two years old when their mother died, and Marguerite had cared for him as only a loving sister can care for a baby brother. She smoothed back the curls from the tiny brow, and the tears began to fall gently on the bed. Little Jamie stirred in his sleep, and Marguerite tripped gently out of the room. The happiest days of her life had been spent here as well as some of the saddest.

"I am very sad to-night," she said, as she sat in the little parlor thinking of her home and her pleasant surroundings. "I must be brave and make my decision. How can I look in those honest eyes and tell him? How can I bear to see one cloud on that noble brow? Would I might give him the answer for which he pleads, but cost what it may I must not break my promise to my dying mother. Kneeling at her bedside, with the little ones around me, I promised to be faithful to my church and to train my little brothers as she had trained me. If, then, they choose a better, a different path, I will have done my duty. Had I foreseen what it would cost me, I wonder if I could have made the promise? Mother died happy but her little daughter is miserable, not only one heart is crushed but two must suffer. Ronald's dear mother would not have him change his religion, it would break her heart and we must make the most of my decision."

Just then the wicket gate swung open, a step which Marguerite must have recognized was heard on the porch, and she looked up and smiled.

"May I come in?" she heard some one ask.

"Certainly, Ronald," she answered. "I have been expecting you."

"Expecting me? what news! then you are pleased to see me?"

"Yes, Ronald, I am more pleased than ever before, for I know it will be a long time, if ever we meet again. It is very hard to say this, and to you, one whom I have loved from childhood. It does not seem possible for me to leave my dear old home, my loving friends and the associations of my childhood, but it must come."

"And why, Margie?" asked Ronald, looking into her face, "you have not ceased to care for me."

"No, nor never will; but you remember how we are divided, to some it seems trifling, but to me, brought up as I have been in my faith, I cannot change. When I think of it I feel as though I sin in thought, and mamma made me promise never to leave my church. I cannot, and yet your love for your faith is as strong as mine, so there is nothing for us to do but to part."

Ronald is surprised at such words from Marguerite. He thought her love for him was greater than her religion. He thought all he had to do was to plead his cause and be accepted. Alas, a bitter disappointment. Marguerite does not look up. The sweet face is lowered to hide the blushes, but he who knew for whom they were meant walked gently to her side and lifted her face in his hands. Never before had she seemed so dear to him. For years he had loved her, and no one else had ever had one thought. She was a Catholic and he a Presbyterian. In her eyes he was a perfect man, her ideal; but the training of her youth kept them divided.

"Margie, is it true you will let the question of religion divide us? Must we, who love each other so dearly, be separated because of that? God meant us for each other. He does not intend us to have this chasm divide us. If we are only true to Him we will see Him at last. Although we worship in different churches, there is but one gate; all must enter through it. I do not feel worthy to touch a hair in your head, yet the love of an honest heart I freely give you."

"Ronald, it is useless. I cannot leave the doctrines of the church in which I was trained. I am grieved to know our paths in life must lie in different directions. You are all in all to me. I fear sometimes you have been almost my idol."

"Margie, do you think you can conquer fate?"

"I would that I could. Why can't you come into my church?"

"Remember, Margie, my dear old mother who trained me in the doctrines of her church; it would hasten her end were I to change. Remember the depth of the chasm between Catholicism and the other religions. Were it any other church we would have no need of all this unhappiness. It is one God we serve; I wish it were through only one church. One of us must yield. Which shall it be?"

"Ronald, I cannot leave my church. I realize the sacredness of my promise. I release you. Let us both forget this happy dream which ends so cruelly and abruptly."

Ida Bell Wells-Barnett
Iola ✒
1862–1931

"For more than forty years Ida B. Wells was one of the most fearless and one of the most respected women in the United States."[1] She was widely known as a crusading editor, journalist, organizer, lecturer, social reformer, and feminist.

Born a slave on the threshold of freedom, 16 July 1862, at Holly Springs, Mississippi, she was the oldest of eight children. Her parents were Jim Wells, son of his master and a highly skilled carpenter, and Elizabeth Warrenton, an expert cook. The two were married in slavery and repeated their vows when freed. Deeply religious, Ida's parents instilled in her biblical teachings and the importance of getting an education. She went to Rust College in her hometown, a Freedmen's Aid school with all grade levels. A "pretty little girl, slightly nut-brown, with delicate features,"[2] she became an exceptional student in the school where her father was a member of the first Trustee Board.

When the yellow fever epidemic of 1878 reached Holly Springs, Ida's parents and their youngest child died. Two other children had passed on earlier, leaving Ida and her four brothers and sisters. Showing at the age of fourteen the strength and determination that marked her all her life, she undertook to keep the family together.

After passing the examination for county schoolteacher, she was assigned a one-room school six miles away. After one term, she was encouraged by a widowed aunt to come to Memphis to teach and live with her. While studying for the city school examination, she taught in Shelby County.

In May 1884, when she was traveling on the Chesapeake & Ohio Railroad to teach in Woodstock, Tennessee, a conductor asked her to move to the smoking car. When she refused, the conductor, with the assistance of the baggage man, tried to force her out. During the fracas, Ida braced her feet on the back of the seat and bit the conductor's hand.

Getting off at the next stop, she returned to Memphis and brought a suit against the railroad. She won the case and was awarded five hundred dollars and damages. In writing of her victory, the white Memphis *Daily Appeal* of 25 December 1884, captioned the story: "A Darky Damsel Obtains a Verdict for Damages against the Chesapeake & Ohio Railroad."[3] Her triumph was short-lived, however, for the railroad appealed and the Supreme Court of Tennessee reversed the decision on 5 April 1887. "It was the first case in which a colored plaintiff in the South had appealed to a state court since the repeal of the Civil Rights Bill by the United States Supreme Court."[4]

Ida qualified to teach in the Memphis school system, and became a primary grade teacher for seven years. To further her education, she attended summer school at Fisk University, studied privately with experienced teachers, and read voraciously.

Her writing talent emerged when she was elected editor of a small church paper, the *Evening Star.* Then, much to her surprise, for she had no newspaper training, she was invited to contribute to the *Living Way,* a Baptist weekly. Adapting the pen name of "Iola," she wrote her first article for the paper on the railroad suit. Soon the young journalist, who had learned to "handle a goose-quill, with diamond point, as easily as any man in the newspaper work,"[5] was in demand. She wrote for the *American Baptist, Detroit Plaindealer, Christian Index, Indianapolis World, Gate City Press,* and *A. M. E. Review,* and edited the "Home" department of *Our Women and Children.*

Called the "brilliant Iola" and "Princess of the Press," she was the first woman to attend the Afro-American Press Convention in Louisville, Kentucky, and was elected assistant secretary. There she read a paper, "Women in Journalism, or, How I would Edit." At the 4 March 1889 meeting in Washington, D.C., she was unanimously elected secretary.

Her opportunity to edit a paper came when she bought a one-third interest in the Memphis *Free Speech and Headlight* in 1889. Not one to hold her tongue or her pen, she wrote an article about the poor conditions of the local black schools, deploring not only the physical structures but the inadequacies of the teachers also. The exposé provoked ill feeling against her among both blacks and whites, and she was not rehired to teach the following year.

She had never particularly enjoyed teaching because of its "confinement and monotony," and now she set out to express what she called her "real me" in newspaper work. Shortening the name of the paper to the *Free Speech*, she devoted full-time to traveling for the paper and making it a success. The *Free Speech* soon became a household word "up and down the Delta." It was printed on pink paper so the illiterate could identify it, and circulation increased from fifteen hundred to four thousand.

On 9 March 1892, the lynching in Memphis of three young black businessmen, owners of the People's Grocery Company and friends of Ida's, changed the direction of her life. Away at the time in Natchez, Mississippi, she returned to write blistering editorials that condemned whites for permitting the lynching and urged blacks to leave the city and go west. Hundreds of blacks began to move away, including entire church congregations. She also encouraged blacks to boycott white businesses, introducing the first black boycott.

In May, Ida B. Wells left an editorial at the paper to be published while she attended the A. M. E. General Conference in Philadelphia, where she was to be the guest of author Frances Ellen Watkins Harper. From there, she was scheduled to go to New York to see T. Thomas Fortune, the brilliant editor of the *New York Age*. While in the company of Fortune, she learned about the destruction of her press by an angry white mob. Her partner, J. C. Fleming, had been run out of town, and friends sent word warning her not to return, for whites were threatening to kill her on sight.

The editorial that ignited the wrath of whites concerned the lynching of black men because of white women: "Nobody in this section believes the old thread-bare lie that Negro men assault white women. If southern white men are not careful they will over-reach themselves and a conclusion will be reached which will be very damaging to the moral reputation of their women."[6]

Now an exile from home, Ida was asked by T. Thomas Fortune to write for the *New York Age*. For the 25 June 1892 issue, she substantiated her Memphis editorial by writing an incisive factual front-page piece on lynching. Four months later, it was published again in pamphlet form and called *Southern Horrors: Lynch Law in All Its Phases* (1892). Her writing aroused the interest of the eminent race leader, Frederick Douglass, who published a letter in the pamphlet citing her as a "Brave woman!" That was the beginning of a lifetime friendship between the two.

Ida B. Well's militant writings against lynching awakened other black women to rally behind her cause. Victoria Earle Matthews, writer and reformer of New York, and Maritcha Lyons, a Brooklyn schoolteacher, led a group of black women to give Ida B. Wells a testimonial at Lyric Hall, 5 October 1892. She was presented with five hundred dollars and a gold brooch in the shape of a pen. This event turned out to be an important occasion in her life, for before a large gathering of prominent black women, she gave her first public lecture on the horrors of lynching.

The testimonial had another historic aspect also, for it laid the groundwork for the beginning of the black women's club movement. Out of it came the Women's Loyal Union. Ida B. Well's ability as an organizer was readily recognized, and Josephine St. Pierre Ruffin of Boston asked her to assist in forming the Woman's Era Club. Earning the title "Mother of Clubs," she helped form women's groups throughout New England and in Chicago, where one was named in her honor. She was an outstanding worker in the National Association of Colored Women and, in 1924, ran for president against Mary McLeod Bethune.

Iola now was receiving numerous requests to speak on the subject of lynching. During April and May of 1893, she traveled to England, Scotland, and Wales, and in 1894 visited England again for six months. Her speeches there led to the formation of an Anti-Lynching Committee. Besieged to write as well as to speak, she was asked to send back articles about her trip to the Chicago daily paper, the *Inter-Ocean* (subsequently the *Herald-Examiner*), writing a column "Ida B. Wells Abroad." She commented in her autobiography that she was the first black to become a regular paid correspondent for a daily paper in the United States.

Always quick to publicize racial disparities, she protested against the barring of blacks from the Chicago World's Fair of 1893. She, along with Frederick Douglass and Frederick J. Loudin, an original Fisk University Jubilee Singer, appealed for funds to publish a pamphlet protesting the discrimination. With money raised through churches, Ida, Douglass, Ferdinand Lee Barnett, and I. Garland Penn published an eighty-one page booklet, *The Reason Why the Colored American Is Not in the World's Columbian Exposition—The Afro-American's Contribution to Columbian Literature*, in July 1893. As a fighter who was not afraid to speak out even against her own people if she thought it was necessary, she raised the ire of black leaders when she refused to endorse the fair officials' "solution" of holding "Colored Jubilee Day," or "Negro Day." Nonetheless, she was just as quick to admit poor judgment. After hearing the stirring speech made by Frederick Douglass for the one-day Negro celebration with thousands in attendance, she conceded the program had "done more to bring our cause to the attention of the American people than anything else which had happened during the fair."[7]

Ida B. Wells settled in Chicago, where she wrote her indictment, *A Red Record: Tabulated Statistics and Alleged Causes of Lynching in the United States, 1892–1893–1894* (1895). This notable work presented both lynching statistics and its history. She joined the staff of the first black Chicago newspaper, the *Conservator*, which was owned by Ferdinand L. Barnett, a widower and attorney. Romance entered the picture, and on 27 June 1895, Ida married Barnett. They had four children, but motherhood did not stop her from continuing her writing and lecturing.

In the role of social reformer, she founded the Negro Fellowship League in the most blighted section of Chicago's South Side. The league gave a refuge to those who were homeless, offered religious services, and helped the unemployed. As the first black woman to be appointed a probation officer, she used the league's services to assist with her work.

She was called upon also to investigate riots in such places as Springfield, Illinois; Elaine, Arkansas; and East St. Louis. Her stories on these events ran in the *Chicago Defender, Broad Ax,* and *Whip.* She carried her mission against mob rule all the way to the White House in 1898. Armed with resolutions from a Chicago rally against lynching, she presented them to President William McKinley. In 1900, she published a pamphlet, *Mob Rule in New Orleans: Robert Charles and His Fight to the Death.*

A firm believer in organizing for unity, she was one of the original group who, with W. E. B. Du Bois, conceived of the National Association for the Advancement of Colored People. Entering the political sphere in 1930, she ran as an independent candidate for state senator. When she lost, she blamed her defeat on the "few women who responded." An aggressive feminist, she organized in January 1913 the first suffrage group composed of black women, the Alpha Suffrage Club, which published a newsletter, the *Alpha Suffrage Record.*

All through her life, Ida B. Wells-Barnett was a dynamic, bold, and strong-minded woman who fought against lynching and for the rights of her people. She spoke her mind whenever the occasion warranted, and because of this, she was frequently "not only opposed by whites, but some of her own people were often hostile, impugning her motives."[8]

She fought a "lonely and almost single-handed fight" against lynching "long before men or women of any race entered the arena."[9] She left her story in an autobiography begun in 1928. Her memoirs were eventually edited by her daughter, Alfreda M. Duster, and published under the title *Crusade for Justice: The Autobiography of Ida B. Wells* (1970).

On 25 March 1931, Ida B. Wells died of uremic poisoning. In 1940, the Chicago Housing Authority named a housing project on the South Side in her honor. Ten years after that, the city designated her as one of the twenty-five outstanding women in Chicago's history.

NOTES

1. Duster, *Crusade for Justice,* p. ix.
2. Hughes, *Famous Negro Heroes,* p. 155.

3. Duster, *Crusade for Justice*, p. 19.
4. Ibid., p. 20.
5. Penn, *Afro-American Press*, p. 408.
6. Duster, *Crusade for Justice*, pp. 65–66.
7. Ibid., p. 119.
8. Ibid., p. xxxi.
9. Ibid., p. xxxii.

SELECTED SOURCES

Primary

Barnett-Wells, Ida B. *Mob Rule in New Orleans: Robert Charles and His Fight to the Death.* Chicago: Author, 1900.
Wells, Ida B. *A Red Record: Tabulated Statistics and Alleged Causes of Lynchings in the United States, 1892–1893–1894.* Chicago: Donohue & Henneberry, 1895.
———. *Southern Horrors: Lynch Law in All Its Phases.* New York: New York Age Print, 1892.

Secondary

Dannet, Sylvia G. L. *Profiles of Negro Womanhood.* Vol. 2, *20th Century.* Yonkers, N.Y.: Educational Heritage, 1966.
Duster, Alfreda M., ed. *Crusade for Justice: The Autobiography of Ida B. Wells.* Chicago: University of Chicago Press, 1970.
Giddings, Paula. *When and Where I Enter: The Impact of Black Women on Race and Sex in America.* New York: William Morrow & Co., 1984.
Hughes, Langston. *Famous Negro Heroes of America.* New York: Dodd, Mead & Co., 1958.
Lerner, Gerda. *Black Women in White America: A Documentary History.* New York: Pantheon Books, 1972.
Loewenberg, Bert James, and Bogin, Ruth. *Black Women in Nineteenth-Century American Life: Their Words, Their Thoughts, Their Feelings.* University Park: Pennsylvania State University Press, 1976.
Majors, Gerri, and Saunders, Doris E. *Black Society.* Chicago: Johnson Publishing Co., 1976.
Majors, Monroe Alphus. *Noted Negro Women, Their Triumphs and Activities.* Chicago: Donohue & Henneberry, 1893.
Mossell, N. F. *The Work of the Afro-American Woman.* 2d ed. Philadelphia: Geo. S. Ferguson Co., 1908.
Noble, Jeanne. *Beautiful, Also, Are the Souls of My Black Sisters: A History of the Black Woman in America.* Englewood Cliffs, N.J.: Prentice-Hall, 1978.
Penn, I. Garland. *The Afro-American Press and Its Editors.* 1891. Reprint. New York: Arno Press and The New York Times Co., 1969.

The Case Stated

The student of American sociology will find the year 1894 marked by a pronounced awakening of the public conscience to a system of anarchy and outlawry which had grown during a series of ten years to be so common, that scenes of unusual brutality failed to have any visible effect upon the humane sentiments of the people of our land.

Beginning with the emancipation of the Negro, the inevitable result of unbridled power exercised for two and a half centuries, by the white man over the Negro, began to show itself in acts of conscienceless outlawry. During the slave *regimé*, the Southern white man owned the Negro body and soul. It was to his interest to dwarf the soul and preserve the body. Vested with unlimited power over his slave, to subject him to any and all kinds of physical punishment, the white man was still restrained from such punishment as tended to injure the slave by abating his physical powers and thereby reducing his financial worth. While slaves were scourged mercilessly, and in countless cases inhumanly treated in other respects, still the white owner rarely permitted his anger to go so far as to take a life, which would entail upon him a loss of several hundred dollars. The slave was rarely killed, he was too valuable; it was easier and quite as effective, for discipline or revenge, to sell him "Down South."

But Emancipation came and the vested interests of the white man in the Negro's body were lost. The white man had no right to scourge the emancipated Negro, still less has he a right to kill him. But the Southern white people had been educated so long in that school of practice, in which might makes right, that they disdained to draw strict lines of action in dealing with the Negro. In slave times the Negro was kept subservient and submissive by the frequency and severity of the scourging, but, with freedom, a new system of intimidation came in vogue; the Negro was not only whipped and scourged; he was killed.

Not all nor nearly all of the murders done by white men, during the past thirty years in the South, have come to light, but the statistics as gathered and preserved by white men, and which have not been questioned, show that during these years more than ten thousand Negroes have been killed in cold blood, without the formality of judicial trial and legal execution. And yet, as evidence of the absolute impunity with which the white man dares to kill a Negro, the same record shows that during all these years, and for all these murders only three white men have been tried, convicted, and executed. As no white man has been lynched for the murder of colored people, these three executions are the only instances of the death penalty being visited upon white men for murdering Negroes.

Naturally enough the commission of these crimes began to tell upon the public conscience, and the Southern white man, as a tribute to the nineteenth century civilization, was in a manner compelled to give excuses for his barbarism. His excuses have adapted themselves to the emergency, and are aptly outlined by that greatest of all Negroes, Frederick Douglass, in an article of recent date, in which he shows that there have been three distinct eras of southern barbarism, to account for which three distinct excuses have been made.

The first excuse given to the civilized world for the murder of unoffending Negroes was the necessity of the white man to repress and stamp out alleged "race riots." For years immediately succeeding the war there was an appalling slaughter of colored people, and the wires usually conveyed to northern people and the world the intelligence, first, that an insurrection was being planned by Negroes, which, a few hours later, would prove to have been vigorously resisted by white men, and controlled with a resulting loss of several killed and wounded. It was always a remarkable feature in these insurrections and riots that only Negroes were killed during the rioting, and that all the white men escaped unharmed.

From 1865 to 1872, hundreds of colored men and women were mercilessly murdered and the almost invariable reason assigned was that they met their death by being alleged participants in an insurrection or riot. But this story at last wore itself out. No insurrection ever materialized; no Negro rioter was ever apprehended and proven guilty, and no dynamite ever recorded the black man's protest against oppression and wrong. It was too much to ask thoughtful people to believe this transparent story, and the southern white people at last made up their minds that some other excuse must be had.

Then came the second excuse, which had its birth during the turbulent times of reconstruction. By an amendment to the Constitution the Negro was given the right of franchise, and, theoretically at least, his ballot became his invaluable emblem of citizenship. In a government "of the people, for the people, and by the people," the Negro's vote became an important factor in all matters of state and national politics. But this did not last long. The southern white man would not consider that the Negro had any right which a white man was bound to respect, and the idea of a republican form of government in the southern states grew into general contempt. It was maintained that "This is a white man's government," and regardless of numbers, the white man should rule. "No Negro domination" became the new legend on the sanguinary banner of the sunny South, and under it rode the Ku Klux Klan, the Regulators, and the lawless mobs, which for any cause chose to murder one man or a dozen as suited their purpose best. It was a long, gory campaign; the blood chills and the heart almost loses faith in Christianity when one thinks of Yazoo, Hamburg, Edgefield, Copiah, and the countless massacres of defenceless Negroes, whose only crime was the attempt to exercise their right to vote.

But it was a bootless strife for colored people. The government which had made the Negro a citizen found itself unable to protect him. It gave him the right to vote, but denied him the protection which should have maintained that right. Scourged from his home; hunted through the swamps; hung by midnight raiders, and openly murdered in the light of day, the Negro clung to his right of franchise with a heroism which would have wrung admiration from the heart of savages. He believed that in that small white ballot there was a subtle something which stood for manhood as well as citizenship, and thousands of brave black men went to their graves, exemplifying the one by dying for the other.

The white man's victory soon became complete by fraud, violence, intimidation and murder. The franchise vouchsafed to the Negro grew to be a "barren ideality," and regardless of numbers, the colored people found themselves voiceless in the councils of those whose duty it was to rule. With no longer the fear of "Negro Domination" before their eyes, the white man's second excuse became valueless. With the Southern governments all subverted and the Negro actually eliminated from all participation in state and national elections, there could be no longer an excuse for killing Negroes to prevent "Negro Domination."

Brutality still continued; Negroes were whipped, scourged, exiled, shot and hung whenever and wherever it pleased the white man so to treat them, and as the civilized world with increasing persistency held the white people of the South to account for its outlawry, the murderers invented the third excuse—that Negroes had to be killed to avenge their assaults upon women. There could be framed no possible excuse more harmful to the Negro and more unanswerable if true in its sufficiency for the white man.

Humanity abhors the assailant of womanhood, and this charge upon the Negro at once placed him beyond the pale of human sympathy. With such unanimity, earnestness and apparent candor was this charge made and reiterated that the world has accepted the story that the Negro is the monster which the Southern white man has painted him. And today, the Christian world feels, that while lynching is a crime, and lawlessness and anarchy the certain precursors of a nation's fall, it can not by word or deed, extend sympathy or help to a race of outlaws, who might mistake their plea for justice and deem it an excuse for their continued wrongs.

The Negro has suffered much and is willing to suffer more. He recognizes that the wrongs of two centuries can not be righted in a day, and he tries to bear his burden with patience for to-day and be hopeful for to-morrow. But there comes a time when the veriest worm will turn, and the Negro feels to-day that after all the work he has done, all the sacrifices he has made, and all the suffering he has endured, if he did not, now, defend his name and manhood from this vile accusation, he would be unworthy even of the contempt of mankind. It is to this charge he now feels he must make answer.

If the Southern people in defense of their lawlessness, would tell the truth and admit that colored men and women are lynched for almost any offense from murder to a misdemeanor, there would not now be the necessity for this defense. But when they intentionally, maliciously and constantly belie the record and bolster up these falsehoods by the words of legislators, preachers, governors and bishops, then the Negro must give to the world his side of the awful story.

A word as to the charge itself. In considering the third reason assigned by the Southern white people for the butchery of blacks, the question must be asked, what the white man means when he charges the black man with rape. Does he mean the crime which the statutes of the civilized states describe as such? Not by any means. With the Southern white man, any *mesalliance* existing between a white woman and a colored man is a sufficient foundation for the charge of rape.

The Southern white man says that it is impossible for a voluntary alliance to exist between a white woman and a colored man, and therefore, the fact of an alliance is a proof of force. In numerous instances where colored men have been lynched on the charge of rape, it was positively known at the time of lynching, and indisputably proven after the victim's death, that the relationship sustained between the man and woman was voluntary and clandestine, and that in no court of law could even the charge of assault have been successfully maintained.

It was for the assertion of this fact, in the defense of her own race, that the writer hereof became an exile; her property destroyed and her return to her home forbidden under penalty of death, for writing the following editorial which was printed in her paper, *The Free Speech*, in Memphis, Tenn., May 21, 1892.

"Eight Negroes lynched since last issue of the 'Free Speech' one at Little Rock, Ark., last Saturday morning where the citizens broke (?) into the penitentiary and got their man; three near Anniston, Ala., one near New Orleans; and three at Clarksville, Ga., the last three for killing a white man, and five on the same old racket—the new alarm about raping white women. The same programme of hanging, then shooting bullets into the lifeless bodies was carried out to the letter. Nobody in this section of the country believes the old thread bare lie that Negro men rape white women. If Southern white men are not careful, they will over-reach themselves and public sentiment will have a reaction; a conclusion will then be reached which will be very damaging to the moral reputation of their women."

But threats cannot suppress the truth, and while the Negro suffers the soul deformity, resultant from two and a half centuries of slavery, he is no more guilty of this vilest of all vile charges than the white man who would blacken his name.

During all the years of slavery, no such charge was ever made, not even during the dark days of the rebellion, when the white man, following the fortunes of war went to do battle for the maintenance of slavery. While the master was away fighting to forge the fetters upon the slave, he left his wife and children with no protectors save the Negroes themselves. And yet during those years of trust and peril, no Negro proved recreant to his trust and no white man returned to a home that had been despoiled.

Likewise during the period of alleged "insurrection," and alarming "race riots," it never occurred to the white man, that his wife and children were in danger of assault. Nor in the Reconstruction era, when the hue and cry was against "Negro Domination," was there ever a thought that the domination would ever contaminate a fireside or strike to death the virtue of womanhood. It must appear strange indeed, to every thoughtful and candid man, that more than a quarter of a century elapsed before the Negro began to show signs of such infamous degeneration.

In his remarkable apology for lynching, Bishop Haygood, of Georgia, says: "No race, not the most savage, tolerates the rape of woman, but it may be said without reflection upon any other people that the Southern people are now and always have been most sensitive concerning the honor of their women—their mothers, wives, sisters and daughters." It is not the purpose of this defense to say one word against the white women of the South. Such need not be said, but it is their misfortune that the chivalrous white men of that section, in order to escape the deserved execration of the civilized world, should shield themselves by their cowardly and infamously false excuse, and call into question that very honor about which their distinguished priestly apologist claims they are most sensitive. To justify their own barbarism they assume a chivalry which they do not possess. True chivalry respects all womanhood, and no one who reads the record, as it is written in the faces of the million mulattoes in the South, will for a minute conceive that the southern white man had a very chivalrous regard for the honor due the women of his own race or respect for the womanhood which circumstances placed in his power. That chivalry which is "most sensitive concerning the honor of women" can hope for but little respect from the civilized world, when it confines itself entirely to the women who happen to be white. Virtue knows no color line, and the chivalry which depends upon complexion of skin and texture of hair can command no honest respect.

When emancipation came to the Negroes, there arose in the northern part of the United States an almost divine sentiment among the noblest, purest and best white women of the North, who felt called to a mission to educate and Christianize the millions of southern ex-slaves. From every nook and corner of the North, brave young white women answered that call and left their cultured homes, their happy associations and their lives of ease, and with heroic determi--

nation went to the South to carry light and truth to the benighted blacks. It was a heroism no less than that which calls for volunteers for India, Africa and the Isles of the sea. To educate their unfortunate charges; to teach them the Christian virtues and to inspire in them the moral sentiments manifest in their own lives, these young women braved dangers whose record reads more like fiction than fact. They became social outlaws in the South. The peculiar sensitiveness of the southern white men for women, never shed its protecting influence about them. No friendly word from their own race cheered them in their work; no hospitable doors gave them the companionship like that from which they had come. No chivalrous white man doffed his hat in honor or respect. They were "Nigger teachers"—unpardonable offenders in the social ethics of the South, and were insulted, persecuted and ostracised, not by Negroes, but by the white manhood which boasts of its chivalry toward women.

And yet these northern women worked on, year after year, unselfishly, with a heroism which amounted almost to martyrdom. Threading their way through dense forests, working in school house, in the cabin and in the church, thrown at all times and in all places among the unfortunate and lowly Negroes, whom they had come to find and to serve, these northern women, thousands and thousands of them have spent more than a quarter of a century in giving to the colored people their splendid lessons for home and heart and soul. Without protection, save that which innocence gives to every good woman, they went about their work, fearing no assault and suffering none. Their chivalrous protectors were hundreds of miles away in their northern homes, and yet they never feared any "great dark faced mobs," they dared night or day to "go beyond their own roof trees." They never complained of assaults, and no mob was ever called into existence to avenge crimes against them. Before the world adjudges the Negro a moral monster, a vicious assailant of womanhood and a menace to the sacred precincts of home, the colored people ask the consideration of the silent record of gratitude, respect, protection and devotion of the millions of the race in the South, to the thousands of northern white women who have served as teachers and missionaries since the war.

The Negro may not have known what chivalry was, but he knew enough to preserve inviolate the womanhood of the South which was entrusted to his hands during the war. The finer sensibilities of his soul may have been crushed out by years of slavery, but his heart was full of gratitude to the white women of the North, who blessed his home and inspired his soul in all these years of freedom. Faithful to his trust in both of these instances, he should now have the impartial ear of the civilized world, when he dares to speak for himself as against the infamy wherewith he stands charged.

It is his regret, that, in his own defense, he must disclose to the world that degree of dehumanizing brutality which fixes upon America the blot of a national crime. Whatever faults and failings other nations may have in their dealings with their own subjects or with other people, no other civilized nation stands condemned before the world with a series of crimes so peculiarly national. It becomes a painful duty of the Negro to reproduce a record which shows that a large portion of the American people avow anarchy, condone murder and defy the contempt of civilization.

These pages are written in no spirit of vindictiveness, for all who give the subject consideration must concede that far too serious is the condition of that civilized government in which the spirit of unrestrained outlawry constantly increases in violence, and casts its blight over a continually growing area of territory. We plead not for the colored people alone, but for all victims of the terrible injustice which puts men and women to death without form of law. During the year 1894, there were 132 persons executed in the United States by due form of law, while in the same year, 197 persons were put to death by mobs who gave the victims no opportunity to make a lawful defense. No comment need be made upon a condition of public sentiment responsible for such alarming results.

The purpose of the pages which follow shall be to give the record which has been made, not by colored men, but that which is the result of compilations made by white men, of reports sent over the civilized world by white men in the South. Out of their own mouths shall the murderers be condemned. For a number of years the Chicago Tribune, admittedly one of the leading journals of America, has made a specialty of the compilation of statistics touching upon lynching. The data compiled by that journal and published to the world January 1st, 1894, up to the present time has not been disputed. In order to be safe from the charge of exaggeration, the incidents hereinafter reported have been confined to those vouched for by the Tribune.

Alice Ruth Moore Dunbar-Nelson

1875–1935

Alice Ruth Moore Dunbar-Nelson was another multidimensional black female writer whose occupations included educator, clubwoman, suffragist, politician, and civic worker. Her writing spanned the late nineteenth and early twentieth centuries, making her a precursor of the Harlem Renaissance, as well as a participant in it. She is readily recognized as having been the wife of the famed black poet, Paul Laurence Dunbar. Possibly because of this, like many accomplished wives, her achievements have been partially obscured by the brighter sun of a husband's prominence.

One of two daughters born to Patricia Wright, a seamstress, and Joseph Moore, a Merchant Marine, "Alice was the rambunctious, temperamental family genius, always having to be calmed down from some emotional peak or another."[1] Alice's genius showed at a youthful age when her first book, *Violets and Other Tales* (1895), was published under her maiden name, Alice Ruth Moore, when she was twenty. Now a collector's item, the book contained a potpourri of sketches, essays, poems, and stories, of which many were published previously in newspapers and magazines. She modestly looked upon her work as "a maiden effort,—a little thing with absolutely nothing to commend it, that seeks to do nothing more than amuse."

Ignoring the author's youth, one critic frowned upon her "maiden effort" as being "one of those lifeless privately printed things which most authors who ever do anything better would like to destroy."[2] Sylvanie F. Williams, who wrote the introduction to *Violets and Other Tales*, was more perceptive and fairminded about the young writer's work: "There is much in this book that is good; much that is crude; some that is poor."[3] Moreover, she envisioned a "bud of promise" unfolding.

Alice's second book, *The Goodness of St. Rocque and Other Stories*, was published four years later by Dodd, Mead, and Company, and was better received. The same critic who had disparaged her first book now saw "some excellent material handled with pleasing effect."[4] Another commented on "its quaint charm and gentle sentiment," written by a "still young" author whose style was "high-flown and generous in its use of adjectives."[5]

Born in New Orleans, 19 July 1875, Alice wrote stories that were almost devoid of black characters. They were rich with the regional flavor of her surroundings, embracing the local scenes, streets, and customs, the blithe spirit of Mardi Gras, and the lives of the mixed-blood Cajuns and Creoles. Reputedly able to speak six of Louisiana's patois, she wove these skillfully into her dialogue.

The fourteen stories in *The Goodness of St. Rocque* are of lost loves, unfaithful lovers, jealousy, death, and disappointment with mostly unhappy endings. Sentimental romance abounds. Three of the stories were in *Violets and Other Tales*; one of them, "Titee," was changed to end happily.[6] *The Goodness of St. Rocque* was the first collection solely of short fiction to be published by a black woman—a fact that has been overlooked.

Alice, however, is remembered more for her poetry, which to date remains uncollected. Her poem, "I Sit and Sew," first published in the *A. M. E. Review*, has been much anthologized in recent years. The verses lament a woman who is relegated to sitting and sewing while men fight the real battle of war. A second popular poem, "April Is on the Way," graced the pages of *Ebony and Topaz* (1927), a collection edited by the godfather of the Harlem Renaissance, Charles S. Johnson. Her "Sonnet," occasionally listed as "Violets" and published in the *Crisis* (August 1917), is frequently referred to as her best.

Alice was also a prolific writer for newspapers and magazines, contributing to the *Crisis*, *Opportunity*, the *Messenger*, and *Collier's*. She wrote the weekly newspaper columns "As in a Looking Glass" for the *Washington Eagle* and "From a Woman's Point of View" and "So It Seems" for the *Pittsburgh Courier*.

Educated at Straight University in New Orleans (now Dillard University), she graduated in 1892 and remained in her hometown to teach. In 1897, she accepted a teaching position in Brooklyn, New York, and pursued further studies at the University of Pennsylvania, Cornell University, and the School of Industrial Art.

While she was teaching and writing, one of her sketches, accompanied by a photograph, was published in the *Monthly Review*, which caught the attention of another aspiring writer, Paul Laurence Dunbar. Captivated by the attractive auburn-haired woman, he wrote to her in care of the magazine, enclosing a poem, "Phyllis," for her to read.

In Dunbar's first letter of 17 April 1895, which set the stage for an Elizabeth Barrett–Robert Browning romance, Dunbar entreated her to "pardon my boldness in addressing you," while presenting his "credentials, with as little egotism as possible."[7]

Through letters, they grew to share each other's writing ambitions, ideas, and experiences. Dunbar's love poured forth in a letter of 13 October 1895: "Isn't there some hope for me? I wish you could read my heart. I love you. I love you. You bring out the best in me. You are an inspiration to me."[8] Alice was won over, and wrote from West Medford, Massachusetts, on 1 December 1897: "My darling: this is the last day of the old year, a year that will always be memorable to me as the one in which I met my Paul and was wooed and won by him."[9]

Before Paul left to lecture in England, they were quietly betrothed. The romance by correspondence went smoother than what followed. Alice's people "looked askance" at the "somewhat offhand way" in which she had fallen in love with a laundrywoman's son who was "black as sin," whereas Alice "had an almost white complexion."[10] And worse, Dunbar wrote "coon songs" for minstrels, which cultured and educated blacks considered derogatory to the race. One of the couple's most heated arguments during their marriage concerned this activity until Dunbar stopped writing the songs.

Alice married Paul in New York, 6 March 1898. A month later, she moved to be with him in Washington, D.C. As writers sharing talents, "there was no competition between them. They criticized and encouraged each other. He encouraged her; she encouraged him."[11] Nevertheless the marriage was stormy. Alice's makeup, "forceful, strong-willed, inquisitive, imaginative, and stubborn,"[12] collided with that of a man who, though much in demand for distant public appearances, was tubercular and becoming addicted to medicinal alcohol. "Accusations of selfishness, infidelity, and cruelty cropped up between them, aggravated by gossip [and] family pressure."[13] The quarrels ended in January 1902 after Paul returned from a reading in South Carolina. "Alice threw him out of the house. They never saw each other again."[14] Dunbar died four years later on 9 February 1906 at the age of thirty-four.

After the breakup, Alice went to Wilmington, Delaware, where she taught and headed the English department at Howard High School until 1920. Here she became more of a public figure in her own right.

She continued to write, and compiled, for the fiftieth anniversary of the Emancipation Proclamation, a book of important speeches entitled *Mas-*

terpieces of Negro Eloquence: The Best Speeches Delivered by the Negro from the Days of Slavery to the Present Time (1914). Included was her own "The Life of Social Service as Exemplified in David Livingstone," which was delivered at Lincoln University, Pennsylvania, on the occasion of the centenary of Livingstone's birth.

She opened new reading vistas for her students when she edited *The Dunbar Speaker and Entertainer* (1920) for "the children of the race." Educator Leslie Pinckney Hill praised it as "the first attempt I have known of directly on the part of any Negro to frame a speaker composed entirely of literature produced by black men and women, and about black men and women."[15]

The collection of poems, speeches, and stories for reading and performing contained eight selections from Alice's works, including a play, as well as several of Paul Laurence Dunbar's writings. The book was named in honor of him, although Alice had married for a third time to Robert J. ("Bobo") Nelson of Harrisburg, Pennsylvania, on 20 April 1916. (Her second was a brief, secret union to Arthur Callis, a Howard High School teacher twelve years younger than she on 19 January 1910.) Together, she and Nelson published and edited the *Wilmington Advocate* newspaper from 1920 to 1922. She also served as associate editor of the *A. M. E. Review*.

A writer and historian, she became much in demand as a lecturer. For the platform, she composed a series of five lectures pertaining to black history called "Romances of the Negro in Our History." Her scholarship was well established when she published a two-part article, "People of Color in Louisiana," in the *Journal of Negro History* (1916–17). The esteemed black scholar, W. E. B. Du Bois, quoted her freely in his classic *The Gift of Black Folk*.

For a time, Alice served as a parole and probation officer, and from 1924 to 1928, she taught at the Industrial School for Colored Girls, which she helped found in Marshallton, Delaware. Following this, she became executive secretary of the American Friends Inter-Racial Peace Committee from 1928 to 1931. An active clubwoman, she participated in the National Federation of Colored Women's Clubs, the Women's International League for Peace and Freedom, the National Association for the Advancement of Colored People, the Association for the Study of Afro-American Life and History, and Delta Sigma Theta (for whose hymn she wrote the lyrics).

A key black figure in Delaware politics, she was a member of the Republican State Committee from 1920 to 1922, although she considered herself an independent. Not liking what she saw in Delaware, she wrote a critical article, "Politics in Delaware," for *Opportunity* (1924), which exposed the state's political racism.

As suffragist and feminist, she composed the essay "The Woman" in *Violets and Other Tales*. It is an example of early black feminist writing by a woman who would not have thought of it as such at the time. The piece voiced her views on the independence of working women who bypass a confining and frequently disappointing marriage.

Alice "produced literature" all the time, leaving two unpublished novels, *This Lofty Oak* and *Confessions of a Lazy Woman*. But she is recalled more as a poet who "wrote sonnets of uncommon skill and beauty."[16]

She died of a heart ailment on 18 September 1935 in a Philadelphia hospital. Her body was cremated in Wilmington, Delaware. Sylvanie F. Williams introduced her to the world of letters as a "'brave new woman who scorns to sigh,' but feels that she has something to say, and says it to the best of her ability."[17] A "brave new woman" she was, working at the brink of a new era of black womanhood and black writing.

NOTES

1. Hull, "Alice Dunbar-Nelson," p. 92.
2. Loggins, *Negro Author*, p. 318.
3. Moore, *Violets and Other Tales*, pp. 10–11.
4. Loggins, *Negro Author*, p. 318.
5. Brawley, *Negro Genius*, pp. 216–17.
6. Hull gives in-depth analysis of her writings in *Color, Sex, and Poetry*.
7. Young, "Paul Laurence Dunbar," p. 320.
8. Ibid., p. 325.
9. Ibid., p. 329.
10. Wagner, *Black Poets*, p. 78.
11. Interview with Pauline A. Young, 14 August 1980, Arden, Delaware.
12. Hull, "Alice Dunbar-Nelson," p. 92.
13. Ibid., p. 93.
14. Wagner, *Black Poets*, p. 79. Hull contends in *Color, Sex, and Poetry* that on a binge one night in 1902, Paul beat Alice and then spread lies about her. After that night, she never saw him again.
15. Nelson-Dunbar, *Dunbar Speaker*, p. 12.
16. Redding, *They Came in Chains*, p. 207.
17. Moore, *Violets and Other Tales*, p. 10.

SELECTED SOURCES

Primary

Dunbar, Alice. *The Goodness of St. Rocque and Other Stories*. New York: Dodd, Mead & Co., 1899.
Dunbar, Alice Moore, ed. *Masterpieces of Negro Eloquence: The Best Speeches Delivered by the Negro from the Days of Slavery to the Present Time*. New York: Bookery Publishing Co., 1914.

Dunbar-Nelson, Alice. *Give Us Each Day: The Diary of Alice Dunbar-Nelson.* Edited by Gloria T. Hull. New York: W. W. Norton & Co., 1984.

Dunbar-Nelson, Alice Moore, ed. *The Dunbar Speaker and Entertainer: Containing the Best Prose and Poetic Selections by and about the Negro Race.* Naperville, Ill.: J. L. Nichols & Co., 1920.

Moore, Alice Ruth. *Violets and Other Tales.* Boston: Monthly Review, 1895.

Secondary

Brawley, Benjamin Griffith. *The Negro Genius: A New Appraisal of the Achievement of the American Negro in Literature and the Fine Arts.* New York: Dodd, Mead & Co., 1937.

Cullen, Countee, ed. *Caroling Dusk: An Anthology of Verse by Negro Poets.* New York: Harper & Brothers, 1927.

Gilbert, Sandra M., and Gubar, Susan. *The Norton Anthology of Literature by Women: The Tradition in English.* New York: W. W. Norton & Co., 1985.

Hull, Gloria T. "Alice Dunbar-Nelson: Delaware Writer and Woman of Affairs." *Delaware History* 17 (Fall–Winter 1976):87–103.

———. *Color, Sex, and Poetry: Three Women Writers of the Harlem Renaissance.* Bloomington and Indianapolis: Indiana University Press, 1987.

Johnson, James Weldon, ed. *The Book of American Negro Poetry.* New York: Harcourt, Brace & Co., 1922.

Loggins, Vernon. *The Negro Author: His Development in America.* New York: Columbia University Press, 1931.

Redding, Jay Saunders. *They Came in Chains: Americans from Africa.* Philadelphia: J. B. Lippincott, 1950.

Wagner, Jean. *Black Poets of the United States: From Paul Laurence Dunbar to Langston Hughes.* Translated by Kenneth Douglas. Urbana: University of Illinois Press, 1973.

Williams, Ora. "Works by and About Alice Ruth (Moore) Dunbar-Nelson: A Bibliography." *CLA Journal* 19 (March 1976):322–26.

Young, Pauline A. "Paul Laurence Dunbar: An Intimate Glimpse." *Freedomways* 12 (Fourth quarter 1972):319–29.

Tony's Wife

"Gimme fi' cents worth o'candy, please." It was the little Jew girl who spoke, and Tony's wife roused herself from her knitting to rise and count out the multi-hued candy which should go in exchange for the dingy nickel grasped in warm, damp fingers. Three long sticks, carefully wrapped in crispest brown paper, and a half dozen or more of pink candy fish for lagniappe, and the little Jew girl sped away in blissful contentment. Tony's wife resumed her knitting with a stifled sigh until the next customer should come.

A low growl caused her to look up apprehensively. Tony himself stood beetle-browned and huge in the small doorway.

"Get up from there," he muttered, "and open two dozen oysters right away; the Eliots want 'em." His English was unaccented. It was long since he had seen Italy.

She moved meekly behind the counter, and began work on the thick shells. Tony stretched his long neck up the street.

"Mr. Tony, mama wants some charcoal." The very small voice at his feet must have pleased him, for his black brows relaxed into a smile, and he poked the little one's chin with a hard, dirty finger, as he emptied the ridiculously small bucket of charcoal into the child's bucket, and gave a banana for lagniappe.

The crackling of shells went on behind, and a stifled sob arose as a bit of sharp edge cut into the thin, worn fingers that clasped the knife.

"Hurry up there, will you?" growled the black brows; "the Eliots are sending for the oysters."

She deftly strained and counted them, and, after wiping her fingers, resumed her seat, and took up the endless crochet work, with her usual stifled sigh.

Tony and his wife had always been in this same little queer old shop on Prytania Street, at least to the memory of the oldest inhabitant in the neighbourhood. When or how they came, or how they stayed, no one knew; it was enough that they were there, like a sort of ancestral fixture to the street. The neighbourhood was fine enough to look down upon these two tumble-down shops at the corner, kept by Tony and Mrs. Murphy, the grocer. It was a semi-fashionable locality, far up-town, away from the old-time French quarter. It was the sort of neighbourhood where millionaires live before their fortunes are made and fashionable, high-priced private schools flourish, where the small cottages are occupied by aspiring school-teachers and choir-singers. Such was this locality, and you must admit that it was indeed a condescension to tolerate Tony and Mrs. Murphy.

He was a great, black-bearded, hoarse-voiced, six-foot specimen of Italian humanity, who looked in his little shop and on the prosaic pavement of Prytania Street somewhat as Hercules might seem in a modern drawing-room. You instinctively thought of wild mountain-passes, and the gleaming dirks of bandit contadini in looking at him. What his last name was, no one knew. Someone had maintained once that he had been christened Antonio Malatesta, but that was unauthentic, and as little to be believed as that other wild theory that her name was Mary.

She was meek, pale, little, ugly, and German. Altogether part of his arms and legs would have very decently made another larger than she. Her hair was pale and drawn in sleek, thin tightness away from a pinched, pitiful face, whose dull cold eyes hurt you, because you knew they were trying to mirror sorrow, and could not because of their expressionless quality. No matter what the weather or what her other toilet, she always wore a thin little shawl of dingy brick-dust hue about her shoulders. No matter what the occasion or what the day, she always carried her knitting with her, and seldom ceased the incessant twist, twist of the shining steel among the white cotton meshes. She might put down the needles and lace into the spool-box long enough to open oysters, or wrap up fruit and candy, or count out wood and coal into infinitesimal portions, or do her housework; but the knitting was snatched with avidity at the first spare moment, and the worn, white, blue-marked fingers, half enclosed in kid-glove stalls for protection, would writhe and twist in and out again. Little girls just learning to crochet borrowed their patterns from Tony's wife, and it was considered quite a mark of advancement to have her inspect a bit of lace done by eager, chubby fingers. The ladies in larger houses, whose husbands would be millionaires some day, bought her lace, and gave it to their servants for Christmas presents.

As for Tony, when she was slow in opening his oysters or in cooking his red beans and spaghetti, he roared at her, and prefixed picturesque adjectives to her lace, which made her hide it under her apron with a fearsome look in her dull eyes.

He hated her in a lusty, roaring fashion, as a healthy beefy boy hates a sick cat and torments it to madness. When she displeased him, he beat her, and knocked her frail form on the floor. The children could tell when this had happened. Her eyes would be red, and there would be blue marks on her face and neck. "Poor Mrs. Tony," they would say, and nestle close to her. Tony did not roar at her for petting them, perhaps, because they spent money on the multi-hued candy in glass jars on the shelves.

Her mother appeared upon the scene once, and stayed a short time; but Tony got drunk one day and beat her because she ate too much, and she disappeared soon after. Whence she came and where she departed, no one could tell, not even Mrs. Murphy, the Pauline Pry and Gazette of the block.

Tony had gout, and suffered for many days in roaring helplessness, the while his foot, bound and swathed in many folds of red flannel, lay on the chair before him. In proportion as his gout increased and he bawled from pure physical discomfort, she became light-hearted, and moved about the shop with real, brisk cheeriness. He could not hit her then without such pain that after one or two trials he gave up in disgust.

So the dull years had passed, and life had gone on pretty much the same for Tony and the German wife and the shop. The children came on Sunday evenings to buy the stick candy, and on week-days for coal and wood. The servants came to buy oysters for the larger houses, and to gossip over the counter about their employers. The little dry woman knitted, and the big man moved lazily in and out in his red flannel shirt, exchanged politics with the tailor next door through the window, or lounged into Mrs. Murphy's bar and drank fiercely. Some of the children grew up and moved away, and other little girls came to buy candy and eat pink lagniappe fishes, and the shop still thrived.

One day Tony was ill, more than the mummied foot of gout, or the wheeze of asthma; he must keep his bed and send for the doctor.

She clutched his arm when he came, and pulled him into the tiny room.

"Is it——is it anything much, doctor?" she gasped.

Æsculapius shook his head as wisely as the occasion would permit. She followed him out of the room into the shop.

"Do you——will he get well, doctor?"

Æsculapius buttoned up his frock coat, smoothed his shining hat, cleared his throat, then replied oracularly,

"Madam, he is completely burned out inside. Empty as a shell, madam, empty as a shell. He cannot live, for he has nothing to live on."

As the cobblestones rattled under the doctor's equipage rolling leisurely up Prytania Street, Tony's wife sat in her chair and laughed,—laughed with a hearty joyousness that lifted the film from the dull eyes and disclosed a sparkle beneath.

The drear days went by, and Tony lay like a veritable Samson shorn of his strength, for his voice was sunken to a hoarse, sibilant whisper, and his black eyes gazed fiercely from the shock of hair and beard about a white face. Life went on pretty much as before in the shop; the children paused to ask how Mr. Tony was, and even hushed the jingles on their bell hoops as they passed the door. Red-headed Jimmie, Mrs. Murphy's nephew, did the hard jobs, such as splitting wood and lifting coal from the bin; and in the intervals between tending the fallen giant and waiting on the customers, Tony's wife sat in her accustomed chair, knitting fiercely, with an inscrutable smile about her purple compressed mouth.

Then John came, introducing himself, serpent-wise, into the Eden of her bosom.

John was Tony's brother, huge and bluff too, but fair and blond, with the beauty of Northern Italy. With the same lack of race pride which Tony had displayed in selecting his German spouse, John had taken unto himself Betty, a daughter of Erin, aggressive, powerful, and cross-eyed. He turned up now, having heard of this illness, and assumed an air of remarkable authority at once.

A hunted look stole into the dull eyes, and after John had departed with blustering directions as to Tony's welfare, she crept to his bedside timidly.

"Tony," she said,—"Tony, you are very sick."

An inarticulate growl was the only response.

"Tony, you ought to see the priest; you mustn't go any longer without taking the sacrament."

The growl deepened into words.

"Don't want any priest; you're always after some snivelling old woman's fuss. You and Mrs. Murphy go on with your church; it won't make *you* any better."

She shivered under this parting shot, and crept back into the shop. Still the priest came next day.

She followed him in to the bedside and knelt timidly.

"Tony," she whispered, "here's Father Leblanc."

Tony was too languid to curse out loud; he only expressed his hate in a toss of the black beard and shaggy mane.

"Tony," she said nervously, "won't you do it now? It won't take long, and it will be better for you when you go—— Oh, Tony, don't— —don't laugh. Please, Tony, here's the priest."

But the Titan roared aloud: "No; get out. Think I'm a-going to

271

give you a chance to grab my money now? Let me die and go to hell in peace."

Father Leblanc knelt meekly and prayed, and the woman's weak pleadings continued,——

"Tony, I've been true and good and faithful to you. Don't die and leave me no better than before. Tony, I do want to be a good woman once, a real-for-true married woman. Tony, here's the priest; say yes." And she wrung her ringless hands.

"You want my money," said Tony, slowly, "and you sha'n't have it, not a cent; John shall have it."

Father Leblanc shrank away like a fading spectre. He came next day and next day, only to see re-enacted the same piteous scene,— the woman pleading to be made a wife ere death hushed Tony's blasphemies, the man chuckling in pain-racked glee at the prospect of her bereaved misery. Not all the prayers of Father Leblanc nor the wailings of Mrs. Murphy could alter the determination of the will beneath the shock of hair; he gloated in his physical weakness at the tenacious grasp on his mentality.

"Tony," she wailed on the last day, her voice rising to a shriek in its eagerness, "tell them I'm your wife; it'll be the same. Only say it, Tony, before you die!"

He raised his head, and turned stiff eyes and gibbering mouth on her; then, with one chill finger pointing at John, fell back dully and heavily.

They buried him with many honours by the Society of Italia's Sons. John took possession of the shop when they returned home, and found the money hidden in the chimney corner.

As for Tony's wife, since she was not his wife after all, they sent her forth in the world penniless, her worn fingers clutching her bundle of clothes in nervous agitation, as though they regretted the time lost from knitting.

I Sit and Sew

I sit and sew—a useless task it seems,
My hands grown tired, my head weighed down with
    dreams—

The panoply of war, the martial tread of men,
Grim faced, stern eyed, gazing beyond the ken
Of lesser souls, whose eyes have not seen Death,
Nor learned to hold their lives but as a breath—
But—I must sit and sew.

I sit and sew—my heart aches with desire—
That pageant terrible, that fiercely pouring fire
On wasted fields, and writhing grotesque things
Once men. My soul in pity flings
Appealing cries, yearning only to go
There in that holocaust of hell, those fields of woe—
But—I must sit and sew

The little useless seam, the idle patch;
Why dream I here beneath my homely thatch,
When there they lie in sodden mud and rain,
Pitifully calling me, the quick ones and the slain?
You need me, Christ. It is no roseate dream
That beckons me—this pretty futile seam
It stifles me—God, *must* I sit and sew?

Part 3

Pre–World War I to the New Negro Movement
1900–1923

The turn of the century saw Afro-Americans at their lowest ebb in their pursuit of social, economic, and political justice. W. E. B. Du Bois looked upon the first part of the twentieth century as "more critical than the Reconstruction years," and historian John Hope Franklin condemned it as a "bleak plateau in freedom's climb." This nadir in black history manifested itself in the literature, which continued the past century's themes of protest, moral living, and racial uplift, but adding standards for race improvement that, it was hoped, would lead to white acceptance.

The women fiction writers who were precursors of the New Negro Movement were not as recognizable as their black male writing counterparts, W. E. B. Du Bois, Paul Laurence Dunbar, Charles W. Chesnutt, and James Weldon Johnson. They were few in number, and young Fisk University student Virginia B. Miller, writing in the school's literary magazine, the *Fisk Herald* (1901), urged Negro women to contribute more to their literature and "show the world that we are capable of succeeding in such attempts."

Pauline E. Hopkins was the first black woman to publish a novel at the beginning of the century. Her *Contending Forces: A Romance Illustrative of Negro Life, North and South* (1900) appeared the same year as Charles W. Chesnutt's *The House Behind the Cedars*, but did not make the same impact as Chesnutt's. Whereas Chesnutt was published by the established white house of Houghton Mifflin, Hopkins's imprint was that of the small newly organized Colored Co-operative Publishing Company of Boston, where she was a shareholder and board of directors member.

In all likelihood, even if Hopkins had chosen to submit her manuscript to a white publisher, it would have been rejected because of its nature. Carole McAlpine Watson has judged it to be "the most forceful protest novel written by a black American woman prior to Ann Petry's *The Street.*" Hopkins's elements of post-Reconstruction lynchings, sexual abuses, and social and economic oppression were not the grist for white publishers' book mills. Also, it is likely that Hopkins, being a race-conscious woman, as she described herself, would have preferred a black publishing company to issue her work.

Contending Forces contributed strongly to the Afro-American feminist literary tradition. Black feminist critic Claudia Tate credits Hopkins with offering "a tentative program for the advancement of black Americans in general and black American women in particular." This is sustained in Hopkins's chapter "The Sewing Circle" in *Contending Forces* in which Mrs. Willis deems "the advancement of the colored woman should be the new problem in the woman question that should float her upon its tide into the prosperity she desired." Mrs. Willis is Hopkins's prototype of a cultured middle-class black woman who leads a comfortable life, is knowledgeable about the race, and wants to counter stereotypes of the black woman's immorality. In her talk to the sewing circle's young women, she praises virtuous women as race builders.

Pauline E. Hopkins has now been recognized in Afro-American literature after lengthy years of neglect by white and black male critics. She came to my attention when I happened upon a small collection of her papers in the Special Collections of the Fisk University Library. Realizing that she was a foremother who deserved to be rediscovered, I published an article about her with the purpose of giving new exposure to a woman who deserves more recognition. She is now being placed in proper perspective by such critics as Claudia Tate, Carole McAlpine Watson, and Vashti Lewis. Just as Hugh M. Gloster thought the publication of Chesnutt's folk stories in the *Atlantic Monthly* represented the "coming-of-age of Negro literature in the United States," so, unheralded, did the publication of Hopkins's *Contending Forces* mark the coming-of-age of the Afro-American feminist literary tradition.

It was eight years after *Contending Forces* appeared that another black woman, Sarah Lee Brown Fleming, published a novel. Her *Hope's Highway* (1918) symbolized the black racial problems of the age and proposed ways of coping with them. Her plot revolves around the national controversy between black leaders Booker T. Washington, who founded the Tuskegee Institute in Alabama and was accepted by whites as the spokesperson for the black race, and W. E. B. Du Bois, Fisk- and Harvard-trained historian and scholar. Washington, an accommodationist, sought to mollify white southerners by advocating social separation of the races and industrial education for his people. Du Bois opposed this line of conciliation, advocating a more assertive stance for equality, suffrage, and the education of the black intelligentsia, the "Talented Tenth."

Fleming's *Hope's Highway*, published three years after Washington's death, obviously borrowed from the national dispute. The story concerns a school in the South, Vance Institute (possibly Tuskegee about which Fleming wrote a poem in her *Clouds and Sunshine*), which changes its curriculum from industrial education to the liberal arts. This act is denounced by a white racist politician, Joe Vardam, whose character is no doubt based on a Mississippi white supremacist of the time, J. K. Vardaman. As a result of Vardam's opposition, "the leader" of the school (who represents Booker T. Washington) dies of a broken heart. Fleming's message for racial acceptance is cast in terms of education and leadership.

Another novel, *The Resentment* (1921) by Mary Etta Spencer, also bears evidence of the Washington–Du Bois conflict. Spencer's "rags to riches" story concerns a young black man who becomes a successful hog-raising entrepreneur, thereby embodying Washington's concept of "business enterprise" for "racial elevation" and self-esteem through entry into the "all-powerful business and commercial world." This is emphasized when the protagonist, Silas Miller, says to himself: "I shall not always be a nigger, I am going to be a business man, and men will take their hats off—well, we'll take our hats off together." Silas is envisioning white men taking their hats off to him in respect for his business accomplishments, which will dignify his racial status.

Lillian E. Wood's novel, *"Let My People Go"* (1922) carried on the inspirational themes of leadership and achievement as anodynes for racial woes. Wood also reiterated Pauline E. Hopkins's message of virtuous black women imparting a positive image to the race—which was incongruous with the drive by the white women of this period to effect social reforms in order to free women from Victorian mores. For black women, ennobling a downtrodden race was more important.

Zara Wright's *Black and White Tangled Threads* (1920) and its sequel, *Kenneth* (1920), reflected the melodramatic romance novels of the nineteenth century. The uniqueness of the first book lay in its mulatto story with a different twist; it showed the effects of miscegenation upon a white antebellum southern family who acknowledges a mulatto as a legitimate family member. The author sermonized for education to support race progress and accord. Wright, like the rest of her female contemporaries, was more concerned with spinning propaganda than presenting a story with a valid plot and characters. This was the weakness in their fiction; nevertheless, their will to write must be acknowledged.

While these novelists were protesting racial injustices and proposing ways to advance the race, Amelia E. Johnson, in her last novel, *Martina Meriden; or, What Is My Motive?* (1901), presented yet another moralistic story revolving around young white characters. Maggie Shaw-Fullilove, another obscure black woman novelist, delivered a different message in *Who Was Responsible?* (1919), published by the Abingdon Press of Cincinnati. I have not seen this book, but it is said to deal with the evils of alcohol, a problem taken up earlier by Frances Ellen Watkins Harper in her poetry and lectures as a temperance worker.

None of these women novelists gained widespread literary recognition. They were black writers at a time when white women writers were prodigious "producers of novels," as Sandra M. Gilbert and Susan Guber have pointed out. Nevertheless they were forming a nucleus of their own, furnishing models for future black women writers.

As in the late nineteenth century, there was a profusion of women poets writing pastoral poems, lyrics, and eulogies. Among these was Myra Viola Wilds, author of *Thoughts of Idle Hours* (1915).

Wilds, a native of Mount Ollie, Kentucky, was a seamstress who began writing poetry after losing her eyesight in 1911. A year later, she had completed a book of fifty-three poems in "her own hand." The last poem, "Waiting in the Shadow," tells of her courage and unflagging spirit while she awaits "the coming of the light." Effie T. Battle, a poet and teacher born in Okolona, Mississippi, of poor parents, wrote poems that appeared in newspapers and magazines. By 1914, she had brought out a volume, *Gleanings from Dixie Land*.

H. Cordelia Ray was more well known, writing what Gloria T. Hull called "mannered bookish poetry." Her career spanned the turn of the century when she published a second book, *Poems*, in 1910. Olivia Ward Bush, a newly appreciated poet and playwright whose career also began in the nineteenth century, gained a reputation as a poet with her book, *Driftwood* (1914). The Thompson sisters, Priscilla Jane and Clara Ann, were represented in anthologies, but not generally admired. Clara Ann's poems in *Songs from the Wayside* (1908) and *A Garland of Poems* (1926) were less antagonistic toward whites than were Priscilla Jane's *Ethiope Lays* (1900) and *Gleanings of Quiet Hours* (1907).

Afro-American women may have been more inclined to write poetry than prose, for it offered a ready means of expressing their creativity. Clara Ann Thompson, for example, wanted to write a novel but never did. Prose writing may have been too time-consuming, or she may have been uncertain of her skills. Many of the writers were self-educated, had only minimal formal schooling, or at best were graduates of normal schools.

It was not until 1918 when Georgia Douglas Johnson published *The Heart of a Woman and Other Poems* that an early twentieth-century black woman poet gained more than a little attention. Johnson's success, prior to the New Negro Movement, can be attributed to a number of circumstances. First, she lived in the East, where the New Negro Movement would take hold, and she was a friend of leading black male literary figures. The eminent anthologist and critic, William Stanley Braithwaite, wrote the introduction to *The Heart of a Woman*, and W. E. B. Du Bois contributed a foreword to her second book, *Bronze: A Book of Verse* (1922). Johnson thus had a foot in the door, which helped her gain recognition for her writing. Modern-day critics have called her work "conventional" and have criticized the "sameness of her themes and manner." Nevertheless, she broke out of the Victorian mold of black women poets by exploring intimate women's themes with "candor of expression."

Afro-American women writers at the outset of the twentieth century now tried their hand at a new genre, drama. Fiction and poetry writers began to experiment with plays, using interracial and intraracial subjects. Angelina Weld Grimké's play *Rachel* (1916) was a precedent-setting model for women playwrights and others.

Alice Dunbar-Nelson's one-act drama, *Mine Eyes Have Seen*, was written near the close of World War I in 1918. Its theme was racism and patriotism, and it was presented by the children of the school where Dunbar taught. The plot concerns Chris, a young black, wrestling over being called to service. He harbors bitter memories of a jealous southern mob burning his family's home because they lived in a "decent house." His father was killed defending it, and Chris, his mother, sister, and brother were forced to flee north. But loyalty to his nation and pride in his race win out as Chris is told by a settlement worker, "your race is calling you to carry on its good name." Dunbar-Nelson used Julia Ward Howe's Civil War song, "The Battle Hymn of the Republic" at the end to drum up the emotions and patriotism of her audience.

Mary Burrill, a Washington schoolteacher, followed a year later with a play published in the *Birth Control Review* entitled *They That Sit in Darkness*. The darkness represents women's ignorance about birth control. Truly a feminist play, as well as one dealing with classism, it deplores the predicament of poor women whose lack of knowledge of birth control dooms them to incessant childbearing, which keeps them locked in poverty and ill health, and restricts them to the home. Malinda Jasper is a poor black rural southern woman who is the mother of ten children, eight living and two dead. She has just had another child, which she had been warned against because of a heart condition. The visiting nurse is permitted by law to tell her only to be "careful." She dies on the day her daughter Lindy is preparing to go to Tuskegee. As a result, Lindy is forced to stay home to care for the children. This may well have been the first black feminist play. It dwelt not on race but on birth control, emphasizing a woman's right to know.

The young century's blatant racism, expressed through disfranchisement, segregation, and the reign of white supremacy, strengthened the awareness of blacks for the need to promote black history and pride in the race. Blacks were being ridiculed in minstrel shows with "coon" songs and "darky" jokes, and white writers were denigrating them in their books. Thomas Dixon's *The Clansman: An Historical Romance of the Ku Klux Klan* (1905) was made into the notorious movie *The Birth of a Nation* by D. W. Griffith, from which he made a fortune.

To counter these negative images, blacks began to compile anthologies and write books of black history and black leaders. They did not realize they were also planting the seeds for the New Negro Movement, which espoused black identity. Alice Dunbar-Nelson's *Masterpieces of Negro Eloquence: The Best Speeches Delivered by the Negro from the Days of Slavery to the Present Time* (1914) included the speeches of Josephine St. Pierre Ruffin, Frances Ellen Watkins Harper, Fanny Jackson Coppin, and Dunbar-Nelson herself. Her second anthology, *The Dunbar Speaker and Entertainer: Containing the Best Prose and Poetic Selections by and about the Negro Race* (1920), was designed to stimulate race pride and knowledge among young people. Also working with black youth in mind, Mrs. Leila Amos Pendleton assembled a history book for children ages twelve to fourteen. Her *Narrative of the Negro* (1912) recorded facts left out of other history books about Afro-Americans' contributions to history. And Laura Eliza Wilkes, a Washington, D.C., teacher, spent six years researching colonial records, state papers, assembly journals, and histories of slavery for her *Missing Pages in American History, Revealing the Services of Negroes in the Early Wars in the United States of America, 1641–1815* (1919).

Collective biographies sought to instill race respect by highlighting black achievers. Elizabeth Ross Haynes *Unsung Heroes* (1921) presented a group of black leaders of the past and the present. Delilah L. Beasley, Los Angeles journalist, concentrated on black pioneers in *The Negro Trail Blazers of California* (1919).

Also during this period, Maud Cuney Hare, a highly intelligent and versatile woman, wrote a biography about her father, *Norris Wright Cuney: A Tribune of the Black People* (1913), which reflected the courage of her father and herself as well. The delineation of a middle-class black family living in the South when racism was rampant is valuable documentation for social and literary history.

Numerous autobiographies recounted religious experiences and postslavery memories. A woman minister continued the personal stories of sexism in the black church in her autobiography, *Life of Mrs.*

Helena Arkansas Mason (1902). A member of the African Methodist Episcopal Church, Mrs. Mason repeats the earlier stories of Jarena Lee and Amanda Berry Smith of male animosity toward female ministers. Born in Quincy, Illinois, in 1864, she spent forty years as an evangelist holding revival services in the Middle West. Baptist ministers, believing only men should preach, tried to thwart her religious activities. Even Bishop B. T. Tanner of her own denomination fought her: "He, Bishop Tanner, spoke against me, and forbid his men having me to help them." Mrs. Mason died in 1924 after having guided more than "100,000 souls to Christ."

Mrs. Frances A. Joseph Gaudet's *He Leadeth Me* (1913), published by herself in New Orleans, tells of living in Mississippi with her grandparents after her father was killed in the Civil War, and then in New Orleans with her mother. Her story is one of courage and endurance in surviving.

Susie King Taylor's *Reminiscences of My Life with the 33d United States Colored Troops Late 1st S.C. Volunteers* (1902) enriched the Civil War saga with a black woman's point of view and offered her reflections on Reconstruction. Another book about war as experienced by black women was *Two Colored Women with the American Expeditionary Forces* (1920) by Addie W. Hunton and Kathryn M. Johnson. It was a singular account of their World War I involvement in France as YMCA welfare workers among black troops. They reported the prejudices and harassments of black soldiers by white officers, and the bigoted attitudes of white secretaries of the YMCA toward black troops and the two women themselves. One black soldier, having fought for two days at the front without food and water, was not allowed to buy a package of cookies when he came across a YMCA hut. Other revelations make for pathetic reading about black soldiers fighting on foreign soil for a freedom not accorded them. Photographs and poems by Georgia Douglas Johnson and Paul Laurence Dunbar are scattered throughout the text.

Through these literary accomplishments, Afro-American women writers were becoming more certain of themselves as a woman force and as writers. Their new confidence was reflected in the founding of the monthly magazine *Woman's Voice* in 1919, a periodical "By Woman—Of Woman—For Woman." An editorial of 1923 addressed the fact that women of color needed a medium, set apart for their progress and achievements.

From these women's writing, it can be seen that they were not silent or idle prior to the New Negro Movement. Although unheralded, they were proving themselves to be the "capable" writers the young Fisk student so wanted them to be.

Chronology of Writings

1900   Frances Ellen Watkins Harper, *Poems*

Pauline E. Hopkins, *Contending Forces: A Romance Illustrative of Negro Life North and South*

Priscilla Jane Thompson, *Ethiope Lays*

1901   Frances Ellen Watkins Harper, *Idylls of the Bible*

Amelia E. Johnson (Mrs. A. E. Johnson), *Martina Meriden; or, What Is My Motive?*

1901–2   Pauline E. Hopkins (Pseudonym, Sarah A. Allen), *Hagar's Daughters, a Story of Southern Caste Prejudice*

1902   Pauline E. Hopkins, *Winona: A Tale of Negro Life in the South and Southwest*

Susie King Taylor, *Reminiscences of My Life with the 33d United States Colored Troops Late 1st S.C. Volunteers*

Helena Arkansas Mason, *Life of Mrs. Helena Arkansas Mason*

1902–3   Pauline E. Hopkins, *Of One Blood; or, The Hidden Self*

1904   Effie Waller, *Songs of the Months*

1905 Pauline E. Hopkins, *A Primer of Facts Pertaining to the Early Greatness of the African Race and the Possibility of Restoration by Its Descendants—with Epilogue*

1907 Priscilla Jane Thompson, *Gleanings of Quiet Hours*

   Walker, Virginia Broughton. *Twenty Years* [!] *Experience of a Missionary*

1908 Clara Ann Thompson, *Songs from the Wayside*

1909 Effie Waller, *Rhymes from the Cumberland*

   Annie L. Campbell Burton, *Memories of Childhood's Slavery Days*

1910 H. Cordelia Ray, *Poems*

   Gertrude Arquene Fisher, *Original Poems*

   Maggie Pogue Johnson, *Virginia Dreams. Lyrics for an Idle Hour; Tales of the Time Told in Rhyme*

   Christina Moody, *A Tiny Spark*

   Katherine Davis Tillman, *Fifty Years of Freedom; or, From Cabin to Congress; a Drama in Five Acts*

1911 Carrie Williams Clifford, *Race Rhymes*

1912 Leila Amos Pendleton, *A Narrative of the Negro*

1913 Maud Cuney Hare, *Norris Wright Cuney: A Tribune of the Black People*

   Mrs. Frances Joseph Gaudet, *He Leadeth Me: An Autobiography by Mrs. Frances Joseph Gaudet*

1914 Alice Moore Dunbar (Alice Moore Dunbar-Nelson), *Masterpieces of Negro Eloquence: The Best Speeches Delivered by the Negro from the Days of Slavery to the Present Time*

   Olivia Ward Bush, *Driftwood*

   Effie T. Battle, *Gleanings from Dixie Land*

1915 Bettiola Heloise Fortson, *(Mental Pearls). Original Poems and Essays*

   Maggie Pogue Johnson, *Thoughts for Idle Hours*

   Myra Viola Wilds, *Thoughts of Idle Hours*

1918 Maud Cuney Hare, *The Message of the Trees; an Anthology of Leaves and Branches*

   Georgia Douglas Johnson, *The Heart of a Woman and Other Poems*

Sarah Lee Brown Fleming, *Hope's Highway*

1919   Maggie Shaw Fullilove, *Who Was Responsible?*

Laura Eliza Wilkes, *Missing Pages in American History, Revealing the Services of Negroes in the Early Wars in the United States of America, 1641–1815*

Delilah L. Beasley, *The Negro Trail Blazers of California*

Mamie Jordan Carver, *As It Is; or, The Conditions under Which the Race Problem Challenges the White Man's Solution*

Charlotte Hawkins Brown, *"Mammy": An Appeal to the Heart of the South*

1920   Alice Moore Dunbar-Nelson, *The Dunbar Speaker and Entertainer: Containing the Best Prose and Poetic Selections by and about the Negro*

Zara Wright, *Black and White Tangled Threads*

Zara Wright, *Kenneth*

Addie W. Hunton and Kathryn M. Johnson, *Two Colored Women with the American Expeditionary Forces*

Carrie Law Morgan Figgs, *Poetic Pearls*

Angelina Weld Grimké, *Rachel: A Play in Three Acts*

Sarah Lee Brown Fleming, *Clouds and Sunshine*

1921   Elizabeth Ross Haynes, *Unsung Heroes*

Carrie Law Morgan Figgs, *Nuggets of Gold*

Mary Etta Spencer, *The Resentment*

1922   Carrie Williams Clifford, *The Widening Light*

Lillian E. Wood, *"Let My People Go"*

J. Pauline Smith, *"Exceeding Riches" and Other Verse*

Georgia Douglas Johnson, *Bronze: A Book of Verse*

1923   Carrie Law Morgan Figgs, *Select Plays: Santa Claus Land, Jepthah's Daughter, The Prince of Peace, Bachelor's Convention*

Pauline Elizabeth Hopkins

1859–1930

At the age of fifteen, Pauline Elizabeth Hopkins won a prize of ten dollars in gold for writing the best essay on the "Evils of Intemperance and Their Remedy." The contest was sponsored by the Congregational Publishing Society of Boston among the colored youth of the local schools. The award for her first writing effort was presented by William Wells Brown, first black novelist and playwright.

Born in Portland, Maine, in 1859,[1] Pauline was the daughter of Northup Hopkins, a Virginian, and Sarah Allen, of Exeter, New Hampshire. William A. Hopkins, a tailor and GAR veteran of the Civil War, became her stepfather. Her mother was a descendant of the Paul brothers, one of whom founded the historic St. Paul Baptist Church in Boston. She was also the grandniece of poet and editor James W. Whitfield. When quite young, she was brought to Boston to live and graduated from the Boston Girls High School.

She began her writing pursuits as a playwright, composing a four-act musical drama, *Peculiar Sam; or, the Underground Railroad* (1879). Later modified to three acts, it was presented as *Slaves' Escape; or the Underground Railroad* at the Oakland Garden by the Hopkins Colored Troubadours, which included Pauline, her mother, and her stepfather, with the famous Hyers Sisters by request and a chorus of over sixty people. Opening on 5 July 1880, it ran for a week before receptive audiences and received commendable reviews. The Hopkins Colored Troubadours also gave recitals and concerts featuring guitar playing by W. A. Hopkins and southern jubilee songs. Pauline was praised by the press for her "beautiful voice" and was called "Boston's favorite Colored Soprano."

Because she needed more financial stability, she studied stenography and in 1892 was hired by two affluent Republican politicians. She went on to become a stenographer for the Bureau of Statistics on the Massachusetts Census of 1895 for four years. During this time, she began to lecture on black history in churches and schools.

Pauline E. Hopkins's recognition as a fiction writer came when she was in her forties and "coincided with the appearance of the fine Negro publication, the *Colored American*, in May, 1900."[2] This monthly illustrated magazine, whose initial cover described it as being "Devoted to Literature, Science, Music, Art, Religion, Facts, Fiction and Traditions of the Negro Race," sold for fifteen cents a copy, or a dollar and a half for a year's subscription. It was the "first significant Afro-American journal to emerge in the twentieth century."[3]

The idea for the magazine came from Walter W. Wallace who, although he had no journalistic experience, envisioned a general magazine of creative and informative writing. In this endeavor, he was joined by three men who formed the Colored Co-operative Publishing Company in Boston. To sustain the company, certificates of deposit were advertised in the magazine, and Pauline E. Hopkins became a shareholder, member of the board of directors, and creditor with the publication of her novel. Her first short story, "The Mystery within Us," was published in the maiden issue of May 1900. Also at this time, it was announced that she would become editor of the Women's Department in June.

In September the Co-operative Publishing Company advertised the forthcoming October publication of her novel, *Contending Forces: A Romance Illustrative of Negro Life in the North and South*. "The book publishing venture was an outgrowth of the magazine . . . and was intended as an outlet for books about Negroes and by Negro authorship."[4] This was indeed a stroke of good fortune for Miss Hopkins to become affiliated with a company that could publish her novel. Copyrighted by her in 1899, she had traveled the women's circuit, reading portions of it to the Women's Era Club of Boston and others.

The romantic historical novel was written in the manner of earlier black nineteenth-century novels, reflecting the problems of the post-Reconstruction era. The intricate story, which begins in the South and concludes in Boston, recounts incidents the author says in her preface actually occurred. It is a tale of miscegenation, family separations caused by slavery, and chaotic love lives enmeshed in jealous intrigue. The tragic mulatto, caught between the hatred of blacks and the scorn of whites, is a prevailing theme, as in most of Miss Hopkins's fiction.

The characters give lengthy discourses on womanhood, prejudice, lynchings, and the uplifting of the race with views derived from the divergent philosophies of Booker T. Washington and W. E. B. Du Bois. The title reflects the contrasting incentives that motivate black leaders. Some are prompted by monetary and self-serving gains; others, more conscious of the race, are moved by humanitarianism. These are the "contending forces" the author perceived as "dooming" the race to "despair."

The complicated plot begins with Charles Montford and his fair-skinned wife, Grace, moving from Bermuda to North Carolina with their slaves and two sons, Charles and Jesse. A diabolical neighbor, Anson Pollock, detects the mixed blood in Grace, but still desires her. Angered by Grace's rejection of him and Montford's plan to free his slaves, Pollock has Montford killed and his slaves sold. Overcome by these events, Grace commits suicide. Charles is bought from Pollock by an English mineralogist who takes him to England. Jesse, Pollock's valet, escapes to Boston. The remainder of the story tells of Jesse's grandchildren, Cora and Will Smith, who portray a proper middle-class black family. Will, dedicated to his race, vies with John Pollock Langely, a self-serving black descendant of Anson Pollock, for the love of a beautiful mulatto, Sappho Clark.

The 402-page novel sold for one dollar and fifty cents. It was promoted by the *Colored American Magazine* as "a book that will not only appeal strongly to the race everywhere, but will have a large sale among the whites."

In May 1903, the *Colored American Magazine* changed hands, and Miss Hopkins was hired to be its literary editor. Of this appointment, she candidly wrote: "I was engaged as literary editor because I was well-known as a race writer, had gained the confidence of my people, and also because there seemed to be at that time, no one else as well qualified to fill the position, for as yet the editing of a high-class magazine was puzzling work even to our best scholars."[5] Miss Hopkins started at a salary of seven dollars a week, which was later raised another dollar after the typist was dismissed and she took over the additional duties. On this, she supported a bedridden mother.

As literary editor of "the strongest Negro organ put upon the market since the days of Frederick Douglass,"[6] she laid the "foundation for a new black journalism,"[7] for which she has not received just recognition. Aligned with a group of radical editors of protest journalism, she, along with W. E. B. Du Bois and Monroe Trotter, fought the powerful accommodationist philosophy of Booker T. Washington. A valiant editor, she "made no attempt to modify the magazine's expressions out of consideration for the white persons from whom most of the support was obtained."[8] Unyielding in her opinion that blacks should not follow a conciliatory line with regard to whites, she promoted the literature of protest by "agitating the south."

She strove to make the magazine a truly literary one, for which she hoped that "Race writers" would enter "an era of strong competition in the field of letters." Through articles on education, religion, politics, music, art, and black history, the publication sought to counter white charges of racial inferiority. Feature articles of an international scope dealt with Africa, Siam, India, Panama, and the Philippines. Well-established and emerging writers were published, such as Frances Ellen Watkins Harper, Angelina Grimké, Gertrude Mossell, Benjamin Griffith Brawley, Olivia Ward Bush, James Corrothers, and William Stanley Braithwaite.

A strong proponent of black history, which, Miss Hopkins lamented, was omitted from textbooks, she wrote a series of biographical sketches on "Famous Women of the Negro Race" and "Famous Men of the Negro Race." She was also a prolific fiction writer for the magazine, producing short stories and three serialized novels. Her first novel to appear in the *Colored American Magazine* was *Hagar's Daughter, A Story of Southern Caste Prejudice*, published in thirty-three chapters from March 1901 to March 1902. For this, she used the pseudonym of Sarah A. Allen, taken from her mother's name, Sarah Allen. Other articles and stories also bore this nom de plume. Hopkins had toyed previously with using a pen name as indicated in an early unpublished manuscript, "One Scene from the Drama of Early Days," an account of the biblical story of Daniel, which she signed Pauline E. Allen.[9]

In her fiction, Miss Hopkins continually dealt with the taboo subject of miscegenation, particularly white men married to mulattoes, and also utilized the themes of social protest and advancement of women. She acknowledged that "'Contending Forces' and my serial story 'Hagar's Daughter' . . . aroused the ire of the white South, male and female, against me."[10]

Two additional serialized novels followed, *Winona: A Tale of Negro Life in the Southwest* (May 1902–October 1902), and *Of One Blood; or, the Hidden Self*, which commenced immediately after *Winona* in November 1902 and concluded in November 1903. All were complicated stories of interracial romance. In reply to a white female reader who indignantly protested the recurring interracial themes, Miss Hopkins replied: "Marriage is made illegal between the races and yet the mulattoes increase. Thus the shadow of corruption falls on the blacks and on the whites, without whose aid the mulattoes would not exist."[11]

Pauline E. Hopkins worked hard and faithfully to make the magazine a success. She traveled throughout the country giving lectures to gain support and was one of the founders of the Colored American League in Boston, which tried to gather subscriptions and business for the publication. Under her editorship, the circulation grew to fifteen thousand. But in 1904, through poor management, the magazine became debt-ridden, and the powerful Booker T. Washington faction moved to take it over and mute its stand against Washington's views. Put up for purchase, it was bought by Washington and Fred R. Moore, an organizer and recording secretary of the National Negro Business League.

The headquarters of the *Colored American Magazine* were moved to New York, and T. Thomas Fortune became editor, while Pauline E. Hopkins was retained as assistant editor at a salary of twelve dollars a week. She accepted the offer on condition that she not be asked "to publicly renounce the rights of my people." After moving to New York, however, she discovered that she was to be "frozen out" for a nephew of Mrs. Booker T. Washington, Roscoe Conklin Simmons. By September, she was "forced to resign." The publishers masked her departure from the staff in the November 1904 issue, saying "On account of ill-health Miss Pauline Hopkins has found it necessary to sever her relations with this magazine."

Miss Hopkins's so-called ill-health did not prevent her from continuing to write. To the South's first black magazine, the *Voice of the South*, she contributed an article, "The New York Subway," in 1904 and a series on "The Dark Races of the Twentieth Century" from February to July 1905. She herself also published a thirty-one-page booklet, *A Primer of Facts Pertaining to the Early Greatness of the African Race and the Possibility of Restoration by Its Descendants—with Epilogue* (1905). Listed as Black Classics Series no. 1, she apparently intended to publish additional ones.

Once again Hopkins became an editor when the black New Era Publishing Company of Boston began *New Era* magazine in 1916. In it, she published a fiction serial, "Topsy Templeton," which purported to be about a "modern Topsy." The story tells of a little girl, daughter of a waitress in a wealthy white family, who is abandoned by her mother. Two white sisters give the child a name and place her with a respectable black family to rear into "noble womanhood." The story's purpose was to show the importance of individual effort in solving the race problem. Miss Hopkins also did biographical pieces for the magazine, which had a short publishing span.

Apparently discouraged by the lack of recognition for her efforts, she retreated from literary circles. To make a living, she went back to work as a stenographer for the Massachusetts Institute of Technology. A freak accident led to a painful death. She was suffering from neuritis, when her liniment-soaked flannel bandages caught fire from an oil stove. She died as a result of the burns on 13 August 1930.

Thus ended the life of a versatile editor, writer, novelist, playwright, and singer. Miss Hopkins had been a black leader inspired by the altruistic aspect of her "contending forces" and placing the welfare of her people above all else.

NOTES

1. The Massachusetts Department of Vital Statistics gives her age as seventy-one at the time of her death in 1930. Dorothy Porter, in the *Dictionary of American Negro Biography,* gives Hopkins's birth date as 1856.
2. Shockley, "Pauline Elizabeth Hopkins," p. 24.
3. Abby Arthur Johnson and Ronald M. Johnson, "Away from Accommodation: Radical Editors and Protest Journalism, 1900–1910," *Journal of Negro History* 62 (July 1977):325.
4. William Stanley Braithwaite, "Negro America's First Magazine," *Negro Digest* 6 (December 1947):24.
5. Hopkins to W. M. Trotter, 16 April 1905, Charles S. Johnson Papers, Fisk University Library, Nashville, Tenn., p. 1.
6. Ibid., p. 8.
7. Johnson and Johnson, "Away from Accommodation," p. 325. An insightful account of Pauline E. Hopkins's tenure as editor of the *Colored American Magazine* is presented in this article.
8. Charles S. Johnson, "The Rise of the Negro Magazine," *Journal of Negro History* 12 (January 1928):13.
9. Pauline E. Hopkins Papers, Fisk University Library, Nashville, Tenn.
10. Hopkins to Trotter, p. 6.
11. Pauline E. Hopkins, "Reply to Letter to the Editor," *Colored American Magazine* 6 (March 1903):399.

SELECTED SOURCES

Primary

Hopkins, Pauline E. *Contending Forces: A Romance Illustrative of Negro Life North and South.* Boston: Colored Co-operative Publishing Co., 1900.

———— [Sarah A. Allen]. *Hagar's Daughters, a Story of Southern Caste Prejudice. Colored American Magazine* 2 (1901–2).

————. *Of One Blood; or, The Hidden Self. Colored American Magazine* 6 (1902–3).

————. *A Primer of Facts Pertaining to the Early Greatness of the African Race and the Possibility of Restoration by Its Descendants—with Epilogue.* Cambridge: P. E. Hopkins & Co., 1905.

————. *Winona: A Tale of Negro Life in the South and Southwest. Colored American Magazine* 5 (1902–3).

Secondary

Bone, Robert A. *The Negro Novel in America.* New Haven: Yale University Press, 1958.

Gloster, Hugh M. *Negro Voices in American Fiction.* 1948. Reprint. New York: Russell & Russell, 1965.

Loggins, Vernon. *The Negro Author: His Development in America.* New York: Columbia University Press, 1931.

Porter, Dorothy B. "Pauline Elizabeth Hopkins." In *Dictionary of American Negro Biography*, edited by Rayford W. Logan and Michael R. Winston. New York: W. W. Norton & Co., 1982.

Shockley, Ann Allen. "Pauline Elizabeth Hopkins: A Biographical Excursion into Obscurity." *Phylon* 33 (Spring 1972):22–26.

Tate, Claudia. "Pauline Hopkins: Our Literary Foremother." In *Conjuring: Black Women, Fiction, and Literary Tradition*, edited by Marjorie Pryse and Hortense J. Spillers. Bloomington: Indiana University Press, 1985.

The Sewing-Circle

Where village statesmen talked with looks profound,
Imagination fondly stoops to trace
The parlor splendors of that festive place.

. . . .

Yes! let the rich deride, the proud disdain,
These simple blessings of the lowly train;
To me more dear,
One native charm than all the gloss of art.

—GOLDSMITH.

Ma Smith was a member of the church referred to in the last chapter, the most prominent one of color in New England. It was situated in the heart of the West End, and was a very valuable piece of property. Every winter this church gave many entertainments to aid in paying off the mortgage, which at this time amounted to about eight thousand dollars. Mrs. Smith, as the chairman of the board of stewardesses, was inaugurating a fair—one that should eclipse anything of a similar nature ever attempted by the colored people, and numerous sewing-circles were being held among the members all over the city. Parlor entertainments where an admission fee of ten cents was collected from every patron, were also greatly in vogue, and the money thus obtained was put into a fund to defray the expense of purchasing eatables and decorations, and paying for the printing of tickets, circulars, etc., for the fair. The strongest forces of the colored people in the vicinity were to combine and lend their aid in making a supreme effort to clear this magnificent property.

Boston contains a number of well-to-do families of color whose tax-bills show a most comfortable return each year to the city treasury.

Strange as it may seem, these well-to-do people, in goodly numbers, distribute themselves and their children among the various Episcopal churches with which the city abounds, the government of which holds out the welcome hand to the brother in black, who is drawn to unite his fortunes with the members of this particular denomination. It may be true that the beautiful ritual of the church is responsible in some measure for this. Colored people are nothing if not beauty-lovers, and for such a people the grandeur of the service has great attractions. But in justice to this church one must acknowledge that it has been instrumental in doing much toward helping this race to help itself, along the lines of brotherly interest.

These people were well represented within the precincts of Mrs. Smith's pretty parlor one afternoon, all desirous of lending their aid to help along the great project.

As we have said, Mrs. Smith occupied the back parlor of the house as her chamber, and within this room the matrons had assembled to take charge of the cutting out of different garments; and here, too, the sewing machine was placed ready for use. In the parlor proper all the young ladies were seated ready to perform any service which might be required of them in the way of putting garments together.

By two o'clock all the members of the sewing-circle were in their places. The parlor was crowded. Mrs. Willis, the brilliant widow of a bright Negro politician, had charge of the girls, and after the sewing had been given out the first business of the meeting was to go over events of interest to the Negro race which had transpired during the week throughout the country. These facts had been previously tabulated upon a blackboard which was placed upon an easel, and occupied a conspicuous position in the room. Each one was supposed to contribute anything of interest that she had read or heard in that time for the benefit of all. After these points had been gone over, Mrs. Willis gave a talk upon some topic of interest. At six o'clock tea was to be served in the kitchen, the company taking refreshment in squads of five. At eight o'clock all unfinished work would be folded and packed way in the convenient little Boston bag, to be finished at home, and the male friends of the various ladies were expected to put in an appearance. Music and recitations were to be enjoyed for two hours, ice cream and cake being sold for the benefit of the cause.

Mrs. Willis was a good example of a class of women of color that came into existence at the close of the Civil War. She was not a *rara avis,* but one of many possibilities which the future will develop from among the colored women of New England. Every city or town from Maine to New York has its Mrs. Willis. Keen in her analysis of human nature, most people realized, after a short acquaintance, in which they ran the gamut of emotions from strong attraction to repulsion, that she had sifted them thoroughly, while they had gained nothing in return. Shrewd in business matters, many a subtle business man had been worsted by her apparent womanly weakness and charming simplicity. With little money, she yet contrived to live in quiet elegance, even including the little journeys from place to place, so adroitly managed as to increase her influence at home and her fame abroad. Well-read and thoroughly conversant with all current topics, she impressed one as having been liberally educated and polished by travel, whereas a high-school course more than covered all her opportunities.

Even today it is erroneously believed that all racial development among colored people has taken place since emancipation. It is impossible of belief for some, that little circles of educated men and women of color have existed since the Revolutionary War. Some of these people were born free, some have lost the memory of servitude in the dim past; a greater number by far were recruited from the energetic slaves of the South, who toiled when they should have slept, for the money that purchased their freedom, or else they boldly took the rights which man denied. Mrs. Willis was one from among these classes. The history of her descent could not be traced, but somewhere, somehow, a strain of white blood had filtered through the African stream. At sixty odd she was vigorous, well-preserved, broad and comfortable in appearance, with an aureole of white hair crowning a pleasant face.

She had loved her husband with a love ambitious for his advancement. His foot on the stairs mounting to the two-room tenement which constituted their home in the early years of married life, had sent a thrill to her very heart as she sat sewing baby clothes for the always expected addition to the family. But twenty years make a difference in all our lives. It brought many changes to the colored people of New England—social and business changes. Politics had become the open sesame for the ambitious Negro. A seat in the Legislature then was not a dream to this man, urged by the loving woman behind him. Other offices of trust were quickly offered him when his worth became known. He grasped his opportunity; grew richer, more polished, less social, and the family broadened out and overflowed from old familiar "West End" environments across the River Charles into the aristocratic suburbs of Cambridge. Death comes to us all.

Money, the sinews of living and social standing, she did not possess upon her husband's death. Therefore she was forced to begin a weary pilgrimage—a hunt for the means to help her breast the social tide. The best opening, she decided after looking carefully about her, was in the great cause of the evolution of true womanhood in the work of the "Woman Question" as embodied in marriage and suffrage. She could talk dashingly on many themes, for which she had received much applause in by-gone days, when in private life she had held forth in the drawing-room of some Back Bay philanthropist who sought to use her talents as an attraction for a worthy charitable object, the discovery of a rare species of versatility in the Negro character being a sure drawing-card. It was her boast that she had made the fortunes of her family and settled her children well in life. The advancement of the colored woman should be the new problem in the woman question that should float her upon its tide into the prosperity she desired. And she succeeded well in her plans: conceived in selfishness, they yet bore glorious fruit in the formation of clubs of colored women banded together for charity, for study, for every reason under God's glorious heavens that can better the condition of mankind.

Trivialities are not to be despised. Inborn love implanted in a woman's heart for a luxurious, esthetic home life, running on well-oiled wheels amid flowers, sunshine, books and priceless pamphlets, easy chairs and French gowns, may be the means of developing a Paderewski or freeing a race from servitude. It was amusing to watch the way in which she governed societies and held her position. In her hands committees were as wax, and loud murmurings against the tyranny of her rule died down to judicious whispers. If a vote went contrary to her desires, it was in her absence. Thus she became the pivot about which all the social and intellectual life of the colored people of her section revolved. No one had yet been found with the temerity to contest her position, which, like a title of nobility, bade fair to descend to her children. It was thought that she might be eclipsed by the younger and more brilliant women students on the strength of their alma mater, but she still held her own by sheer force of will-power and indomitable pluck.

The subject of the talk at this meeting was: "The place which the virtuous woman occupies in upbuilding a race." After a few explanatory remarks, Mrs. Willis said:

"I am particularly anxious that you should think upon this matter seriously, because of its intrinsic value to all of us as race women. I am not less anxious because you represent the coming factors of our race. Shortly, you must fill the positions now occupied by your mothers, and it will rest with you and your children to refute the charges brought against us as to our moral irresponsibility, and the low moral standard maintained by us in comparison with other races."

"Did I understand you to say that the Negro woman in her native state is truly a virtuous woman?" asked Sappho, who had been very silent during the bustle attending the opening of the meeting.

"Travelers tell us that the native African woman is impregnable in her virtue," replied Mrs. Willis.

"So we have sacrificed that attribute in order to acquire civilization," chimed in Dora.

"No, not 'sacrificed,' but pushed one side by the force of circumstances. Let us thank God that it *is* an essential attribute peculiar to us—a racial characteristic which is slumbering but not lost," replied Mrs. Willis. "But let us not forget the definition of virtue—'Strength to do the right thing under all temptations.' Our ideas of virtue are too narrow. We confine them to that conduct which is ruled by our animal passions alone. It goes deeper than that—general excellence in every duty of life is what we may call virtue."

"Do you think, then, that Negro women will be held responsible for all the lack of virtue that is being laid to their charge today? I mean, do you think that God will hold us responsible for the *illegitimacy* with which our race has been obliged, as it were, to flood the world?" asked Sappho.

"I believe that we shall not be held responsible for wrongs which we have *unconsciously* committed, or which we have committed under *compulsion*. We are virtuous or non-virtuous only when we have a *choice* under temptation. We cannot by any means apply the word to a little child who has never been exposed to temptation, nor to the Supreme Being 'who cannot be tempted with evil.' So with the African brought to these shores against his will—the state of morality which implies will-power on his part does not exist, therefore he is not a responsible being. The sin and its punishment lies with the person *consciously* false to his *knowledge* of right. From this we deduce the truism that 'the civility of no race is perfect whilst another race is degraded.'"

"I shall never forget my feelings," chimed in Anna Stevens, a school teacher of a very studious temperament, "at certain remarks made by the Rev. John Thomas at one of his noonday lectures in the Temple. He was speaking on 'Different Races,' and had in his vigorous style been sweeping his audience with him at a high elevation of thought which was dazzling to the faculties, and almost impossible to follow in some points. Suddenly he touched upon the Negro, and with impressive gesture and lowered voice thanked God that the mulatto race was dying out, because it was a mongrel mixture which combined the worst elements of two races. Lo, the poor mulatto! despised by the blacks of his own race, scorned by the whites! Let him go out and hang himself!" In her indignation Anna forgot the scissors, and bit her thread off viciously with her little white teeth.

Mrs. Willis smiled as she said calmly: "My dear Anna, I would not worry about the fate of the mulatto, for the fate of the mulatto will be the fate of the entire race. Did you never think that today the black race on this continent has developed a race of mulattoes?"

"Why, Mrs. Willis!" came in a chorus of voices.

"Yes," continued Mrs. Willis, still smiling. "It is an incontrovertible truth that there is no such thing as an unmixed black on the American continent. Just bear in mind that we cannot tell by a person's complexion whether he be dark or light in blood, for by the working of the natural laws the white father and black mother produce the mulatto offspring; the black father and white mother the mulatto offspring also, while the *black father* and *quadroon* mother produce the black child, which to the eye alone is a child of unmixed black blood. I will venture to say that out of a hundred apparently pure black men not one will be able to trace an unmixed flow of African blood since landing upon these shores! What an unhappy example of the frailty of all human intellects, when such a man and scholar as Doctor Thomas could so far allow his prejudices to dominate his better judgment as to add one straw to the burden which is popularly supposed to rest upon the unhappy mulattoes of a despised race," finished the lady, with a dangerous flash of her large dark eyes.

"Mrs. Willis," said Dora, with a scornful little laugh, "I am not unhappy, and I am a mulatto. I just enjoy my life, and I don't want to die before my time comes, either. There are lots of good things left on earth to be enjoyed even by mulattoes, and I want my share."

"Yes, my dear; and I hope you may all live and take comfort in the proper joys of your lives. While we are all content to accept life, and enjoy it along the lines which God has laid down for us as individuals as well as a race, we shall be happy and get the best out of life. Now, let me close this talk by asking you to remember one maxim written of your race by a good man: 'Happiness and social position are not to be gained by pushing.' Let the world, by its need of us along certain lines, and our intrinsic fitness for these lines, push us into the niche which God has prepared for us. So shall our lives be beautified and our race raised in the civilization of the future as we grow away from all these prejudices which have been the instruments of our advancement according to the intention of an All-seeing Omnipotence, from the beginning. Never mind our poverty, ignorance, and the slights and injuries which we bear at the hands of a higher race. With the thought ever before us of what the Master suffered to raise all humanity to its present degree of prosperity and intelligence, let us cultivate, while we go about our daily tasks, no matter how inferior they may seem to us, beauty of the soul and mind, which being transmitted to our children by the law of heredity, shall improve the race by eliminating *immorality* from our midst and raising *morality* and virtue to their true place. Thirty-five years of liberty have made us a new people. The marks of servitude and oppression are dropping slowly from us; let us hasten the transformation of the body by the nobility of the soul."

For of the soul the body form doth take,
For soul is form and doth the body make,

quoted Dora.

"Yes," said Mrs. Willis with a smile, "that is the idea exactly, and well expressed. Now I hope that through the coming week you will think of what we have talked about this afternoon, for it is of the very first importance to all people, but particularly so to young folks."

Sappho, who had been thoughtfully embroidering pansies on white linen, now leaned back in her chair for a moment and said: "Mrs. Willis, there is one thing which puzzles me—how are we to overcome the nature which is given us? I mean how can we eliminate passion from our lives, and emerge into the purity which marked the life of Christ? So many of us desire purity and think to have found it,

301

but in a moment of passion, or under the pressure of circumstances which we cannot control, we commit some horrid sin, and the taint of it sticks and will not leave us, and we grow to loathe ourselves."

"Passion, my dear Miss Clark, is a state in which the will lies dormant, and all other desires become subservient to one. Enthusiasm for any one object or duty may become a passion. I believe that in some degree passion may be beneficial, but we must guard ourselves against a sinful growth of any appetite. All work of whatever character, as I look at it, needs a certain amount of absorbing interest to become successful, and it is here that the Christian life gains its greatest glory in teaching us how to keep ourselves from abusing any of our human attributes. We are not held responsible for compulsory sin, only for the sin that is pleasant to our thoughts and palatable to our appetites. All desires and hopes with which we are endowed are good in the sight of God, only it is left for us to discover their right uses. Do I cover your ground?"

"Yes and no," replied Sappho; "but perhaps at some future time you will be good enough to talk with me personally upon this subject."

"Dear child, sit here by me. It is a blessing to look at you. Beauty like yours is inspiring. You seem to be troubled; what is it? If I can comfort or strengthen, it is all I ask." She pressed the girl's hand in hers and drew her into a secluded corner. For a moment the floodgates of suppressed feeling flew open in the girl's heart, and she longed to lean her head on that motherly breast and unburden her sorrows there.

"Mrs. Willis, I am troubled greatly," she said at length.

"I am *so* sorry; tell me, my love, what it is all about."

Just as the barriers of Sappho's reserve seemed about to be swept away, there followed, almost instantly, a wave of repulsion toward this woman and her effusiveness, so forced and insincere. Sappho was very impressionable, and yielded readily to the influence which fell like a cold shadow between them. She drew back as from an abyss suddenly beheld stretching before her.

"On second thoughts, I think I ought to correct my remarks. It is not really *trouble*, but more a desire to confirm me in my own ideas."

"Well, if you feel you are right, dear girl, stand for the uplifting of the race and womanhood. Do not shrink from duty."

"It was simply a thought raised by your remarks on morality. I once knew a woman who had sinned. No one in the community in which she lived knew it but herself. She married a man who would have despised her had he known her story; but as it is, she is looked upon as a pattern of virtue for all women."

"And then what?" asked Mrs. Willis, with a searching glance at the fair face beside her.

"Ought she not to have told her husband before marriage? Was it not her duty to have thrown herself upon his clemency?"

"I think not," replied Mrs. Willis dryly. "See here, my dear, I am a practical woman of the world, and I think your young woman builded wiser than she knew. I am of the opinion that most men are like the lower animals in many things—they don't always know what is for their best good. If the husband had been left to himself, he probably would not have married the one woman in the world best fitted to be his wife. I think in her case she did her duty."

"Ah, that word 'duty.' What is our duty?" queried the girl, with a sad droop to the sensitive mouth. "It is so hard to know our duty. We are told that all hidden things shall be revealed. Must repented and atoned-for sin rise at last to be our curse?"

"Here is a point, dear girl. God does not look upon the constitution of sin as we do. His judgment is not ours; ours is finite, his infinite. *Your* duty is not to be morbid, thinking these thoughts that have puzzled older heads than yours. *Your* duty is, also, to be happy and bright for the good of those about you. Just blossom like the flowers, have faith and *trust*." At this point the entrance of the men made an interruption, and Mrs. Willis disappeared in a crowd of other matrons. Sappho was impressed in spite of herself, by the woman's words. She sat buried in deep thought.

There was evidently more in this woman than appeared upon the surface. With all the centuries of civilization and culture that have come to this grand old world, no man has yet been found able to trace the windings of God's inscrutable ways. There are men and women whose seeming uselessness fit perfectly into the warp and woof of Destiny's web. All things work together for good.

Priscilla Jane Thompson

1871–1942

Priscilla Jane Thompson was the first of the female poets in the family of John Henry and Clara Jane Gray Thompson to publish a book of poetry. As in the case of her older sister, Clara Ann, a birth date was never mentioned in biographical summaries, only the birthplace, Rossmoyne, Ohio.[1] The family tombstone in the old Colored American Cemetery, Cincinnati, Ohio, now the United American Cemetery, gives her birth date as 1871, and the year of her death as 1942.[2]

Priscilla attended school in Rossmoyne, and received additional private instruction. She could have taught, but instead, because of ill health, she spent her days writing, publishing, and selling her own works. She became known as an elocutionist through her public readings.

Her first book of poetry, *Ethiope Lays* (1900), was dedicated to an older brother, Garland Yancey (1865–1938), a "friend and warder" from whom she "imbibed truth" and who in her "riper years," soothed her "grief and cares away." Both Priscilla and Clara lived with Garland, father figure of their household. When poet brother Aaron Belford (1873–1929) married in 1902, he moved to Indianapolis, Indiana, and set up a print shop. He too was a self-published poet.

Priscilla mourned a "foster-mother" in her elegy "To a Deceased Friend," which is included in *Ethiope Lays* and *Gleanings of Quiet Hours*

(1907). The friend, identified in the second book as Mrs. Polly Dixon, was asked by the poet's dying mother to "ever guard her orphan brood." The surrogate mother did not live long enough to wear the mantle, for she too died when Priscilla was young.

As stated by the author, the purpose of her now-rare *Ethiope Lays* was "to picture the real side of my race . . . their patience, fortitude and forbearance." The book contains narrative poems of slavery and freedom—"Freedom at McNealy's," "My Father's Story," and "The Old Freedman"—and one poem about lynching, "A Southern Scene." Additional verses concern nature, religion, and death.

In the context of today, some might single out two of her romantic poems as woman-identified. Her four-stanza "Alberta" is a love-sick youthful song to a "lovely little dame." Here, the author pleads:

> Thou surely know I loveth thee,
>   For when I'd show my feeling,
>   Thou seemst in modesty to thwart,
> The flow of love words from my heart,
> By chaff and laughter pealing;
>   Oh, show thy own true self to me!
>   And let me show my love to thee,
>   Do shy Alberta.[3]

Others, however, might see it as a poem written by a female imagining a male in love with a maid. The same impassioned verse is repeated in "Evelyn," where Priscilla writes:

> Evelyn, sweet Evelyn,
>   List to my lay;
> Forsooth you have made me to sing;
>   Your sweet midnight eyes, and your smiles, fair dove,
> Have prompted my heart-chords to ring.[4]

Those who would wish to place them in the safe realm of non-woman-identified poems might cite the lines in the last verse of "Alberta" where the "hand" of Alberta is sought, which in those days would have been unthinkable for a female, and in "Evelyn," where at the end, the poet asks her to "favor my suit." The suit could refer, for some, to male clothing, and for others, to courtship—which might simply reflect the paradoxes of a poet's point of view.

Priscilla, as a poet, was overshadowed by Clara and Aaron Belford, but as a proponent of the strength and beauty of blackness, she was outstanding.

Her "Address to Ethiopia" is an early twentieth-century black woman's rallying cry to her race:

> Oh rise in union great and strong!
>   Hold each black brother dear;
> And form a nation of thine own,
>   Despite thy tyrant's jeers!
>
> We need not reek in blood and groans,
>   This is a war within;
> We need but conquer cow'ring self,
>   And rise a man with men.[5]

Just as Priscilla Thompson envisioned black strength in unity, she also glorified the beauty and majesty of black women long before the Harlem Renaissance poets. In "The Muse's Favor," she acutely observes, "Naught of thy due in verse to see."

Her *Gleanings of Quiet Hours* repeats several of the poems in *Ethiope Lays*, although not "Alberta" and "Evelyn." There is more humor in this volume, particularly in her dialect poems, "A Domestic Storm" and "An Afternoon Gossip."

Unlike Clara Ann, neither Priscilla nor Aaron Belford are included in *An Anthology of Verse by American Negroes*; nevertheless, they are mentioned in the book's "Biographical and Critical Notes," more than likely to show contrasts in their works. Professor White, one of the editors, takes strong exception to Priscilla's race poems in *Ethiope Lays*, maintaining that the volume is filled with a keen, crude, indiscriminate sense of race. The white critic further charges: "She exhorts the Negroes to rise against oppression and patronage."[6]

For a southern white professor to read such militant poems by a black woman, whose parents were but a short step out of slavery, was probably a difficult experience. He continued to attack her poetry for having "a sullen uncomprehending, illiterate hatred" of race. Now, Priscilla was not college educated, but she was certainly not illiterate. She wrote out of her own limited experiences and her imagination; she was a black woman surviving in racist times. Little wonder she had to publish her own books. Professor White was a little kinder in his assessment of *Gleaning of Quiet Hours*, noting the "new poems showed considerable improvement; still there are occasional raw crudities of the same fundamental lack of education."[7]

Priscilla, like Clara Ann, did not marry. Her "Knight of My Maiden Love" poem, whether fantasy or reality, speaks of one, "stalwart and manly," whom she secretly admires. But she does not confess her feelings to him because "maidens must modest be."[8]

The poet's ill health prevented her from working. Tuberculosis was common among blacks during that time: her "The Consumptive" could have described her own or another's battle with the disease. In it, she writes of the mental anguish of a tubercular who travels to consult various physicians for a cure. The poem is a protest against disease and death at a young age:

I am dying of consumption;
 Oh my God can this be true?
I, so fresh, so young, so hopeful,
 Pass away like morning dew?[9]

Nevertheless, she lived to the age of seventy-one, passing on before her sister, Clara Ann. Her poems are "gleanings" from the life of a small-town black woman poet who was ahead of her time, who envisioned and wrote of black women's splendor and the strength of her race.

NOTES

1. Dabney's *Cincinnati's Colored Citizens*, p. 319, and Yenser's *Who's Who in Colored America, 1938–1939–1940*, p. 365.
2. The family tombstone was located for me by Connie Harris, a librarian at the Cincinnati Public Library for birth and death dates.
3. Thompson, *Ethiope Lays*, p. 17.
4. Ibid., p. 39.
5. Ibid., p. 94.
6. White and Jackson, *Anthology of Verse*, p. 233.
7. Ibid.
8. Thompson, *Ethiope Lays*, p. 26.
9. Ibid., p. 90.

SELECTED SOURCES

Primary

Thompson, Priscilla Jane. *Ethiope Lays*. Rossmoyne, Ohio: Published by the author, 1900.
———. *Gleanings of Quiet Hours*. Rossmoyne, Ohio: Published by the author, 1907.

Secondary

Coyle, William. *Ohio Authors and Their Books; Biographical Data and Selective Bibliographies for Ohio Authors, Native and Resident, 1796–1950*. Cleveland, Ohio: World Publishing Co., 1962.

Dabney, Wendell P. *Cincinnati's Colored Citizens, Historical, Sociological and Biographical*. Cincinnati, Ohio: Dabney Publishing Co., 1926.

Sherman, Joan R. *Invisible Poets: Afro-Americans of the Nineteenth Century*. Urbana: University of Illinois Press, 1974.

White, Newman Ivey, and Jackson, Walter Clinton. *An Anthology of Verse by American Negroes*. Durham, N.C.: Trinity College Press, 1924.

Who's Who in Colored America; A Biographical Dictionary of Notable Living Persons of African Descent in America, 1938–1939–1940. 5th ed. Brooklyn, N.Y.: Who's Who in Colored America, 1940.

The Muse's Favor

Oh Muse! I crave a favor,
   Grant but this one unto me:
Thou hast always been indulgent—
   So I boldly come to thee.

For oft I list thy singing—
   And the accents, sweet and clear,
Like the rhythmic flow of waters,
   Fall on my ecstatic ear.

But of Caucasia's daughters,
   So oft I've heard thy lay,
That the music, too familiar—
   Falls in sheer monotony.

And now, oh Muse exalted!
   Exchange this old song staid,
For an equally deserving—
   The oft slighted, Afric maids.

The Muse, with smiles consenting,
   Runs her hand the strings along,
And the harp, as bound by duty—
Rings out with the tardy song.

The Song

Oh, foully slighted Ethiope maid!
With patience, bearing rude upbraid,

With sweet, refined, retiring, grace,
And sunshine ling'ring in thy face,
With eyes bedewed and pityingly
   I sing of thee, I sing of thee.

Thy dark and misty curly hair,
In small, neat, braids entwineth fair,
Like clusters of rich, shining, jet,
All wrapt in mist, when sun is set;
Fair maid, I gaze admiringly,
   And sing of thee, and sing of thee.

Thy smooth and silky, dusky skin,
Thine eyes of sloe, thy dimple chin,
That pure and simple heart of thine,
'Tis these that make thee half divine;
Oh maid! I gaze admiringly,
   And sing of thee, and sing of thee.

Oh modest maid, with beauty rare,
Whoe'er hath praised thy lithe form, fair?
Thy tender mien, thy fairy tread—
Thy winsome face and queenly head?
Naught of thy due in verse I see,
   All pityingly I sing of thee.

Who've dared to laud thee 'fore the world,
And face the stigma of a churl?
Or brook the fiery, deep, disdain—
Their portion, who defend thy name?
Oh maiden, wronged so cowardly,
   I boldly, loudly, sing of thee.

Who've stood the test of chastity,
Through slav'ry's blasting tyranny,
And kept the while, their virtuous grace,
To instill in a trampled race?
Fair maid, thy equal few may see;
   Thrice honored I, to sing of thee.

Let cowards fear thy name to praise,
Let scoffers seek thee but to raze;
Despite their foul, ignoble, jeers,

A worthy model thou appear,
Enrobed in love and purity;
   Oh who dare blush, to sing of thee?

And now, oh maid, forgive I pray.
The tardiness of my poor lay;
The weight of wrongs unto thee done—
Did paralyze my falt'ring tongue,
'Twas my mute, innate, sympathy—
   That staid this song, I sing to thee.

Knight of My Maiden Love

Knight of my maiden love,
   Stalwart and manly—
Ever my yearning heart searcheth for thee;
   Searcheth the busy crowd;
   Hearken its babble loud;
Yearning in secret, thy dear face to see.

Knight of my maiden love,
   Stalwart and manly—
Tender thy words were, and tender thy mien;
   Deep in my loving heart,
   Thee, hath I set apart—
Prince of my fancy, and lord of my dream.

Knight of my maiden love,
   Stalwart and manly—
Calm and composed in thy presence I seem;
   This is my sex decree—
   Maidens must modest be;
And manly courage hath made thee my dream.

Knight of my maiden love,
   Stalwart and manly—

'Tis not thy noble form, I love the best;
   Nay, 'tis thy tenderness,
   Tempered with manliness,
Forming a noble heart, deep in thy breast.

Susie Baker King Taylor
Susie King Taylor

1848–1912

In writing of her life, Susie Baker King Taylor left a small treasure to Afro-American women's writings: her *Reminiscences of My Life in Camp with the 33d United States Colored Troops Late 1st S.C. Volunteers* (1902). The autobiography stands out as an account of a black woman laundress who assumed an unofficial role as nurse and teacher to the first regular army of freed blacks during the Civil War.

She dedicated her book to Col. Thomas Wentworth Higginson, who also had written about his experiences with the soldiers as commander in his *Army Life in a Black Regiment* (1870). A longtime supporter of women's rights, Higginson perceptively capsuled the book's "peculiar interest" in his introduction, when he noted: "Actual military life is rarely described by a woman, and this is especially true of a woman whose place was in the ranks, as the wife of a soldier and herself a regimental laundress. No such description has ever been given, I am sure, by one thus connected with a colored regiment . . . delineated from the woman's point of view."[1]

The personal narrative also links the author's life as a nineteenth-century black woman to the beginning of the twentieth century. It shows that even until the latter part of her life, Susie was involved in devoting her energies to her race.

Like other black women of the turbulent nineteenth century, her life was formed by the historical events that brought on the Civil War. She was one of those who are commonly referred to as being at the right place at the right time.

Her parents, Raymond and Hagar Ann Reed Baker, were slaves on the Grest Farm, Liberty County, about thirty-five miles from Savannah, Georgia. Born on 6 August 1848, she was the first of nine children, of whom three died in infancy. When Susie was around seven years old, she was allowed to go to Savannah to live with her grandmother, Dolly Reed. Wanting her grandchildren to have what she had not had, Mrs. Reed sent Susie and her brother to the house of a freed widow, Mrs. Woodhouse, to learn to read and write. Because the teacher operated a clandestine school for blacks in her kitchen, the children had to wrap their books in paper to prevent whites from realizing what was taking place.

Susie studied under Mrs. Woodhouse for two years or more and then went to another teacher, Mrs. Mary Beasley. By May 1860, Mrs. Beasley had taught her all she knew and dismissed her. Determined to learn more, Susie had a white playmate, Kate O'Connor, give her lessons, but these instructions ended after four months when Kate entered a convent. Luck was with Susie, however, for James Blouis, their landlord's high school son, had taken a liking to Susie's grandmother and agreed to continue the studies. The schooling was interrupted when Blouis was ordered to the front in the middle of 1861 with the Savannah Volunteer Guards.

When Union forces advanced on Fort Pulaski, 1 April 1862, Susie was sent to the country to live with her mother. After the fort was captured, she joined her uncle and his family who sailed to St. Catherine Island, where they landed under the protection of the Union fleet. She remained there for two weeks, until thirty of them were transported by gunboat to St. Simon's Island, where she saw the "Yankee" for the first time. While on the boat, the captain discovered that she could read and write. This information was passed on, and Susie was asked to take charge of a school for children. Herself only fourteen years old, the dark-skinned, slender youth, friendly to all, became the schoolmistress of forty children and a few adults.

It was on the island that she met and married Sergeant Edward King, a literate noncommissioned officer in the First South Carolina Volunteers, Company E, which became the Thirty-third United States Colored Infantry. Along with her husband, she had a number of relatives in Company E.

The couple was uprooted when Capt. C. T. Trowbridge came to the island in August 1862 to enlist men for his regiment. By October, orders had been given to evacuate, and Susie enrolled in the army as a laundress to follow her husband to Camp Saxton, Beaufort, South Carolina.

Because she could read and write, her job as laundress receded to the background, for she was always being called upon for other services. She took charge of Company E's mail, reading letters and writing them for illiterate soldiers. When time allowed, she and her husband gave many the lessons they craved.

In February 1863, smallpox broke out in camp, and Susie, who had been vaccinated, helped with the sick. She kept her "blood purged" by constantly drinking sassafras tea. Because she was sensitive to suffering and willing to sacrifice for the welfare of the soldiers, her volunteer services as a nurse did much to aid the overburdened medics. She wrote that she was glad to be permitted to go with the regiment and care for the sick and afflicted comrades.

While at Camp Shaw, she visited the hospital in Beaufort, where she met Clara Barton, war nurse and guiding founder of the Red Cross. Susie sometimes accompanied Miss Barton when she made her hospital rounds and was impressed by her "devotion and care of those men."

At one time, she was one of only two women with the regiment, the other being the quartermaster's wife. Susie learned to handle a musket and shoot accurately. She bragged that she could take a gun apart and put it together again.

Devoted to the army of ex-slaves whose assignment was to blockade the southern coast, she went on skirmishes with them, and accompanied them when they set out to capture Jacksonville, Florida, on 10 March 1863. Writing about the sickening spectacle of the battle, she noted the "gruesome sight" of "fleshless heads and grinning jaws," and of "limbs blown off." For the injured, she tried to relieve them by binding up their wounds and giving them water. To ring a change on their hospital diet of dry meat, dip toast, and tea without milk, she made custard out of turtle eggs and condensed milk.

On 9 February 1866, word was received to muster out the regiment. In Colonel Trowbridge's General Orders, he praised the "valor" and "heroism" of the First South Carolina Volunteers, "the first black regiment that ever bore arms in defense of freedom on the continent of America."[2] He commended the men who had served "for long and weary months, without pay or even the privilege of being recognized as soldiers,"[3] noting that the "little band" had grown into an army of 140,000 black soldiers.

Susie, whose services also came to an end now, had benefited her country for four years and three months without pay or official recognition. Her reward was satisfaction in doing for others. But as would be expected, her experiences left bitter memories, and she wrote: "I can and shall never forget that terrible war until my eyes close in death."[4]

Susie and her husband returned to Savannah where she opened a school on Oglethorpe Street. She had twenty pupils whom she charged a dollar a month, and she taught them until the Beach Institute offered free schooling.

Adding to her problems, her husband died 16 September 1866, while she was awaiting the birth of her son. A year later, she started another school in Liberty County, Georgia, operating it for twelve months. But country life did not agree with her, and she returned to Savannah to open a night school for adults. This ended in 1868 when the Beach Institute founded a similar school without charge to its students.

Susie put in a claim in 1872 for her husband's bounty, which amounted to one hundred dollars, and to support herself, she found employment as a laundress with a family who went north. Finding living there better than in the South, she decided to make her home in Boston. There she entered domestic service, subsequently marrying Russell L. Taylor in 1879.

When she became a housewife, she found time to promote her interest in "the boys in blue," both black and white. In 1886, she helped organize Corps 67 of the Women's Relief Corps, an auxiliary to the Grand Army of the Republic. For this, she acted as guard, secretary, and treasurer for three years and then president in 1893.

The tumultuous racial strife that emerged after the war caused her to question whether the loss of lives had been worthwhile. Her remarkable chapter, "Thoughts on Present Conditions," expressed the concern of a black woman who had served her country, but now wondered if it had been in vain. She weighed the benefits of a war for freedom against the injustices and inequities now blighting the South.

A harsh confrontation with racism occurred on 3 February 1898, when she had to go to help her son in Shreveport, Louisiana. Traveling with Nickens and Company as an actor in *The Lion's Bride*, he had become seriously ill. En route to his bedside, Susie had her first encounter with segregation when she was told to ride in the car for colored people. Finding her son recovering from a hemorrhage, she tried to secure a sleeper to take him home for proper medical attention, since he could not sit up. But unable to travel in one because of her color, she was forced to stay with him until he died.

On 11 October 1901, her second husband died. And it was in October of 1912 that Susie's own life ended. Fortunately, for us, she had been persuaded to write of herself. By doing so, she avoided, unlike so many black women, becoming lost to history.

NOTES

1. Taylor, *Army Life*, p. xi.
2. Ibid., p. 47.
3. Ibid.
4. Ibid., p. 50.

SELECTED SOURCES

Primary

Taylor, Susie King. *Reminiscences of My Life with the 33d United States Colored Troops Late 1st S.C. Volunteers*. Boston, 1902.

Secondary

Dannett, Sylvia F. L. *Profiles of Negro Womanhood*. Vol. 1, *1619–1900*. Yonkers, N.Y.: Educational Heritage, 1964.
Katz, William Loren. *Eyewitness: The Negro in American History*. New York: Pitman Publishing Co., 1967.
Loewenberg, Bert James, and Bogin, Ruth. *Black Women in Nineteenth-Century American Life: Their Words, Their Thoughts, Their Feelings*. University Park: Pennsylvania State University Press, 1976.
McPherson, James M. *The Negro's Civil War: How American Negroes Felt and Acted during the War of the Union*. New York: Vintage Books, 1965.
Quarles, Benjamin. *The Negro in the Civil War*. Boston: Little, Brown, 1953.

On Morris and Other Islands

About the first of June, 1864, the regiment was ordered to Folly Island, staying there until the latter part of the month, when it was ordered to Morris Island. We landed on Morris Island between June and July, 1864. This island was a narrow strip of sandy soil, nothing growing on it but a few bushes and shrubs. The camp was one mile from the boat landing, called Pawnell Landing, and the landing one mile from Fort Wagner.

Colonel Higginson had left us in May of this year, on account of wounds received at Edisto. All the men were sorry to lose him. They did not want him to go, they loved him so. He was kind and devoted to his men, thoughtful for their comfort, and we missed his genial presence from the camp.

The regiment under Colonel Trowbridge did garrison duty, but they had troublesome times from Fort Gregg, on James Island, for the rebels would throw a shell over on our island every now and then. Finally orders were received for the boys to prepare to take Fort Gregg, each man to take 150 rounds of cartridges, canteens of water, hard-tack, and salt beef. This order was sent three days prior to starting, to allow them to be in readiness. I helped as many as I could to pack haversacks and cartridge boxes.

The fourth day, about five o'clock in the afternoon, the call was sounded, and I heard the first sergeant say, "Fall in, boys, fall in," and they were not long obeying the command. Each company marched out of its street, in front of their colonel's headquarters, where they rested for half an hour, as it was not dark enough, and they did not want the enemy to have a chance to spy their movements. At the end of this time the line was formed with the 103d New York (white) in the rear, and off they started, eager to get to work. It was quite dark by the time they reached Pawnell Landing. I have never forgotten the good-bys of that day, as they left camp. Colonel Trowbridge said to me as he left, "Good-by, Mrs. King, take care of yourself if you don't see us again." I went with them as far as the landing, and watched them until they got out of sight, and then I returned to the camp. There was no one at camp but those left on picket and a few disabled soldiers, and one woman, a friend of mine, Mary Shaw, and it was lonesome and sad, now that the boys were gone, some never to return.

Mary Shaw shared my tent that night, and we went to bed, but not to sleep, for the fleas nearly ate us alive. We caught a few, but it did seem, now that the men were gone, that every flea in camp had located my tent, and caused us to vacate. Sleep being out of the question, we sat up the remainder of the night.

About four o'clock, July 2, the charge was made. The firing could be plainly heard in camp. I hastened down to the landing and remained there until eight o'clock that morning. When the wounded arrived, or rather began to arrive, the first one brought in was Samuel Anderson of our company. He was badly wounded. Then others of our boys, some with their legs off, arm gone, foot off, and wounds of all kinds imaginable. They had to wade through creeks and marshes, as they were discovered by the enemy and shelled very badly. A number of the men were lost, some got fastened in the mud and had to cut off the legs of their pants, to free themselves. The 103d New York suffered the most, as their men were very badly wounded.

My work now began. I gave my assistance to try to alleviate their sufferings. I asked the doctor at the hospital what I could get for them to eat. They wanted soup, but that I could not get; but I had a few cans of condensed milk and some turtle eggs, so I thought I would try to make some custard. I had doubts as to my success, for cooking with turtle eggs was something new to me, but the adage has it, "Nothing ventured, nothing done," so I made a venture and the result was a very delicious custard. This I carried to the men, who enjoyed it very much. My services were given at all times for the comfort of these men. I was on hand to assist whenever needed. I was enrolled as company laundress, but I did very little of it, because I was always busy doing other things through camp, and was employed all the time doing something for the officers and comrades.

Thoughts on Present Conditions

Living here in Boston where the black man is given equal justice, I must say a word on the general treatment of my race, both in the North and South, in this twentieth century. I wonder if our white fellow men realize the true sense or meaning of brotherhood? For two hundred years we had toiled for them; the war of 1861 came and was ended, and we thought our race was forever freed from bondage, and that the two races could live in unity with each other, but when we read almost every day of what is being done to my race by some whites in the South, I sometimes ask, "Was the war in vain? Has it brought freedom, in the full sense of the word, or has it not made our condition more hopeless?"

In this "land of the free" we are burned, tortured, and denied a fair trial, murdered for any imaginary wrong conceived in the brain of the negro-hating white man. There is no redress for us from a government which promised to protect all under its flag. It seems a mystery to me. They say, "One flag, one nation, one country indivisible." Is this true? Can we say this truthfully, when one race is allowed to burn, hang, and inflict the most horrible torture weekly, monthly, on another? No, we cannot sing, "My country, 'tis of thee, Sweet land of Liberty"! It is hollow mockery. The Southland laws are all on the side of the white, and they do just as they like to the negro, whether in the right or not.

I do not uphold my race when they do wrong. They ought to be punished, but the innocent are made to suffer as well as the guilty, and I hope the time will hasten when it will be stopped forever. Let us remember God says, "He that sheds blood, his blood shall be required again." I may not live to see it, but the time is approaching when the South will again have cause to repent for the blood it has shed of innocent black men, for their blood cries out for vengeance. For the South still cherishes a hatred toward the blacks, although there are some true Southern gentlemen left who abhor the stigma brought upon them, and feel it very keenly, and I hope the day is not far distant when the two races will reside in peace in the Southland, and we will sing with sincere and truthful hearts, "My country, 'tis of thee, Sweet land of Liberty, of thee I sing."

Clara Ann Thompson

1869–1949

In the foreword to her second book of verse, *A Garland of Poems* (1926), Clara Ann Thompson expressed her unrealized desire to be a novelist instead of a poet. Here she declared: "I have always loved poetry, still my wish has been, to be not a poet, but a novelist. But it seems that the Muse had other plans for me and I have always found myself giving expression to my thoughts in verse."[1]

The call of the muse was strong in the Thompson family. Clara Ann had a sister, Priscilla Jane (discussed earlier), and a brother, Aaron Belford, who were poets also. Aaron, unable to find a publisher for his works, bought a printing press and brought out his own books. James Whitcomb Riley wrote an introduction to the second edition of his *Echoes of Spring* (1907), which gained him some recognition. The three poets were the children of John Henry and Clara Jane Gray Thompson, former Virginia slaves, who lived in Rossmoyne, Ohio, near Cincinnati.

Biographical sketches do not provide a birth date for Clara Ann.[2] But her obituary in the *Cincinnati Enquirer* stated that she was eighty years old at her death in 1949, which would place her birth in 1869.[3]

Clara lived almost all of her life in Rossmoyne with Priscilla and an older brother, Garland Yancey. *A Garland of Poems* was dedicated to her brother "In Recognition of his unfailing kindness and affection." There was another brother who died young, as indicated in a poem "To My Dead Brother," which began *Songs from the Wayside* (1908).

Clara Ann was educated in the public schools of Rossmoyne and received private tutorage. She taught school away from Rossmoyne for a year and then returned to devote the rest of her life to writing poetry and giving readings from her books. She became known as a "fine elocutionist."

The poet's first book, *Songs from the Wayside*, was published by herself. According to white critic Newman Ivey White, the collection of thirty-seven poems was of "better quality than those of her brother and sister"; however, he denounced her breadth of view, her intensity, and her lack of imagination and culture.[4] The critic, viewing her through the eyes of a white man, obviously did not take into consideration Miss Thompson's race, background limitations, or motivation.

Clara Ann's poems concerned religion, hope, family, nature, and death. Her poems in dialect—"Uncle Rube's Defense," "Uncle Rube on the Race Problem," and "Uncle Rube to the Young People"—give folksy handed-down advice on race issues. A feeling of race pride is strong in them. Her frequently anthologized poem, "Mrs. Johnson Objects" conveys an insightful half-humorous message about blacks who place themselves above poor whites.

In 1921, she published a single poem in book form, "What Means This Bleating of the Sheep," which was later included in *A Garland of Poems*. Her race poems in her last book attempted to strike a common denominator about what she termed "both sides of the subject," white and black.

Clara Ann remained single, although her hand in marriage was probably sought. Her poem "If Thou Shouldst Return" speaks of a spurned lover about whom she has second thoughts: "If thou shouldst return to claim me thy bride, / How gladly thy fate would I share."

In her later years, Clara Ann lived with a niece in Cincinnati. There she taught catechism at the St. Andrew Episcopal Church. When she died, she was the last of the trio of family poets. She rests in an unmarked grave in the United American Cemetery.

NOTES

1. Thompson, *A Garland of Poems*, p. 9.
2. Coyle, in *Ohio Authors*, mistakenly gives her birth date as around 1875, and Sherman, in *Invisible Poets*, estimates it as 1887.
3. *Cincinnati Enquirer*, 20 March 1949. The death age of eighty is also in the records of the Colored American Cemetery statistics given to me by the Union Baptist Church, Cincinnati, Ohio.
4. White and Jackson, *Anthology of Verse*, p. 233.

SELECTED SOURCES

Primary

Thompson, Clara Ann. *A Garland of Poems*. Boston: Christopher Publishing House, 1926.
———. *Songs from the Wayside*. Rossmoyne, Ohio: Published by the author, 1908.

Secondary

Coyle, William. *Ohio Authors and Their Books; Biographical Data and Selective Bibliographies for Ohio Authors, Native and Resident, 1796–1950*. Cleveland, Ohio: World Publishing Co., 1962.
Dabney, Wendell P. *Cincinnati's Colored Citizens; Historical, Sociological and Biographical*. Cincinnati, Ohio: Dabney Publishing Co., 1926.
Sherman, Joan R. *Invisible Poets: Afro-Americans of the Nineteenth Century*. Urbana: University of Illinois Press, 1974.
Stetson, Erlene. *Black Sister: Poetry by Black American Women, 1746–1980*. Bloomington: Indiana University Press, 1981.
White, Newman Ivey, and Jackson, Walter Clinton. *An Anthology of Verse by American Negroes*. Durham, N.C.; Trinity College Press, 1924.
Who's Who in Colored America; A Biographical Dictionary of Notable Living Persons of African Descent in America, 1938–1939–1940. 5th ed. Brooklyn, N.Y.: Who's Who in Colored America, 1940.

Uncle Rube on the Race Problem

"How'd I solve de Negro Problum?"
   Gentlemen, don't like dat wo'd!
'Mind me too much uv ol' slave times,
   When de white man wus de lo'd.

Spoutin' roun' about "My niggahs,"
   Knockin' us fum lef' to right,
Sellin' us, like we wus cattle,
   Drivin' us fum mawn till night,—

Oh, you say I'm off de subjec';
   Am a little off, I see,—
Well, de way to solve de problum,
   Is, to let de black man be.

Say, "you fail to ketch my meanin'?"
   Now, dat's very plain to me,
Don't you know, you whites is pickin'
   On de blacks, continu'ly?

Jes' pick up de mawnin' papah,
   Anywhaur you choose to go,
When you read about de black man,
   You may bet it's somepin low.

It's all right to tell his meanness,
   Dat's, pervided it is true;
But, why, in de name uv blazes,
   Don't you tell de good things too!

No, I ain't a-cussin' either!
   Et my blood was young an' waum,
Guess I'd sometimes, feel like cussin',
   How you whites is takin' on,

Still, I don't hol' wid dat business,
   Leave dat, fah you whites to do—
Cussin' an' a-suicidin',
   When de whole land b'longs to you.

Den, agin, ez I wus sayin',—
   Ef a black man makes a mawk,
Seems you white-folks will go crazy,
   Try'n' to keep him in de dawk.

An', ef he don't watch his cornahs,
   An' his head ain't mighty soun',
Fust he knows: some uv you white-folks
   Done reached up, an' pulled him down.

Whut you say? I'm too hawd on you?
   Whut you 'spected me to do,
When you axed me, my opinion?
   Tell you somepin' wusn't true?

Co'se dah's some exceptions 'mong you,
   An' I ain't denyin' it;
But dah's might few, I tell you,
   Dat kin say: "Dis shoe don't fit."

Yes, you say some blacks is "on'ry";
 So is many uv de whites;
But de black race mus' be perfec',
 'Fo we git ou' "equal rights."

Foreign whites, fum ev'ry nation,
 Finds a welcome in dis lan',
Yet, dah seems to be no welcome
 Fah de native cullud man.

You don't have to "tote his skillet,"—
 Ez de folks in Dixie say,—
Only, when you see him strugglin',
 Don't you git into his way.

Co'se, ef you is got a mind to,
 You kin lend a helpin' han',
But de best help you kin give him,
 Is, to treat him like a man.

Look at all de great improvement,
 He has made since he wus free;
Yet, de white-folks keep a-wond'ring,
 Whut's his future go'n' to be.

All time talkin' 'bout his meanness,
 An' de many things he lack,
Makin' out dey see no progress,
 Doe dey're try'n' to hol' him back.

Oh, it ain't no use in talkin',
 Ef you whites would jest play faiah,
All de wranglin' 'bout dis problum,
 Soon would vanish in de aiah.

Once dey couldn't find no method,
 Dat would put down slavery,
Till it like to split de country,
 Den, dey set de black man free.

Dat's de way wid dis race problum:
 Ef de white-folks had a min',
Dey could fin' a answer to it,
 Like dey did de other time.

Co'se, dah's two sides to dis problum,
    An dah's things de blacks should do,
But I'm talkin' 'bout you white-folks,
    And de pawt dat b'longs to you.

"Don't know whaur to place de black man?"
    He will fin' his place;—You'll see!
Like de foreign whites is doin'
    When you learn to let him be.

"Den, you feah amalgamation?"
    When de black man takes his stan',
Don't you know he'll squar' his shoulders,
    Proud, dat he's a Af'ican?

In dis lan', to be a black man,
    Isn't called a lucky thing;
An' dat's why some fools among us,
    Think it smawt to mingle in.

An' you white-folks isn't blameless,
    Some uv you is in dat too,—
Takin' ev'ry mean advantage,
    Dat is in yo' powah to do.

But, de race will reach a station,
    Whaur de blindes' one kin see,
Dat 'tis good to be a black man,
    Jest ez sho', ez sho' kin be.

Den, agin, sometimes I'm thinkin',
    Dat dis 'malgamation fright's
Jes' got up by you smawt white-folks,
    Keep fum givin' us ou' rights.

Fah, ef now; in all her trials,
    Mos' uv us stick to de race,
You know well, we won't fahsake her,
    When she gits a honored place.

"Be a nation in a nation?"
    Now you're talkin' like a fool!
Whut you mean by "'Plur'bus unyun?—"
    Many nations 'neath one rule.

Not go'n' back on dat ol' motto,
    Dat has made yo' country's name,
Jest because de race you brung here,
    Ax you fah a little claim?

Well, I 'spec' I mus' be goin',
    Gittin' kinder late, I see;
Guess nex' time "Ol' Rube" is passin',
    Gentlemen, you'll let him be.

Oh, you say, "you bah no malice,"
    Well, Id ruther have it so,
But I'll hol' up fah my people,
    Whethah folks like it or no.

Henrietta Cordelia Ray
H. Cordelia Ray ✒

1849?/1850?/1852?–1916

Henrietta Cordelia Ray was a nineteenth-century poet whose literary output continued into the early part of the twentieth century, peaking when her major collection of verse, *Poems* (1910), was published.

H. Cordelia Ray, as she signed her name, was born into a well-to-do family whose roots extended to the Indian and English bloodlines of the first blacks of Cape Cod, New England. Her father, Reverend Charles B. Ray, a Congregationalist minister, was an Abolitionist, editor of the *Colored American*, and black leader. Cordelia was the daughter of Reverend Ray's second marriage to Charlotte Augusta Burrough.

The year of the poet's birth in New York varies among the sources. Hallie Q. Brown's *Homespun Heroines* places it as 1849; Joan R. Sherman's *Invisible Poets* tentatively gives it as 1852; and William H. Robinson, Jr., in his *Early Black American Poets*, points to 1850. The Ray family consisted of two boys and five girls; two of the girls died before reaching adulthood.

Cordelia was very close to her oldest sister, Florence. Together they published a seventy-nine-page biography of their father, *Sketch of the Life of Rev. Charles B. Ray* (1887). A memorial poem by Cordelia to him introduced the memoir.

Another sister, Charlotte E. Ray, was the first black woman to receive a law degree in this country when she graduated from Howard University in

1872. She was admitted to the bar of the District of Columbia and became Washington's first black woman lawyer.

Cordelia, like her sisters, was "well-born, well-bred and enjoyed all the advantages accruing to her position in a family where birth, breeding and culture were regarded as important assets."[1] She was the muse of the family, the dreamer, and the recluse. Both she and the more outgoing Florence received pedagogy degrees from the University of the City of New York in 1891. Cordelia also finished the Sauveneur School of Languages and was reputed to have been fluent in French, Greek, Latin, and German.

Wanting to emulate Florence, she became a schoolteacher, serving in the girls' department of Colored Grammar School No. 1, in 1868. During the 1890s, she transferred to No. 80 where Florence taught and poet Charles L. Reason was principal. But the routine of teaching was dull and stifling to Cordelia's creative impulses. She preferred writing and traveling to the confines of the classroom. When she retired through length of service, she conducted private lessons in music, mathematics, and languages, and taught English literature to teachers. "Happy with her friends, her books, her writings, her charities, she lived a simple, blameless life."[2]

Cordelia was the epitome of the gentlewoman whom nineteenth- and some early twentieth-century black women writers characterized as untouched by the worldly. She was defined as modest, quiet, kind, affable, reserved, and brainy. Neither she nor Florence married, instead living together on Woodside, Long Island. When Florence died, Cordelia dedicated a poem to her entitled "Heart-Sister."

H. Cordelia Ray gained attention as a poet when William E. Matthews read her eight-line *Commemoration Ode or Lincoln/ written for the occasion of the/ unveiling of the Freedman's monument/ in Memory of Abraham Lincoln/* 14 April 1876. Congress had declared a holiday for the event, and thousands of people gathered for a parade and speeches in Washington's Lincoln Park to observe the eleventh anniversary of the president's death and the Emancipation Proclamation. President Grant unveiled the seventeen-thousand-dollar bronze statue of Lincoln by Thomas Ball. The idea for the monument was first conceived by a woman, ex-slave Charlotte Scott of Ohio, who in 1865 gave five dollars toward it when she heard of Lincoln's assassination. John M. Langston made the acceptance speech, and Frederick Douglass delivered the oration for the day. Cordelia's ode was read in the best of company.

The poet wrote prolifically in the last part of the nineteenth century, and some of her poems appeared in the *A. M. E. Review.* Her verses received mixed reactions, but most agreed that they lacked passion, emotion, and vitality. The poems in her first privately published twenty-nine-page *Sonnets* (1893) were later included in her larger collection *Poems.* Of this work, Jessie

Redmon Fauset wrote in a review, "The quality of the verse is uneven, but much of it is very, very good."[3]

"Nature, Christian idealism and morality, love, and literature" were purported to be Cordelia's "major poetic concerns."[4] She wrote poems to Abolitionists, other poets, and her family. Her verses strongly reflected her cultural background and aloofness from reality.[5] She was believed to have "suppressed natural feelings and thoughtful scrutiny of human relationships, actions, and ideas to serve as a Muse for whom poetry was more a skill than an art, more a penmanship exercise than a new, complex creation of heart and mind."[6]

The poet lived in an idyllic world, and viewed her surroundings from the genteelness of her black middle-class northern upbringing. Nevertheless, it was the world she knew and loved. She died in 1916.

NOTES

1. Brown, *Homespun Heroines*, p. 172.
2. Ibid., p. 173.
3. Jessie Fausett, "What to Read," *Crisis* 4 (August 1912):183.
4. Sherman, *Invisible Poets*, p. 134.
5. For an analysis of Ray's poetry, see Sherman, *Invisible Poets*.
6. Ibid., p. 134.

SELECTED SOURCES

Primary

Ray, H. Cordelia. *Poems*. New York: Grafton Press, 1910.

Secondary

Brown, Hallie Q. *Homespun Heroines and Other Women of Distinction*. Xenia, Ohio: Aldine, 1926.

Kerlin, Robert T. *Negro Poets and Their Poems*. Washington, D.C.: Associated Publishers, 1923.

Sherman, Jean R. *Invisible Poets: Afro-Americans of the Nineteenth Century*. Urbana: University of Illinois Press, 1974.

Stetson, Erlene. *Black Sister: Poetry by Black American Women, 1746–1980*. Bloomington: Indiana University Press, 1981.

White, Newman Ivey, and Jackson, Walter Clinton. *An Anthology of Verse by American Negroes*. Durham, N.C.: Trinity College Press, 1924.

Wilson, Joseph Thomas. *Emancipation: Its Course and Progress, from 1481 B.C. to A.D. 1875*. Hampton, Va.: Normal School Steam Power Press Point, 1882.

Verses to My Heart's-Sister

We've traveled long together,
   O sister of my heart,
Since first as little children
   All buoyant, we did start
Upon Life's checkered pathway,
   Nor dreamed of aught save joy;
But ah! To-day can tell us
   Naught is without alloy.

Rememb'rest thou the gambols
   Of those sweet, early days,
When siren Fancy showed us
   Our dreams through golden haze?
Ah, well thou dost remember
   The mirth we then did share,
The sports, the tasks, the music,
   The all-embracing prayer.

Somehow my own sweet sister,
   Our heart-strings early twined;
Some rare bond of affection
   Of tastes and aims combined,
Made us, e'en in our Springtime,
   Soul-sister fond and leal;
And how that love has strengthened
   The years can well reveal.

We've seen our loved ones vanish
   Far from our yearning gaze,
Into the peace of Heaven.
   O those sad, saddest days,
When we two clung together,
   So lonely and forlorn,
With our crushed hearts all quiv'ring,
   All bruised, and scarred and torn.

So nearer clung we, sister,
   And loved each other more;

The tendrils of our natures
    Twined closer than before.
We could speak to no other
    Of those sweet, holy things,
So tender yet so nameless,
    Which sorrow often brings.

The troubles that have thickened
    Around our daily path,
We've borne together, sister,
    And oft when courage hath
Grown feeble, and the future
    Was dark with naught of cheer,
Could one have faced the conflict
    Without the other near?

And sister, dear Heart's-Sister,
    When all the mystery
Of this strange life is ended
    In Immortality,
We'll love each other dearly
    As now we do, and more;
For sacred things in Heaven
    Grow richer than before.

And shall not those sweet loved ones
    Missed her so long! so long!
Join with us in the music
    Of an all-perfect song?
We feel a gladder cadence
    Will thrill their rapt'rous strain,
When we are with them, sister,
    All, ne'er to part again!

So now as here we linger,
    May ours be happy days!
O generous-hearted sister,
    In all Life's winding ways
May we have joy together!
    And this I fondly pray,—
God bless thee, dear Heart's-Sister!
    Forever and for aye!

The Enchanted Shell

Fair, fragile Una, golden-haired,
With melancholy, dark gray eyes,
Sits on a rock by laughing waves,
Gazing into the radiant skies;

And holding to her ear a shell,
A rosy shell of wondrous form;
Quite plaintively to her it coos
Marvelous lays of sea and storm.

It whispers of a fairy home
With coral halls and pearly floors,
Where mermaids clad in glist'ning gold
Guard smilingly the jeweled doors.

She listens and her weird gray eyes
Grow weirder in their pensive gaze.
The sea birds toss her tangled curls,
The skiff lights glimmer through the haze.

O strange sea-singer! what has lent
Such fascination to thy spell?
Is some celestial guardian
Prisoned within thee, tiny shell?

The maid sits rapt until the stars
In myriad shining clusters gleam;
"Enchanted Una," she is called
By boatmen gliding down the stream.

The tempest beats the restless seas,
The wind blows loud, fierce frown the skies;
Sweet, sylph-like Una clasps the shell,
Peace brooding in her quiet eyes.

The wind blows wilder, darkness comes,
The rock is bare, night birds soar far;
Thick clouds scud o'er the gloomy heav'ns
Unvisited by any star.

Where is quaint Una? On some isle,
Dreaming 'mid music, may she be?
Or does she listen to the shell
In coral halls within the sea?

The boatmen say, on stormy nights
They see rare Una with the shell,
Sitting in pensive attitude.
Is it a vision? Who can tell?

Maud Cuney Hare

1874–1936

As a biographer, playwright, anthologist, music historian, and musician prior to and during the New Negro Movement, Maud Cuney Hare's literary contributions have been overshadowed by her reputation in the field of music.[1] In Hare's ground-breaking study, *Negro Musicians and Their Music* (1936), Clarence Cameron White, well-known black composer and musician, wrote of her: "One who does not already know of the versatility of this remarkably talented woman will doubtless be amazed at the diversified character of her activities."[2]

This introduction, written in January 1936, is of prime importance, for it documents the legacy of Maud Cuney Hare. She died the next month, on 13 February in Boston, three days before her sixty-second birthday.

The multitalented woman was born in Galveston, Texas. Much of her early life can be gleaned from her biography about her father, *Norris Wright Cuney: A Tribune of the Black People* (1913), published by the Crisis Publishing Company of the National Association for the Advancement of Colored People. Norris Cuney was a prominent black leader of Galveston and a nationally known Texas Republican. He was one of eight children born to plantation owner Colonel Philip Cuney and his slave mistress, Adeline Stuart, whom he set free. The family moved to Houston, and at the age of thirteen, Cuney was sent to Pittsburgh to continue his schooling.

Cuney's public service began in Texas in 1869, when he was appointed sergeant-at-arms for the Twelfth Texas Legislature and later, a school director of Galveston County in 1871. The following year, he was appointed inspector of customs for the District of Texas. In 1875, he was the Republican candidate in the race for Galveston's mayor, in which he was defeated. Wanting to be independent, Cuney started a stevedoring business in 1883, which employed five hundred blacks to load and unload vessels passing through Galveston's port.

Maud Cuney Hare's mother was Adelina Dowdie, a "handsome" daughter of a Woodville, Mississippi, white planter, who came to Texas in 1864, and a mulatto slave. Adelina married Cuney at the age of sixteen in 1871, while she was preparing for the teaching profession. Maud Cuney Hare's mother was active in "charitable organizations" and "social uplift." She had a "beautiful dramatic soprano voice" and sang for various causes.

The biography provides glimpses into Maud Cuney Hare's young life as a black middle-class southern girl growing up in comfort with loving parents who exposed her to literature, music, and drama. She was, in all probability, brought up in a finer environment than some of the white girls her age in Galveston at the time. Her home life was happy and warm, shutting out the outside forces of mob violence against blacks and the social injustices her father was fighting.

The harshness of the winds of racial bias confronted her at the New England Conservatory of Music in Boston, where her parents sent her to "complete her general education and also get musical training." There she and another black student lived in the Conservatory's home. But in October, her father received a letter from the executive committee of the school requesting that he find his daughter a place to stay outside of the home. The letter told of the committee's distress, but more of its bigotry: "We have a large number of pupils who are affected by race prejudices, and the Home must be conducted so as to insure the comfort and satisfaction of the largest number possible."[3] Her father responded indignantly: "You request my cooperation in surrendering to the demands of prejudice, by withdrawing my daughter; I cannot help you."[4]

Maud Cuney Hare bravely stayed on, suffering "many petty indignities," but "insisting upon proper treatment." She furthered her musical studies under private tutors Emil Ludwig, a student of Anton Rubinstein, and Edwin Klaber, a student of Franz Liszt.

She entered the teaching profession, one of the few occupations open to educated black women, becoming director of music at the Deaf, Dumb and Blind Institute in Austin, Texas, 1897–98. Other positions included posts at the settlement program of the Institutional Church of Chicago, 1900–1901, and the State Normal and Industrial College for Negroes at Prairie View, Texas, 1903–4.

In 1906, she returned to Boston, which she made her permanent home after marrying William Hare, a member of an old Boston family. She gave concert tours and lectures with baritone William Howard Richardson to whom she dedicated her book, *Negro Musicians and Their Music*. She founded the Musical Arts Studio, and fostered a "Little Theatre" movement among the blacks in Boston.

A folklorist, she collected songs from Mexico, the Virgin Islands, Puerto Rico, and Cuba. At home, she was the first to collect the Creole music of New Orleans, publishing some in a twenty-four-page booklet, *Six Creole Folk-Songs with Original Creole and Translated English Text*, with her own music arrangements and translations. Writing on music, she contributed to the *Musical Quarterly, Musical Observer, Christian Science Monitor*, and *Musical America*, and edited a column of music notes for the *Crisis*.

Reflecting her long-standing appreciation for poetry, which her father read to her as a child, was her volume *The Message of the Trees: An Anthology of Leaves and Branches* (1918). William Stanley Braithwaite wrote the introduction to this book, which held poems on the theme of trees. The work has been overlooked because of its nonblack theme and paucity of black poets. Thus, the extent of her literary knowledge has been unappreciated.

She displayed yet another talent when she wrote the play *Antar of Araby* (1929), based on the life of Antar Bin Shaddah, black Arabian warrior and poet. The play was the first by a black to introduce a foreign character.

As Clarence Cameron White said of her: "To do any one of these things well would be a distinct achievement, but to do all of these acceptedly as Mrs. Hare has done is truly amazing."[5] Her works and life should not go unnoticed.

NOTES

1. In Eileen Southern's *Biographical Dictionary of Afro-American and African Musicians*, she is listed as a writer.
2. Hare, *Negro Musicians*, p. xi.
3. Hare, *Norris Wright Cuney*, p. 132.
4. Ibid., p. 133.
5. Hare, *Negro Musicians*, p. XII.

SELECTED SOURCES

Primary

Hare, Maud Cuney. *Antar of Araby*. In *Plays and Pageants from the Life of the Negro*, edited by Willis Richardson. Washington, D.C.: Associated Publishers, 1930.
———. "Folk Music of the Creoles." In *Negro: Anthology Made by Nancy Cunard, 1931–1933*. 1934. Reprint. New York: Negro Universities Press, 1969.

————. *The Message of the Trees: An Anthology of Leaves and Branches*. Boston: Cornhill Co., 1918.

————. *Negro Musicians and Their Music*. Washington, D.C.: Associated Publishers, 1936.

————. "Negro Music in Porto Rico." In *Negro: Anthology Made by Nancy Cunard, 1931–1933*. 1934. Reprint. New York: Negro Universities Press, 1969.

————. *Norris Wright Cuney: A Tribune of the Black People*. New York: Crisis Publishing Co., 1913.

Secondary

Dannett, Sylvia G. L. *Profiles of Negro Womanhood*. Vol. 1, *1619–1900*. Yonkers, N.Y.: Educational Heritage, 1964.

Southern, Eileen. *Biographical Dictionary of Afro-American and African Musicians*. Wesport, Conn.: Greenwood Press, 1982.

Home Life

The twelfth ward in Galveston, in which we always lived, was in the East End of the city, near the beach. Our house, which was a modest one, was in every sense a home.

My mother was not strong and spent much time out doors with her flowers. There were roses—red, pink and white, and the yellow Marechal Neil; borders of violets, daffodils and jonquils in the spring, and asters and chrysanthemums in the fall, with cape jasmine, well known in Texas, but now rare and precious to me, after years of life in the Northeast.

Back of the house were orange trees, plum and pomegranate, the purple fig and mulberry trees, where we used to read perched upon seats among the branches. Mother cared zealously for her flowers until Easter, when the yard, awakened by the spring, would be stripped and the flowers carried to the hospital.

Our home life was particularly happy. The three married brothers lived within a radius of three blocks. There were seven cousins, and as we were near the same age, we were companionable and always warm friends. We found much pleasure on the beach and in the surf. Father, who enjoyed surf bathing, went often with us.

Christmas and New Years were of course our gayest holidays. There was always a generous Santa Claus, but father gave his personal gifts on the first day of the year. The night before, we always had a family party enlivened by the visits of intimate friends. Father enjoyed reading aloud the poems of the old year, always closing with "Ring out the old, ring in the new." As midnight approached, we would guess the minute and all troop out doors to see the stars shining on the new-old world.

"Open house" was held on New Years Day, with the reception for the grown-ups.

Christmas with the children's party and the candle-lighted tree, always brought us books galore. Our first introduction to New England was through a treasured Christmas book—"A Family Flight Around Home," by Edward Everett Hale and his sister.

Father cared but little for current fiction. He read deeply, preferring early Hebrew, Greek and Roman history. He was fond of the classics, and in poetry, enjoyed Byron, perhaps next to Shakespeare. He often read aloud to us, and we liked to listen, although there were many things which we could not understand.

Shakespeare was his beloved poet, and he knew him intimately. Father's enthusiasm awakened the interest of my boy cousins, and the two brothers, Richard and Wright, who bore my father's name, used to commit to memory long passages, and in the dining room made cheerful by an open fire, they rehearsed scenes from Shakespeare's plays. We young children of the family, Nisi, Philip, Daisy, my brother Lloyd and I, composed the audience and thought the actors very wonderful.

A retainer and faithful friend of ours limped in his walk. Father said he walked like Richard III, and often when this man came into his presence, would softly quote in an affectionate, quizzing undertone, passages from the play.

Father, intensely sympathetic and generous to a fault, was often imposed upon. Mother continually reprimanded him for going on bond for some repentant law-breaker, who had pleaded for a chance to reform and, usually, to run away; or for bestirring himself to get work for some unfortunate who repaid him by opposing him in the next election.

There were certain men in Galveston who invariably opposed him in any convention, or in any of his public undertakings, but who came to him whenever they were out of work. Mother argued against his assisting them, but in spite of the fact that his kindness was abused, he was not soured. He met every argument smilingly and repeated the phrase: "Forgive them, they know not what they do."

He had a hatred of form and ceremony and was impatient with creed and dogma. While he belonged to no church, he had the heart and soul of a Christian, and was a follower of the Lowly Nazarene.

The term "Nigger" was hateful in the extreme to father and was never used in our home. Upon one occasion, when we attended the theatre in Boston to see the Kendalls—(he never entered a theatre in the South)—father was incensed at Mr. Kendall's free use of the word Nigger on the stage, and both the play and the English actor were lowered in his estimation.

Our home was a music-loving one. Mother played the piano and sang. Father's appreciation was not that of the ultra-modern school. He liked the old songs of Ireland, martial strains and melodies from the old Italian operas.

The correction of our childish faults lay chiefly in mother's hands, for father could not withstand tears or pleadings. However, he taught us self-control and always cautioned my brother and me, to "Do as you please, but please to do right." He was particularly sensitive and tender in his affections. No wish of mine was ever left ungratified, and nothing would put him in a more furious rage than any question of my ill treatment. It was so in later years. He remained my worshipping and worshipped father.

Little time did he give to pleasure, for life took a strong hold on him. He continually shortened his sleeping hours in order to have more time for his work—an unfortunate habit, for he early suffered from insomnia, a condition due, no doubt, to overwork, and his nervous desire to lengthen his working day. Aside from his private business, in his work for better racial conditions, the demands on his time were enormous. He was no "holiday politician" and, imperious and impetuous as he was in action, he fought his battles with sincerity and earnestness.

At three o'clock father was usually at home, unless detained on one of the ships that the longshore men might be loading far out in the harbor. The close of the dinner hour was one of the happiest periods of the day. Father, sipping his claret, his only dinner wine, followed by the inevitable cigar—he smoked incessantly—would in these moments of leisure, talk of the world happenings of the day, or engage in discussion with mother over some book they were reading. I remember particularly their talk of Mrs. Ward's Robert Elsmere.

Olivia Ward Bush Banks
Olivia Ward Bush

1869–1944

Olivia Ward Bush has been rescued from literary oblivion by her great-grand-daughter, Bernice F. Guillaume. Most of the information in this biographical sketch has been derived from Guillaume's painstaking research.[1]

Olivia Ward Bush received some small recognition as a poet on the threshold of the new century, when her *Original Poems*, a little book of twelve poems, was published in 1899. A larger collection, *Driftwood*, appeared fifteen years later and was praised by Paul Laurence Dunbar, who felt it "should be an inspiration to the women of our race." Because she was a contributor to the *Colored American Magazine*, the publishers publicized the work by announcing in the June 1900 issue: "'Driftwood and Other Poems,' by Mrs. Olivia Ward Bush, will soon make its debut in the literary world." One of her poems, "A Picture," was also printed, the editors saying it was "written expressly" for the magazine to give readers a sampling "of the extreme descriptiveness which characterizes her writings." Mrs. Bush also reported news of the Northeastern Federation of Women's Clubs for the *Colored American Magazine*, as well as contributing articles.

Although she has been omitted from black poetry anthologies, Olivia Ward Bush was noted in early bibliographical poetry lists compiled by bibliophile Arthur A. Schomburg, *A Bibliographical Checklist of American Negro*

Poetry (1916), and librarian Dorothy B. Porter, *North American Negro Poets: A Bibliographical Checklist of Their Writings 1760–1944* (1945).

Driftwood contains poems and three prose pieces in nine sections with seashore headings, such as "Driftwood," "Bits," "Lights Along the Shore," and "The Tide Surges." There are poems to black and white leaders and writers, and others with themes of nature, religion, race, and family.

Mrs. Bush's literary output spanned the nineteenth and twentieth centuries. A flexible writer who adapted her style to the changing trends in Afro-American writing, she was a precursor of the Negro Renaissance period, as well as a participant when it came to fruition in the twenties.

The writer was born four years after the Civil War at Sag Harbor, Long Island, New York, 27 February 1869. Her father, Abraham Ward, and mother, Eliza Draper, were both of African and Indian blood, descendants of the Montauk Indian tribe of Long Island. Abraham was "reputed a Mormon."[2] Taking advantage of the sect's view of polygamy, he was married also to another woman between 1865 and 1869. Her mother died when Olivia was only nine months old. When her father moved to Providence, Rhode Island, in November 1869, he married again, and Olivia went to live with her mother's sister, Maria Draper. Maria was like a mother to Olivia, and the two became very close. Olivia dedicated *Driftwood* to her aunt, about whom she wrote: she "loved me unceasingly, labored untiringly, Sacrificing willingly for me her own life's interest."

Olivia's aunt saw her through Providence High School where she prepared to enter the nursing profession. In 1889, she married Frank Bush in Providence, and they had two daughters, Rosamund and Marie. The couple divorced sometime between 1895 and 1910. Olivia, left with the responsibility of rearing two children alone, returned to live with her aunt.

As she grappled with her psychological and economic difficulties, Olivia discovered that her "two loves" were drama and literature. She became assistant drama director for the Robert Gould Shaw Community House in Boston at the beginning of the century and considered "the dramatic art to be her best *metiér*."[3] She then channeled her creative talents in that direction.

Sometime in the 1920s, she married Anthony Banks.[4] The couple lived in Chicago, where Olivia worked as a drama instructor in the public schools and operated the Bush-Banks School of Expression for dramatic acting. After fourteen years in Chicago, she made her home in New Rochelle and New York City during the depression. She worked as a staff writer for the *Westchester Record-Courier,* where she wrote a cultural arts column. "Her articles were a forum of support for the Negro Renaissance and its aspiring artists, such as Langston Hughes, Richmond Barthé, and baritone John Greene."[5] Although older than the Renaissance luminaries, she perceived the importance of the period and actively participated in it. She was a friend of Countee Cullen, W. E. B. DuBois, Paul Robeson, and John Hope.

Because of her mixed heritage, she realized its special complexities and kept a two-story studio in New York where "'reconciliation groups' of mixed ethnicity shared viewpoints, performances and exhibitions."[6] Employed by the federal WPA, she acted as drama coach for Adam Clayton Powell, Sr.'s Abyssinia Community Center. Her work as a playwright has been neglected, except for the sixteen-page *Memories of Calvary*, a religious Easter pageant published with no date; however, James V. Hatch and Omanii Abdullah in their *Black Playwrights, 1832–1977* (1977) place its publication in 1915. Included with the play are five Easter poems, which the author states could be used "between the two scenes at the conclusion."

Always mindful of her Indian ancestry, Olivia wrote *Indian Trails*, a three-act play of "rich romanticism," based on the Montauks.[7] Maggie Walker, prominent black banker, is said to have been among those who tried to have it produced. Two other plays, *Shadows*, a "dramatic monologue" in dance and poetry that "exalts Afro-primitivism and stresses the need for African research,"[8] and *A Shantytown Scandal*, a one-act play decrying the "insensitivity among black women," were never produced or published.

Mrs. Bush also wrote some stories in dialect about a sharp-witted black woman of the times: Aunt Viney survives with humor and wisdom during the depression years, expounding on people, places, and things. These too were unpublished and have only recently been discovered.[9]

Olivia Ward Bush Banks left an unfinished autobiography, *The Lure of the Distance*. But because of Guillaume, she is no longer so distant from us.

NOTES

1. Bernice F. Guillaume has written a dissertation on Bush, "The Life and Work of Olivia Ward Bush (Banks), 1869–1944," Tulane University, 1983.
2. Bernice F. Guillaume, "Olivia Ward Bush," *Negro History Bulletin*, p. 32.
3. Ibid.
4. Letter received from Bernice F. Guillaume, 28 January 1983.
5. Guillaume, "Olivia Ward Bush," p. 33.
6. Ibid.
7. Ibid.
8. Ibid.
9. Ibid.

SELECTED SOURCES

Primary

Bush, Olivia Ward. *Driftwood*. Providence, R.I.: Atlantic Printing Co., 1914.
———. *Memories of Calvary: An Easter Sketch*. Philadelphia: A. M. E. Book Concern, 1915.
———. *Original Poems*. Providence, R.I.: Press of Louis A. Basinet, 1899.

Secondary

Guillaume, Bernice F. "Olivia Ward Bush: Factors Shaping the Social and Cultural Outlook of a Nineteenth-Century Writer." *Negro History Bulletin* 43 (April–June 1980):32–34.

Hatch, James V., and Abdullah, Omanii. *Black Playwrights, 1823–1977: An Annotated Bibliography of Plays*. New York: R. R. Bowker, Co., 1977.

Voices

I stand upon the haunted plain
    Of vanished day and year,
And ever o'er its gloomy waste
    Some strange, sad voice I hear.
Some voice from out the shadowed Past;
    And one I call Regret,
And one I know is Misspent Hours,
    Whose memory lingers yet.

Then Failure speaks in bitter tones,
    And Grief, with all its woes;
Remorse, whose deep and cruel stings
    My painful thoughts disclose.
Thus do these voices speak to me,
    And flit like shadows past;
My spirit falters in despair,
    And tears flow thick and fast.

But when, within the wide domain
    Of Future Day and Year
I stand, and o'er its sunlit Plain
    A sweeter word I hear,
Which bids me leave the darkened Past
    And crush its memory—
I'll hasten to obey the Voice
    Of Opportunity.

Fancies

Mid parted clouds, all silver-edged,
   A gleam of fiery gold,
A dash of crimson-varied hues,
   The Sunset Story's told.

A mirrored lake 'tween mossy banks,
   A lofty mountain ridge,
A cottage nestling in the vale
   Seen from a ruined bridge.

A woman longing to discern
   Beyond the gleam of gold
A rush of memory, a sigh,
   And Life's strange tale is told.

Georgia Blanche Douglas Camp Johnson
Georgia Douglas Johnson🖋
1877–1966

Although Georgia Douglas Johnson was a prolific writer prior to and during the New Negro Movement, little was written about her life until 1931. In that year students Theresa Scott Davis and Charles Y. Freeman, under the aegis of Arthur A. Schomburg, wrote a paper entitled "A Biographical Sketch of Georgia Douglas Johnson and Some of Her Works" for the now defunct YMCA Graduate School in Nashville, Tennessee. The seventeen-page study is of value for documenting Mrs. Johnson's little known early life, since she supplied most of the information herself. Because of this, Davis and Freeman were "able to obtain some of the more intimate glimpses" regarding her background.

Georgia Blanche Douglas Camp Johnson was born 10 September 1877 in Atlanta, Georgia.[1] Her formative years were spent in Rome, about sixty miles from Atlanta. She was the daughter of Laura Jackson and George Camp. "Her paternal grandfather was an Englishman who moved to this country with his parents in the early days and settled in Marietta, Georgia. His family was wealthy and he was quite musical. He died in his middle thirties in the midst of a brilliant and ambitious career."[2]

Her maternal grandmother was an Indian, and her grandfather, a black bridge builder, "both of whom died early in life leaving the care of seven young children to the oldest daughter, Laura, fourteen at the time."[3] In talk-

346

ing about her mother, who was a maid, Mrs. Johnson described her as having "primitive ideas" and resenting her daughter's dominating childhood personality; nevertheless, she said, she was a person with a "great big loving heart." Protective of her mother's privacy, she asked Davis and Freeman to "step very lightly on my early history. My mother still lives and while she is uneducated, she has a great reticence and is unusually shy."[4]

Laura married three times. During her last union, she gave birth to two half brothers and one half sister to Georgia. As the first child, Georgia grew up very lonely, for her mother worked all day. An aunt on her mother's side—whom she characterized as being "big-hearted," "uneducated," but "proud" of her niece—tried to dispell some of the loneliness by dispensing the love and attention she so much needed.

Georgia began her education in Rome and then attended a public school in Atlanta, where she was the teacher's pet. She was quite good in reading, recitations, and calisthenics, but poor in spelling and arithmetic. After transferring to Storr's School in the seventh grade, she was happier because the New England teachers were "splendid."

Her loneliness followed her all through school, so that she became withdrawn and isolated. She entered Atlanta University's Normal School, where she "experienced the first real homey sympathetic atmosphere" of her life; nevertheless, she continued to be apart even from her three roommates. This was attributed to her fastidiousness about friendships. Concerning those days, she recollected: "There were girls in school whom I would have liked to be associated with but I was too proud to seek them and I had no material offerings to make to attract superior girls."[5]

To compensate for her estrangement, she bought a violin and taught herself to play. Thus began her interest in music, which later had an effect on her writing. When graduation came from Normal School in 1893,[6] she cried during the last night, for it meant leaving a place that had been a "haven" to her.

Her teaching career began in Marietta, Georgia, the birthplace of her mother. After a time, she returned to Atlanta to become an assistant principal. She resigned to go to Cleveland, Ohio, to study piano, harmony, and voice, and then attended the Oberlin Conservatory of Music during 1902–3. Music was her "first and strongest passion, composition mainly," which she gave up professionally for "there seemed no outlet."[7]

She married Henry Lincoln Johnson, an Atlanta attorney and prominent member of the Republican party on 28 September 1903. They had two sons, Henry Lincoln, Jr., and Peter Douglas. During this part of her life, she began to write stories and poems, sending them out to newspapers and small magazines. She taught music, performed as organist for the Congregational church, and wrote songs.

When her husband was appointed recorder of deeds by William Howard

Taft, the family moved to Washington, D.C. There he died suddenly in 1924. As a gesture of appreciation for his services to the Republican party, President Calvin Coolidge appointed Mrs. Johnson to be commissioner of conciliation in the Department of Labor.

She educated her sons at the best of schools. Peter, who died in 1957, attended Williston Seminary, Dartmouth College, and Medical School at Howard University. Henry Lincoln, Jr., went to Asburnham Academy, Bowdoin College, and Howard University's law school.

As an artistically motivated woman, Georgia Douglas Johnson was not a conventional housewife. She was not even an especially good cook, for she spent most of her time on her writing and reading books; she was known as an omnivorous reader.

Searching for creative outlets, she tried charcoal sketching and oil painting, which she eventually gave up. She was first inspired to write poetry after reading one of William Stanley Braithwaite's poems about a rose, nurtured by a child, which tries to bloom in a New York City window. In the end poetry writing won out over her early desire to compose music: "I dreamed of being a composer—wrote songs, many of them. The words took fire and the music smouldered and so, following the lead of friends and critics, I turned my face toward poetry and put my songs away for a while."[8]

She became the "first colored woman after Frances Harper to gain general recognition as a poet."[9] Her youthful loneliness carried over into her lyric poetry. Her first book, *The Heart of a Woman* (1918), contained poems of love, disappointment, regrets, passion, and sorrow. In the introduction, Braithwaite calls the poems "intensely feminine" and praises her openness as a woman writing about women, "lifting the veil" of "woman's nature." The first poem, "The Heart of a Woman," is the most memorable.

Johnson was criticized, however, because nothing in the book concerns race. In answer to this, she published *Bronze: A Book of Verse* (1922), her only book of poems with racial themes. About *Bronze*, she wrote to poet and anthologist Arna Bontemps, "My first book was *The Heart of a Woman*. It was not at all race conscious. Then, some one said—She had no feeling t [sic] all for the race. So I wrote BRONZE—it is entirely racial."[10] As such, it received more attention and plaudits. The illustrious scholar and editor of the *Crisis*, W. E. B. Du Bois, wrote the introduction, commenting, "Her word is simple, sometimes trite, but it is singularly sincere and true, and as a revelation of the soul struggle of the women of a race it is invaluable."[11] And the literary reviewers of the *Crisis*, Alain LeRoy Locke and Jessie Redmon Fauset, wrote, "In *Bronze*, Mrs. Johnson has at last come to her own—if not also in a peculiar way, *into* her own."[12]

Thirty years later, Cedric Dover detected another dimension in *Bronze*: "The subject is still the heart of a woman, but now it is the heart of a colored woman aware of her social problem and the potentiality of the so-called hybrid."[13] *Bronze* certainly reflected much of Mrs. Johnson's life as a person of mixed blood, a fact that she was said to have been proud of but that deeply concerned her. Her poems "Cosmopolite," "Fusion," "The Octoroon," and "Aliens" address the theme of alienation; for example, in "The Octoroon," she wrote "One drop of midnight in the dawn of life's pulsating stream / Marks her an alien from her kind, a shade amid it gleam."

Cedric Dover, himself an Eurasian, called her "the most prolific poet of the 'half-caste,'" and compared her to Langston Hughes and Eurasian George Walker. "She was the first to give to peoples of mixed origin the pride in themselves that they so badly needed."[14]

Her third book, *An Autumn Love Cycle* (1928), was published during the heyday of the New Negro Movement, but she returned now to what she loved most to write about: a woman's heart. Candidly and without apology, she said, "My third attempt was a book that had no thought of race consciousness—just poetry—the dreams and longings of the heart—An Autumn Love Cycle."[15] She did not like to write about "things that make the heart heavy," wanting to forget her "special call to sorrow and live as happily" as she could.

Alain LeRoy Locke, a prime figure of the Harlem Renaissance, and patron of black literary people, contributed the foreword to *An Autumn Love Cycle*, acknowledging that the author had committed herself to documenting the "feminine heart." He lauded her frank writing about the "experiences of love," for in "seeking a pure lyric gold, Mrs. Johnson has gone straight to the mine of the heart."[16] In her writing from the heart, Cedric Dover discerned a "strong note of frank hedonism" in her poems, which was "almost unique amongst the woman poets of her generation."[17] He wrote of her as one who "sings the pleasures of loving today, sorrowing tomorrow, and loving again the day after."[18] Mrs. Johnson's well-known "I Want to Die While You Love Me" is in this collection. She composed music for the poem, and the song was sung by Harry Burleigh on Victor Records.[19]

Love, the focal point of her poems, spilled over into her real world. She wanted everyone to love and be loved, and as a result, she sponsored a Lonely Hearts Club for people to meet and correspond throughout the country. She assigned the members categories, according to their education, age, place of residence, marital status, and experience in life.[20] Coinciding with this, she issued a Washington social letter which cost two dollars a year. One Lonely Hearts prospective member called her club a "Godsend to lonesome girls."

Georgia Douglas Johnson also wrote columns entitled "Homely Philosophy," "Wise Sayings," and "Beauty Hints" for twenty-eight black newspapers. In 1941, she started an interracial column for the *Amsterdam News* to foster a better understanding between the races. She was an ardent proponent of brotherhood. One of her many unpublished works was a book, *Bridge to Brotherhood*, which she wrote to "foster and promote good feeling between the races." It combined eighty poems with songs and music.

She wrote in her historic home at 1461 South Street, N.W., surrounded by flowers in her yard and window boxes to cheer passersby. Saturday evening gatherings were held in her home, which she christened Half-way House, for she considered herself "half-way between everybody and everything and I bring them together." Her weekly open houses attracted a "free-wheeling jumble of the gifted, famous, and odd."[21]

Among the guests were W. E. B. Du Bois, Angelina W. Grimké, Alice Dunbar-Nelson, Sterling Brown, Langston Hughes, Alain LeRoy Locke, Jean Toomer, Richard Bruce Nugent, and whites Zona Gale, Vachel Lindsay, and Waldo Frank. Supplementing the literary coterie, according to Henry Lincoln, Jr., who served refreshments, were prisoners to whom she had written in jail and invited to her home when they were released. At one time, she had projected writing about her "Literary Salon," the only one in Washington, D.C., "where many of the splendid young writers of the present-day received their contactual inspiration."

Georgia Douglas Johnson thrived on friendship. She mailed cards with original poems on them to friends across the country. She adopted as "sons" Langston Hughes, Glenn Carrington, and Harold Jackman. Harold was her most beloved, and he served as an emotional prop and supporter for her creative endeavors.

Zona Gale, to whom *Bronze* was dedicated, introduced her to play writing. *Blue Blood*, a drama about the intermixture of races, won *Opportunity* magazine's second prize in 1926, and her most famous one-act play, *Plumes*, was awarded *Opportunity*'s first prize the following year. This folk drama recounts the story of a mother who is torn between using fifty dollars she has saved for a fine funeral to bury the next member of the family or to pay for an operation that might save her daughter's life. While she is trying to make up her mind, the child dies. Other published plays in anthologies include the historical *Frederick Douglass, William and Ellen Craft*, and a drama about lynching, *A Sunday Morning in the South*, which was first published in Hatch's *Black Theater* (1974).

She wrote many unpublished short stories, some under the pseudonym of Paul Tremain, and others with Gypsy Drago. Seventeen of those written with Drago were culled from his life as a man who did not know he was black until the age of thirty. Her "The Skeleton" won a first prize through the *Washington Tribune*.

Georgia tried in vain to get her book, *The Black Cabinet*, being *The Life of Henry Lincoln Johnson*, published. The biography of her husband was to have told "the true story of Republican politics in the South from the Reconstruction to 1924." And almost until her death, she tried to interest publishers in another book, *White Men's Children*, with a theme of the "interplay of bloods."

Despite her creative output in her early years, she was unable to obtain philanthropic aid "for a clearing space, elbow room in which to think and write and live beyond the reach of the wolf's fingers."[22] She was turned down for grants by the Guggenheim, Whitney, and Rosenwald foundations. To her "son," Jackman, she wrote: "You would be surprised to know how many foundations I have tried, and more surprised to learn that . . . each one, said 'no,' but *most* surprised to learn that I have still high hopes."[23]

She wrote steadily until her death in 1966, remaining till the end in her Half-Way House, which by now had become ringed by urban blight. She stayed on with her books, writing, memories, and dashed hopes, becoming known as "the old woman with the headband and the tablet around her neck."[24] The tablet with pencil was in readiness to write down "an idea, a word, a line for a poem."[25] Even as an octogenarian, she stayed mentally alert, studying journalism at nearby Howard University.

Her last book, *Share My World* (1962), was a small privately published collection of thirty-seven poems. In 1965, she was awarded a doctor of literature degree from Atlanta University. To Davis and Freeman, she confided that an appropriate epitaph for her would be "She tried." She did more than try, however: she succeeded.

NOTES

1. Biographical sources have listed the year of birth as 1886, but the date 1877 was verified by the Registrar's Office at Atlanta University. The Davis and Freeman paper gives 10 September 1886, and her birthplace as Rome, Georgia; however, neither the location nor the date of birth was given to Davis and Freeman by Mrs. Johnson in her letter to them. Gloria T. Hull in *Color, Sex, and Poetry* gives the birth date as 10 September 1880. In an interview with Henry Lincoln Johnson, Jr., he believed that his mother was born in Rome, but gave only 10 September as a birth date, with no year.
2. Davis and Freeman, "A Biographical Sketch," p. 3.
3. Ibid.
4. Johnson to Davis and Freeman, n.d., Special Collections, Fisk University Library, Nashville, Tenn.
5. Ibid., p. 2.
6. Contrary to Hull's date of 1896, Johnson is listed in the Atlanta University Catalog as finishing in the Normal Class of 1893.
7. Johnson to Davis and Freeman, p. 3.
8. Davis and Freeman, "A Biographical Sketch," p. 7.
9. Johnson, *American Negro Poetry*, p. 181.
10. Johnson to Bontemps, 19 July 1941, Harold Jackman Collection, Robert W. Woodruff Library, Atlanta University, Atlanta, Ga.

11. Johnson, *Bronze*, p. 7.
12. Alain LeRoy Locke and Jesse Fauset, "Notes on the New Books," *Crisis* 25 (February 1923):161.
13. Cedric Dover, "The Importance of Georgia Douglas Johnson," *Crisis* 59 (December 1952):634.
14. Ibid., p. 635. Another poet prior to Johnson and Hughes, Joseph S. Cotter, Jr., also wrote of mixed heritage in his poem, "The Mulatto to His Critics," in his collection, *The Band of Gideon and Other Lyrics* (1918).
15. Letter to Bontemps.
16. Johnson, *An Autumn Love Cycle*, p. xix.
17. Dover, "Importance," p. 634.
18. Ibid., p. 635.
19. The Schomburg catalog has Burleigh as the composer of the music. The song was copyrighted by Mrs. Johnson in 1949.
20. Henry Lincoln Johnson, Jr., interview with author, Washington, D.C., 12 July 1978.
21. Lewis, *Harlem*, p. 127.
22. Davis and Freeman, "A Biographical Sketch," p. 7.
23. Johnson to Jackman, 2 March 1950. Countee Cullen Collection, Robert W. Woodruff Library, Atlanta University, Atlanta, Ga.
24. Hatch, *Black Theatre*, p. 211.
25. Ibid.

SELECTED SOURCES

Primary

Johnson, Georgia Douglas. *An Autumn Love Cycle*. New York: Harold Vinal, 1928.
———. *Bronze: A Book of Verse*. Boston: B. J. Brimmer Co., 1922.
———. *The Heart of a Woman and Other Poems*. Boston: Cornhill Co., 1918.
———. *Share My World: A Book of Poems*. Washington, D.C.: Half-Way House, 1962.

Secondary

Adoff, Arnold. *The Poetry of Black America: An Anthology of the 20th Century*. New York: Harper & Row, 1973.
Brown, Sterling A.; Davis, Arthur P.; and Lee, Ulysses, eds. *The Negro Caravan: Writings by American Negroes*. New York: Dryden Press, 1941.
Catalog of Writings by Georgia Douglas Johnson. Washington, D.C.: Half-Way House, n.d.
Cullen, Countee. *Caroling Dusk: An Anthology of Verse by Negro Poets*. New York: Harper & Brothers, 1927.
Davis, Theresa Scott, and Freeman, Charles Y. "A Biographical Sketch of Georgia Douglas Johnson and Some of Her Works." Nashville, Tenn.: Y.M.C.A. Graduate School, 1931.
Ellington, Mary Davis. "Plays by Negro Authors with Special Emphasis upon the Period 1916 to 1934." Master's thesis, Fisk University, 1934.

Fletcher, Winona. "Georgia Douglas Johnson." In *Afro-American Writers from the Harlem Renaissance to 1940. Dictionary of Literary Biography*, vol. 51, edited by Trudier Harris and Thadious M. Davis. Detroit, Mich.: Gale Research, 1987.

Hatch, James V. *Black Theater, U.S.A.: Forty-five Plays by American Negroes, 1847–1974*. New York: Free Press, 1974.

Hughes, Langston, and Bontemps, Arna, ed. *The Poetry of the Negro, 1746–1970*. Rev. ed. New York: Doubleday & Co., 1970.

Hull, Gloria T. *Color, Sex, and Poetry: Three Women Writers of the Harlem Renaissance*. Bloomington and Indianapolis: Indiana University Press, 1987.

Johnson, James Welson, ed. *The Book of American Negro Poetry*. Rev. ed. New York: Harcourt, Brace & Co., 1931.

Kerlin, Robert T. *Negro Poets and Their Poems*. Washington, D.C.: Associated Publishers, 1923.

Lewis, David Levering. *When Harlem Was in Vogue*. New York: Alfred A. Knopf, 1981.

Lock, Alain LeRoy, and Gregory, Montgomery, eds. *Plays of Negro Life: A Source-Book of Native American Drama*. New York: Harper & Brothers, 1927.

Peplow, Michael W., and Davis, Arthur. *The New Negro Renaissance*. New York: Holt, Rinehart, & Winston, 1975.

White, Newman Ivey, and Jackson, Walter Clinton. *An Anthology of Verse by American Negroes*. Durham, N.C.: Trinity College Press, 1924.

The Heart of a Woman

The heart of a woman goes forth with the dawn,
As a lone bird, soft winging, so restlessly on,
Afar o'er life's turrets and vales does it roam
In the wake of those echoes the heart calls home.

The heart of a woman falls back with the night,
And enters some alien cage in its plight,
And tries to forget it has dreamed of the stars
While it breaks, breaks, breaks on the sheltering bars.

I Want to Die While You Love Me

I want to die while you love me
    While yet you hold me fair,

While laughter lies upon my lips
  And lights are in my hair.

I want to die while you love me
  And bear to that still bed
Your kisses—turbulent, unspent,
  To warm me when I'm dead.

I want to die while you love me
  Oh, who would care to live,
'Til love has nothing more to ask
  And nothing more to give.

Old Love Letters

Old love letters
How they bring
Back the tang and glow of spring
Waking with a stab of bliss
Some, almost forgotten, kiss.

Old love letters:
My eyes dim
Through the mist that shadows them
As I read, I know, I know.
I was loved once—long ago.

Cosmopolite

Not wholly this or that,
But wrought
Of alien bloods am I,
A product of the interplay
Of traveled hearts.
Estranged, yet not estranged I stand
All comprehending;

From my estate
I view earth's frail dilemma;
Scion of fused strength am I,
All understanding,
Nor this nor that
Contains me.

Sarah Lee Levy Lindo McDowell Brown Fleming

Sarah Lee Brown Fleming ✒

1875–1963

Sarah Lee Brown Fleming has been unnoticed as an early novelist and poet of the twentieth century. Her books were not mentioned in *Jet*'s brief historical capsule about her.[1] She is remembered more for her social and civic contributions than for her writing.

When she was two and a half years old, Sarah Lee Brown was brought to Brooklyn, New York to live from Charlestown, South Carolina, where she had been born on 10 January 1875. Her mother was Elizabeth Levy McDowell, and her father, Samuel Brown, a chef.

As a schoolgirl, Sarah decided that she wanted to be a teacher, then an unheard-of idea, since there were no black teachers in Brooklyn at the time. This ambition was further hindered by her parents, who gave her no encouragement. During her senior year, she asked her father to buy her a coat. He refused, telling her that she should go to work as a domestic, for she would never be a teacher. Her last winter in school, she had to wear a man's old gray coat sweater, despite the severity of the weather. But determined to go on, she said she would rather die than not get an education.[2]

Because she did indeed become Brooklyn's first black schoolteacher, she gained considerable attention and made her initial mark on life. After marrying Dr. Richard Stedman Fleming, a dentist, she moved to New Haven, Connecticut, in 1906. Her husband added another first to the family legacy by becoming the first black dentist in the state. Concerned over the dental health of schoolchildren, he opened his office to them free of charge. The Flemings had a son and daughter who followed in their footsteps, Harold becoming a prominent dentist and Dorothy, a social worker with teenage groups.

Mrs. Fleming always possessed a strong interest in literary pursuits, and despite the energy she poured into community work, she managed to write songs, plays, musicals, skits, short stories, and essays. She felt that her writing would be better, however, if she were able to improve her mind.[3] Thus, she tried to strengthen her educational background by taking correspondence courses, particularly in creative writing. She was a familiar figure at Yale University where she enrolled in special classes and lecture courses. William Lyon Phelps at Yale was one of her literary mentors. A great reader, she kept her home filled with books as well as music.

Her *Hope's Highway* (1918) is a message novel, which, despite family breakups, reunions, escapes, and romances, promotes education as a means of race building. The war is over and the ex-slaves in the small southern town of Santa Maria are trying to elevate themselves. They are opposed by Joe Vardam, a diabolical poor white politician, whose aim is to keep the blacks down by weeding out their leadership.

Vardam destroys the Vance Institute, named after a kind slave master, John Vance, who has left half his wealth and land to erect a school for former slaves. Enoch Vance, a slave who has taken his master's name, has been freed prior to the Emancipation that he might get an education and return to help his race rise from ignorance. He is called the "Leader" by his people.

When Vardam forces the school to drop its liberal arts courses, the Leader dies of a broken heart. At his funeral, young Tom Brinley vows to take his place. Soon recognized by Vardam as a potential force in the town, Tom is railroaded to a chain gang.

With the aid of another jailed leader, Tom escapes to New York, where his mother has moved. He changes his name to Frank Hope, gets a job, and goes to school. When trailed by Vardam, he, with the assistance of two white friends, escapes to England. He returns for a trial, is vindicated, and goes back to finish Oxford. He soon resigns a position as a writer for the London *Times* to join the French army where he becomes a hero. But wanting to return home, Tom goes back to Santa Maria to reopen Vance Institute and lead his people to a "greater freedom." The author concludes with the premise that by obtaining an education, black people can turn the "rough road of ignorance into the happy highway of hope."[4]

Two years later, Fleming wrote *Clouds and Sunshine* (1920), which was dedicated to her son and daughter. A book of verse, it contains a mixture of happy and sorrowful poems, a few in dialect, and others concerning race. Besides her novel and poetry, Sarah Lee Brown Fleming contributed two biographical histories to Hallie Q. Brown's *Homespun Heroines*. One was of Eliza Gardner, temperance worker and clubwoman, who operated an Underground Railroad station in Boston; the second concerned Josephine St. Pierre Ruffin, suffragist and clubwoman.

Sarah Fleming has been extolled as a black woman achiever for her community and club work. Like Victoria Earle Matthews, she was greatly concerned with the plight of young black women migrating to northern cities. Realizing the need for a place to shelter them while they searched for jobs, she organized the New Haven Women's Civic League, part of a national organization, in 1929.[5] With the aid of Mary McLeod Bethune, she succeeded in convincing the league to help found the Phillis Wheatley Home for Girls in 1936. It operated for seventeen years.

Her work in helping homeless girls and children of destitute families earned her an added first as a black woman when she was chosen to be Connecticut's Mother of the Year in 1952. On 27 April 1955, she was cited in the House of Representatives by U.S. Representative Albert W. Cretella of Connecticut for her "civic, welfare and political achievements."[6] Mrs. Fleming was the recipient of many other awards and honors. The New Haven chapter of the National Association of Negro Business and Professional Women's Clubs gave her the Sojourner Truth Scroll for "meritorious community achievements," and the Connecticut Valley branch of the NAACP honored her with its "Hat's Off" award in 1952 for making an "outstanding contribution to the advancement of colored people."

Like her fictional leaders in *Hope's Highway*, Sarah Fleming led the way for her people, but the New Haven papers never informed their readers of her literary works during her life or afterward. She died five days before her eighty-seventh birthday.

NOTES

1. "Yesterday in Negro History," *Jet* 26 (30 April 1964):11.
2. Letter from Dorothy Fleming, February 1983. The author wishes to acknowledge Dorothy Fleming's significant personal information about her mother.
3. Ibid.
4. Fleming, *Hope's Highway*, p. 156.
5. A brief history of the Women's Civic League can be found in the *New Haven Register*, 6 March 1955.
6. "A Tribute for Mrs. Sarah Lee Fleming," *Congressional Record*, 27 April 1955, p. 5186.

SELECTED SOURCES

Primary

Fleming, Sarah Lee Brown. *Clouds and Sunshine*. Boston: Cornhill, Co., 1920.
———. *Hope's Highway*. New York: Neale Publishing Co., 1918.

Secondary

Gloster, Hugh M. *Negro Voices in American Fiction*. New York: Russell & Russell, 1965.
Kerlin, Robert T. *Negro Poets and Their Poems*. Washington, D.C.: Associated Publishers, 1923.

John Vance

John Vance's name was held in reverence by every Negro in and around Santa Maria. How many Black men and women in slavery had heard of this good man and prayed that some day they might become his property! Often, on moonlight nights, he would listen to the singing of his slaves, as they sat in their cabin doors, voicing the familiar plantation melodies,—the effect of which was marvelous,—as it passed from door to door on the balmy breezes. One song that particularly pleased their master was:

Lord, I'd rather go to Glory, Lord, I'd rather go to Glory, Lord, I'd rather go to Glory, than to leave this master kind.

John Vance was in the habit of visiting his slaves in their cabins, he would talk with them, and thus he became a part of their lives. He never had occasion to whip a slave, never kept an overseer, neither did he ever have a runaway. When a slave became in any way obstinate or unruly, the master would only have to suggest in a kindly way, that perhaps the bondman would like another master; and, almost invariably, he would get the result he desired. He could count upon the fingers of one hand,—out of a thousand or more slaves that he owned,—the few cases he could not handle.

Being of a very sympathetic nature, he often wanted to help many a one who yearned for an education; for if there was any aristocrat in the South who desired to change the existing laws regarding educating slaves, John Vance truly was one. As soon as freedom came, he secured teachers for those of the adults that desired to learn, while the children were compelled to spend a certain number of hours each day in the schoolroom. Indeed, his was the first institute for Blacks in the South, being the forerunner of the many organizations that were established for this race by loyal Northern supporters.

The young Negro lad, Enoch, whom John Vance specially favored, was born upon the Vance plantation, as was his mother. His father had been bought by Vance from a neighboring slaveholder,— who had lost heavily in speculation. The father of Enoch had courted and married Enoch's mother; and when the son was born his mother felt that the boy was destined to be a Moses to his people.

Knowing how Enoch's mother yearned for an education, and seeing the same desire manifested by the lad, John Vance hoped that he might be able to start him on the road of knowledge. He was fortunately able to do this, by giving the lad his freedom and sending him to that greatest of Western colleges, which has ever held and which still holds open the "Door of Hope" to all who would enter therein. Thus Enoch developed into a true leader of his people, for he was the first Negro qualified to teach the Blacks in the South after Emancipation.

When John Vance lay dead in the Big House, Negroes came from far and near to view the abode of this true lover of humanity. Many, too poor to buy flowers, wrought wreaths out of wild flowers and lay them at the entrance of the Big House. Children could be seen strewing flowers in the familiar spots and along the roads he frequented. Men and women wept like babies, as from their cabins they saw the body of their dearest friend borne to its final resting-place.

After the closing up of the Big House, the late owner's widowed sister, who had made her home with him, returned North to her husband's people. The division of his lands was made according to John Vance's dying wish, which gave his belongings to the ex-slaves that had served him faithfully. And these same people, by their frugality, became the hope of the South, while by their efforts great business enterprises were launched,—enterprises that to-day, together with the Institute, are the pride of the Black South.

This institute was a haven for the Negro. Located picturesquely at the entrance of Santa Maria and overlooking the Bay of Joan, it seemed almost a temple in a land of promise, and, flocking to its doors, came from all parts of the world, those eager to learn.

Enoch first made the curriculum cover those things that his people most needed,—agriculture and manual training; for he was aware that a people just emerging from slavery could need nothing more than the rudiments of education. As time advanced, however, other departments were added, and finally from the Leader's school emerged men and women fitted for every vocation in life.

The Leader was heralded far and wide for his great achievements. Even abroad he was talked of, and educators of distant lands visited his institute, for the purpose of studying his methods of instruction. Great men from different parts of the country either gave their support financially or otherwise to the Vance Institute, and from its example other schools sprang up, heralding, as did their Alma Mater, "Higher education for the Black man."

This system of enlightenment in the course of time became unpopular with a certain element in the South,—an element that crowded in after slavery from the mountainous districts to the west of Santa Maria, or that came in by immigration. And, as the slaveholding aristocracy passed out by death or migration, these people became leading figures, soon wielding the political ax that chopped down all things that were unfavorable to them,—among them, the political status of the Negro, whom they considered to be growing too powerful. Throughout the South, state after state disfranchised the Blacks and decreed against higher education for them. Thus, because of legislative interference, the great ambition of the Leader's life was blighted.

Joe Vardam, an enemy to the cause of the Blacks, worked his way forward politically, fighting with tooth and nail to have the whole educational curriculum changed, so far as higher education for Blacks was concerned.

Realizing that he was utterly powerless to contend with this powerful demagogue, the Leader was compelled to bend to his will and strike out from his course of study psychology, sociology, comparative literature, law, theology, mathematics, and the classics.

"We don't want any Niggers reading Latin and Greek," Joe Vardam would say. "Soon they'll be wantin' to call on us and be askin' to marry our daughters."

The Leader remembered that his former master had often been upbraided in the State Conventions by this fellow, and he remembered, too, that Vardam had once shaken his fist in John Vance's face, remarking:

"If I ever get a chance to deal a blow at these damned Blacks, I'll deal some blow; believe me!"

True to his oath he dealt a deadly blow, and the Leader, hurt to the soul,—having had all his fond hopes blighted, and being powerless to ask, in the name of the law, protection in the exercise of a right that he considered sacred,—died of a broken heart, in the very prime of his manhood, leaving to the world the memory of a well-spent life.

Charlotte Hawkins Brown
1882 ?/1883 ?/1884 ?–1961

Charlotte Hawkins Brown's eighteen-page *"Mammy": An Appeal to the Heart of the South* (1919) is a short story like Victoria Earle's *Aunt Lindy: A Story Founded on Real Life.* Because it was published in book form, it has sometimes been listed erroneously as a novel. *"Mammy"* has other similarities to Earle's work. In both, characters speak in dialect and elderly female ex-slaves are protagonists in a post–Civil War setting. Both narratives were supposed to have derived from observations from life.

Brown gives her source in the introduction where she tells of an "incident" in Sedalia, North Carolina: a wealthy white spinster died and was survived by her "faithful colored servant, 'Granny Polly,' who for more than a half century had answered to every beckon and call from gardener to house-maid."[1] Granny Polly, who lived in a former slave cabin behind the big house, was bequeathed only twenty-five dollars and thus had to live with a grandchild. Brown saw Granny Polly as "but one of many [mammies] who are left destitute in old age by those she has been faithful to unto death."[2] This provides the pivot for her story.

Aunt Susan, the protagonist, is the prototype of Granny Polly. Once the mammy for the Brethertons, an aristocratic Virginia slaveholding family, she and her "Ole Man" (there was also an Old Man in Earle's story) still live in a ramshackle slave cabin not far from the Brethertons' spacious home. They are now too old to work, but are allowed to spend their last days on the land to survive as best they can.

Brown's Aunt Susan aptly fits Deborah Gray White's description of a black mammy as being "a woman completely dedicated to the white family, especially to the children of that family."[3] She also suits Zora Neale Hurston's "mule of the race." The story's theme, then, is about black faithfulness to whites regardless of treatment and white forgetfulness of black loyalty. Bearing this out is Brown's dedication to her "Good Friend Mrs. Chas. Duncan McIver": "It is with gratitude I acknowledge her personal interest in the colored members of her household and trust that many others may follow her example."[4]

The Brethertons are not like Brown's friend, Mrs. Duncan, however. Too old to be of service anymore, Mammy and her Ole Man have been half forgotten by the Brethertons but Mammy has not forgotten them. She dies trying still to be a Mammy to the family.

The uniqueness of this work is twofold. First, it is an excellent example of fiction by a black woman that has been totally ignored, and second, it was written by a woman who was known more for her work as an educator than for her creativity. The story well illustrates Brown's artistic talent, like that possessed by many black women leaders, such as Alice Dunbar-Nelson, Frances Ellen Harper Watkins, and Victoria Earle Matthews. Charlotte Hawkins as a schoolgirl exhibited her creative nature when she did crayon portraits for her friends to earn extra money. The principal of her high school, Ray Green Huling, commented on her "insatiable thirst for art." This later was expressed in her musical and writing pursuits.

Charlotte was born in Henderson, North Carolina; the place is agreed upon by biographers, but the birth date is given variously as 1882, 1883, and 1884. "Little is known of her father, Edmund H. Hight, a brick mason, who had apparently not married her mother and had separated from the family by the time that Charlotte was born."[5]

Her mother, Caroline Frances Hawkins, took her at the age of seven to join other blacks migrating to Boston. When Charlotte was twelve, she envisioned her role as a leader: "My desire for leadership had asserted itself, and in the city of Cambridge I had organized a little kindergarten department in the Sunday School of the Union Baptist Church."[6]

Charlotte graduated from the Ellston Grammar School in Cambridge, where she was chosen to speak for the exercise. She continued on to Cambridge English High School. Just before graduating, she went to work caring for a baby in order to save money for a silk slip to wear underneath an organdy dress for commencement. While pushing the baby carriage down the streets of Cambridge and reading Virgil, she was stopped by a white woman, obviously captivated by the sight.

Later, her principal informed her that the woman was Alice Freeman Palmer, the second president of Wellesley College and a member of the Board of Education. This encounter was a stroke of luck, for Mrs. Palmer became her benefactress. When Charlotte expressed the desire to her mother to attend Radcliffe College, her mother did not see the need for further study, but did agree to her going to Normal School. Mrs. Palmer voluntarily paid her expenses at the State Normal School in Salem.

Charlotte, however, left in 1901 prior to graduation to take a position as a teacher at Bethany Institute, an American Missionary Association school in McLeansville, North Carolina, near Greensboro. When the AMA closed its one- and two-teacher schools, Charlotte was asked by the community to remain.

After returning to Boston, she discussed with Mrs. Palmer a plan to start a school. Mrs. Palmer was receptive to the idea and sought financial support from her friends. Charlotte began the school in 1902 in a renovated log cabin, naming it the Alice Freeman Palmer Institute. After the death of Mrs. Palmer in Paris, it was changed to the Palmer Memorial Institute. The school eventually grew to become a distinguished preparatory institution for blacks. It was sometimes referred to as a finishing school because of Charlotte's heavy emphasis on social manners and behavior which she instilled in the young ladies and gentlemen in attendance.

Social decorum had been infused early in Charlotte's life when she overheard a white woman say to her mother: "Caroline, if there be anything like a colored *lady*, I want you to be one."[7] Charlotte published a book about manners, *The Correct Thing to Do, to Say, to Wear* (1941), where she credits her mother for teaching her to be "kind, polite and generous"—all markings of a "lady." The book was used as a guide for the students at Palmer, as well as elsewhere, and Charlotte came to be called "the first lady of social graces." Charlotte must have felt as other women builders of her race that acting in a refined way would earn white respect.

Through her vigorous fund-raising activities, the institute expanded to cover 350 acres. She also managed to study at Wellesley, Simmons College, and Harvard University. For her work as an educator, she received six honorary degrees and was inducted into the North Carolina Board of Education's Hall of Fame in 1926.

Her impressive community leadership merged with her other ventures. She organized the North Carolina State Federation of Negro Women's Clubs, acting as its second president in 1915. With the club, she founded the Efland Home for Wayward Girls. In 1919, she developed the Commission on Interracial Cooperation, taking "a more radical and uncompromising stance than her contemporaries, Josephine St. Pierre Ruffin, Mary McLeod Bethune, and Margaret M. Washington."[8] This was a new perception of her, since she had been labeled as "conservative or paternistically inclined." This was often the feeling of the younger generation, which could not conceive of the constraints under which Jim Crowism had to be fought in the early twentieth century. Brown opposed racial discrimination by bringing lawsuits and openly spoke against lynchings.

She married Edmund S. Brown on 12 June 1911. The marriage was "short-lived." They had no children, but Charlotte reared six belonging to relatives, one of whom was Maria Cole, wife of Nat "King" Cole—a marriage that caused some controversy in black society.

Charlotte Hawkins Brown resigned as president of Palmer Memorial Institute in 1952, but stayed on as vice president of the Board of Trustees and director of finances. She died in a hospital in Greensboro on 11 January 1961. She had consigned the writing of fiction to an unimportant niche in her life, placing the education of her people above her creative endeavors. Fortunately, there is "Mammy" to remind us of her talent.

NOTES

1. Brown, "Mammy," p. vii.
2. Ibid., p. viii.
3. White, Ar'n't I a Woman?, p. 49.
4. Brown, "Mammy," p. vi.
5. Tillman, Negro Biography, p. 65.
6. Daniel, Women Builders, p. 134.
7. Bardolph, Negro Vanguard, p. 171.
8. Tillman, Negro Biography, p. 66.

SELECTED SOURCES

Primary

Brown, Charlotte Hawkins. *The Correct Thing to Do, to Say, to Wear.* Boston: Christopher Publishing House, 1941.
———. *"Mammy": An Appeal to the Heart of the South.* Boston: Pilgrim Press, 1919.

Secondary

Bardolph, Richard. *The Negro Vanguard.* New York: Vintage Books, 1961.
Daniel, Sadie Iola. *Women Builders.* Washington, D.C.: Associated Publishers, 1931.
Dannett, Sylvia G. L. *Profiles of Negro Womanhood.* Vol. 2, *20th Century.* Yonkers, N.Y.: Educational Heritage, 1966.
Marteena, Constance H. *The Lengthening Shadow of a Woman: A Biography of Charlotte Hawkins Brown.* Hicksville, N.Y.: Exposition Press, 1977.

Tillman, Elvena. "Charlotte Hawkins Brown." In *Dictionary of American Negro Biography*, edited by Rayford W. Logan and Michael R. Winston. New York and London: W. W. Norton & Co., 1982.

White, Deborah Gray. *Ar'n't I a Woman? Female Slaves in the Plantation South*. New York and London: W. W. Norton & Co., 1985.

"Mammy": An Appeal to the Heart of the South

If there is any word that arouses emotion in the heart of a true Southerner, it is the word, "Mammy." His mind goes back to the tender embraces, the watchful eyes, the crooning melodies which lulled him to rest, the sweet old black face. "What a memory!" he exclaims.

The old cabin leaning far towards the rising sun told that its day was far spent. Here and there, a sill seemed held up by a post, one end of which was buried deep in the ground about eight or ten feet away from the flint rock foundation—a true relic of slavery days.

It was the only one of its kind in the neighborhood, but the land on which it stood was eyed by real estate dealers and owners who vied with each other as to the purchase of this extraordinarily valuable piece of property. The yard had a look of desolation and neglect, yet the sweet-scented magnolias, roses and syringas, now almost covered with vines, told that long ago a lover of art and beauty had lent a charm to this now forlorn hovel.

The back yard of the cabin opened into the back yard of a regal looking mansion, once the home of one of Virginia's prominent governors. Its stately, massive columns gave it the style and dignity of architecture removed a hundred years from the twentieth century. This spacious residence was occupied by the fourth or fifth generation of the Brethertons, the mere mention of whose name gave tone and color to any picture of social life in Virginia. Like many of their kind, the Brethertons had fought and lost, and all that was left to them after the sixties were the home and the name which made a Bretherton hold his head high even though his feet were bare.

The Brethertons had been compelled to sell, acre by acre, the large farm on which a thousand or more negroes had spent days of toil. Costly residences now enclosed them, until only Aunt Susan and her "Ole Man," as she called him, could point to the spot that marked the slave quarters fifty years before.

Aunt Susan had been the "Mammy" of the family for years before the war. She loved to recall the words of old Colonel Bretherton, who said to her as the last man of the family joined the Confederate army, to bind closer the chains that held her people: "Susan, take care of my wife and children, and if I never come back, stay here; if they starve, starve with them . . . if they die, die with them."

The old Colonel never returned, and though Aunt Susan heard the voice of freedom calling to her a few years afterwards, she had given her word to the Colonel and she kept it until the day of her death.

The "ole man" had been Colonel's body-guard. It was he who brought the news of Colonel's death; his own strong arm had borne the fainting Mistress to the couch of down, but now he sat by the fireside in the old cabin, a paralytic, scarcely able to help himself.

Three times a day for forty years as regular as a clock, dear Aunt Susan went back and forth to the "white folks'" house, and cooked the food that the Brethertons thrived on.

The sons grew to manhood and married. Their children and their children's children climbed up on Mammy's knee, nursed often from Mammy's bosom, for one daughter had given her life to give to the world a new life, and this new life lived and thrived from blood of Mammy's blood, flesh of Mammy's flesh. This child called "Edith," because she was the image of her girl mother, Edith, always seemed "near" to Mammy. She was now a young "Miss" at Boarding School, and Mammy's famous beaten biscuits always adorned her lunch when she was leaving, and were never missing from the Thanksgiving box. Then, there was something so historically romantic about the reference when Edith could say to the girls, "My dear old black Mammy baked the biscuits just for me. She's been a servant in our family for forty years or more." This statement carried with it a degree of aristocracy that only a Southerner can appreciate.

Mammy had long ago laid to rest her own little babe, as she always spoke of him, although he had grown to manhood long before. He had offered her a home and every comfort in the North; she preferred the cabin, it seemed—no, it was not the cabin, for ofttimes, on bitter cold nights when the winds would whistle, she would kneel and ask God to be a foundation for the old cabin, until the coming of another day, for each moment she thought it would rock its last time. But, ah, the solemn promise to the Colonel, "till I die!"

Mammy was getting old and rheumatism had set in, so the "white folks" had to get a younger woman to do the cooking, but she must be on hand to do the seasoning, because a Bretherton would not eat a meal at Stone Ledge, as the old Mansion was called, unless Mammy had a hand in it.

The days went by wearily for Mammy's "ole man," but the sweet patience with which the loyal soul watched over him was beautifully pathetic. "Ole Missus don't come no more to see us, and de young 'uns has forgotten us," he thought.

The old ties of former days had been broken between him and the friends of his own race; they had moved away. New folks who had no interest in him had come to town. Sometimes Mammy would find him helpless at the wood pile where he had presumed upon the strength of his one good side to lighten her burden to get the wood.

"Ole man," she would say, "I don' tole you to stay in de house and let me wait on you; you done been faithful to me and de white folks for many a year, and dere ain't no use in frettin' 'cause you ain't young and spry." And Mammy would heave a sigh, for growing signs of neglect had weighed heavily on her, since old Mrs. Bretherton hadn't been able to get around.

"Sometimes dere ain't any wood, and sometimes dere ain't much left on the table for my old man. Things am gettin' kind o' curious. Dese here young folks ain't got no time for us. Dey jest like to p'int at us for the family's sake," thought she, but to encourage "Pappy," as she sometimes called him, she spoke out in jolly tones, "Go long, Pappy, 'twice a child an' once a man,' Colonel used to say; and I 'spec' you's done reached dat second childhood. You want dese young 'uns running down here a-climbin' on your knees like dey use to," and she turned her face to hide the tears. "We'se been faithful; dese hands hab nursed ebry child in dat Bretherton family. I'se laid 'em on my lap and hugged 'em to my breast,—lors a mussy, I lubs dem children, but little Miss Edith is the only one that thinks enough of Mammy to come down here to de old cabin and see how we-uns is libin'."

"Bless ma soul, Christmas is coming, and I looks for her like robins do the spring; she brings sunshine," said Pappy.

Miss Edith came home, bringing some of her friends from the North who attended St. Mary's school—one of the most select boarding-schools in the country. She wanted to give them a taste of a Southern Christmas.

The very interesting course in sociology in school had attacked the cabin life in which the white people had forced the negroes to live, and Edith had become popular by telling of her beloved Mammy, and how she had found shelter within reach of them for forty years, how her mother, grandmother and great-grandmother had cared for her and met her every need. Everybody had warmed up to Edith because of this interesting account of "negro fidelity" and "white devotion."

Hardly had Edith exchanged greetings with the home folks before she realized that it would be perfectly natural for the girls to want to see this beautiful picture of service and gratitude. She began to talk it over with her mother (by the way, this mother was a new one whom Edith's father had chosen for her long before Mammy had given up her claim to be the child's sole guardian).

"Mother," said Edith, "it would never do to carry the girls down to the 'ole cabin.' I know it's spotless, but it looks as if it would tumble down every minute, and when I was there last fall, Mammy had a wash tub on top of the bed to catch the large drops of rain."

"Why didn't you tell your papa?" said her mother.

"Mother," Edith answered, "I did, but papa said the old folks hadn't long to live, and as soon as they were dead the cabin would be torn down and the property would be for sale, and he said it was useless to spend any money on it."

"Well, don't let the situation worry you, little girl," remarked her mother, "your friends will be having such a gay time that the question of sociology in these quarters will not enter their thoughts."

But in spite of Mrs. Bretherton's desire to brush aside the thought of neglect of the two old folks who had been faithful so long, she could not wholly dismiss it.

"Listen, Edith," said her mother, "we ought to do more for Mammy. This winter when your papa's business was about to fail, Mammy somehow or other noticed that something had happened. It was really necessary to cut down the food supply. She sought the confidence of your grandmother, who loves Mammy as a sister, you know; Granny told her all. Edith, it would have brought tears to your eyes if you had seen them weeping on each other's shoulders. I saw Granny count out ten one hundred dollar bills that Mammy handed to her which she said she had kept as her son's "surance money.'

"We all thought that boy worthless. I could not understand, but I followed Mammy to the back door. I saw her look towards heaven as she said earnestly, 'Till I die.'"

The tears trickled down Edith's cheeks, but like most young people, it was an emotion for the moment. She went back into her world of gayety and forgot that Mammy lived.

The holidays came to a close with a blinding snowstorm.

Early in the morning of January sixth, Mammy rose and peeped out, to see the snow piled up high. "Pappy," she called, "Mammy's child leaves dis morning, and ain't nary beaten biscuit dere to put in her lunch. Dese hands ain't never failed dat child, and de snow ain't going to make dem fail dis mornin'."

Pappy sighed. "Mammy, white folks don't care long for us lak dey used to—we's gettin' old and no 'count."

She protested, however, dressing in the meantime. She pried the door open, while a mass of snow fell on the inside. The wind whistled. Bundled up in a shawl, she sought the garden gate, but just as the gate clicked, an avalanche of snow from the roof of Stone Ledge fell, burying beneath it all that was in its path.

An impatient little girl wondered why Mammy didn't come to give her the beaten biscuits.

Late in the afternoon, Pappy grew weary of waiting and watching for her who never stayed away so long. Eating the bread and milk which she always provided for his breakfast did not satisfy him for the day. Soon a whistle, and then a young man rushed into the cabin crying, "Mammy, Mammy, come quick, Grandma is dead."

But no Mammy answered.

Pappy, excited, hobbled to the door just in time to see the snow melting. The red bandanna of his mate of fifty years told the story. "Until I die!" She had kept her vow to the last. He swooned to the floor, and how long he lay there no one knows.

Green Hill Cemetery is a beautiful place, and the most prominent in it is marked by a monument of a soldier in uniform—the "Colonel."

Here his good wife's remains were laid to rest amidst the funeral rites of Church and state.

A new board marked the last resting-place of "Mammy," to which she journeyed in the county wagon.

Outside the County Home, occasionally, is seen an old man counting his years into a century, who murmurs unceasingly: "White folks don't care long for us lak dey use to—we's gettin' ole and no 'count."

A sign "For Sale" marks the place where Mammy once lived.

Each year the Brethertons make a pilgrimage to Green Hill Cemetery to plant flowers, but only the kind honeysuckle creeps over the grave of the body in ebony whose soul was whiter than snow.

Angelina Weld Grimké

1880–1958

It would be impossible to write about Angelina Weld Grimké without delving into her unique family background. Angelina, poet, short-story writer, and dramatist, was named after her history-making great-aunt, Angelina Emily Grimké Weld, on the white side of the family tree.

Aunt Angelina, wife of Abolitionist Theodore Dwight Weld, and her sister, Sarah Moore Grimké, were the rebellious daughters of an aristocratic Charleston, South Carolina, slaveholder, Judge John Faucheraud Grimké. Horrified by slavery, they retreated to live in the North, where Angelina and Sarah became very strong proponents for women's rights as well as Abolitionists. They "were and remained the *only* Southern white *women* in the abolition movement."[1]

It was not until Angelina Weld was sixty-three and Sarah seventy-six that they became aware of the existence of two colored nephews in the family.[2] Archibald Henry and Francis James were the sons of a brother, Henry Grimké, who "regarded a slave as less than a horse," and Nancy Weston, a comely slave woman on Caneacre, the Grimké plantation thirteen miles outside of Charleston. The young black men were students at Lincoln University in Pennsylvania when the sisters made their discovery.

Angelina and Sarah immediately recognized the nephews and helped them to further their education. Francis went on to graduate from Princeton

373

Theological Seminary in 1878, and Archibald finished Harvard Law School in 1874. The nephews were offered the warmth and hospitality of the Grimké-Weld Hyde Park home in Massachusetts. There they met many important and influential people, who had an affect on their lives and careers.

Archibald, Angelina's father, practiced law in Boston. He edited the *Hub* newspaper from 1883 to 1885, wrote books, and served as consul to Santo Domingo. Because of his distinguished career, he was awarded the coveted Spingarn Medal in 1919 for "service to his race."

Sarah E. Stanley, the mother of Angelina, was a writer and member of a prominent white Boston family. She defied the customs of the day by marrying Archibald on 19 April 1879. Angelina was born the following year on 27 February. The mixed union was short-lived, for Sarah soon left her husband and child. She died in 1898, when Angelina was eighteen years old.

Angelina was reared as a well-to-do young black girl in Boston by a doting father, who "constantly exhorted her to be good, study hard, be a lady, make him proud."[3] She received advantages and an education few black or white girls were privileged to have in the nineteenth century. She was educated at the Carleton Academy in Northfield, Minnesota; the Cushing Academy in Ashburnham, Massachusetts; the Girl's Latin School in Boston; and the Boston Normal School of Gymnastics.

Like most educated black women of the times, she entered the teaching profession. She taught English in Washington, D.C., at the Armstrong Manual Training School and the historic Dunbar High School, noted for its high quality of faculty and graduates.

For models as a writer, she had not only her father but Uncle Francis and his wife, diarist and poet Charlotte Forten Grimké. No doubt, the period she lived with "Aunt Lottie" had an impact on her writing pursuits. It was to her that Angelina dedicated her elegy, "To Keep the Memory of Charlotte Forten Grimké."

Without a mother and with a very busy father who left her at home because she was too young to join him when he served four years as consul in Santo Domingo, 1894–98, she was, in all likelihood, lonely. Writing helped fill this void, providing an outlet for her thoughts, pent-up passions, and imagination. The loneliness is mirrored in much of her poetry, which is touchingly melancholy.

As a poet, she became a familiar contributor to magazines and anthologies of the Harlem Renaissance. Sixteen of her poems appeared in Countee Cullen's classic *Caroling Dusk*. They were also featured in the pages of the *Crisis* and *Opportunity* magazines, although none was collected for publication. The poems were conventional verses on nature, love, life, and death. She was considered an imagist poet in the mode of the "old lapidaries," who wrote from her own private emotions about what she felt and saw in a sensitive, poignant, and beautiful way.

Gloria T. Hull, who exhumed Grimké from near literary oblivion, said of her work: "Grimké's poetry is very delicate, musical, romantic, and pensive and draws extensively on the natural world for allusions and figures of speech."[4] Hull found some of her unpublished poetry lesbian in nature. Of this, she wrote: "Most of these lyrics either chronicle a romance which is now dead or record a cruel and unrequited love."[5]

Her prose carried the same element of sadness with the always accompanying death wish so evident in her poetry. In a short piece, "Black Is, As Black Does," in the *Colored American Magazine*, she has a dream on a "dark, rainy morning," in which she fantasizes that "a great feeling of peace came upon me and that all my cares were falling from me, and rolling away—away into infinity."[6] In this dream, she awakens to a beautiful and peaceful pastoral setting, where a woman in white, illuminated by a soft, white light above her head, tells her that she is in heaven. Hearing this, she is delighted: "I was happy, *so* happy." Published when the author was twenty, it clearly spoke of the death wish that permeated her work.

Grimké's most memorable contribution as a writer was a play, *Rachel*. It is reputed to have begun the "actual history of drama by Negro authors" when it was presented in 1916 as "one of the first dramas of Negro authorship performed by Negro actors."[7] *Rachel* was first produced at the Myrtilla Miner Normal School, 3 and 4 March 1916. It was sponsored by the Drama Committee of the NAACP of Washington, D.C. Subsequent productions were at the Neighborhood Playhouse in New York and in Cambridge, Massachusetts. The program stated the significance of the play: "This is the first attempt to use the stage for race propaganda in order to enlighten the American people relative to the lamentable condition of ten millions of Colored citizens in this free republic."[8]

The propaganda aspect upset some members of the NAACP's Drama Committee, who, as a result, helped found the Howard Players for "promoting the purely artistic approach and the folk-drama idea."[9] Eventually the organization served to counter similar plays characterized by Alain LeRoy Locke as "puppets of protest and propaganda."

The play concerns the Lovings, a middle-class black family, consisting of Mrs. Loving, a son, Tom, and a daughter, Rachel. When the father and a half brother are lynched in the South, the family flees north. The drama exposes black northern life, the effects of racial prejudice on black schoolchildren, and job discrimination. It follows the attempts of the Lovings to cope in racist white urban America during the formative years of the twentieth century. The central character, Rachel, adopts a little boy whose parents have died of smallpox. When she learns of his mistreatment and that of a friend's daughter by white teachers and students, she is profoundly affected. "She rejects marriage and, therefore, forfeits motherhood, the dream of her young heart."[10]

When the play was published in 1920, it became the first in book form by an Afro-American woman. It followed William Wells Brown's *The Escape, or, a Leap for Freedom* (1858) and Joseph S. Cotter, Sr.'s *Caleb, the Degenerate* (1903). *Rachel* was compared to Ibsen by Jessie Redmon Fauset, editor and writer for the *Crisis,* although she felt that as a bit of propaganda, it left something to be desired. Lillie Buffum Chace Wyman was so ecstatic over the play that she issued a pamphlet about it, *Angelina W. Grimké's Drama of Rachel and the Lynching Evil.*

When Angelina's father died in 1930, it was reported that she was "devastated." She gave up teaching and moved to New York to write, residing on West 151st Street. She lived quietly, surrounded with the "violet, lavender, grey" memories of her life. Her longtime friend, poet Georgia Douglas Johnson, who affectionately called her "Nina," kept up a friendship from Washington, D.C. She shared poems, news, and invitations to visit. Johnson must have sensed Grimké's self-destructive thoughts, for at one time, she wrote to her consolingly: "Do not think that your fame has grown dim nor the exploits of your father and uncle."[11]

Angelina died at the age of seventy-eight on 19 June 1958. She was returned for burial to Washington, D.C. Her painful life was over, and the long sought kiss of death was finally bestowed.

NOTES

1. Gerda Lerner, "The Grimké Sisters and the Struggle against Race Prejudice," *Journal of Negro History* 48 (October 1973):277.
2. Ibid., p. 289.
3. Gloria T. Hull, "'Under the Days,'" p. 74.
4. Ibid., p. 79. For more aspects on Grimké's private life and poetry, see Hull's *Color, Sex, and Poetry.*
5. Ibid., p. 78.
6. Angelina W. Grimké, "Black Is, As Black Does," *Colored American Magazine* 1 (August 1900):160.
7. Ellington, "Plays by Negro Authors," p. 2.
8. Locke and Gregory, *Plays of Negro Life,* p. 414.
9. Ibid.
10. Jeanne-Marie A. Miller, "Angelina Weld Grimké: Playwright and Poet," *CLA Journal* 21 (June 1978):516. Miller includes an examination of Grimké's unpublished plays.
11. Johnson to Grimké, 6 December 1955, Grimké papers, Moorland-Spingarn Research Center, Howard University, Washington, D.C.

SELECTED SOURCES

Primary

Grimké, Angelina W. *Rachel: A Play in Three Acts*. Boston: Cornhill Co., 1920.

Secondary

Adoff, Arnold. *The Poetry of Black America: Anthology of the 20th Century*. New York: Harper & Row, 1973.

Barksdale, Richard, and Kinnamon, Keneth. *Black Writers of America: A Comprehensive Anthology*. New York: Macmillan Co., 1972.

Bernikow, Louise, ed. *The World Split Open: Four Centuries of Women Poets in England and America, 1552–1950*. New York: Vintage Books, 1974.

Brown, Sterling A.; Davis, Arthur P.; and Lee, Ulysses, eds. *The Negro Caravan: Writings by American Negroes*. New York: Dryden Press, 1941.

Cullen, Countee. *Caroling Dusk: An Anthology of Verse by Negro Poets*. New York: Harper & Brothers, 1927.

Ellington, Mary Davis. "Plays by Negro Authors with Special Emphasis upon the Period from 1916 to 1934." Master's thesis, Fisk University, 1934.

Hatch, James V. *Black Theater, U.S.A.: Forty-five Plays by Black Americans, 1847–1974*. New York: Free Press, 1974.

Hughes, Langston, and Bontemps, Arna, eds. *The Poetry of the Negro, 1747–1970*. Rev. ed. New York: Doubleday & Co., 1970.

Hull, Gloria T. *Color, Sex and Poetry: Three Women Writers of the Harlem Renaissance*. Bloomington: Indiana University Press, 1987.

———. "'Under the Days'": The Buried Life and Poetry of Angelina Weld Grimké." In *Home Girls: A Black Feminist Anthology*, edited by Barbara Smith. New York: Kitchen Table: Women of Color Press, 1983.

Kerlin, Robert T. *Negro Poets and Their Poems*. Washington, D.C.: Associated Publishers, 1923.

Locke, Alain LeRoy, ed. *The New Negro: An Interpretation*. New York: Albert and Charles Boni, 1925.

Locke, Alain LeRoy, and Gregory, Montgomery, eds. *Plays of Negro Life: A Sourcebook of Native American Drama*. New York and London: Harper & Row, 1927.

Stetson, Erlene. *Black Sister: Poetry by Black American Women, 1746–1980*. Bloomington: Indiana University Press, 1981.

Grass Fingers

Touch me, touch me,
Little cool grass fingers,
Elusive, delicate grass fingers.

With your shy brushings,
Touch my face—
My naked arms—
My thighs—
My feet.
Is there nothing that is kind?
You need not fear me.
Soon I shall be far beneath you,
For you to reach me, even,
With your tiny, timorous toes.

A Mona Lisa

I.

I should like to creep
Through the long brown grasses
    That are your lashes;
I should like to poise
    On the very brink
Of the leaf-brown pools
    That are your shadowed eyes;
I should like to cleave
    Without sound,
Their glimmering waters,
    Their unrippled waters,
I should like to sink down
    And down
        And down . . .
            And deeply drown.

II.

Would I be more than a bubble breaking?
    Or an ever-widening circle
    Ceasing at the marge?
Would my white bones

Be the only white bones
Wavering back and forth, back and forth
  In their depths?

At April

Toss your gay heads,
  Brown girl trees;
Toss your gay lovely heads;
Shake your downy russet curls
All about your brown faces;
Stretch your brown slim bodies;
Stretch your brown slim arms;
Stretch your brown slim toes.
Who knows better than we
With the dark, dark bodies,
What it means
When April comes a-laughing and a-weeping
Once again
At our hearts?

Zara Wright

?–?

A rarely mentioned novelist, Zara Wright of Chicago penned a rambling melodramatic romantic novel entitled *Black and White Tangled Threads* (1920), which was privately published and printed by Bernard and Miller. Wright, like other early black women writers, wrote it with the altruistic view of "hoping to interest and possibly benefit someone." The work was dedicated to her deceased husband, J. Edward Wright, who "inspired" her to write it.

The not-so-tragic mulatto theme has characters traversing the continents of America and Europe during antebellum and postwar times. The book skirts the hardships of slavery and the impact of the Civil War to dwell on the "tangled skeins of threads" stitching together the personal lives of blacks and whites in miscegenation and relationships. The inevitable motif of racial uplift is also included. The *Chicago Defender* called the book "remarkable" and praised its author: "To read this story will be convincing proof that as a writer, Mrs. Wright is unexcelled."[1] The book sold for $2.50.

The protagonist, beautiful Zoleeta Andrews, is the product of an interracial marriage between Harold Andrews, a white slave master's son, and Mildred Yates, a pretty slave. In order to marry, the couple flee to England, where they remain until they die. At their deaths, Zoleeta is left alone but wealthy. Her white uncle, Paul Andrews, brings her back to live in the South on the family plantation and to be educated in the North with his daughter, Aline, and niece, Catherine Marceaux.

Zoleeta possesses the virtues of a good Victorian heroine, like all nineteenth-century and early twentieth-century black female protagonists. She is kind, considerate, unselfish, loving, and unvengeful despite the misfortunes visited upon her by a jealous and racist aunt, Claretta Marceaux, mother of Catherine. Zoleeta triumphs over Claretta's schemes to prevent her marriage to a rich white Englishman, Lord Blankleigh, who knows of Zoleeta's mixed blood. The couple goes to live in England where Zoleeta gives birth to a son, Allen.

Upon hearing a missionary lecture on the "semi-civilized, ignorant negroes who lived in the southern part of the United States of America," Zoleeta is horrified by "the exaggerated picture drawn of that race of people from which she descended."[2] Wanting to prove the missionary wrong, she decides to return to America to uplift her race by changing "the attitude of the Southern whites and the calm indifference of the prejudiced Northerner."[3] She embarks on a one-woman mission to lecture to the blacks and whites in America. Since, to do this, she must leave her son and husband and their life of luxury, this is indeed a noble sacrifice: "She crucified herself on the altar of duty for the betterment of her mother's people."[4]

Since Zoleeta looks white, the author does not specify whether she lectures as a white or black Lady Blankleigh. Wright does say "she sought companionship among the wealthy and influential whites and the middle class as well,"[5] a choice of friends that cuts short the intent of her mission. In addition, while in America, Lady Blankleigh gives birth to a daughter, Agnes, who is not made aware of her African ancestry—substantiating that Zoleeta passes as a white lady while trying to uplift her mother's people. The ending is a happy one: after the family is reunited in America after eighteen years apart, they return to England to live in palatial splendor.

A subplot has Zoleeta's racist cousin, Catherine, married to an artist, Guy Randolph. They, too, go abroad to live in Italy.. But when Guy learns that he has some African blood, the race-hating Catherine deserts him and their son, Kenneth. This story was extended into a sequel, *Kenneth* (1920), which follows the life of Kenneth Randolph as he becomes a successful lawyer in a small Kentucky town. Kenneth looks white and is believed to be so by the townspeople. He becomes engaged to Dian Blair, daughter of the town's prejudiced banker. On his father's advice, Kenneth reveals his race to Dian, who assures him that she still loves him and that the secret will be kept between themselves.

Although the novel's title is *Kenneth*, the story also involves Phillip Grayson, his best friend. Phillip is an unmistakably black physician, handsome, cultured, and refined. Another uncommon situation is introduced when Alice, sister of Dian, falls madly in love with Phillip, after a failed romance with Kenneth. But Phillip informs her that he is in love with a black woman, Odene Lester, who lives elsewhere. More involvements, jealousies, deaths, and hidden racial identities entangle the plot.

This book, too, has characters traveling to and from Europe amid any number of melodramatic developments. Alice dies with Phillip's name on her lips, and Phillip and Odene finally get together in their later years. They adopt a baby girl whom they, as forgiving blacks, name after the one who caused them the most trouble, Alice.

Prolonging the conclusion is Agnes's visit to America and her infatuation with Kenneth. Lady Blankleigh still has not informed her daughter of her African heritage. Talking to Kenneth about her feelings toward blacks, Agnes tells him "if she had a drop of Negro blood in her, she would cut herself and let it flow out."[6] She adds: "I do not care how fair one is; I could tell if they were contaminated with Negro blood."[7] Another surprise involves Dian ascertaining through old letters that she descends from Lady Blankleigh's family; thus she is Agnes's second cousin and the real heiress to the Blankleigh estate. After a succession of more complicated episodes, Kenneth and Dian go to live in England as nobility.

Zara Wright's characters are all immensely wealthy, which, of course, eliminates the mundane problems of making a living. Those of African descent have little in common with the blacks of the time, nor do they identify with them except for occasionally admitting bloodlines to family and lovers, which doesn't happen very often. Wright's books, then, are fairy tales created by a fanciful imagination building on nineteenth-century models and adding a few twists of her own.

NOTES

1. *Chicago Defender*, 25 December 1920, p. 8.
2. Wright, *Black and White Tangled Threads*, p. 161.
3. Ibid., pp. 164–65.
4. Ibid., p. 170.
5. Ibid., p. 168.
6. Wright, *Kenneth*, p. 310.
7. Ibid.

SELECTED SOURCES

Primary

Wright, Zara. *Black and White Tangled Threads*. 1920. Reprint. New York: AMS Press, 1975.
———. *Kenneth*. 1920. Reprint. New York: AMS Press, 1975.

The Little Orphan

Some years later Paul received a letter from his brother, telling him that Harold's wife had died two years previous, leaving him a sweet little daughter. The letter also assured Paul that Harold's days were numbered, according to the doctor's statement which said that he might possibly live six or eight weeks. He begged Paul to come and take his little daughter home, assuring him that she was well provided for.

"I came to India soon after my marriage," continued the letter, "and by careful investments and close application to business, have become a successful merchant, more than doubling my wealth."

When Paul received this letter, he was filled with consternation. He felt that he could not do the thing that his brother had not only asked him, but expected him to do.

"No. It is impossible to take that child into my home with a taint of slavery clinging to her ancestors," said he. "I could not let my daughter associate with her. It is not to be thought of."

His sister agreed with him and declared it was an outrageous imposition for Harold to shift his negro child on them. However, it was decided that Paul should hasten to his brother's bedside, take the child and place her in some institution until she became of age, making no other plans for her future, but trusting to time, circumstances and existing conditions to adjust matters satisfactorily to all concerned.

Paul left without delay and it was only by traveling night and day that he succeeded in reaching his brother's side before death claimed him. As he listened to his brother he was convinced that his marriage had been a supremely happy one. Although he seemed loath to leave his little daughter, he appeared anxious to meet his wife, who had preceded to realms above. (Paul had not yet seen his brother's child, and therefore was much disturbed because he felt that he could not heed his brother's last request and asked himself how he could refuse to make his brother's last hours happy.) He was visibly agitated, knowing that his brother's eyes were scanning his face, perhaps reading perplexity and indecision there.

Presently there was a gentle, hesitating rap on the half open door. A sweet, childish voice said "Papa, may I come in?" Feeling sure of her welcome and scarcely waiting for a reply, she softly entered the room. Upon beholding the beautiful child, Paul Andrews was speechless with surprise. She showed no trace of the blood of her mother's people, and was by far the prettiest child he had ever seen. He marveled at the beauty and grace of this little girl scarcely six years old.

The father, propped up in bed, looked on and felt that he could die in peace when he saw his brother open his arms and say: "Darling, come to your uncle." She, unhesitatingly went to him, clasped her little arms around his neck and with her head pillowed on his breast, rested contentedly there. Ah! who knows by what instinct this little girl felt so content in the clasp of her uncle's arms, though she had never seen him before. Was it some unseen power that made it plain to this little innocent child that in her uncle's arms she would find a haven of rest, a shelter and protection from life's tempestuous storms in the trying days to come? Who knows?

Paul Andrews registered a vow as he stroked the long glossy curls of his niece, to stand by her through life. Little did he think at that time that he would be called upon to defend and protect her from the treachery of those who should have felt near and dear to her through ties of blood. When the time came he did not hesitate to do his duty by his dead brother's child.

Unclasping the little arms from around his neck, he glanced at his brother and realized that the Messenger had come—that Zoleeta was an orphan. Before she could realize that her father had gone to join her mother, her uncle had led her from the room. He told her that her father was now with her mother. At first, she was inconsolable, but after the first paroxysm of grief was over, she allowed her uncle to caress her while he explained that she would have two cousins to play with and they would love her dearly, for he had resolved to take Harold's child home and rear her in a befitting manner.

In looking over Harold's papers, he found two letters, one addressed to himself and one to Zoleeta to be given her when she became of age. Paul read his at once. His attention was called to a curiously carved ebony box that had been given his brother by an exiled prince, who lost most of his possessions and was forced into exile by existing conditions in his country. The death of the prince soon followed. This box was in an iron safe filled with precious stones, worth a king's ransom. Paul opened the casket containing the jewels and never had he in his life beheld such jewels representing a vast fortune. He hastily closed the box, resolving to say nothing of its contents until Zoleeta was old enough to understand and appreciate their value.

Paul worked hard to settle up his brother's affairs, but it was some weeks before he was ready to sail for home. He wrote his sister informing her of the death of their brother Harold. He also informed her that he would bring their orphaned niece home with him. When she read the letter she became very indignant because he had not placed the child in some institution as they had agreed to do.

Paul and Zoleeta finally arrived. Zoleeta's aunt was dismayed at the sight of the most beautiful child that she had ever seen. She was amazed at this lovely graceful child, who had no badge to proclaim to the world that she had descended from the degraded race of negroes of the South. She could not understand it, and hated her dead brother's child for her rare loveliness. She had no love in her heart for her little orphaned niece; no compassion for this helpless child, thrown on her care.

Paul took Zoleeta by the hand and led her to his sister, saying: "Claretta, this is Harold's child." His sister made no attempt to welcome the little stranger to either her heart or her home, and, for an instant, seemed inclined to repulse the child, but a look from her brother changed her mind. She spoke a few cold words to her niece and it was plain to be seen that the little girl would have had a hard time in her new home had it not been for her uncle and Cousin Aline. As it was, there were many times that her little heart ached so badly that she wished she was up in the bright blue sky with her own dear father and mother.

Turning to his sister's daughter, he said: "Catherine, I have brought you a little new cousin. I hope you will help to make her happy." That little miss scarcely spoke to Zoleeta. She knew not why, but she saw that her mother was not pleased and felt that she must show her displeasure, also. Before Paul could speak to his daughter Aline, she had thrown her arms around her little cousin's neck telling her how glad she was to see her.

"I am so glad that you are going to stay with us always," said Aline as she led Zoleeta to see her little pet birds. Catherine followed, but said nothing.

When the cousins had left the room, Paul turned to his sister and said: "Claretta, that is our dead brother's child. Will you not help me to care for her and make her happy in her new home? Women know just what to do for little girls and Zoleeta is a sweet, lovable child. I was in hopes that you would love her for Harold's sake."

"You will find out that you have made a mistake by bringing the child here," replied Claretta, becoming more indignant as she continued, "and if after years, she develops traits and habits of her mother's people to the exclusion of the better blood flowing in her veins, causing us shame and humiliation, you must remember that I warned you and you will have no one to blame but yourself. In a few years, our daughters will make their bows to the world and a girl as beautiful as Zoleeta promises to be will prove detrimental to their prospects. Of course," continued she, "Catherine has enough beauty of her own and will not be disturbed by the beauty of Harold's child, but Aline is such a meek little creature that the chances are that she will be outshone by Zoleeta."

Paul was not disconcerted by this outburst of temper from his sister and was firm in his decision that each one should have an equal chance when they entered the social world.

Neither Zoleeta nor her cousins were aware of the secret of her parentage, and Paul impressed upon his sister that under no circumstances were they to be enlightened. There were old servants about the place who remembered their young master Harold, and that he had gone abroad and married, and who were not surprised when Mr. Andrews brought home the little orphan, telling them that his brother and wife had died abroad, leaving a little daughter who would henceforth remain in his home. No one, of course, had attached any importance to the disappearance of Mildred Yates, as it was not infrequent in those days for slaves to take advantage of every opportunity to escape. Paul felt that as no one except himself and sister knew the secret of Zoleeta's parentage, it was perfectly safe.

Mary Etta Spencer

?–?

The life history of Mary Etta Spencer remains to be researched. In 1929, *Opportunity* magazine published her short story, "Beyond the Years." It told of a retired rural one-room schoolteacher who returns for a reunion with her students and learns of their lives in adult years. There is no biography for her in the publication's "Who's Who" column for contributors. Whether this was by the author's choosing is not known.

Eight years prior to the publication of her story, she wrote a novel, *The Resentment*. A bit of the author's life can be glimpsed from its dedication to her mother from whom she claimed to have derived her literary talent. The novel was written in the vein of an inspirational racial success story for young boys and girls. More than likely, it was intended for a Sunday school book by the A. M. E. Book Concern which published it.

The "rags to riches" principal character, Silas Miller, has been hired out by his father to work for Mr. Baxter, a wealthy white southern farmer. A visit by Mr. Walker, an affluent cattle rancher, impels Silas to chart a new direction for his life when he hears the rancher tell of his childhood as an orphan mistreated by his employers. Mr. Walker explains that it was his resentment over a long-standing injustice that motivated his drive to become successful.

Upon hearing this, Silas thinks of his own resentment at being ridiculed and called "nigger" by his employers. He decides to buy a pig and start a farm. From this small beginning, Silas goes on to become the "hog king of the state," working his way from a simple litter of six hogs in a back lot to a 300-acre farm and thousands of the best hogs in the country.

In the beginning, Silas is helped by his sister, Nett, before she leaves to attend a nursing school in Philadelphia. Nett is the epitome of goodness, virtue, honesty, unselfishness, and kindness. She gives up a lucrative position supervising nurses in a hospital to take a low-paying job as a community nurse in a slum inhabited by poor black migrants from the South.

Silas and his sister marry into middle-class families—Silas to an attorney's daughter and Nett to a doctor. Nett, prompted by her love for humanity, takes a monetary gift from her wealthy brother to build an annex to the hospital where she formerly worked, so that black women can be served by their own race and, yes, by their own sex—a feminist outlook, which would not have been interpreted as such at the time. Nett, too, succeeds, like her brother, but in a different way, through service to her people.

Mary Etta Spencer's story and novel concerned achievement. It is possible that she was the schoolteacher in "Beyond the Years," but it is certain that she was a member of that small cadre of black women writers whose main desire was to inspire the boys and girls of their race, as Spencer wrote, "to become a man or woman of worth."

SELECTED SOURCES

Primary

Spencer, Mary Etta. "Beyond the Years." *Opportunity* 7 (October 1929):311–13.
———. *The Resentment*. Philadelphia: A. M. E. Book Concern, 1921.

Secondary

Watson, Carole McAlpine. *Prologue: The Novels of Black American Women, 1891–1965*. Westport, Conn.: Greenwood Press, 1985.

Little Silas

"Come on, come on there, boy, you must think you are owner of half this county instead of being a good-for-nothing 'nigger.' Come, hurry up, we have got lots of work to do today, with the sun two hours high already. And, by the way, a gentleman, a Mr. Walker, will be here today. He is one of the richest ranchmen in the West. Don't for good-ness sake, forget your manners, and please remember to take off your hat to him. He is a great man, and your kind must honor him," said Mr. Baxter with a twinkle in his eye.

Mr. Baxter was a wealthy white Southern farmer. He was talking to Silas Miller, a little colored boy.

Silas had been hired to Mr. Baxter by his father about a year before our story begins. He was then a boy barely fourteen years old, small and delicate for his age. His mother died when he was twelve years old, leaving four children—Silas being the oldest. Two years later, his father married again.

It was the custom in the rural districts of the South for parents to hire their children out as soon as they were old enough to do a little work for small sums of money, monthly; and, very often, for food and clothing only. Silas, not being so strong, was not put to work so soon, but his father hired him to Mr. Baxter when he was fourteen years old, to do light work. Poor little fellow; at first he was so lonely, there being no children there. He missed the merry fun-making of his little brothers and sister.

He was made to sleep over the kitchen stairs, away from the other part of the house. He would have died from fright had he not believed in God. On entering the dark room (he was not allowed to have a light because they were afraid he would set the house afire through carelessness), he would kneel beside the bed and ask God to send "Mamma" to stay with him. Such childish faith! In the next few moments he would be in dreamland.

Humble and poor as they were at home, this child would have given worlds (had they been his to give) to have remained with them.

He was permitted to go home two Sundays in each month. He looked forward to these days as the happiest days of his young life.

Silas had lived here over a year, amidst luxury and wealth. He did not have to work hard, yet little consideration was shown him, the fact being he was only a Negro boy.

At work, he was a little slow, but what he did was well done. "Silas is an unusually bright and quick-witted boy, and I doubt whether he shall be contented to work as a laborer for other farmers long. Of course, we don't want him to know what we think of him; it would make him feel important, yet we all love him and would hate to part with him," said Mr. Baxter in speaking of him to his friends.

Little did Mr. Baxter know that he had said the words that, in years to come, would make Silas Miller one of the richest and most independent men of his race.

While at work that morning, hot tears ran down Silas' face, his heart ached. "Why must I be reminded every day that I am a Negro, I try so hard to do what is right? But, it is always 'Nigger.'" He looked at his dark, brown-skinned hands and wondered why God made some white and others black. Stamping his foot upon the ground, he said, "But there is one thing certain, I shall not always be called a 'nigger,' I am going to be a business man, and men will take their hats off— well, we'll take our hats off to each other."

Dinner over, Mrs. Baxter asked her husband to let Silas stay and help her. She wanted him to motor to town with her and then help with the supper. Silas was elated because he was very anxious to see this man that they all seemed so excited about.

Dressed in his Sunday clothes, with a white straw hat and a black tie, he was a picture, in spite of his color.

"Now, Silas, don't forget to take off your hat and say, 'Good afternoon, sir,'" said Mrs. Baxter for the twentieth time since they started. "Yes'm," replied Silas slowly, wishing that she could think of something to talk about besides the taking off of hats.

They arrived in town just as the train steamed into the station. Mrs. Baxter stood upon the platform scanning every face as the passengers descended from the train. At length, she exclaimed, "Oh, there he is." Walking up to a tall, well-groomed man. "How do you do, Mr. Walker?"

"Well, well, Mrs. Baxter, I'm fine, thank you; how are you, and all of the family?" he asked as he shook her hand.

"Very well," replied Mrs. Baxter, smiling.

During this conversation Silas stood looking; he saw a fine example of a successful business man. His forty-odd years rested lightly upon his shoulders. His gray hair gave decidedly a touch of distinction to his appearance. He was an alert, progressive ranchman from a Western State. Silas admired this stately, refined looking man, and hoped with all his heart that he would not use the word "nigger." He stood with hat in hand waiting and wishing that he would speak to him. He felt slighted at not being noticed when Mrs. Baxter said, "Come, Mr. Walker, my car is over here," pointing to a beautiful car a short distance away.

Mr. Walker had not noticed that the boy was with them until they reached the car, and saw Silas struggling to lift his heavy baggage into the car. "Hello there, little fellow; are you with us?"

"Yes, sir," Silas answered, his hat still in his hand.

Seeing that the baggage was far too heavy for his child strength, he said, "Don't, child, don't! Let me help you."

"I can get it in, sir, if you give me time." Silas was afraid of being called "good-for-nothing" before this great man.

"Yes, my child, I shall have to give you ten years, I'm afraid, you get hold of that end," pointing to the lighter side, "and I will take this end; now, both together."

Then Mr. Walker did what few colored boys of the South had seen a white man do. He took the little brown hands into his soft, white ones with their glittering diamonds, shook them and asked, "What is your name?"

"Silas Miller, sir."

"Well, Silas, I am indeed glad to know you." The child did not know what to say, but he did the right thing—he smiled and bowed his head, then he put on his hat.

As they motored home, Silas wondered if Jesus was any nicer than this man. Mrs. Baxter also saw that Mr. Walker was different from the men of the South, but said nothing.

That night they sat down to a real Southern supper of fried chicken and waffles. As Silas served the supper, he could not help noticing Mr. Walker's cultured and refined manner. Each time he was served, he said "Thank you," or bowed his head. "Ain't he grand?" thought Silas. "I do hope he will stay two whole weeks."

Silas got up early the next morning and by ten o'clock had all of his work done. Mr. Baxter wondered what had come over the boy. "He worked well before, but now he is a wonder," he said to his wife.

Lillian E. Wood

?–?

Bishop Robert E. Jones of the African Methodist Episcopal Church wrote the introduction to Lillian E. Wood's novel, *"Let My People Go"* (1922), a not so surprising gesture since the book was published by the A. M. E. Book Concern. The bishop's sketchy information about the author notes that she had been a teacher for twenty years, which gave her an advantage in gaining the confidence of people so that she might learn their real-life backgrounds.

The author's fictionalized coverage of racial injustices and whites' subjugation of blacks encompasses nearly all the race's ordeals of the period, as seen in the life of Robert ("Bob") McComb. There are accounts of lynchings, mob violence, and social confrontations. Adding more fuel to the racial fires are the problems of blacks who migrated to the North and of black World War I soldiers in America and Europe. Tying together the episodes is the love story of Bob and Helen Adams.

Orphaned at the age of fourteen, Bob carries with him his mother's motto: "Be somebody." He is befriended by his white employer, Mr. Carson, who sends him away to college. On the train, he meets Helen, a returning senior at the school. Always a gentleman, Bob rescues her from a drunken white man intent on harassing her.

Bob studies hard and heads his class each year. It is on the eve of commencement when his spiritual call to lead occurs. Looking out his window, he sees a white mob moving through the streets, bent on hanging, burning, and running the "niggers" out of town. He goes outside, where his classmates are watching. The boys decide to follow the whites who are suddenly met by a challenging crowd of men from the black section. A melee ensues, broken up by the arrival of the police. Bob lectures his classmates, cautioning them that violence is not the way to be recognized as a man.

Later that night, the rumor circulates that blacks are going to dynamite the sheriff's house. Bob's benefactor, Mr. Carson, has come to see him graduate and is staying at the hotel next to the sheriff's home. Fearful of Mr. Carson's safety, he goes to the center of the city alone. There he meets eight hundred angry black men and women surging toward Main Street.

Bob bravely mounts a box to stop them. Being a "natural orator," he subdues the mob and they return to their homes. Walking back to the school, he passes a night service being held by a group of black women. When they begin to sing "Go down, Moses, Let my people go!" Bob suddenly feels impelled spiritually to lead, to be a black Moses for his people and deliver them from white oppression.

Bob becomes a superleader in various guises. He joins the army and meets Helen again, who is now a nurse. When he is seriously wounded, she nurses him back to health. Romance blossoms and they marry after the war. Bob goes on to excel as a lawyer, politician, organizer, and congressman. While in Congress, he succeeds in getting an antilynching bill passed.

Bishop Jones's introduction interestingly centers on Helen rather than the protagonist, Bob. The bishop bestows praises on Helen for winning "victories" over "the flesh and devil," by keeping her "virtue and noble womanhood" intact.[1] The chapter that recounts what the bishop refers to as "Helen's escape" from a fall into disgrace, "The Cloud with a Silver Lining," presents a subtle lesson to young ladies about how to cope with male crudities and advances, and thereby uphold black womanhood.

Wood's novel is filled with messages about coping with injustice, forgiveness, and raising the masses; she insists there are good and bad people in both races. She, too, had faith in the emerging black woman. Through the lips of Bob McComb, she says: "The women are taking an interest in public affairs now, and when educated, good women, with their fine instincts, take hold of affairs, there'll be a change."[2]

With this, Lillian E. Wood summed up the new black woman: she should combine the virtue of the nineteenth century with the progressivism of the twentieth.

NOTES

1. Wood, *"Let My People Go,"* p. 7.
2. Ibid., p. 106.

SOURCE

Primary

Wood, Lillian E. *"Let My People Go."* Philadelphia: A. M. E. Book Concern, 1922.

The Cloud With a Silver Lining

He plants His footsteps on the sea
And rides upon the storm.

Helen watched the soldiers march away, straining her eyes to see as long as she could the figure of her *own* soldier. With a lightened heart she ordered her baggage sent to the depot and wended her way into the crowded city. She determined to start at once for St. Louis. She chose a Southern route, because the trains by the other routes were all gone for the day and she did not care to stay in New York all night. True, she might have secured a sleeper and started about midnight, but Helen was unused to sleepers, and she was in a hurry to be off. She secured a good seat, settled herself in the luxurious cushions, and went to sleep. She would take advantage of this coach as long as she could. At B——, Virginia, she must enter the Jim-Crow car, she knew.

She slept until the time for the change. She left the train and entered the waiting-room. She found she had missed her Western train and that she would have to wait several hours. It was past midnight, and she reluctantly seated herself in the little waiting-room assigned to the race, and looked around. It was dark and dirty; the air was close, and a great lonely feeling came over her. She wished she and Bob didn't have to wait. She wanted him *now*. She took from her bag a book she had bought on the way to the station in New York. Soon she was lost to all surroundings, so intensely interested was she in the reading.

Suddenly she was startled by a chorus of oaths and vile language. A crowd of Negro men came into the waiting-room. They were working men, miners, carrying dinner-pails. Evidently they had to take an early train. Their clothes were black, greasy, and ill-smelling. She drew herself from them as far as possible, and tried to read on. The odor of liquor and tobacco alone was unbearable, and the vile talk continued. Some of the men, however, were quiet; for they threw themselves down on the benches and floor and slept heavily.

Two of the younger men began to notice Helen. She felt that they were staring at her. She could stand it no longer, so she got up and sauntered out of the room. She walked to the other side of the depot. Glancing into the waiting-room for whites, she found it vacant. It looked comfortable, and there was no one to enjoy it. What if she should go in and sit down? Quickly she resolved to do so, and seated herself in a corner of the room, again burying herself in her book. The station-master came in, glanced at her, and said nothing. A policeman looked in at the door, saw her, and passed on.

Presently some white people came into the room and seated themselves on the other side. For some minutes they took no notice of her. Then she heard a child's voice.

"See, Daddy, theuh's a nigguh gul!"

"O John! Baby's right. How scandalous! Why do they puhmit such things? Do go and have huh sent out," said a woman's voice.

John evidently was used to obeying, for he rose at once and left the room.

In a few minutes the station-master stood before Helen.

"Look here!" he began and then stopped for fully two minutes. As Helen looked up, he instinctively took off his hat and bowed. Then, as if regretting the action, he quickly replaced his hat and continued: "This is a white waiting-room! Didn't you understand?"

"I cannot stay in there with those men!" answered Helen. "They're too rough."

"You're right. I'll speak to them and make them behave themselves. But you can't stay in here! I wouldn't mind it, Miss, but people object," he explained.

"Very well," said Helen, rising at once and walking out of the room.

The station-master went into the waiting-room for colored passengers and spoke to the men, telling them to stop their talk, to sit up, and if they could not behave themselves, to go outside.

They obeyed; those lying on the floor seated themselves, and others stopped their vile talk. But Helen could not make up her mind to go back into the close, tobacco-and-alcohol-laden atmosphere of that room, and so she stood outside, leaning against the wall until the train came.

She was glad to get a seat in the car. The men filled the small apartment, but they soon arrived at the mines, and Helen had few traveling companions.

Arriving at St. Louis, she went at once to the hospital and renewed her friendship with the girls. They had a pleasant time together. Helen told of her experiences while in army service, all except that too closely connected with Robert McComb. She had her trunk sent out to the hospital and stayed there two days. It was not long, however, until she was busy again. There was a call for a nurse from the hospital; it was considered a very difficult case, and there was none of the regular force competent yet to take the place. The doctors knew Helen's capabilities and recommended her. Just before she went to the case, she received a letter from Bob. He was then starting with his men to Camp J——. It was filled with love and hope.

She found her place a large airy house on one of the principal residence streets. The patient was a white child of ten, who had typhoid fever. Helen had to be with her almost constantly for three weeks. During those weeks she received at least six letters from Bob, and she knew about his successes and pleasures in the South, but nothing, of course, of the terrible tragedy he had witnessed. The last letter stated that he would start on Monday morning for Chicago. That Sunday morning, which Bob spent in such agony of soul, little Jenny was much better and able to sit up in bed.

Helen went to church in the morning after she had cared for her patient and made her comfortable for the day. She left her with her mother. The sermon was excellent and at the service Helen met some old friends and walked home, thinking happily of the coming years as companion and wife of Robert McComb. Ah, Helen! it was nearer than you thought.

The next day she went to the hospital for an hour. The crisis was past with the child, and she knew she could safely leave her for some time now each day. She had a pleasant time with the girls. During this call she told them of the young officer who had been so near death's door and who had recovered almost by a miracle. She was glad soon that she had told them.

Blest be the tempest, kind the storm,
Which drives me nearer home.

396

Helen was humming this over to herself as she approached the mansion. There was a beautiful park with flowers and trees and fountains in front of the residence. She walked briskly up the path. Her patient must be ready for her dinner and somebody might give her what she ought not to have. She was not looking to left or right and did not notice the form of her patient's father reclining on one of the park benches. She was nearly to the steps when a hand was laid upon her arm and she was dragged to the shade of a large rosebush. She was terribly frightened. A deathly pallor overspread her face and she trembled from head to foot. She saw that it was the master of the house.

"Helen, darling, I love you. I must take you with me!" whispered the man.

The strength of an Amazon seemed to come to her, and she wrested herself from his grasp and gave him a push! Then she ran and gained the walk. As she did so she ran against another man, who caught her in his arms and pressed a kiss upon her lips. This time she did not struggle, for through her tears she saw the dark, handsome face of Robert McComb! Without a word, he turned and walked to the gate, carrying his dearest girl. He hailed a passing cab, ordered the chauffeur to take them to the Colored Hospital, placed Helen inside, and sprang in himself.

"How *did* it happen, Bob, that you came?" asked Helen, laughing and crying at the same time.

"I had to come North a day earlier. In fact, I hardly know how I came to be on that train, but when the porter called 'St. Louis,' I just felt that I must see you. I found the address of your letters, so here I am," answered Bob, taking off her hat and smoothing her hair. "And I have made up my mind this minute, unless you say 'No!' that you and I will never part till death. You're going with me to Chicago, aren't you dear? We'll make it, somehow, and it shall be together after this."

"Oh, my Captain Bob, yes, I'll go now," answered Helen, laying her head upon his shoulder, sobbing like a child.

At the hospital Helen telephoned to her patient's mother, saying that she would not return. The lady did not seem surprised. What had she seen from the window? Poor woman! The janitor was sent after her suitcase, and Helen received by him the amount due for her services. Bob sent out into the city and made arrangements for something very important. He returned for lunch at the hospital.

"In the morning at ten. I can't get everything ready until then," he said after lunch. "Rest now. I will come for you then."

"Yes, dear," answered Helen happily.

She retired at once and slept, and arose refreshed and smiling.

"This is my wedding day!" she said.

Then she committed to God the new life upon which she was entering, dressed, and went down to breakfast.

Promptly at ten Bob came and brought with him a clergyman, pastor of the church Helen had attended in St. Louis. In the private parlor, surrounded by nurses, the servants, and all patients who were able to be brought from their rooms, Helen Adams became Mrs. Robert McComb.

Amid showers of rice and old shoes, Captain McComb and his bride entered the cab, were driven to the depot, and, after checking their baggage, boarded a train for Chicago, the happiest two people in the whole world.

Part 4

The New Negro Movement
1924–1933

Black women writers became more prominent with the rise of the New Negro Movement, an epoch Alain Locke described as a "spiritual coming of age" in his *The New Negro: An Interpretation* (1925). Locke rejoiced to see blacks "rising above the past levels of inferiority in living, thinking and being," as evidenced in their burgeoning art, literature, music, and history.

This black awakening has been given various labels, ranging from the New Negro Renaissance, the Negro Renascence, the Harlem Renaissance (the most commonly used), and the New Negro Movement. For this work, I will use the designation, the New Negro Movement, because of its broad impact not only on the artistic, cultural, and intellectual flowering of Afro-Americans but also on the social, political and economic conditions that affected all regions of the country.

Scholars differ also on the dates of its beginning and its end. Some have placed the origin as far back as 1903, when W. E. B. Du Bois published *The Souls of Black Folks: Essays and Sketches*. Benjamin Brawley pinpointed its roots "in the throes of the World War," when returning black soldiers realized they had another freedom to fight-for—their own at home. Others picked the year 1925 when Locke's *The New Negro* was published. Ending dates have been placed variously at the Harlem riots of 1935 and the Wall Street market crash in 1929, when Langston Hughes wryly noted, "We were no longer in vogue."

Since the New Negro Movement's dates can be fixed to suit particular purposes, this book will use as its starting point the publication of Jessie Redmon Fauset's novel of 1924, *There Is Confusion* (which predates Locke's *The New Negro*), and its termination the year of Fauset's last novel, *Comedy, American Style*, in 1933. The year 1924 was not picked solely out of female scholarly partisanship, but also because this was the time when Charles S. Johnson, godfather of the New Negro Movement, decided to sponsor an informal coming-out party at the Civic Club in New York on 21 March to celebrate the publication of Fauset's novel.

Additionally, the occasion introduced a group of younger Negro members of the Writers' Guild that included Countee Cullen, Langston Hughes, Eric Walrond, Gwendolyn Bennett, Regina Anderson Andrews, and Jessie Fauset herself. Spontaneous remarks memorialized the gathering of illustrious persons, white and black, who saw "new currents" in Negro literature. Praising the black literary renaissance were Alain Locke, W. E. B. Du Bois, James Weldon Johnson, Horace Liveright, and Carl Van Doren. The function was captured in a dedication poem by Gwendolyn Bennett, who embraced the new spirit of her fellow writers and herself. As if distilling the future, she proclaimed: "And there are those who feel the pull / Of seas beneath the skies."

Different now from the earlier part of the century, multiple forces were providing an impetus for the expression of Afro-American writers' creativity. White publishers and magazine editors, smitten with the New Negro fever, were not only considering more works by blacks but publishing them too. This reversal could have been prompted by the realization that there was a white readership for black books out there.

Publishers, white private foundations, and individuals handed out awards to encourage and honor black writers. Publishers Boni and Liveright in 1926 offered a one-thousand-dollar prize for the "best novel on Negro life" by a black. The William E. Harmon Foundation proferred gifts for distinguished achievement, one of which Nella Larsen won for *Quicksand*. Amy Spingarn contributed money to the *Crisis* magazine for literary prizes, as did Harlem's roving white author, Carl Van Vechten, to *Opportunity*.

The increasing number of black publications helped liberate the voices of black women writers, who were contributors and in some cases editors and founders. New York City's black ghetto, Harlem, became a mecca for black artists and writers. Here was located the Urban League's *Opportunity* magazine, founded in 1923 with Charles S. Johnson as editor. Some of the women writers gracing its pages as prize winners for poetry, short stories, essays, and plays were Georgia Douglas Johnson, Gwendolyn Bennett, Lucy Oriel Williams, Anita Scott Coleman, Dorothy West, Zora Neale Hurston, Helene Johnson, Mae V. Cowdery, Marian Cuthbert, Esther Popel Shaw, and May Miller.

The *Crisis*, official organ of the NAACP launched earlier in 1910, had Jessie Redmon Fauset, midwife of the New Negro Movement, as literary editor. Standing out among its contributors were poets Effie Lee Newsome, Marjorie Marshall, and Beatrice M. Murphy, short-story writers Brenda Ray Moryck and Maude Irwin Owens, and playwright Marita O. Bonner.

Magazines outside of New York also proliferated. Boston's *Saturday Evening Quill*, founded by a group of young black writers, contained short stories by Dorothy West, Gertrude Schalk, Florence Marion Harmon, and Edythe Mae Gordon. The latter's story, "Subversion," published in the first issue, was one of the O. Henry Memorial Award Prize Stories of 1928. Philadelphia had Nellie Bright's *Black Opals*; Los Angeles, the *Ink Slingers*; and Washington, D.C., Howard University's the *Stylus*, which first published Zora Neale Hurston.

Of these small literary magazines, the best remembered is Harlem's *Fire!* which had Gwendolyn Bennett and Zora Neale Hurston as associate staff members. *Fire!* which was published 1926, represented the younger writers who were rebelling against conventional writing. The magazine elicited outrage from orthodox black critics and survived for only one issue. Coincidentally, copies of the journal stored in a warehouse were destroyed by fire.

Greater numbers of black book publishers supported black writers by producing books that white publishers normally would reject.

Moreover, organizations entered the field of publishing. The Crisis Publishing Company of the NAACP brought out Maud Cuney Hare's biography, *Norris Wright Cuney: A Tribune to His People*. The National Urban League published Charles S. Johnson's *Ebony and Topaz: A Collectanea* (1927), which featured women writers Mae V. Cowdery, Jessie Redmon Fauset, Georgia Douglas Johnson, Alice Dunbar-Nelson, Zora Neale Hurston, Angelina W. Grimké, and Dorothy R. Peterson. And the National Association of Colored Women published Elizabeth Lindsay Davis's *Lifting as They Climb*.

The black church had long been active in publishing black books—the African Methodist Episcopal Church started this in 1817. Its A. M. E. Book Concern was responsible for Mary Etta Spencer's *The Resentment*; Lillian E. Wood's *"Let My People Go"*; Katherine Davis Tillman's *Fifty Years of Freedom; or, From Cabin to Congress; a Drama in Five Acts*, which was based on the life of Benjamin Banneker; and Tillman's one-act domestic play, *Aunt Betsy's Thanksgiving*. The National Baptist Publishing Board issued Myra Viola Wilds's *Thoughts of Idle Hours*.

Newspapers also brought out books. The *Iowa State Bystander*'s publisher was responsible for Sue M. Wilson Brown's *The History of the Order of the Eastern Star among Colored People*, and private individuals formed publishing companies. W. E. B. Du Bois and Granville Dill founded the Du Bois and Dill Publishing Company, which sponsored Elizabeth Ross Haynes's *Unsung Heroes*. Black historian Carter G. Woodson originated the Associated Publishers in Washington, D.C., which included Maude Cuney Hare's *Negro Musicians and Their Music* and Sadie Iola Daniel's *Women Builders* on its list.

Some black women authors published their own works using black job printers whose imprints appeared on the title page. Such was the Press of R. L. Pendleton, Washington, D.C., which printed Laura Eliza Wilkes's *Missing Pages in American History, Revealing the Services of Negroes in the Early Wars in the United States* and Leila Amos Pendleton's *A Narrative of the Negro*. Murray Brothers Printing Company, also in Washington, D.C., issued Mamie Jordan Carver's *As It Is; or, the Conditions under Which the Race Problem Challenges the White Man's Solution*. Others, such as Delilah Beasley and Frances Gaudet, used their own names as publishers.

Although Afro-American women writers were at work in regions throughout the country, Harlem was their major center. Writing in *The*

New Negro, Elsie Johnson MacDougal saw Harlem, "more than any-where else," as a place where the black woman was freed "from the cruder handicaps of primitive household hardships and the grosser forms of sex and race subjugations." There McDougal knew "dram-atists, poets, and novelists" who were "enjoying a vogue in print."

Women, then, were sharing in the literary harvest of the times, but not as much as black male writers. Alain Locke singled out the year 1928 as representing a "floodtide of the present Negrophile Movement," for more books were published by and about blacks than in the decade past. Nevertheless, only two books were published by Afro-American women that year—Georgia Douglas Johnson's *An Au-tumn Love Cycle* and Nella Larsen's *Quicksand*. As Erlene Stetson suc-cinctly put it: "If the Renaissance had a gender, it was male." The patronizing attitude of black male writers and critics toward black women writers forestalled their literary recognition. For example, W. E. B. Du Bois's foreword to Georgia Douglas Johnson's *Bronze* used the condescending words of *simple* and *trite* to describe it.

The differences in interests, subject matter, and writing styles between males and females added to the schism. While black males like Claude McKay, Wallace Thurman, and Langston Hughes were writing in a realistic style of race assertion, primitivism, and sex, the in themes of the New Negro Movement, women writers tended to cling to outdated Victorian themes and conventional styles.

The women were constricted by their sex. As in the last years of the nineteenth century, they were still set on saving the race and being "proper" women, goals that placed constraints on their imagi-nation. As black feminist critic Barbara Christian put it, "The garb of uninhibited passion wears better on a male, who after all, does not have to carry the burden of the race's morality or lack of it."

The women who wrote what males smirkingly called "genteel" novels and "possy" poems came from middle-class backgrounds that had inculcated them with the standards of refinement and Victorian virtues that surfaced in their writings. Adding to their self-imposed inhibitions were their husbands and fathers who restricted them phys-ically and mentally through what Alice Dunbar-Nelson called "the white male's attitude of woman's place built on the rock of southern chivalry." This was all the more anomalous since white women writers were abandoning Victorianism in favor of more liberal attitudes.

For all that, one can glimpse through the veil of Victorian restraints indications that black women were not that far behind their white counterparts. Georgia Douglas Johnson's poetry contained recurring references to the heart and love. Angelina Grimké's subtle eroticism pervaded her poetry in a way that Gloria T. Hull has identified as woman-to-woman in nature, designating "A Mona Lisa," in particular. Grimké's "Grass Fingers" also could be read as a woman-to-woman poem, as evidenced by the lines "Elusive, delicate grass fingers" and "For you to reach me, even / With your tiny timorous toes." Clearly no male would have such sensitive fingers or little toes.

The diary of Alice Dunbar-Nelson from 1921 to 1931, entitled *Give Us Each Day* and edited by Gloria T. Hull, reveals Dunbar-Nelson's lesbian affairs in real life, an unspoken subject among middle-class blacks of her time, even between those involved as can be seen through Dunbar-Nelson's own camouflaged words to her lovers.

In Nella Larsen's *Quicksand*, Helga Crane's Swedish admirer, painter Axel Olsen, may have been speaking of the author herself when he notes the "contradictions" between her outward properness and the qualities his portrait of her illuminates. Larsen could have been exposing the repressed sexual and emotional impulses in herself and other black middle-class women.

Jessie Fauset, derided by Claude McKay for being "prim," dealt with her own warring forces by encouraging black radical male writers to do what she could not. To compensate, she acquired the relatively harmless affectation of smoking Salomes cigarettes of different colors, which probably matched her clothes.

Zora Neale Hurston, because of her background and naturally uninhibited personality, was the most unreserved of the writers. Born to poor sharecropper parents in an all-black southern town in Florida, she left home at an early age to strike out on her own. Thus unsheltered, Hurston was free of the middle-class proprieties and prejudices that Jessie Fauset derided in her novels. Since Hurston was aggressive, free-spirited, and astute enough to take advantage of white patronage like some of the black male writers, she became a target for black and white male displeasure. White sociologist Edwin Embree, although bowing to Hurston's brilliance, deplored her personality, informing her "discoverer," Charles S. Johnson, that she needed "discipline both intellectually and personally." Engrossed in folklore expeditions, she moved only on the fringe of the New Negro Movement and did not write her novels until afterward.

The two leading women novelists of the New Negro Movement, Fauset and Larsen, strengthened links in the Afro-American feminist literary tradition. Fauset has been much maligned by black and white male critics for her "middle-class novels of manners," which showed that blacks were no different from whites. Frequently quoted Robert A. Bone, a white critic of Fauset, ridiculed her novels and relegated her to the "Rear Guard" of the New Negro Movement writers.

Today with the mounting awareness of the Afro-American feminist literary tradition, black feminist critic Deborah E. McDowell in her "The Neglected Dimension of Jessie Fauset," sees Fauset as a "quiet rebel, a pioneer black feminist," whose "characters were harbingers of the movement for women's liberation from the constrictions of cultural conditioning." Like Frances Ellen Watkins Harper, Fauset believed the importance of "the pursuit of happiness to the black woman." McDowell's Fauset is one who dared to write "about women taking charge of their own lives and declaring themselves independent of social conventions."

Fauset's literary rebellion shines through in the bold themes of "incest," "exploitative sexual affairs," and "promiscuity," all long ignored by male critics. The feminist attitude is adroitly rendered in the characters' dialogue and the romantic twists. Angela Murray in *Plum Bun* feels it isn't "decent for women to have to scrub and work and slave and bear children and sacrifice their looks and their pretty hands." And Angela's free-thinking friend, Martha, tells her how to "play the game" with men by not giving too much or "we lose ourselves."

Nella Larsen, too, was reduced to Bone's "Rear Guard." Larsen's themes, like Fauset's, dealt with the black bourgeoisie, passing, and a new "tragic mulatto." Passing also became a popular theme for whites with great numbers of masters' ex-slave descendants crossing over for convenience, or for economic, political, or social reasons. Popular white novelist Vera Caspary wrote a sensational novel, *The White Girl* (1929), about a black New York woman who, because she hates her race, passes for white. When she is blackmailed by a West Indian elevator boy, she commits suicide.

Larsen's Irene Redfield in *Passing* posed for the ease of shopping and sipping tea in white Chicago hotels, and Fauset's Angela Murray, characterized in *Plum Bun*, summed up her reasons by saying, "I am both white and Negro and look white. Why shouldn't I declare for the one that will bring me the greatest happiness, prosperity and respect?"

Larsen's two novels, *Quicksand* and *Passing*, uncovered the effects of racism and sexism on the lives of their black female protagonists. *Quicksand*, in the context of today's genres, could fall into the realm of an autobiographical novel, for it echoed the life of its author. Like Fauset, Larsen also was quietly feminist about her work. At a time when black churches were considered sacrosanct pillars of the black community, Larsen dared to delineate a crude unpolished black southern minister in the form of Reverend Mr. Pleasant Green, who takes advantage not only of the women in his church but of his wife also. In the pulpit, Green propounds religion as a solace for black peoples' woes, thus keeping the poor and illiterate congregation wrapped in poverty and ignorance rather than proposing other, more worldly solutions. Larsen portrayed sexism through Helga's domination by the Reverend Green physically, emotionally, and economically. Her *Passing* has been freshly interpreted by Claudia Tate in "Nella Larsen's *Passing*: A Problem Interpretation" as a "skillfully executed and enduring work of art." And she uncovered another layer of meaning in *Passing* when she detected themes of "jealousy, psychological ambiguity, and intrigue." If Tate's interpretation is accurate, this would place Larsen in the avant-garde of black women authors of psychological novels.

Fauset and Larsen, then, are two complex literary foremothers whose works, however, have not been emulated by present-day black women writers as has Zora Neale Hurston, who is extravagantly admired.

A never-mentioned serial novel of the period, *Vagrant Love* by Marjorie Wilson, was published in the *Chicago Defender*. The plot concerns the trials and tribulations of urban blacks within the framework of a story of a young black woman, Georgia Morse from Georgia, who leaves to seek a better life in New York. The narration reflected the contemporary influx of black emigrants who were leaving the South for the North. This serial ended after eleven installments in September 1928.

Afro-American women poets seem to have fared better with the black male literary critics. As with the novelists, women verse writers were generally branded as minor and not in the same league of Langston Hughes, Countee Cullen, and Claude McKay. On the other hand, Arthur P. Davis and Saunders Redding, bastions of conventional critical analyses, lauded the women poets who "eschewed racial themes" as being "generally better poets than men." They went on to add, however, that the poetry of Johnson, Grimké, and Dunbar-Nelson tended "more to prettiness than profundity, more to surface than to substance."

Making up this circle of minor poets were Georgia Douglas Johnson, Anne Spencer, Jessie Fauset, Angelina Weld Grimké, Helene Johnson, Effie Lee Newsome, and Gwendolyn Bennett. Anne Spencer, like Georgia Douglas Johnson, antedated the New Negro Movement. She has been rated above Johnson in the quality of her writing, although Johnson was more prolific. Erlene Stetson likes Spencer's "polished diction" and "quality." Gloria T. Hull admires the feminist side of her work, her "sense of woman-self" and "female identity" which comes through in her poems. Sterling Brown assigns her to the lofty heights of "the most original of all Negro women poets." Spencer's sensitivity to women's plight seethes in her "Lady, Lady" where she writes:

Lady, lady, I saw your face.
Dark as night withholding a star . . .
The chisel fell, or it might have been
You had borne so long the yoke of men.

Georgia Douglas Johnson, like Harper in the previous era, was the most popular. She published her poems in book form, which brought her more public attention. She is often belittled for her poems of the heart, which her white contemporary and friend, Sara Teasdale, wrote also. Pulitzer Prize winner Teasdale was more successful, however, for she had an appreciative audience.

The younger women poets were less traditional in their verse and wrote to a greater extent of race. Of these, Gloria T. Hull places Helene Johnson at the forefront, for her "work most reflects the themes which are commonly designated as the characteristic ones of the Renaissance." Johnson wrote "in the new colloquial folk-slang style popular during that time." Helene Johnson extolled blackness, black pride, and black life. In her "Sonnet to a Negro in Harlem," she rhapsodized over a black man: "You are disdainful and magnificent— / Your perfect body and your pompous gait." Gwendolyn Bennett, another of the younger poets, glorified the beauty of black women, lifting them to a new level. Her "To a Dark Girl" poeticized "I love you for your brownness, / And the rounded darkness of your breast."

Hull blames the relegation of these female poets to a minor status on the fact they "did not produce and publish enough." But, on the other hand, to produce requires time and energy. As women writers who also worked and took care of their husbands and family, it is remarkable that they published as much as they did. Jessie Fauset wrote her novels after school and during the summer months; Georgia Douglas Johnson wrote after a hard day's work as a stenographer. Even Fauset, who published more novels than any of the other writers and won the respect of the white literary establishment (they gave her an autograph party at Macy's, the first black to have this honor), still bore the stigma of "minor." The truth of the matter is that any woman who writes in a sexist society, regardless of how well or how much, will be considered minor until *major* is no longer synonymous with *male*. Has anyone said that Alice Walker is on the same level as Ralph Ellison or Richard Wright?

Hull's second reason for the women's poets' secondary value is that they did not "parley their talent into fame." True, black women writers were self-effacing about their works, which could be why Grimké, Spencer, and Bennett did not try to publish collections of their poems. Even in the nineteenth century, the women writers in their prefaces were invariably modest, purporting to write not for themselves but for their race's benefit. In her preface to *Morning Glories*, for example, Josie D. Henderson Heard asked: "Will you accept a Bunch of "Morning Glories, freshly plucked and with the Dew Drops still upon them? Coming, as they do, from a heart that desires to encourage and inspire the youth of the Race." And Myra Iola Wilds in *Thoughts of Idle Hours* informed her readers that she wrote her poems to "cheer the soul," not seeking "Wealth, Fame or Place." Eloise Bibb presented her work in *Poems* with almost unbelievable humility: "I timidly present this little volume to the public with a full knowledge of its many faults. Indeed, I sometimes feel greatly frightened at my own temerity, and wonder how I would feel should an able critic deign to censure me as I deserve."

If James Weldon Johnson had not stumbled upon Spencer's

poems scattered about her house while he was visiting her, would she, because of her diffidence, have ended up in the ghostly line of lost black women poets?

As black women whose self-assignment was as guardians of the family and the race, they probably did not look upon themselves as writers as seriously as did the males. The New Negro Movement women writers acted more as mothers, sisters, and confidantes to male writers rather than as their peers. Georgia Douglas Johnson had her "sons"—Langston Hughes, Harold Jackman, and Glenn Carrington, all of whom sought that aspect in women. Similarly, Anne Spencer shared her Lynchburg home as a gathering place for the New Negro Movement male figures. Jessie Fauset held her Sunday teas, and Regina Andrews and Ethel Ray Nance had an open-door policy in their Harlem apartment as literary confidantes.

In spite of the women writers being consigned to the back of the New Negro Movement's literary bus, they unassertively continued to pour their talents into their work. Aside from producing fiction and poetry, they began to explore more fully the genre of play writing, emulating their model, Angelina Weld Grimké. As with other literary art forms, the *Crisis* and *Opportunity* magazines supported the genre through publication and prizes. Some of the winners were Georgia Douglas Johnson, Mary Burrill, Eulalie Spence, May Miller, R. A. Gaines-Shelton, Marita O. Bonner, and Myrtle Smith Livingstone.

Most of the plays had interracial or intraracial themes of racism, miscegenation, black history, and folk drama. Eulalie Spence was an exception with her drama *Undertow* (1929), whose characters could have been any color. Playwright historian James V. Hatch in his *Black Theater, U.S.A.: Forty-five Plays by Black Americans* (1974) identifies her as being perhaps "one of the first to write black characters into a non-racial plot." The play is based on the eternal triangle theme of a man, Dan, married to Hattie, whom he does not love. He chances upon a past love, Clem, who revives old feelings. When he asks his wife for a divorce, she refuses, and in a heated argument, he pushes her. Hattie falls, hits her head against a mantle, and dies.

A second unusual play was *The Church Fight* (1925), a *Crisis* prize-winner by Ruth Gaines-Shelton, who was a grandmother when she wrote it. A comedy, Hatch singles it out as "one of the few written by black playwrights of the period." The play is a satire about church politics with characters having allegorical names like Sister Instigator,

Sister Meddler, Sister Two-Face, and Brother Judas. Its humor and authenticity withstands the test of time.

Marita Bonner's *The Purple Flower* (1928) was a precursor of the sixties' "black revolution" and was published also in the *Crisis*. Bonner examined the idea of a revolution to conquer the "White Devils" (this before Malcolm X) who have held the race down and away from the purple-flower-of-life-at-its-fullest.

Other women left historical chronicles for posterity. Sadie Iola Daniel's *Women Builders* (1931) gave "seven sketches of Negro women who have definitely contributed to the development of the Negro youth." Hattie Quinn Brown, writer, elocutionist, and teacher at Wilberforce for whom the Central State Library is named, published *Homespun Heroines and Other Women of Distinction* (1926). As the reason for writing a book of "history-making women of our race," Brown said she wanted "to preserve for future reference an account of black women, their life and character and what they accomplished under the most trying and adverse circumstances." The book is invaluable for its accounts of black women who might have vanished from memory if not for her foresightedness.

The year 1933, when Fauset's fourth and last novel, *Comedy, American Style* came into being, Elizabeth Lindsay Davis did what was thought of as "a labor of love" with her *Lifting as They Climb*, a historical record of black clubwomen, their organizations, and activities. The book complements Hallie Quinn Brown's earlier work with its biographical data and photographs.

The New Negro Movement writers wrote in all genres, instituting firsts in certain areas and strengthening those they had already created. They advanced both Afro-American literature and the Afro-American feminist literary tradition. Black historian David L. Lewis has acknowledged that there was no telling what Jessie Fauset could have done if she had been a man. Turning his phrase to include all the women writers, there is no telling what they could have done if they had worked under fewer racist, sexist, and classist constraints and had been at least as free as the black male writers of the age. For all that, they accomplished much against great odds.

Chronology of Writings

1924   Jessie Redmon Fauset, *There Is Confusion*

1925   Sue M. Wilson Brown, *The History of the Order of the Eastern Star among Colored People*

         Hallie Quinn Brown, *Our Women: Past, Present, and Future*

         Hallie Quinn Brown, *Tales My Father Taught Me*

1926   Clara Ann Thompson, *A Garland of Poems*

         Hallie Quinn Brown, *Homespun Heroines and Other Women of Distinction*

1927   Eulalie Spence, *Fool's Errand: A Play in One Act*

         Eulalie Spence, *Foreign Mail*

         Nettie Arnold Plummer, *Out of the Depths; or, The Triumph of the Cross*

1927–28   Marjorie Wilson, *Vagrant Love*

1928   Georgia Douglas Johnson, *An Autumn Love Cycle*

         Nella Larsen, *Quicksand*

1929   Jessie Redmon Fauset, *Plum Bun: A Novel without a Moral*

        Nella Larsen, *Passing*

1931   Jessie Redmon Fauset, *The Chinaberry Tree: A Novel of American Life*

        Sadie Iola Daniel, *Women Builders*

1932   Mazie Earhart Clark, *Garden of Memories*

1933   Elizabeth Lindsay Davis, *Lifting as They Climb*

        Jessie Redmon Fauset, *Comedy, American Style*

Jessie Redmon Fauset Harris
Jessie Redmon Fauset

1882–1961

According to Fauset biographer Carolyn Wedin Sylvander, "Jessie 'Redmona' Fauset was born 27 April 1882 in Camden County, Snow Hill Center Township, New Jersey, to Redmon Fauset, age forty-five, and Annie Seamon Fauset, age thirty-seven, their seventh child."[1] This date and place varies from those given in other sources, which cite the years 1882, 1884, 1885, and 1886 with Philadelphia as the birthplace. Fauset herself, in Countee Cullen's *Caroling Dusk*, stated that she was born in Philadelphia. Joseph J. Feeney, S.J., who has also sought to set the record straight, identified 26 April 1882 as the correct date and Frederickville, Camden County, as the place.[2] Both Sylvander and Feeney used the Fauset family Bible for documentation. The discrepancy between the two as to place is accounted for by Feeney's quoting the librarian of Camden County, who noted that in 1882 Frederickville was a part of Snow Hill, New Jersey, a community of freed slaves.[3]

Fauset's reluctance to reveal her date of birth, Feeney reasoned, could have reflected the fact that she belonged "to that era which considered it improper to mention—or even to know—a woman's age; in this period, too, women generally preferred to be thought younger than they were."[4] When Fauset's mother died shortly after her birth, her father took her to Philadelphia to live. (This may be why the author claimed Philadelphia as her birthplace.) There he married Bella Huff, a widow with three children. The couple had three more children, one of whom was writer and educator Arthur Huff Fauset, owner of the family Bible.

Sylvander refutes another legend about Fauset, that she was born into the black middle class. They were children of an African Methodist Episcopal minister, Arthur Huff Fauset pointed out, adding, "our family was poor, one might say, dreadfully poor,"[5] dependent upon church collection plates for existence. In gauging Reverend Fauset's economic status, Sylvander reasoned that "given the large number of children to support, and the probable expense of illness and death among the oldest children, some poverty seems not at all unlikely in Jessie Fauset's first twenty years."[6] On the other hand, he speculated, if one looked at their "type of life" rather than their economic status, the Fausets could have been identified as middle class because they were "of a Negro cultured class or intelligentsia."

Jessie's father instilled in her an ambition to become a schoolteacher, the status symbol occupation for black women. In preparation, she had an outstanding record at the Philadelphia High School for girls, where she was the only black in her class. She was awarded a scholarship to Cornell University, becoming one of the first black women to attend the school in 1901–5. A classical languages major, she was the first black woman to be admitted to Phi Beta Kappa.

At Cornell, she became an ardent admirer of W. E. B. Du Bois, director for publications and research for the NAACP. She began corresponding with him in 1903, the year her father died. Through Du Bois, she obtained a summer teaching position at his alma mater, Fisk University, in 1904 in order to acquire experience before she graduated. Having lived in a white neighborhood and matriculated in predominantly white schools, she expressed to Du Bois her desire to work in the South to get acquainted with another class of her people.[7]

Upon graduating from Cornell, she ran head-on into racism in the City of Brotherly Love, which refused her a teaching position in the Philadelphia high schools. She had to go to nearby Baltimore to teach at the black Douglas High School for the year 1905–6. Afterward, she transferred to the historic Dunbar High School in Washington, D.C., to teach French and Latin.

On leave in 1918–19, she worked toward a master's degree at the University of Pennsylvania. While doing this, she was a writer and "Looking Glass" columnist for the *Crisis* magazine, official organ of the NAACP. Finding the smell of ink more exciting than the classroom, she resigned from Dunbar High in 1919 and moved to New York to become literary editor for the *Crisis* in October.

She strove to develop the publication through her versatility, intellect, imagination, and hard work. The publication outsold Charles S. Johnson's

Opportunity with a monthly circulation of sixty thousand. Fauset encouraged the young radical writers of the Harlem Renaissance by giving counsel and publishing their work. She discovered Langston Hughes, Jean Toomer, and Countee Cullen. In Hughes's autobiography, *The Big Sea,* he named Jessie Fauset along with Charles S. Johnson and Alain Locke as one of the "three people who midwifed the so-called New Negro literature into being."

Through her own short stories, essays, poetry, reviews, critiques, and translations, Fauset added immeasurably to the stature of the *Crisis.* Her skill with words, interpretations, knowledge, and background of world travel made her an outstanding essayist on national and international topics. Her essay, "The Gift of Laughter," in Alain Locke's *The New Negro,* is considered a classic.

Although she wrote poetry, she is hardly considered as a major or even a minor poet. She wrote of love, romance, and nature. Her best-known poems are "La Vie C'est La Vie" (in which historian David L. Lewis saw a secret passion for Du Bois), "Noblesse Oblige," and "Words! Words!"

In 1920–21, Fauset, as literary editor, and Augustus Granville Dill, business manager, piloted into print Du Bois's idea for *The Brownies' Book, A Monthly Magazine for the Children of the Sun.* Designed for youngsters six to sixteen, it contained stories, biographies, songs, pictures, and games. The magazine's lofty purpose was to "teach Universal Love and Brotherhood for all little folks—black and brown and yellow and white." For these pages, Fauset wrote "hundreds of signed and unsigned stories, poems, dialogues, biographies, articles, and did the editing of manuscripts and correspondence with contributors as well."[8]

Along with her writing, she lectured, organized literary groups, and traveled abroad. Her second trip to Paris in 1921, for the Second Pan-African Congress, was sponsored by her Delta Sigma Theta sorority. While there, she lectured in London on Negro women in the United States. She returned to Europe for a year in 1924 to study at the Sorbonne and the Alliance Française which awarded her a certificate in French. During the same year, she made her first trip to Africa. She went overseas again in 1934, visiting Paris, Gibraltar, Naples, Rome, Seville, and Morocco. Her articles pertaining to her travels abroad enhanced her reputation as a writer and journalist.

In February 1926, she resigned as literary editor of the *Crisis.* David L. Lewis attributed the resignation to "personal friction" with Du Bois. It appears that Du Bois objected to the publication of "an excess of socially unredeeming art" (writings of the radical group) and was embarrassed by "a financial debt," which "made Du Bois less chivalrous" to her. Lewis cites a loan of $2,500 to Du Bois from Fauset and her sister, Helen Fauset Lanning, in 1923 that created the tension. When the sisters asked for payment, "Du Bois coldly refused."[9] This very large sum is reduced in Sylvander's account to $588.85, which she states was repaid in late March.[10] A final break with the *Crisis* came in March 1927, when Fauset gave up her status as contributing editor.

Having enjoyed the experience of working with writing and writers, she was reluctant to return to teaching. She asked Arthur Spingarn "to assist her in finding work as a publisher's reader, as a social secretary for a private family, 'preferably a woman,' or with a New York foundation."[11] Her varied experience with the *Crisis* indeed qualified her, but prejudices existed in the publishing houses then more than ever, and she was forced to return to the classroom.

She taught French at DeWitt Clinton High School from 1927 to 1944. It was while she held this position that she began the most noted segment of her literary career, the writing of four novels. She wrote in the afternoons and during summer vacations, "doing a little every day rather than waiting for the correct mood, or for uninterrupted leisure."[12]

The writing of her first book, *There Is Confusion* (1924), at the age of forty-two was prompted by reading an unrealistic novel, *Birthright* (1922), by white writer T. S. Stribling. To her, the story was not indicative of actual Negro life. *There Is Confusion* was the first novel to depict black middle-class people.

Publisher Boni and Liveright's book jacket advertised the book as portraying "the new society that is growing up among the Northern Negroes." Some twenty-five years later, critic Hugh M. Gloster gave it a new historical dimension by calling it a "trail-blazer" in showing "bourgeois Negroes" as "interesting subjects for literary treatment," and most of all, for being "the first nationally recognized novel by an American colored woman."[13]

A saga, the novel portrays the intertwined lives of two black families, the Marshalls of New York and the Byes of Philadelphia, spanning World War I and two continents. Its themes comprise black middle-class values, manners, and history, classism, intraracial color biases, sexism, and passing. An abundance of characters and subplots are presented, featuring romance, separations, reunions, and mishaps. The "confusion" is that of racism affecting blacks in a white society.

Joanna Marshall, youngest of the Marhsalls, is the beautiful, light-skinned (as are all of Fauset's female heroines) principal character. Ambitious and snobbish, she aspires to become a famous singer and dancer, despite the odds against her because of her race. She motivates her friend, antiwhite Peter Bye, a poor but respectable descendant of the aristocratic white Byes of Philadelphia, to go to medical school.

Class-conscious, Joanna breaks up a budding romance between her brother Philip and Maggie Ellersley, who is not of a "good" middle-class family. Maggie marries an older man, Henderson Neal, whom she finds out is a gambler. This pushes her further down society's totem pole. Through a series of trials, adversities, and coincidences, the proper lovers are reunited in Paris during the war. At the conclusion, Peter and Joanna marry, and Maggie has a few brief moments of happiness with Philip before he dies of war wounds.

The novel was rejected by one publisher because "white readers just don't expect Negroes to be like this,"[14] but black critics were delighted with the new black literary image. Montgomery Gregory in his *Opportunity* review (June 1924) praised the work for presenting to whites "a milieu of its civilization of which it has been totally ignorant . . . the more cultured class of Negroes." Staid critic and anthologist William Stanley Braithwaite extolled the author as "the potential Jane Austen of Negro literature."[15]

Fauset's second novel, *Plum Bun: A Novel without a Moral* (1929) was issued by New York publisher Frederick A. Stokes. The title is taken from the Mother Goose rhyme, "To Market, to Market," and the book is divided into five parts.[16] It's main theme is passing; the book examines its effects on black family life, as well as on the one who has crossed over.

When her parents die, pretty Angela Murray, who is lighter in complexion than her sister, Virginia, decides to leave her home in Philadelphia and go to New York. Living in Greenwich Village, she rejects her family roots by changing her name to Angèle Mory, and passes for white because of the advantages.

She studies art at Cooper Union and is pressed into a destructive affair with a spoiled rich white playboy, Richard Fielding. After being discarded by Fielding, she falls for Anthony Cross, a South American black who, ironically, she discovers is also passing. Fauset's characteristic theme of the tangled love lives of family members emerges when Virginia comes to New York to live in Harlem. Although in love with her childhood friend in Philadelphia, Matthew Henson, Virginia becomes engaged to Anthony, not realizing her sister loves him. All ends well, however, when the sisters marry the two men of their hearts. As for passing, Angela, missing her sister and people, returns to her race.

This book too met with favorable commentaries from blacks and whites. Braithwaite went so far as to say it was Fauset's "most perfect artistic achievement, and the most balanced force of interracial experience."[17]

In seeking a publisher for her third novel, *The Chinaberry Tree: A Novel of American Life* (1931), Fauset once more encountered resistance because of the type of characters that were thought to be difficult for white readers to believe or, more likely, to face. Zona Gale, a white friend and popular writer, came to her aid by promoting the book with an introduction. Discussing Fauset's so-called unbelievable black characters, she wrote: "It seems strange to affirm,—as news for many,—that there is in America a great group of Negroes of education and substance who are living lives of quiet interests and pursuits, quite unconnected with white folk save as these are casually met."[18] Fauset also defended her book in a foreword giving her raison'd être: "I have depicted something of the homelife of the colored American who is not being pressed too hard by the Furies of Prejudice, Ignorance, and Economic Injustice. And behold he is not so vastly different from any other American, just distinctive."[19]

Fauset said that the story of Aunt Sal, Laurentine, and Melissa was "literally true," one that she had heard when fifteen years old. The setting is a small town, Red Brook, New Jersey, where Aunt Sal (Sarah Strange), a maid, has an illicit romance with her white mistress's son, Francis Holloway. As a result of the affair, Aunt Sal has an illegitimate daughter, Laurentine. Holloway cannot marry Aunt Sal, but scandalizes the town by providing her with a nice white house with a chinaberry tree ordered especially from Alabama for her backyard and arranging a lifetime income from his family's factory.

When maliciously told by a playmate that she has bad blood, Laurentine withdraws into herself. Life changes for her, however, when Judy, her mother's sister, comes to visit and encourages her to be more outgoing. Judy becomes very friendly with the Forten family, particularly the father, Sylvester, who is known as a rake. Mysteriously, Judy suddenly leaves town, but years later, her daughter, Melissa Paul, comes to live with Aunt Sal and Laurentine. Even though Melissa is dependent upon Aunt Sal, she feels above both Laurentine and her mother because of Laurentine's birth out of wedlock.

Melissa becomes enamored of Mallory Forten, who is forbidden by Laurentine to come to the house, for she resents Melissa's air of superiority. Mallory and Melissa contrive to meet at night under the chinaberry tree. When it is known the couple plan to marry, the secret comes out that the two are actually half brother and half sister. As usual, there is a pat ending of happiness with Melissa going back to her first love, Asshur Lane, and Laurentine, rejected by Phil Hackett, finding love with Dr. Stephen Denleigh.

The story was a bold one for its day, with a woman writing about miscegenation, incest, interracial love, and black middle-class conventions. Dr. Denleigh called the involvement a "Greek Tragedy." Perhaps it was, Afro-American style.

Fauset's fourth novel, *Comedy, American Style* (1933), takes color prejudices within the race and, again, passing as its main ingredients. Olivia Blanchard, who is light enough to pass and sometimes does, is a hater of black skin. Self-willed and domineering, she deliberately marries a fair-skinned Harvard medical doctor, Christopher Cary. They live in a white neighborhood of Philadelphia with their two children, Teresa and Christopher, both of whom look white. When a third child, Oliver, is born browner than the others, he incurs the scorn of his mother. Mrs. Blanchard's color fanaticism practically ruins the family. Teresa is prodded into marrying a tight-fisted French professor while she and her mother, both of them passing, are visiting in France. The husband makes her life miserable. Oliver commits suicide when he discovers why his mother hates him. Christopher manages to find happiness by marrying a childhood friend, Phebe Grant, whose blonde hair and blue eyes are acceptable to his mother, but not her poor family background. Mrs. Blanchard finally ends up living as white in Paris alone, for her son-in-law will not have her. She attempts to exist on the small pittance her husband can send after he has been ruined by the depression.

Jessie Fauset's books have been disparaged because she wrote of the black bourgeoisie and apparently, also, because she too was of that class (which is disconcerting since it is white and black academic bourgeois who criticize her). But she wrote what she wanted and what she knew best: the early twentieth-century black middle class, and its snobbery, hypocrisy, pettiness, clannishness, and narrow-mindedness; its hopes and frustrated ambitions in a racist society.

What is more, she exposed the problems and concerns of black women in the context of the roles society assigned them. Sylvander rightfully felt that the double jeopardy of being black and female "lends a helpful insight into some of Fauset's plots and themes."

Such characters as Angela, Joanna, Phebe, and Maggie are industrious and ambitious women with a certain degree of independence. Joanna in *There Is Confusion* views love at one time as an entrapment into marriage: "a household of children, the getting of a thousand meals, picking up laundry, no time to herself for meditation, or reading."[20] When the talented females in Fauset's work succumb to marriage, they are expected by their husbands to subordinate careers for home and children. It would be interesting to know if Fauset herself thought of marriage in this vein, since she was single at the time.

Sexism is perceived by Angela Murray in *Plum Bun* during an age when it was not recognized as such: "She knew that men had a better time of it than women, coloured men than coloured women, white men than white women."[21] Angela realizes too that if she were a man, she might have been president, but she was a woman and could not possibly be.

In her male-female relationships, Fauset drew a still timely picture of the games men and women play for personal objectives. For Angela, marriage to Fielding would provide the security, riches, and protection she wants, whereas Fielding desires only a nonbinding sexual affinity.

Although the panorama of black middle-class conventions, morals, standards, manners, and female-male relationships is examined in her works, many black and white critics—unlike Sylvander and Jeanne Noble—have ignored these significant elements in her writings. Robert Bone belittled her novels, calling them "uniformly sophomoric, trivial, and dull."[22] Even black feminist critic Barbara Christian found fault with her works: "Her fiction does not capture the essence of the upper-middle-class Negro society . . . because her characters lack critical insight and complexity, and because her plots seldom rise beyond the level of melodrama."[23]

Nevertheless, Fauset, the author, was the prototype of the new breed of Afro-American women writers who were emerging. She was sophisticated, a world traveler, attractive, and highly intelligent. She pursued a multifaceted literary career as critic, literary editor, journalist, poet, short-story writer, and essayist. An independent woman, she did not marry until the age of forty-seven. Her husband was Herbert Hill, an insurance broker with the New York branch of Victory Life Insurance Company and a war veteran.

The couple lived in New York until the early forties when they moved to Montclair, New Jersey. After her husband's death in 1958, she lived in Philadelphia with her stepbrother, Earl Huff. Unfortunately, Jessie Fauset's fine mind deteriorated before her death of heart failure on 30 April 1961.

Her novels have been accorded more respect in recent years as a result of the new awareness of the problems she wrote about. We may hope that even greater recognition will be bestowed in the future upon this black woman writer who "by choosing unpopular topics for her fiction . . . challenged the preconceptions of the publishing industry and opened the way for literature which would appear in succeeding decades."[24]

NOTES

1. Sylvander, *Fauset*, p. 23.
2. Joseph J. Feeney, S.J., "A Small Centennial Tribute: Establishing the Correct Birthdate and Birthplace of Jessie Fauset, Novelist and Critic," *Minority Voices* 4 (Fall 1980):71. This birth date has been verified by Marion Fauset, sister of Arthur Huff Fauset.
3. Ibid., p. 72.
4. Ibid., p. 71.
5. Sylvander, *Fauset*, p. 25.
6. Ibid., pp. 25–26.
7. Ibid., p. 31.
8. Ibid., p. 115.
9. Lewis, *When Harlem Was in Vogue*, p. 177.
10. Sylvander, *Fauset*, p. 66.
11. Ibid., p. 65.
12. Starkey, "Jessie Fauset," p. 218.
13. Gloster, *Negro Voices*, p. 132.
14. Starkey, "Jessie Fauset," p. 219.
15. Braithwaite, "Novels of Jessie Fauset," p. 50.
16. Joseph J. Feeney, S.J., wrote an analysis of the title in "Black Childhood as Ironic: A Nursery Rhyme Transformed in Jessie Fauset's Novel, *Plum Bun*," *Minority Voices* 4 (Fall 1980):65–69.

17. Braithwaite, "Novels of Jessie Fauset," p. 52.
18. Fauset, *Chinaberry Tree*, p. vii.
19. Ibid., p. ix.
20. Fauset, *There Is Confusion*, p. 95.
21. Fauset, *Plum Bun*, p. 88.
22. Bone, *Negro Novel*, p. 101.
23. Christian, *Black Women Novelists*, p. 43.
24. Abbey Arthur Johnson, "Literary Midwife: Jessie Redmon Fauset and the Harlem Renaissance," *Phylon* 34 (June 1978):153.

SELECTED SOURCES

Primary

Fauset, Jessie. *The Chinaberry Tree: A Novel of American Life*. New York: Frederick A. Stokes Co., 1933.
———. *Comedy, American Style*. New York: Frederick A. Stokes Co., 1931.
———. *Plum Bun: A Novel without a Moral*. New York: Frederick A. Stokes Co., 1929.
———. *There Is Confusion*. New York: Boni & Liveright, 1924.

Secondary

Bone, Robert A. *The Negro Novel in America*. New Haven: Yale University Press, 1958.

Braithwaite, William Stanley. "The Novels of Jessie Fauset," In *The Black Novelist*, edited by Robert Hemenway. Colombus, Ohio: Charles E. Merrill Publishing Co., 1970.

Brawley, Benjamin. *The Negro Genius: A New Appraisal of the Achievement of the American Negro in Literature and the Fine Arts*. New York: Dodd, Mead & Co., 1937.

Brown, Sterling, A.; Davis, Arthur P.; and Lee, Ulysses, eds. *The Negro Caravan: Writings by American Negroes*. New York: Dryden Press, 1941.

Christian, Barbara. *Black Women Novelists: The Development of a Tradition, 1892–1976*. Westport, Conn.: Greenwood Press, 1980.

Cullen, Countee. *Caroling Dusk: An Anthology of Verse by Negro Poets*. New York: Harper & Brothers, 1927.

Dannett, Sylvia F. L. *Profiles of Negro Womanhood*. Vol. 2, *20th Century*. Yonkers, N.Y.: Educational Heritage Library, 1966.

Davis, Arthur P. *From the Dark Tower: Afro-American Writers 1900 to 1960*. Washington, D.C.: Howard University Press, 1974.

Davis, Arthur P., and Redding, Saunders. *Cavalcade: Negro American Writing from 1760 to the Present*. Boston: Houghton Mifflin Co., 1971.

Gloster, Hugh M. *Negro Voices in American Fiction*. 1948. Reprint. New York: Russell & Russell, 1965.

Kerlin, Robert T. *Negro Poets and Their Poems*. Washington, D.C.: Associated Publishers, 1923.

Lewis, David Levering. *When Harlem Was in Vogue*. New York: Alfred A. Knopf, 1981.

Locke, Alain LeRoy, ed. *The New Negro: An Interpretation.* New York: A. and C. Boni, 1925.

McDowell, Deborah E. "The Neglected Dimension of Jessie Redmon Fauset." In *Conjuring: Black Women, Fiction, and Literary Tradition*, edited by Marjorie Pryse and Hortense J. Spillers. Bloomington: Indiana University Press, 1975.

Noble, Jeanne. *Beautiful, Also, Are the Souls of My Black Sisters: A History of the Black Woman in America.* New Jersey: Prentice-Hall, 1978.

Perry, Margaret. *Silence to the Drums: A Survey of the Literature of the Harlem Renaissance.* Westport, Conn.: Greenwood Press, 1976.

Sato, Hiroko. "Under the Harlem Shadow: A Study of Jessie Fauset and Nella Larsen." In *The Harlem Renaissance Remembered*, edited by Arna Bontemps. New York: Dodd, Mead & Co., 1972.

Sims, Janet L. "Jessie Redmon Fauset (1885–1961): A Selected Annotated Bibliography." *Black American Literature Forum* 14 (Winter 1980):147–52.

Singh, Amritjit. *The Novels of the Harlem Renaissance: Twelve Black Writers, 1923–1933.* University Park: Pennsylvania State University Press, 1976.

Starkey, Marion C. "Jessie Fauset." *Southern Workman* 61 (May 1932):217–20.

Sylvander, Carolyn Wedin. *Jessie Redmon Fauset, Black American Writer.* Troy, N.Y.: Whitston Publishing Co., 1981.

———. "Jessie Redmon Fauset (1882–1961)." In *Afro-American Writers from the Harlem Renaissance to 1940*, Dictionary of Literary Biography, vol. 51, edited by Trudier Harris and Thadious M. Davis. Detroit, Mich.: Gale Research, 1987.

Watson, Carole McAlpine. *Prologue: The Novels of Black American Women, 1891–1965.* Westport, Conn.: Greenwood Press, 1985.

Rejection

Angela took the sketch of Hetty Daniels to school. "What an interesting type!" said Gertrude Quale, the girl next to her. "Such cosmic and tragic unhappiness in that face. What is she, not an American?"

"Oh yes she is. She's an old coloured woman who's worked in our family for years and she was born right here in Philadelphia."

"Oh coloured! Well, of course I suppose you would call her an American though I never think of darkies as Americans. Coloured,— yes that would account for that unhappiness in her face. I suppose they all mind it awfully."

It was the afternoon for the life class. The model came in, a short, rather slender young woman with a faintly pretty, shrewdish face full of a certain dark, mean character. Angela glanced at her thoughtfully, full of pleasant anticipation. She liked to work for character, preferred it even to beauty. The model caught her eye, looked away and again turned her full gaze upon her with an insistent, slightly incredulous stare. It was Esther Bayliss who had once been in the High School with Angela. She had left not long after Mary Hastings' return to her boarding school.

Angela saw no reason why she should speak to her and presently, engrossed in the portrayal of the round, yet pointed little face, forgot the girl's identity. But Esther kept her eyes fixed on her former school-mate with a sort of intense, angry brooding so absorbing that she forgot her pose and Mr. Shields spoke to her two or three times. On the third occasion he said not unkindly, "You'll have to hold your pose better than this, Miss Bayliss, or we won't be able to keep you on."

"I don't want you to keep me on." She spoke with an amazing vindictiveness. "I haven't got to the point yet where I'm going to lower myself to pose for a coloured girl."

He looked around the room in amazement; no, Miss Henderson wasn't there, she never came to this class he remembered. "Well after that we couldn't keep you anyway. We're not taking orders from our models. But there's no coloured girl here."

"Oh yes there is, unless she's changed her name." She laughed spitefully. "isn't that Angela Murray over there next to that Jew girl?" In spite of himself, Shields nodded. "Well, she's coloured though she wouldn't let you know. But I know. I went to school with her in North Philadelphia. And I tell you I wouldn't stay to pose for her not if you were to pay me ten times what I'm getting. Sitting there drawing from me just as though she were as good as a white girl!"

Astonished and disconcerted, he told his wife about it. "But I can't think she's really coloured, Mabel. Why she looks and acts just like a white girl. She dresses in better taste than anybody in the room. But that little wretch of a model insisted that she was coloured."

"Well she just can't be. Do you suppose I don't know a coloured woman when I see one? I can tell 'em a mile off."

It seemed to him a vital and yet such a disgraceful matter. "If she is coloured she should have told me. I'd certainly like to know, but hang it all, I can't ask her, for suppose she should be white in spite of what that little beast of a model said?" He found her address in the registry and overcome one afternoon with shamed curiosity drove up to Opal Street and slowly past her house. Jinny was coming in from school and Hetty Daniels on her way to market greeted her on the lower step. Then Virginia put the key in the lock and passed inside. "She is coloured," he told his wife, "for no white girl in her senses would be rooming with coloured people."

"I should say not! Coloured, is she? Well, she shan't come here again, Henry."

Angela approached him after class on Saturday. "How is Mrs. Shields? I can't get out to see her this week but I'll be sure to run in next."

He blurted out miserably, "But, Miss Murray, you never told me that you were coloured."

She felt as though she were rehearsing a well-known part in a play. "Coloured! Of course I never told you that I was coloured. Why should I?"

But apparently there was some reason why she should tell it; she sat in her room in utter dejection trying to reason it out. Just as in the old days she had not discussed the matter with Jinny, for what could the latter do? She wondered if her mother had ever met with any such experiences. Was there something inherently wrong in "passing?"

Her mother had never seemed to consider it as anything but a lark. And on the one occasion, that terrible day in the hospital when passing or not passing might have meant the difference between good will and unpleasantness, her mother had deliberately given the whole show away. But her mother, she had long since begun to realize, had not considered this business of colour or the lack of it as pertaining intimately to her personal happiness. She was perfectly satisfied, absolutely content whether she was part of that white world with Angela or up on little Opal Street with her dark family and friends. Whereas it seemed to Angela that all the things which she most wanted were wrapped up with white people. All the good things were theirs. Not, some coldly reasoning instinct within was saying, because they were white. But because for the present they had power and the badge of that power was whiteness, very like the colours on the escutcheon of a powerful house. She possessed the badge, and unless there was someone to tell she could possess the power for which it stood.

Hetty Daniels shrilled up: "Mr. Henson's down here to see you."

Tiresome though his presence was, she almost welcomed him to-night, and even accepted his eager invitation to go to see a picture.

"It's in a little gem of a theatre, Angela. You'll like the surroundings almost as much as the picture, and that's very good. Sawyer and I saw it about two weeks ago. I thought then that I'd like to take you."

She knew that this was his indirect method of telling her that they would meet with no difficulty in the matter of admission; a comforting assurance for Philadelphia theatres, as Angela knew, could be very unpleasant to would-be coloured patrons. Henson offered to telephone for a taxi while she was getting on her street clothes, and she permitted the unnecessary extravagance for she hated the conjectures on the faces of passengers in the street cars; conjecture, she felt in her sensitiveness, which she could only set right by being unusually kind and friendly in her manner to Henson. And this produced undesirable effects on him. She had gone out with him more often in the Ford, which permitted a modicum of privacy. But Jinny was off in the little car to-night.

At Broad and Ridge Avenue the taxi was held up; it was twenty-five minutes after eight when they reached the theatre. Matthew gave Angela a bill. "Do you mind getting the tickets while I settle for the cab?" he asked nervously. He did not want her to miss even the advertisements. This, he almost prayed, would be a perfect night.

Cramming the change into his pocket, he rushed into the lobby and joined Angela, who, almost as excited as he, for she liked a good picture, handed the tickets to the attendant. He returned the stubs. "All right, good seats there to your left." The theatre was only one storey. He glanced at Matthew.

"Here, here, where do you think you're going?"

Matthew answered unsuspecting: "It's all right. The young lady gave you the tickets."

"Yes, but not for you; she can go in, but you can't." He handed him the torn ticket, turned and took one of the stubs from Angela, and thrust that in the young man's unwilling hand. "Go over there and get your refund."

"But," said Matthew and Angela could feel his very manhood sickening under the silly humiliation of the moment, "there must be some mistake; I sat in this same theatre less than three weeks ago."

"Well, you won't sit in there to-night; the management's changed hands since then, and we're not selling tickets to coloured people." He glanced at Angela a little uncertainly. "The young lady can come in——"

Angela threw her ticket on the floor. "Oh, come, Matthew, come."

Outside he said stiffly, "I'll get a taxi, we'll go somewhere else."

"No, no! We wouldn't enjoy it. Let's go home and we don't need a taxi. We can get the Sixteenth Street car right at the corner."

She was very kind to him in the car; she was so sorry for him, suddenly conscious of the pain which must be his at being stripped before the girl he loved of his masculine right to protect, to appear the hero.

She let him open the two doors for her but stopped him in the box of a hall. "I think I'll say good-night now, Matthew; I'm more tired than I realized. But,—but it was an adventure, wasn't it?"

His eyes adored her, his hand caught hers: "Angela, I'd have given all I hope to possess to have been able to prevent it; you know I never dreamed of letting you in for such humiliation. Oh how are we ever going to get this thing straight?"

"Well, it wasn't your fault." Unexpectedly she lifted her delicate face to his, so stricken and freckled and woebegone, and kissed him, lifted her hand and actually stroked his reddish, stiff, "bad" hair.

Like a man in a dream he walked down the street wondering how long it would be before they married.

Angela, waking in the middle of the night and reviewing to herself the events of the day, said aloud: "This is the end," and fell asleep again.

The little back room was still Jinny's, but Angela, in order to give the third storey front to Hetty Daniels, had moved into the room which had once been her mother's. She and Virginia had placed the respective head-boards of their narrow, virginal beds against the dividing wall so that they could lie in bed and talk to each other through the communicating door-way, their voices making a circuit from speaker to listener in what Jinny called a hair-pin curve.

Angela called in as soon as she heard her sister moving, "Jinny, listen. I'm going away."

Her sister, still half asleep, lay intensely quiet for another second, trying to pick up the continuity of this dream. Then her senses came to her.

"What'd you say, Angela?"

"I said I was going away. I'm going to leave Philadelphia, give up school teaching, break away from our loving friends and acquaintances, and bust up the whole shooting match."

"Haven't gone crazy, have you?"

"No, I think I'm just beginning to come to my senses. I'm sick, sick, sick of seeing what I want dangled right before my eyes and then of having it snatched away from me and all of it through no fault of my own."

"Darling, you know I haven't the faintest idea of what you're driving at."

"Well, I'll tell you." Out came the whole story, an accumulation of the slights, real and fancied, which her colour had engendered throughout her lifetime; though even then she did not tell of that first hurt through Mary Hastings. That would always linger in some remote, impenetrable fastness of her mind, for wounded trust was there as well as wounded pride and love. "And these two last happenings with Matthew and Mr. Shields are just too much; besides they've shown me the way."

"Shown you what way?"

Virginia had arisen and thrown an old rose kimono around her. She had inherited her father's thick and rather coarsely waving black hair, enhanced by her mother's softness. She was slender, yet rounded; her cheeks were flushed with sleep and excitement. Her eyes shone. As she sat in the brilliant wrap, cross-legged at the foot of her sister's narrow bed, she made the latter think of a striking dainty, colourful robin.

"Well you see as long as the Shields thought I was white they were willing to help me to all the glories of the promised land. And the doorman last night,—he couldn't tell what I was, but he could tell about Matthew, so he put him out; just as the Shields are getting ready in another way to put me out. But as long as they didn't know it didn't matter. Which means it isn't being coloured that makes the difference, it's letting it be known. Do you see?

"So I've thought and thought. I guess really I've had it in my mind for a long time, but last night it seemed to stand right out in my consciousness. Why should I shut myself off from all the things I want most,—clever people, people who do things, Art,—" her voice spelt it with a capital,—"travel and a lot of things which are in the world for everybody really but which only white people, as far as I can see, get their hands on. I mean scholarships and special funds.

patronage. Oh Jinny, you don't know, I don't think you can understand the things I want to see and know. You're not like me——"

"I don't know why I'm not," said Jinny looking more like a robin
than ever. Her bright eyes dwelt on her sister. "After all, the same
blood flows in my veins and in the same proportion. Sure you're not
laying too much stress on something only temporarily inconvenient?"

"But it isn't temporarily inconvenient; it's happening to me
every day. And it isn't as though it were something that I could help.
Look how Mr. Shields stressed the fact that I hadn't told him I was
coloured. And see how it changed his attitude toward me; you can't
think how different his manner was. Yet as long as he didn't know,
there was nothing he wasn't willing and glad, glad to do for me. Now
he might be willing but he'll not be glad though I need his assistance
more than some white girl who will find a dozen people to help her
just because she is white." Some faint disapproval in her sister's face
halted her for a moment. "What's the matter? You certainly don't
think I ought to say first thing: 'I'm Angela Murray. I know I look
white but I'm coloured and expect to be treated accordingly!', Now
do you?"

"No," said Jinny, "of course that's absurd. Only I don't think
you ought to mind quite so hard when they do find out the facts. It
seems sort of an insult to yourself. And then, too, it makes you lose
a good chance to do something for—for all of us who can't look like
you but who really have the same combination of blood that you
have."

"Oh that's some more of your and Matthew Henson's philosophy. Now be practical, Jinny; after all I am both white and Negro and
look white. Why shouldn't I declare for the one that will bring me
the greatest happiness, prosperity and respect?"

"No reason in the world except that since in this country public
opinion is against any infusion of black blood it would seem an awfully decent thing to put yourself, even in the face of appearances,
on the side of black blood and say: 'Look here, this is what a mixture
of black and white really means!'"

Angela was silent and Virginia, feeling suddenly very young, almost childish in the presence of this issue, took a turn about the
room. She halted beside her sister.

"Just what is it you want to do, Angela? Evidently you have some
plan."

She had. Her idea was to sell the house and to divide the proceeds. With her share of this and her half of the insurance she would go to New York or to Chicago, certainly to some place where she could by no chance be known, and launch out "into a freer, fuller life."

"And leave me!" said Jinny astonished. Somehow it had not dawned on her that the two would actually separate. She did not know what she had thought, but certainly not that. The tears ran down her cheeks.

Angela, unable to endure either her own pain or the sight of it in others, had all of a man's dislike for tears.

"Don't be absurd, Jinny! How could I live the way I want to if you're with me. We'd keep on loving each other and seeing one another from time to time, but we might just as well face the facts. Some of those girls in the art school used to ask me to their homes; it would have meant opportunity, a broader outlook, but I never dared to accept because I knew I couldn't return the invitation."

Under that Jinny winced a little, but she spoke with spirit. "After that, Angela dear, I'm beginning to think that you *have* more white blood in your veins than I, and it was that extra amount which made it possible for you to make that remark." She trailed back to her room and when Hetty Daniels announced breakfast she found that a bad headache required a longer stay in bed.

Nella Marian Larsen Imes
Nella Larsen ✒
1891?/1893?–1964

When Nella Larsen's first novel, *Quicksand* (1928), came out during the New Negro Movement, it was acclaimed by W. E. B. Du Bois as "the best piece of fiction that Negro America has produced since the heyday of Chesnutt."[1] Some thirty years later, the controversial white critic Robert Bone praised it as "the best [novel] of the period, with the exception of Jean Toomer's *Cane*."[2]

The author's life has proved to be as interesting as her work. Anthologist Arthur P. Davis charged her with being "the most elusive [of the New Negro authors] in the matter of biographical details, especially dates."[3] Her elusiveness was noted also at the time of the book's publication in a *Chicago Defender* front-page article which said "so little has been and is known about the author."

She was dubbed "Madame X" by the *Amsterdam News* society editor, Thelma E. Berlack, when she interviewed the novelist. In this exchange, Larsen informed Berlack that she was thirty-five years of age and born in Chicago.[4] Her mother was Danish and her father a Danish West Indian.

Larsen was an attractive woman. She was medium brown-skinned, dark-haired, and petite, standing five feet, two inches. For her day, she was considered a "modern woman," for she smoked, wore short dresses, and did not believe in religion or churches, although the latter came to be the turning point for her protagonist, Helga Crane, in *Quicksand*.

Nella Larsen lived in a five-room apartment on West 135th Street in New York, which was likened to a "Greenwich Village studio" with its many books, colorful pillows, and flowers, the whole bearing a striking resemblance to Helga Crane's room at the black college of Naxos. When *Quicksand* came out, the author had been married nine years to Dr. Elmer Samuel Imes, a pioneering black physicist, Fisk University graduate, and University of Michigan Ph.D. They were wed in the chapel of Union Theological Seminary.

The writer's father died when she was very young. Her mother remarried one of her own nationality and had a second daughter. (When *Quicksand* appeared, they lived in California.) "At eight, Nella and her white half-sister attended a small private school in which most of the children were of Scandinavian or German ancestry."[5]

Larsen attended Fisk University's Normal School Department for one year. The school catalogue of 1907–8 lists her name as Nellie Marie Larsen from Chicago. This leads to speculation that she may have changed her name when she later lived in Denmark; perhaps Nella Marian was more to her liking. She made fair grades at Fisk, none exceeding eighty-seven, with the highest in mythology and algebra. After leaving Fisk, which may have been lonely for her (as Helga Crane felt about Naxos), she attended the University of Copenhagen for three years. She may have lived with her mother's relatives, although her father's "people lived in Denmark," also.

Returning to the States, she entered the Lincoln School for Nurses, Bronx, New York, which had an outstanding reputation for preparing black women for the profession. She completed the three-year program in 1915 in a class of eleven. From 1915 to 1916, she was head nurse at the John A. Andrew Hospital and Nurse Training School at Tuskegee, Alabama. But one year of the Deep South and a black school took its toll, and she returned to New York.

She became an assistant superintendent of nurses at Lincoln Hospital for a year and performed social service work for the Board of Health. She left the field of nursing to become an employee of the New York Public Library at the Countee Cullen Regional Branch in September 1921. She took library training courses for a year in 1922–23 and then became a librarian at the Seward Park Branch Library. A year later, she was placed in charge of the children's room at the Countee Cullen Branch.

Because of health problems, she requested a year's leave in October 1925 and resigned in January 1926. With time on her hands, she apparently wrote *Quicksand* while recuperating. Working with books and meeting writers who visited the library, coupled with her own love of books, may have been the factors encouraging her to try her hand at writing.

She credited Carl Van Vechten, author and white literary patron of black talent, for discovering her. "Five months in her head and six weeks on the typewriter is the time it took her to write her book."[6] Walter White, author and future executive secretary of the NAACP, also adopted her as another protégé in his group of young artists and writers. After making revisions he suggested, she sold the book to Alfred A. Knopf.

The author became a luminary among the select male New Negro clique of writers. The Women's Committee of the NAACP held a Sunday evening autograph tea for her on 20 May 1928. There she was introduced by James Weldon Johnson, who magnanimously endorsed all black women writers. When presenting her, he remarked that there should be a real place for the woman novelist of the group because of her background of achievement contributing to the upward climb of the race. Other notable people attending the gathering were Mrs. W. E. B. Du Bois, Alain Locke, Dr. and Mrs. Rudolph Fisher, Grace Nail Johnson, and Harold Jackman. *Quicksand* won the Harmon Foundation literary award of a bronze medal and one hundred dollars for "distinguished achievement among Negroes."

The novel appears to be autobiographical, with parallels to the author's life. The plot revolves around Helga Crane and her search for self. She is the attractive daughter of a black gambling father and a white immigrant mother, Karen Nilssen. She teaches at Naxos, where she becomes dissatisfied with the black school's hypocrisy, its stifling of student initiative, and its rigid discipline, and with blacks trying to imitate whites in order to uplift the race. She leaves and returns to Chicago. There she is rejected by her white uncle Peter who has educated her but is now married to a woman who wants to ignore that branch of her husband's family tree. To survive, Helga accepts a job as speech editor for a black woman leader, Mrs. Hayes-Rore. Through her, Helga gets a job with a black insurance company in New York and lives with Mrs. Hayes-Rore's niece.

In New York, Helga observes and participates in Harlem's glittering society life, but again she becomes bored and restless. Upon receiving an unexpected check from her uncle, she goes to Copenhagen to visit her mother's people. There, because of the novelty of her race, she is a social success. She is wined and dined and wooed by an important artist whose proposal she rejects. Finally, tired of a sea of white faces, she becomes "homesick" for her own people and departs.

Back in New York, the matter of her sexual fulfillment becomes important as she continues her quest for identity. When Dr. Robert Anderson, former principal at Naxos to whom she was once attracted, kisses her at a party and then apologizes, she feels ridiculed and is indignant. Caught in a web of emotional confusion, she walks aimlessly one evening in the rain and stumbles into a storefront church where a visiting southern country minister, the Reverend Pleasant Green, is preaching. She is converted by him and, moreover, becomes his wife.

Her odyssey from the South to New York, then to Copenhagen and back to New York, now ends in the rural South. Here she feels she is caught in quicksand: she is married to a prosaic man she has grown to hate, she has a baby every year, and she is stifled by uncultivated southern women who believe their lot is ordained by God. Lying in her bed after a difficult child-birth, she disdains the white man's God and the religion that "ailed the whole Negro race in America." The novel ends with her sinking even deeper in the mire: there is no escape now, for she is expecting her fifth child.

Adelaide Cromwell Hill summed up the significance of *Quicksand* in her introduction: "*Quicksand* helps us to see how one Black woman viewed the problem of the Black community, its relation to White society, the survival of the individual Black person in a totally White society abroad, and the basic problem of sex as it expresses itself for Black women and for those males, Black or White, available or attractive to them."[7]

Arthur P. Davis called Helga Crane a "superb creation" and "the most intriguing and complex character in Renaissance fiction." Du Bois perceived the character of Helga as a fresh approach for his era, seeing her as being "typical of the new, honest, young fighting Negro woman—the one in whom 'race' sits negligibly and life is always first."

Critics have cited the tragic mulatto and racism as the dominant themes in *Quicksand*. But in the light of today's feminist consciousness, Hortense E. Thornton offers another dimension: "When one considers the complex events of the novel, it becomes possible to argue that Helga's tragedy was perhaps more a result of sexism than of racism."[8] Thornton argues that Helga's tragic end results from her being a woman caught in the web of black and white male domination.

Critic Deborah E. McDowell looks upon Helga as a woman torn between "sexual repression and expression," desiring "sexual fulfillment and a longing for social respectability."[9] Helga believes that through marriage she can be free to release her sexual tension and remain a proper woman too—a concept reflecting the Victorian principle that sex outside of wedlock is unacceptable. But in marriage, Helga is caught in the "quicksand" of repeated pregnancies and babies. Here again Thornton's view of male domination over Helga is repeated.

One year following the publication of *Quicksand*, Larsen produced a second novel, *Passing* (1929). Its setting is the black bourgeois society of Harlem. It portrays the pretentious values, conventions, and life-styles of the black "jet set"—a picture of black people denying their blackness.

There are two major characters. Clare Kendry, the Chicago-born daughter of a drunken white father and a black mother, crosses over into the white world to better her lot. She marries John Bellew, a white banking agent who despises blacks, and has one daughter who is abroad in school. The other protagonist is Irene Redfield, Clare's childhood friend. Irene is married to a black physician, has two sons, and lives comfortably in New York. Irene is light enough to pass, but she does so only to shop and to eat in the better restaurants.

After years apart, the two women meet accidentally in a Chicago hotel, and Clare indicates that she wants to renew their friendship. She is aggressive, pretty, hard, and selfish, yet she manages to convey a semblance of "warmth and passion" akin to the theatrical. She confides to Irene that in passing, she misses black people, their laughter, their talk, and their fun. She intrudes into the life of Irene and her family and friends by making furtive trips to Harlem, where she enjoys the parties, luncheons, and balls.

But Irene soon realizes that her husband is attracted to Clare, and she feels threatened. When John follows Clare to a Harlem party, he is shocked to find that he has married a "damned dirty nigger." Witnessing the scene between them, Irene fears that Clare might now have to return to her own and, as a free woman, will jeopardize her marriage. At this point, Clare falls out of a sixth-floor window at the party, which creates a perplexing melodramatic ending to the novel. The reader is left wondering whether Irene pushed her intentionally, she fell accidentally, or she committed suicide.

The story of Clare is told indirectly as she is seen through the eyes of Irene. In a paradoxical interpretation of *Passing*, Mary Mabel Youman has suggested that it is really Irene who is "passing" by imitating whites while living as a black. Irene, she says, has "'passed' into the conventionalized, mechanized, non-humane white world" by adopting their values and losing "her black heritage of spontaneity, freedom from convention, and zest for life."[10]

Passing did not receive the accolades of *Quicksand*. Hoyt Fuller, in a chauvinistic introduction to one edition of the novel, compared it to "the easy worldliness of a Katherine Mansfield and the deliberate scene-setting of a mediocre home magazine story-teller."[11] But in contrast to Fuller's evaluation, Hugh M. Gloster called it "one of the significant studies of its kind in American fiction."

Feminist McDowell in a more recent consideration has spotted an unexplored subplot of lesbianism in *Passing*: "Though, superficially, Irene's is an account of Clare's passing for white and related issues of racial identity and loyalty, underneath the safety of that surface is the more dangerous story—though not named explicitly—of Irene's awakening sexual desire for Clare."[12] She backs this claim by citing the erotic narrative descriptions and dialogue of the encounters between Clare and Irene, and notes that this theme has been passed over by critics. She may be right: most of the earlier critics were males, or females who at the time would have been reluctant to express such a view for fear of being labeled lesbian. Moreover, the idea would have been countered by the argument that women in those days wrote like that. In any event, McDowell credits Larsen for being "something of a pioneer, a trailblazer in the Afro-American female literary tradition" for her "treatment of black female sexuality."[13]

Both of Larsen's novels represented a coming out of the Victorian closet for black women in reckoning with their sexuality. After *Quicksand* and *Passing*, Larsen published no more novels, although, says biographer Thadious M. Davis, "She remained committed to her writing during 1932 and 1933 when she began a fourth novel as well as a fifth in collaboration with Edward Donahoe, a young white writer."[14]

She is believed to have become despondent when accusations of plagiarism and a divorce from Imes affected her personal and literary life. In January 1930, Larsen had published a short story, "Sanctuary," which was embellished by Winold Reiss drawings and published in the *Forum*. The narrative's setting is the rural South, where Jim Hammer, a ne'er-do-well, shoots a man who tries to stop him during a burglary attempt. Jim seeks refuge from the law at the home of Annie Poole, mother of his friend Obadiah. Annie's dislike for white people overrides her contempt for Jim, and she hides him in a feather bed. When the white sheriff comes, she learns that it was her son who was shot and killed. Despite this, she does not expose Jim because he is black.

Letters were written to the *Forum* about the story's resemblance to another tale, "Mrs. Adis" by Shelia Kaye-Smith published in the *Century* eight years earlier. Replying to the accusations, Larsen sent drafts of the story to her editor who supported her. She also wrote a letter to the *Forum* defending herself, stating that the story was told to her by an old Negro woman who was an inmate at the Lincoln Hospital and Home between 1912 and 1915. She contended the story was now considered "folklore," for there were hundreds like it, sometimes involving a "woman's brother, husband, son, lover."[15]

Her divorce from Elmer Imes (to whom *Quicksand* was dedicated) in 1933 was the subject of rumors and sensational black news stories at the time. The marriage had long been on the rocks. When Imes went to organize the physics department at Fisk University in 1929, his wife was not with him; being the recipient of a Guggenheim Fellowship in 1930 offered her a convenient out. The first black woman to receive such an award in creative writing, she was to use it for European travel and write a novel on "the different effects of Europe and the United States on the intellectual and physical freedom of the Negro." While abroad, she was said to have had "an affair with an Englishman."

Pipe-smoking Imes was brilliant, suave, charming, and well-read, with a reputation as a "Beau Brummel." Eugene Gordon of the *Boston Post* selected him In 1931 as one of the thirteen most gifted blacks in the United States. Fisk's white president Thomas Elsa Jones wanted his faculty's unions to be stable, and he may have sensed something amiss in the Imes marriage. As a result, thinking that comfortable accommodations might entice Mrs. Imes to stay on campus upon her return from Europe, he offered Imes one of the three new houses to be constructed for faculty in 1930.

Imes chose an English cottage of brick and stucco, which was built to his specifications and still stands on Morena Street. It was rumored that the house was designed for "two people who did not get along." Nevertheless, despite the lovely house, Mrs. Imes was rarely seen on campus. She is remembered now as a precise and intense woman who was a nervous bridge player. When she and Imes were among company, the tension between them was evident. Mrs. Imes no doubt was aware (as was everyone else) of her husband's liaison with a vivacious white staff member. (At his death of cancer in New York in 1941, the woman brought his ashes back to scatter over the campus.)

The Imes marriage at times must have been tempestuous. During their breakup, in 1933, Imes wrote the university president that he wanted to vacate the house: he needed to cut down on expenses and his ailing mother was coming to live with him. He felt, too, that with a smaller place, "there would be less chance of Mrs. Imes' return to upset things."[16] Nella Larsen and her mother-in-law, a woman who looked white and, unlike her daughter-in-law, was quite conventional, did not get on together. Imes's mother refused to leave her Memphis home to live with her son "as long as Mrs. Imes is in it." On a previous visit, she had had a "too ghastly time while she [Nella Larsen] was there." Imes spoke of his marriage as an "agony" and was willing to "sacrifice to meet Mrs. Imes conditions for leaving."[17] On the other hand, his wife's ill temper could have concerned her husband's extramarital activities.

These circumstances—the charges of plagiarism and her broken marriage—may or may not have had an effect on Larsen's subsequent literary silence. It may have been that she was simply bereft of ideas for another novel or that she lacked discipline. Or she may have needed more support to encourage her. The Harlem Renaissance was in decline when she came back from Europe. The black literary circle was gone, and white publishers and patrons had lost interest in blacks.

She did take an active interest for a while in racial problems, becoming the assistant secretary of the newly formed Writers' League against Lynching in December 1933. The organization, composed of prominent black and white writers, was founded to fight mob murder and violence, which had become even more outrageous in the South.

To earn a living, Larsen did not reenter the field of librarianship.

Rather she returned to nursing at Bethel Hospital, helping others to overcome their pain while trying to forget her own.

An aloof and private woman, it was thought that like her creation, Helga Crane, she may have been haunted by her mother's rejection and her lack of love and family roots. In any event, she died as anonymously as she had lived her later life. A friend found her dead of heart failure at her home on Second Avenue, 30 March 1964. The death certificate gave her occupation as "nurse." She was interred in the Cypress Hills Cemetery in Brooklyn, New York, on 6 April. Her literary life had been buried over thirty years before.

NOTES

1. W. E. B. Du Bois, "Two Novels," *Crisis* 35 (June 1928):202.
2. Bone, *Negro Novel*, p. 97.
3. Arthur P. Davis, *Dark Tower*, p. 94.
4. The 28 May 1928 article would place her birth year in 1893; however, when applying for employment with the New York Public Library, Larsen's birth was recorded as 13 April 1891. The latter date is used by Thadious M. Davis.
5. Arthur P. Davis, *Dark Tower*, p. 95.
6. Thelma E. Berlack, "New Author Unearthed Right Here in Harlem," *Amsterdam News*, 23 May 1928.
7. Larsen, *Quicksand* (Collier ed.), p. 12.
8. Thornton, "Sexism as Quagmire," p. 288.
9. Larsen, *Quicksand and Passing*, p. xvii.
10. Youman, "Nella Larsen's Passing," p. 236.
11. Larsen, *Passing* (Collier ed.), p. 18.
12. Larsen, *Quicksand and Passing*, p. xxvi.
13. Ibid., p. xxxi.
14. Thadious M. Davis, "Nella Larsen," *Afro-American Fiction Writers*, p. 190.
15. Larsen, "The Author's Explanation," p. 42.
16. Imes to Jones, 22 July 1933, Thomas Elsa Jones Papers, Fisk University Library, Nashville, Tenn.
17. Ibid.

SELECTED SOURCES

Primary

Larsen, Nella. "The Author's Explanation." *Forum*, Supp. 4, 83 (April 1930):4142.
———. *Passing.* New York and London: Alfred A. Knopf, 1929. Reprint. New York: Arno Press and The New York Times Co., 1969; New York: Collier Books, 1971.
———. *Quicksand.* New York and London: Alfred A. Knopf, 1928. Reprint. New York: Negro Universities Press, 1969; New York: Collier Books, 1971.

———. *Quicksand and Passing.* Edited and with an Introduction by Deborah E. McDowell. American Women Writers Series. New Brunswick, N.J.: Rutgers University Press, 1986.

———. "Sanctuary." *Forum* 83 (January 1930):15–18.

Secondary

Bone, Robert A. *The Negro Novel in America.* New Haven: Yale University Press, 1958.

Christian, Barbara. *Black Women Novelists: The Development of a Tradition, 1892–1976.* Westport, Conn.: Greenwood Press, 1980.

Davis, Arthur P. *From the Dark Tower: Afro-American Writers 1900–1960.* Washington, D.C.: Howard University Press, 1974.

Davis, Thadious M. "Nella Larsen." In *Afro-American Fiction Writers from the Harlem Renaissance to 1940.* Dictionary of Literary Biography, vol. 51, edited by Trudier Harris and Thadious M. Davis. Detroit, Mich.: Gale Research, 1987.

Huggins, Nathan Irvin. *Harlem Renaissance.* New York: Oxford University Press, 1971.

Lewis, David Levering. *When Harlem Was in Vogue.* New York: Alfred A. Knopf, 1981.

Mays, Benjamin E. *The Negro's God as Reflected in His Literature.* 1938. Reprint. New York: Russell & Russell, 1968.

Peplow, Michael W., and Davis, Arthur P. *The New Negro Renaissance: An Anthology.* New York: Holt, Rinehart & Winston, 1975.

Perry, Margaret. *Silence to the Drums: A Survey of the Literature of the Harlem Renaissance.* Westport, Conn.: Greenwood Press, 1976.

Sato, Hiroko. "Under the Harlem Shadow: A Study of Jessie Fauset and Nella Larsen." In *The Harlem Renaissance Remembered,* edited by Arna Bontemps. New York: Dodd, Mead & Co., 1972.

Singh, Amritjit. *The Novels of the Harlem Renaissance: Twelve Black Writers, 1923–1933.* University Park: Pennsylvania State University Press, 1976.

Tate, Claudia. "Nella Larsen's Passing: A Problem of Interpretation." *Black American Literature Forum* 14 (Winter 1980):142–46.

Thornton, Hortense E. "Sexism as Quagmire: Nella Larsen's *Quicksand.*" *CLA Journal,* 16 (March 1973):285–301.

Washington, Mary Helen. "Nella Larsen: Mystery Woman of the Harlem Renaissance." *MS* 9 (December 1980):44–50.

Whitlow, Roger. *Black American Literature: A Critical History.* Chicago: Nelson Hall, 1973.

Youman, Mary Mabel. "Nella Larsen's *Passing:* A Study in Irony." *CLA Journal* 18 (December 1974):235–41.

The Abyss

It began, this next child-bearing, during the morning services of a breathless hot Sunday while the fervent choir soloist was singing: "Ah am freed of mah sorrow," and lasted far into the small hours of Tuesday morning. It seemed, for some reason, not to go off just right. And when, after that long frightfulness, the fourth little dab of amber humanity which Helga had contributed to a despised race was held before her for maternal approval, she failed entirely to respond properly to this sop of consolation, for the suffering and horror through which she had passed. There was from her no pleased, proud smile, no loving, possessive gesture, no manifestation of interest in the important matters of sex and weight. Instead she deliberately closed her eyes, mutely shutting out the sickly infant, its smiling father, the soiled midwife, the curious neighbors, and the tousled room.

A week she lay so. Silent and listless. Ignoring food, the clamoring children, the comings and goings of solicitous, kind-hearted women, her hovering husband, and all of life about her. The neighbors were puzzled. The Reverend Mr. Pleasant Green was worried. The midwife was frightened.

On the floor, in and out among the furniture and under her bed, the twins played. Eager to help, the church-women crowded in and, meeting there others on the same laudable errand, stayed to gossip and to wonder. Anxiously the preacher sat, Bible in hand, beside his wife's bed, or in a nervous half-guilty manner invited the congregated parishioners to join him in prayer for the healing of their sister. Then, kneeling, they would beseech God to stretch out His all-powerful hand on behalf of the afflicted one, softly at first, but with rising vehemence, accompanied by moans and tears, until it seemed that the God to whom they prayed must in mercy to the sufferer grant relief. If only so that she might rise up and escape from the tumult, the heat, and the smell.

Helga, however, was unconcerned, undisturbed by the commotion about her. It was all part of the general unreality. Nothing reached her. Nothing penetrated the kind darkness into which her bruised spirit had retreated. Even that red-letter event, the coming to see her of the old white physician from downtown, who had for a long time stayed talking gravely to her husband, drew from her no interest. Nor for days was she aware that a stranger, a nurse from Mobile, had been added to her household, a brusquely efficient woman who produced order out of chaos and quiet out of bedlam. Neither did the absence of the children, removed by good neighbors at Miss Hartley's insistence, impress her. While she had gone down into that appalling blackness of pain, the ballast of her brain had got loose and she hovered for a long time somewhere in that delightful borderland on the edge of unconsciousness, an enchanted and blissful place where peace and incredible quiet encompassed her.

After weeks she grew better, returned to earth, set her reluctant feet to the hard path of life again.

"Well, here you are!" announced Miss Hartley in her slightly harsh voice one afternoon just before the fall of evening. She had for some time been standing at the bedside gazing down at Helga with an intent speculative look.

"Yes," Helga agreed in a thin little voice, "I'm back." The truth was that she had been back for some hours. Purposely she had lain silent and still, wanting to linger forever in that serene haven, that effortless calm where nothing was expected of her. There she could watch the figures of the past drift by. There was her mother, whom she had loved from a distance and finally so scornfully blamed, who appeared as she had always remembered her, unbelievably beautiful, young, and remote. Robert Anderson, questioning, purposely detached, affecting, as she realized now, her life in a remarkably cruel degree; for at last she understood clearly how deeply, how passionately, she must have loved him. Anne, lovely, secure, wise, selfish. Axel Olsen, conceited, worldly, spoiled. Audrey Denney, placid, taking quietly and without fuss the things which she wanted. James Vayle, snobbish, smug, servile. Mrs. Hayes-Rore, important, kind, determined. The Dahls, rich, correct, climbing. Flashingly, fragmentarily, other long-forgotten figures, women in gay fashionable frocks and men in formal black and white, glided by in bright rooms to distant, vaguely familiar music.

It was refreshingly delicious, this immersion in the past. But it was finished now. It was over. The words of her husband, the Reverend Mr. Pleasant Green, who had been standing at the window looking mournfully out at the scorched melon-patch, ruined because Helga had been ill so long and unable to tend it, were confirmation of that.

"The Lord be praised," he said, and came forward. It was distinctly disagreeable. It was even more disagreeable to feel his moist hand on hers. A cold shiver brushed over her. She closed her eyes. Obstinately and with all her small strength she drew her hand away from him. Hid it far down under the bed-covering, and turned her face away to hide a grimace of unconquerable aversion. She cared nothing, at that moment, for his hurt surprise. She knew only that, in the hideous agony that for interminable hours—no, centuries—she had borne, the luster of religion had vanished; that revulsion had come upon her; that she hated this man. Between them the vastness of the universe had come.

Miss Hartley, all-seeing and instantly aware of a situation, as she had been quite aware that her patient had been conscious for some time before she herself had announced the fact, intervened, saying firmly: "I think it might be better if you didn't try to talk to her now. She's terribly sick and weak yet. She's still got some fever and we mustn't excite her or she's liable to slip back. And we don't want that, do we?"

No, the man, her husband, responded, they didn't want that. Reluctantly he went from the room with a last look at Helga, who was lying on her back with one frail, pale hand under her small head, her curly black hair scattered loose on the pillow. She regarded him from behind dropped lids. The day was hot, her breasts were covered only by a nightgown of filmy *crêpe*, a relic of prematrimonial days, which had slipped from one carved shoulder. He flinched. Helga's petulant lip curled, for she well knew that this fresh reminder of her desirability was like the flick of a whip.

Miss Hartley carefully closed the door after the retreating husband. "It's time," she said, "for your evening treatment, and then you've got to try to sleep for a while. No more visitors tonight."

Helga nodded and tried unsuccessfully to make a little smile. She was glad of Miss Hartley's presence. It would, she felt, protect her from so much. She mustn't, she thought to herself, get well too fast. Since it seemed she was going to get well. In bed she could think, could have a certain amount of quiet. Of aloneness.

In that period of racking pain and calamitous fright Helga had learned what passion and credulity could do to one. In her was born angry bitterness and an enormous disgust. The cruel, unrelieved suffering had beaten down her protective wall of artificial faith in the infinite wisdom, in the mercy, of God. For had she not called in her agony on Him? And He had not heard. Why? Because, she knew now, He wasn't there. Didn't exist. Into that yawning gap of unspeakable brutality had gone, too, her belief in the miracle and wonder of life. Only scorn, resentment, and hate remained—and ridicule. Life wasn't a miracle, a wonder. It was, for Negroes at least, only a great disappointment. Something to be got through with as best one could. No one was interested in them or helped them. God! Bah! And they were only a nuisance to other people.

Everything in her mind was hot and cold, beating and swirling about. Within her emaciated body raged disillusion. Chaotic turmoil. With the obscuring curtain of religion rent, she was able to look about her and see with shocked eyes this thing that she had done to herself. She couldn't, she thought ironically, even blame God for it, now that she knew that He didn't exist. No. No more than she could pray to Him for the death of her husband, the Reverend Mr. Pleasant Green. The white man's God. And His great love for all people regardless of race! What idiotic nonsense she had allowed herself to believe. How could she, how could anyone, have been so deluded? How could ten million black folk credit it when daily before their eyes was enacted its contradiction? Not that she at all cared about the ten million. But herself. Her sons. Her daughter. These would grow to manhood, to womanhood, in this vicious, this hypocritical land. The dark eyes filled with tears.

"I wouldn't," the nurse advised, "do that. You've been dreadfully sick, you know. I can't have you worrying. Time enough for that when you're well. Now you must sleep all you possibly can."

Helga did sleep. She found it surprisingly easy to sleep. Aided by Miss Hartley's rather masterful discernment, she took advantage of the ease with which this blessed enchantment stole over her. From her husband's praisings, prayers, and caresses she sought refuge in sleep, and from the neighbors' gifts, advice, and sympathy.

There was the day on which they told her that the last sickly infant, born of such futile torture and lingering torment, had died after a short week of slight living. Just closed his eyes and died. No vitality. On hearing it Helga too had just closed her eyes. Not to die. She was convinced that before her there were years of living. Perhaps of happiness even. For a new idea had come to her. She had closed her eyes to shut in any telltale gleam of the relief which she felt. One less. And she had gone off into sleep.

And there was that Sunday morning on which the Reverend Mr. Pleasant Green had informed her that they were that day to hold a special thanksgiving service for her recovery. There would, he said, be prayers, special testimonies, and songs. Was there anything particular she would like to have said, to have prayed for, to have sung? Helga had smiled from sheer amusement as she replied that there was nothing. Nothing at all. She only hoped that they would enjoy themselves. And, closing her eyes that he might be discouraged from longer tarrying, she had gone off to sleep.

Waking later to the sound of joyous religious abandon floating in through the opened windows, she had asked a little diffidently that she be allowed to read. Miss Hartley's sketchy brows contracted into a dubious frown. After a judicious pause she had answered: "No, I don't think so." Then, seeing the rebellious tears which had sprung into her patient's eyes, she added kindly: "But I'll read to you a little if you like."

That, Helga replied, would be nice. In the next room on a high-up shelf was a book. She'd forgotten the name, but its author was Anatole France. There was a story, "The Procurator of Judea." Would Miss Hartley read that? "Thanks. Thanks awfully."

"'Lælius Lamia, born in Italy of illustrious parents,'" began the nurse in her slightly harsh voice.

Helga drank it in.

"'. . . For to this day the women bring down doves to the altar as their victims. . . .'"

Helga closed her eyes.

"'. . . Africa and Asia have already enriched us with a considerable number of gods. . . .'"

Miss Hartley looked up. Helga had slipped into slumber while the superbly ironic ending which she had so desired to hear was yet a long way off. A dull tale, was Miss Hartley's opinion, as she curiously turned the pages to see how it turned out.

"'Jesus? . . . Jesus—of Nazareth? I cannot call him to mind.'"

"Huh!" she muttered, puzzled. "Silly." And closed the book.

Appendix A

Biographical Sketches of Notable Afro-American Women Writers of the New Negro Movement Who Did Not Publish Books or Publish Them Prior to 1933

Andrews, Regina Anderson (1901–)

Chicago-born librarian, playwright, and occupant once of the famed 580 St. Nicholas Avenue apartment in Harlem, where she, Ethel Ray Nance, and Luella Tucker provided a social and intellectual atmosphere for the writers and artists in their "Dream Haven." Regina Andrews attended Wilberforce University, the University of Chicago, City College of New York, and Columbia University's library school. She began her library experience at the historic 135th Street Branch of the New York Public Library and, after a prestigious career, retired from the Washington Heights Branch in 1947.

She was one of the organizers of the Harlem Experimental Theatre, along with Jessie Fauset, Harold Jackman, Dorothy Williams, and others. Her two plays, *Climbing Jacob's Ladder* and *Underground*, were produced by the Harlem Experimental Theatre in 1925 and 1931. A recipient of many civic awards, Andrews (along with Jessie Fauset and Gwendolyn Bennett) was honored among ten black women at the 1939 New York World's Fair.

Bennett, Gwendolyn (1902–1981)

A talented poet as well as artist, Gwendolyn Bennett came from Giddings, Texas. She was the first black woman to be elected to the Felter Library Society and Dramatic Society of Girls High School in Brooklyn, New York. She enrolled in the fine arts department of Teachers College for two years before taking the normal art course at Pratt Institute, which she completed in 1924.

Her first teaching position was at Howard University as an instructor in design, watercolor, and crafts. In 1924, she was awarded the Thousand Dollar Foreign Scholarship by the Alpha Sigma chapter of Delta Sigma Theta sorority. She sailed to Cherbourg, France, in June of the next year to study at the Académie Julian, the Académie Coloraossi, and the École de Pantheon.

On her return in the summer of 1926, she became an assistant to the editor of *Opportunity* magazine. Her Ebony Flute column of literary and artistic news began in August. She wrote short stories, some of which appeared in *Ebony and Topaz* and *Fire!* Her poems were published in *Opportunity* and *Palms*, and have been reprinted in various anthologies. Her poetry was said to have "equalled her art."

Bennett's drawings appeared in the *Crisis* and *Messenger*, and she and Aaron Douglas were the first black artists to receive a Barnes Foundation Fellowship in 1927. Sandra Y. Govan, who wrote a dissertation on Bennett, places her death as 30 May 1981 in Kutztown, Pennsylvania.

Coleman, Anita Scott (1890–1960)

Anita Scott Coleman was a poet, short-story writer, and essayist. As a Los Angeles schoolteacher, she taught long enough to consider it the most interesting work she had ever done. She enjoyed children for whom she frequently wrote and, at one time, operated a boarding home for them.

Her father was a Cuban who purchased her mother as a slave,

but later fought in the Civil War on the Union side. Anita was born in Mexico, state of Sonora, city of Guaymas, and attended school in Silver City, New Mexico, where she had moved.

When *Opportunity* magazine awarded her a second prize in 1926 for "The Dark Horse," a personal experience sketch, she was an ex-teacher, married and living on a ranch with children. The same year, she received another second prize from the Amy Spingarn Contest in Literature and Art sponsored by the *Crisis* for her essay "Unfinished Masterpieces."

Besides the *Crisis* and *Opportunity* magazines, her work appeared in *Half-Century, Southwest Review,* the *Messenger, Competitor,* and *Flash,* as well as in the anthologies *Ebony Rhythm* and *An Anthology of Contemporary Verse: Negro Voices.*

Under the pseudonym of Elizabeth Stapleton Stokes, she wrote a book of verse, *Small Wisdom* (1937), and won a *Crisis* third prize for her short story "Three Dogs and a Rabbit" in 1925. She published two more books of poetry under her own name, *Reason for Singing* (1948) and the posthumous *The Singing Bells* (1961), which featured pictures by Claudine Nankivel.

Delany, Clarissa Scott (1901–1927)

Clarissa Scott was born in Tuskegee, Alabama, where her eminent father, Emmett J. Scott, was secretary to Booker T. Washington. In keeping with her middle-class milieu, she attended Bradford Academy in New England for three years before entering Wellesley College. "Beautiful and talented," she was a magazine cover girl the year she graduated. She taught at the elite Dunbar High School in Washington, D.C., but after three years, she decided that teaching was not her métier.

She married Hubert Delany in 1926. After completing "A study of Delinquency and Neglect among Negro Children in New York City," she settled on being a housewife. She contributed to the *Crisis, Opportunity,* and *Palms,* as well as *Caroling Dusk, Negro Poets and Their Poems,* and *American Negro Poetry.* Her budding writing career was abruptly terminated by her untimely death at the age of twenty-six. Angelina W. Grimké eulogized her in a poem, "To Clarissa Scott Delany," in *Ebony and Topaz.* A moving tribute to her in *Opportunity* (November 1927) stated in part: "With a well-trained and restlessly searching mind, a magnificent and sturdy idealism and all of the impetuous zeal of youth, she was superbly poised for life; and quietly she left it."

Dickinson, Blanch Taylor (1896–?)

In *Opportunity* (July 1927), Blanche Taylor Dickinson wrote from her home in Sewickley, Pennsylvania: "As far back as I can remember I have had the urge to write poetry and stories." As a gifted poet, she won a special Buckner prize for her poem "A Sonnet and a Rondeau." Her work can be found in the *Crisis, Ebony and Topaz, A Rock against the Wind,* and *Caroling Dusk.*

Blanche Taylor Dickinson was born on a farm in Franklin, Kentucky, on 15 April 1896. She attended Bowling Green Academy and Simmon's University, and studied in various summer schools. She never earned a degree, but taught for several years in Kentucky. As a writer, she was first published in the *Franklin Favorite,* and afterward, such newspapers as the *Louisville Leader, Chicago Defender,* and *Pittsburgh Courier.*

Hurston, Zora Neale (1891?/1901?/1903?–1960)

At long last, this complex and individualistic woman has been accorded her proper niche as a distinguished Afro-American woman writer. Her life story is legendary now, having been reexamined and memorialized in a multitude of articles, essays, and books—to such an extent, in fact, that there almost exists a Zora Neale Hurston cult. Always different from others, even as a child, she was born in Eatonville, Florida, an all-black town where her father was mayor. Eatonville later provided the material for her stories and research. Her birth date has been a mystery, made more so by Hurston's conflicting accounts. Professor Cheryl Wall of Rutgers University has placed it from the census records as 7 January 1891, ten years before the frequently used date of 1 January 1901.

After her mother died, Hurston left home in search of a better future. She supported herself by working as a maid and manicurist. She received her high school diploma from Morgan College's preparatory school in 1918. (The school awarded her an honorary doctor of literature degree in 1939.) She attended Howard University for two years, where she met one of her mentors, Alain Locke. She joined his Stylus literary society and had her first short story, "John Redding Goes to Sea," published in the society's literary magazine, the *Stylus,* in May 1921.

Her writing caught the eye of another New Negro Movement godfather, Charles S. Johnson, editor of *Opportunity*, who invited her to New York. Johnson published her second story, "Spunk," in 1925, for which she won *Opportunity*'s first literary contest. This was followed the next year by her play, *Color Struck*, which won second place.

She then moved to New York in January of that year, starry-eyed and virtually penniless. Johnson and Locke took her under their wing and introduced her to persons of means. She was awarded a scholarship to Barnard College and became secretary, then chauffeur to white novelist Fannie Hurst. While in school, her writing activities continued. Blending in well with the rebellious mood of the young New Negro Movement writers, she helped publish and contributed to the controversial one-issue *Fire!*

At Barnard, she came under the influence of anthropologist Franz Boas, who guided her research after graduation. She left the thriving artistic Harlem scene to collect folklore. Although absent during the flowering of the New Negro Movement, biographer Robert Hemenway felt that she was an important contributor to the Renaissance spirit. Her research was supported by foundation grants and white Renaissance godmother Mrs. Rufus Osgood Mason.

The most prolific and enduring of the post–New Negro Movement women writers, Hurston continued to publish even while staying at the St. Lucie County Welfare Home in Florida in 1958, where she wrote part time for the Fort Pierce *Chronicle*. She died penniless and in partial obscurity in 1960. Her Fort Pierce grave remained unmarked until Alice Walker, editor of *I Love Myself When I Am Laughing . . . And Then Again When I Am Looking Mean and Impressive: Zora Neale Hurston Reader* (1979), placed a tombstone on it.

The erratic, rebellious, her-own-woman writer published seven books—two of folklore, *Mules and Men* (1935) and *Tell My Horse* (1938); an autobiography, *Dust Tracks on the Road* (1942); and four novels, *Jonah's Gourd Vine* (1934), *Their Eyes Were Watching God* (1937), *Moses, Man of the Mountain* (1939), and *Seraph on the Suwanee* (1948).

Johnson, Helene Hubbell (1907–)
A cousin to writer Dorothy West, Helene Hubbell Johnson was born in Boston. She attended the public schools and Boston University. When she went to New York in 1926 to become a student at the Extension Division of Columbia University, she became involved in

the Harlem segment of the New Negro Movement. Her poetry ap peared in *Opportunity, Vanity Fair, Palms*, the *Literary Digest*, the *Saturday Evening Quill*, and New York dailies. James Weldon Johnson enthusiastically noted that her "earliest work bore the stamp of a genuine poet." He admired her "colloquial style" and "true lyric talent." Arna W. Bontemps looked upon her as one of the youngest of those who brought about the Harlem Renaissance. She has been the recipient of a number of poetry awards.

Miller, May (1899–)

May Miller's (Mrs. John Sullivan) literary talent came into view during the New Negro Movement when her one-act play, *The Bog Guide*, won *Opportunity*'s third prize in 1925. The following year, a second play, *The Cuss'd Thing*, won honorable mention. After that, she became a short-story writer and poet of note.

The daughter of writer and scholar Kelly Miller, she was born in Washington, D.C. A graduate of Howard University, she did additional study at American and Columbia universities. Miller taught speech and dramatics at Frederick Douglass High School in Baltimore. She has been a lecturer, reader, and poet-in-residence at Mammouth College, University of Wisconsin, Milwaukee, and the Phillips Exeter Academy. In 1972, she recorded for the Library of Congress Collection of Poets Reading Their Own Works. For three years, she was coordinator for performing poets, a project sponsored by the Friends of the Arts in the Public Schools of the District of Columbia.

She coedited with Willis Richardson *Negro History in Thirteen Plays* (1935), which included four of her own. She has published poetry and short stories in the *Crisis, Opportunity*, the *Antioch Review, Common Ground*, the *Nation*, and anthologies. Her poems have been collected in *Into the Clearing* (1959), *Poems* (1962), *The Clearing and Beyond* (1974), and *Dust of Uncertain Journey* (1975).

Newsome, Effie Lee (1885–1979)

Effie Lee Newsome described herself as a "children's muralist, author and librarian." She wrote verses and short stories for children and young adults, nature sketches, and biographies for the *Crisis, Opportunity, Phylon*, and *Child Craft*. She served as the Little Page editor of the *Crisis*. Although most of her writing was for children, she wrote some for adults.

Newsome was born in Philadelphia, Pennsylvania, and lived most of her life in Wilberforce, Ohio, where she was a librarian for the Cook Laboratory School of Central State College. She graduated from Wilberforce University in 1904 and did further study at Oberlin College's Academy, 1904–5, the Academy of Fine Arts, 1907–8, and the University of Pennsylvania, 1911–14. Her book of poetry, *Gladiola Gardens*, was issued in 1940.

Popel, Esther (?–?)

A poet and essayist, Esther Popel Shaw was born in Harrisburg, Pennsylvania, where her family had lived since 1826, when her paternal grandfather, at the age of six, was brought there by free-born parents. She received her education at Dickinson College and Columbia University. A Phi Beta Kappa, she taught French and Spanish at Shaw Junior High School in Washington, D.C.

Opportunity magazine published her poetry, awarding her honorable mention in its 1925 poetry contest for "Cat and the Saxophone." She reviewed books, lectured, and read her poetry to various groups. In her later years, she was editor of the *Lincoln Reporter*, a monthly bulletin of the Lincoln Congregational Temple, 1951–52.

An active clubwoman, she served as corresponding secretary for the National Association of College Women. Following an address for the Women's Club in Lawrenceville, New Jersey, the Woman's Press of the national board of the YWCA published her "Personal Adventures in Race Relations" (1946).

Christmas of 1934, she privately printed a limited edition of her poems, *A Forest Pool*. The book was distributed to close friends as gifts: "Because / (My ego whispers soft' to me) / You care!"

Spencer, Anne (1882–1975)

Anne Spencer was born Annie Bethel Scales Bannister in Henry Country, Virginia, on a plantation. Four years later, her mother took her to Bramwell, West Virginia, to live. She could not read or write until she was eleven years old. When her mother sent her to Virginia Seminary and Normal School in Lynchburg in September 1893, she found that she had a lot of learning to do. This she did, graduating in 1899 at the age of seventeen as valedictorian of her class. She then taught for a while in Maybeury and Elkhorn, Virginia.

She married Edward A. Spencer, a schoolmate at the seminary, in May 1901. Two years later, they moved into a house practically built by her husband at 1313 Pierce Street. Behind it, Anne Spencer had her famous garden and little cottage, Edankraal, constructed by her husband for her retreat. There she did her reading, thinking, writing, and tending to her cherished garden.

The Spencers' house eventually became a center for New Negro Movement figures to visit, meet, and talk with the poet. W. E. B. Du Bois, James Weldon Johnson, Georgia Douglas Johnson, Langston Hughes, Claude McKay, Sterling Brown, and Paul Robeson were a few of the prominent guests. Anne Spencer lifted the curtain to another part of the country for the New Negro intellectuals. It was as a guest in 1919 that James Weldon Johnson "discovered" her as a poet by reading some of the poems she had scattered about the house. He sent one to H. L. Mencken, who was impressed. It became her first published poem, "Before the Feast at Shushan" printed in the *Crisis* (February 1920). Johnson gave her her pen name, Anne Spencer. An admirer of her poetry, he praised her high degree of maturity in verse. Sterling Brown, poet, writer, and critic, called her a "first-rate poet," and immortalized her in a poem, "To a Certain Lady in Her Garden."

Anne Spencer published less than thirty of her poems, and her career lasted just over ten years. She scribbled thousands of poems on pieces of paper, which were accidentally thrown out by house cleaners. Professor J. Lee Greene, in his valuable biography, *Time's Unfading Garden: Anne Spencer's Life and Poetry* (1971), made forty-two of the fifty extant poems available in an appendix to his book.

Anne Spencer wrote conventional poetry, little of it about race, but her personal life was highly unconventional. She waged battles against school segregation and Jim Crowism in Lynchburg. As an early civil rights activist, she was the founder of the first permanent chapter of the NAACP in Lynchburg. She defied social customs and propriety by wearing pantsuits in public when other women did not. Her husband pampered her, letting her do as she pleased. She was admittedly not a housekeeper. She had her writing and her garden to occupy her time. There were always people about to do the domestic chores and take care of their three children, two girls and a boy.

When the children reached college age, she went to work to help with expenses. She became the first librarian at Dunbar High School, where she had a record of being an excellent and caring librarian who introduced black children to books and life beyond Lynchburg. Many of the books in the segregated school library were her personal ones. She remained at Dunbar High for twenty-three years.

In May 1975, shortly before her death on 27 July, Virginia Seminary and College conferred upon her an honorary doctor of letters. Two years later, on Saturday, 26 February 1977, the Anne Spencer House and Garden, 1313 Pierce Street, Lynchburg, was dedicated as a historic landmark.

West, Dorothy (1910?/1912?–)

At the age of seven, Dorothy West decided that she wanted to be a writer because "words were the most beautiful things in the world." One of the few still living personages of the New Negro Movement, she was an only child of a Boston middle-class family. Her father, a generation older than her mother, was an ex-slave. Because of a paucity of male family members, she was brought up in a "society of women."

Dorothy West was educated at Girls Latin High School and Boston University. It was when she entered Columbia University's School of Journalism that she became an active part of the New Negro Movement scene. The youngest of the new writers, she was only seventeen and a half when her short story "The Typewriter" won second place in *Opportunity*'s contest of 1926. The story was reprinted in the *Mahashakti*, a magazine in Benares, India. She published stories in the *Boston Post*, the *Saturday Evening Quill*, and the *New York Daily News*, as well as in anthologies.

She remained in Harlem for ten years after the New Negro Movement waned and the Great Depression set in. She wrote and participated in the Theatre Guild. For a while, she was a welfare relief social worker and then conducted interviews and wrote for the Federal Writers' Project.

Like some black writers, she became disenchanted with the times, and briefly espoused communism. In the mid-thirties, she went to Russia with a group to make a propaganda film about the plight of American blacks, but the film was not released. With the money from the venture, however, she started and edited a black quarterly, *Challenge*, whose name was changed to *New Challenge*.

In 1948, her novel, *The Living Is Easy*, was published and has been reprinted by the Feminist Press. She still resides on Martha's Vineyard, where she continues to write and publish.

Appendix B

Additional Selected Sources to Afro-American Women Writers, 1900–1933, and Notable Afro-American Women Writers of the New Negro Movement

Adoff, Arnold. *The Poetry of Black America: Anthology of the 20th Century.* New York: Harper & Row, 1973.

Bell, Roseann P.; Parker, Bettye J.; and Guy-Sheftall, Beverly, eds. *Sturdy Black Bridges: Visions of Black Women in Literature.* Garden City, N.Y.: Anchor Books, 1979.

Bernikow, Louise. *The World Split Open: Four Centuries of Women Poets in England and America, 1552–1950.* New York: Vintage Press, 1974.

Cromwell, Otelia; Turner, Lorenzo Dow; and Dykes, Eva B., eds. *Readings from Negro Authors for Schools and Colleges, with a Bibliography of Negro Literature.* New York: Harcourt, Brace & Co., 1931.

Cullen, Countee. *Caroling Dusk: An Anthology of Verse by Negro Poets.* New York: Harper & Brothers, 1927.

Davis, Arthur P., and Redding, Saunders, eds. *Cavalcade: Negro American Writing from 1760 to the Present.* Boston: Houghton Mifflin Co., 1971.

Davis, Arthur P. *From the Dark Tower: Afro-American Writers 1900 to 1960.* Washington, D.C.: Howard University Press, 1974.

Ellington, Mary Davis. "Plays by Negro Authors with Special Emphasis upon the Period from 1916 to 1934." Master's thesis, Fisk University, 1934.

Fisk University Library. *Dictionary Catalog of the Negro Collection of the Fisk University Library.* 6 vols. Boston: G. K. Hall & Co., 1974.

Bontemps, Arna, ed. *The Harlem Renaissance Remembered: Essays Edited with a Memoir.* New York: Dodd, Mead & Co., 1972.

Giddings, Paula. *When and Where I Enter: The Impact of Black Women on Race and Sex in America.* New York: William Morrow & Co., 1984.

Gilbert, Sandra M., and Gubar, Susan. *The Madwoman in the Attic: The Woman Writer and the Nineteenth-Century Literary Imagination.* New Haven and London: Yale University Press, 1984.

———. *The Norton Anthology of Literature by Women: The Tradition in English.* New York: W. W. Norton & Co., 1985.

Gloster, Hugh M. *Negro Voices in American Fiction.* 1948. Reprint. New York: Russell & Russell, 1965.

Greene, J. Lee. *Time's Unfading Garden: Anne Spencer's Life and Poetry.* Baton Rouge and London: Louisiana State University Press, 1977.

Harris, Trudier, and Davis, Thadious M., eds. *Afro-American Writers before the Harlem Renaissance.* Dictionary of Literary Biography, vol. 50. Detroit, Mich.: Gale Research Co., 1986.

———. *Afro-American Writers from the Harlem Renaissance to 1940.* Dictionary of Literary Biography, vol. 51. Detroit, Mich.: Gale Research Co., 1987.

Hatch, James V., and Abdullah, Omani. *Black Playwrights, 1823–1977: An Annotated Bibliography of Plays.* New York: R. R. Bowker, 1977.

Hatch, James V., ed. *Black Theater, U.S.A.: Forty-five Plays by Black Americans, 1847–1974.* New York: Free Press, 1974.

Hemenway, Robert E. *Zora Neale Hurston: A Literary Biography.* Urbana: University of Illinois Press, 1977.

Howard University, Founders Library, Moorland Foundation. *Dictionary Catalog of the Jesse E. Moorland Collection of Negro Life and History.* 9 vols. Boston: G. K. Hall & Co., 1962.

Huggins, Nathan Irvin, ed. *Voices from the Harlem Renaissance.* New York: Oxford University Press, 1976.

Hughes, Langston, and Bontemps, Arna, eds. *The Poetry of the Negro, 1746–1970.* Rev. ed. Garden City, N.Y.: Doubleday & Co., 1970.

Hull, Gloria T.; Scott, Patricia Bell; and Smith, Barbara, eds. *All the Women Are White, All the Blacks Are Men, but Some of Us Are Brave: Black Women's Studies.* Old Westbury, N.Y.: Feminist Press, 1982.

Hurston, Zora Neale. *Dust Tracks on a Road: An Autobiography.* 2d ed. Edited and with an introduction by Robert Hemenway. Urbana and Chicago: University of Illinois Press, 1984.

Iaciofana, Carol. "The Sun Doesn't Set on Dorothy West." *Sojourner* 7 (April 1982):15.

Johnson, Charles Spurgeon, ed. *Ebony and Topaz: A Collectanea.* New York: *Opportunity: Journal of Negro Life,* National Urban League, 1927.

Johnson, James Weldon, ed. *The Book of American Negro Poetry.* New York: Harcourt, Brace & Co., 1931.

Joyce, Donald Franklin. *Gatekeepers of Black Culture: Black-Owned Book Publishing in the United States, 1817–1981.* Westport, Conn.: Greenwood Press, 1983.

Kellner, Bruce, ed. *The Harlem Renaissance: A Historical Dictionary for the Era.* Westport, Conn. and London: Greenwood Press, 1984.

Kerlin, Robert T. *Negro Poets and Their Poems.* Washington, D.C.: Associated Publishers, 1923.

Mitchell, Lofton. *Black Drama: The Story of the American Negro in the Theater.* New York: Hawthorn Books, 1967.

Murphy, Beatrice, ed. *An Anthology of Contemporary Verse: Negro Voices.* New York: Henry Harrison, 1928.

———. *Ebony Rhythm: An Anthology of Contemporary Negro Verse.* New York: Exposition Press, 1948.

New York Public Library, Schomburg Collection of Negro Literature and History. *Dictionary Catalog.* 9 vols. Boston: G. K. Hall & Co., 1962.

Noble, Jeanne. *Beautiful, Also, Are the Souls of My Black Sisters: A History of the Black Woman in America.* Englewood Cliffs, N.J.: Prentice-Hall, 1978.

Porter, Dorothy Burnett. *North American Negro Poets: A Bibliographical Checklist of Their Writings, 1760–1944.* Hattiesburg, Miss.: Book Farm, 1945.

————. *A Working Bibliography of the Negro in the United States.* Ann Arbor, Mich.: Xerox, University Microfilms, 1969.

Richardson, Marilyn, ed. *Maria W. Stewart: America's First Black Woman Political Writer, Essays and Speeches.* Bloomington: Indiana University Press, 1987.

Richardson, Willis, and Miller, May. *Negro History in Thirteen Plays.* Washington, D.C.: Associated Publishers, 1933.

Rush, Theressa Gunn; Myers, Carol Fairbanks; and Arata, Esther Spring. *Black American Writers Past and Present: A Biographical and Bibliographical Dictionary.* 2 vols. Metuchen, N.J.: Scarecrow Press, 1975.

Schomburg, Arthur A. *A Bibliographical Checklist of American Negro Poetry.* New York: Charles F. Heartman, 1916.

Showalter, Elaine, ed. *The New Feminist Criticism: Essays on Women, Literature, and Theory.* New York: Pantheon Books, 1985.

Stetson, Erlene, ed. *Black Sister: Poetry by Black American Women, 1746–1980.* Bloomington: Indiana University Press, 1981.

Walker, Alice, ed. *I Love Myself When I Am Laughing, and Then Again When I Am Looking Mean and Impressive: A Zora Neale Hurston Reader.* Old Westbury, N.Y.: Feminist Press, 1979.

Washington, Mary Helen, ed. *Invented Lives: Narratives of Black Women, 1860–1960.* Garden City, N.Y., Anchor Press/Doubleday & Co., 1987.

Whiteman, Maxwell. *A Century of Fiction by American Negroes, 1853–1952: A Descriptive Bibliography.* Philadelphia: Albert Saifer, 1955.

Williams, Ora. *American Black Women in the Arts and Social Sciences: A Bibliographic Survey.* Rev. ed. Metuchen, N.J., and London: Scarecrow Press, 1978.

Wright, Odessa Mae. "Achievements of Negro Women Since 1865." Master's thesis, State University of Iowa, 1931.

Work, Monroe N. *A Bibliography of the Negro in Africa and America.* 1928. Reprint. New York: Octagon Books, 1970.

Source Notes

Lucy Terry Prince
  "Bars Fight." From George Sheldon, "Negro Slavery in Old
  Deerfield," *New England Magazine* 8 (March–August 1893): 56.
Phillis Wheatley
  "On Being Brought from Africa to America"; "To S. M., a Young
  African Painter, on Seeing His Works"; "On Imagination"; "A
  Funeral Poem on the Death of C. E., and Infant of Twelve
  Months." From Phillis Wheatley, *Poems on Various Subjects, Religious and Moral* (London: Printed for A. Bell, Bookseller, Aldgate, 1773), pp. 18, 114, 65, 69.
Ann Plato
  "To the First of August"; "Advice to Young Ladies"; "Forget
  Me Not"; "Education." From Ann Plato, *Essays; Including Biographies and Miscellaneous Pieces in Prose and Poetry* (Hartford, 1841), pp. 114, 66, 106–7, 26–27.
Zilpha Elaw
  [Mrs. Elaw.] From Zilpha Elaw, *Memoirs of the Life, Religious Experience, Ministerial Travels and Labours of Mrs. Zilpha Elaw, an American Female of Color; Together with Some Account of the Great*

Religious Revivals in America (London: Published by the author, 1846), pp. 1–7.

Jarena Lee.

"My Call to Preach the Gospel." From Jarena Lee, *Religious Experience and Journal of Mrs. Jarena Lee, Giving an Account of Her Call to Preach the Gospel* (Philadelphia, 1849), pp. 10–13.

Nancy Gardener Prince

"Her Return Back to Jamaica, and State of Things at That Time." From Mrs. Nancy Gardener Prince, *A Narrative of the Life and Travels of Mrs. Nancy Prince*. 3d ed. (Boston: Published by the author, 1856), pp. 57–63.

Frances Ellen Watkins Harper

"The Slave Mother." From Frances Ellen Watkins, *Poems on Miscellaneous Subjects* (Boston, J. B. Yerrinton & Son, Printers, 1854), pp. 6–8.

"The Two Offers." From the *Anglo-African Magazine* 1 (September–October 1859): 288–291, 311–313. Reprint. (New York: Arno Press and New York Times, 1968).

Charlotte L. Forten

[Emancipation Day in St. Helena Island.] From Charlotte L. Forten, *The Journal of Charlotte L. Forten*. Edited by Ray Allen Billington (New York: Dryden Press, 1953), pp. 153–57.

"A Parting Hymn"; "The Angel's Visit." From William Wells Brown, *The Black Man: His Antecedents, His Genius, and His Achievements* (New York: Thomas Hamilton; Boston: R. F. Wallcut, 1863), pp. 191; 196–99.

Harriet E. Adams Wilson

"A New Home for Me." From Mrs. H. E. Wilson, *Our Nig; or, Sketches from the Life of a Free Black, in a Two-Story White House, North. Showing That Slavery's Shadows Fall Even There* (Boston: Printed by Geo. Rand & Avery, 1859), pp. 24–29. Reprint. With introduction and notes by Henry Louis Gates, Jr. (New York: Random House, Vintage Books, 1983).

Harriet Ann Jacobs

"The Jealous Mistress." From Harriet Jacobs [Linda Brent, pseud.], *Incident in the Life of a Slave Girl*. Edited by L. Maria Child (Boston, 1861), pp. 49–57.

Frances Anne Rollin Whipper

"The Council Chamber—President Lincoln." From Frances A.

Rollin [Frank A. Rollin, pseud.], *Life and Public Service of Martin R. Delany* (Boston: Lee & Shepard, 1868), pp. 166–75.

Elizabeth Hobbs Keckley

"The Secret Life of Mrs. Lincoln's Wardrobe in New York." From Elizabeth Keckley, *Behind the Scenes; or, Thirty Years a Slave, and Four Years in the White House* (New York: G. W. Carleton, 1868), pp. 267–72, 302–8.

Clarissa Minnie Thompson

"De Verne or Herbert—Which?" From Clarissa Minnie Thompson, "Treading the Winepress; or, A Mountain of Misfortune," *Boston Advocate* 1, no. 2 (1885–86).

Miss Garrison

"Churches and Religion." From Miss Garrison, "A Ray of Light," *A. M. E. Church Review* 6 (1889–90):96–102.

Amelia Etta Hall Johnson

"The Reunion." From Amelia E. Johnson, *Clarence and Corinne; or, God's Way* (Philadelphia: American Baptist Publication Society, 1890), pp. 169–79.

Josephine Delphine Henderson Heard

"To Whittier"; "The Black Sampson." From Josephine D. (Henderson) Heard, *Morning Glories* (Philadelphia: Published by the author, 1890), pp. 11; 88–89.

Emma Dunham Kelley-Hawkins

"Joy and Sorrow." From Emma D. Kelley-Hawkins [Forget-me-not, pseud.], *Megda* (Boston: James H. Earle, 1891), pp. 319–23.

Victoria Earle Matthews

Aunt Lindy: A Story Founded on Real Life (New York: J. J. Little & Co., 1893), pp. 3–16.

Frances Ellen Watkins Harper

"School-Girl Notions." From Frances E. W. Harper, *Iola Leroy; or, Shadows Uplifted* 3d ed. (Boston: James H. Earle, 1895), pp. 97–108.

"A Double Standard." From Frances E. W. Harper, *Atlanta Offerings: Poems* (Philadelphia, 1895), pp. 12–14.

Anna Julia Haywood Cooper

"The Higher Education of Women." From Anna J. Cooper, *A Voice from the South: By a Black Woman of the South* (Xenia, Ohio: Aldine Printing House, 1892), pp. 48–79.

Amanda Berry Smith

[The General Conference at Nashville.] From Amanda Berry Smith, *An Autobiography; the Story of the Lord's Dealings with Mrs. Amanda Smith, the Colored Evangelist; Containing an Account of Her Life Work of Faith, and Her Travels in America, England, Ireland, Scotland, India and Africa, as an Independent Missionary* (Chicago: Meyer & Brother, 1893), pp. 198–201, 204.

Eloise Bibb Thompson

"Gerarda"; "Tribute." From Eloise Bibb, *Poems* (Boston: Monthly Review Press, 1895), pp. 36–43; 98.

Marie Louise Burgess

"Marguerite Earle." From Marie Louise Burgess, *Ave Maria* (Boston: Press of the Monthly Review, 1895), pp. 5–14.

Ida Bell Wells-Barnett

"The Case Stated." From Ida B. Wells, *A Red Record: Tabulated Statistics and Alleged Causes of Lynchings in the United States, 1892–1893–1894* (Chicago: Donohue & Henneberry, 1895), pp. 7–17.

Alice Ruth Moore Dunbar-Nelson

"Tony's Wife." From Alice Dunbar, *The Goodness of St. Rocque and Other Stories* (New York: Dodd, Mead & Co., 1899), pp. 19–33.

"I Sit and Sew." From Alice Moore Dunbar-Nelson, ed., *The Dunbar Speaker and Entertainer: Containing the Best Prose and Poetic Selections by and about the Negro Race* (Naperville, Ill.: J. L. Nichols & Co., 1920), pp. 145.

Pauline Elizabeth Hopkins

"The Sewing Circle." From Pauline E. Hopkins, *Contending Forces, a Romance Illustrative of Negro Life North and South* (Boston: Colored Co-operative Publishing Co., 1900), pp. 141–157.

Priscilla Jane Thompson

"The Muses Favor"; "Knight of My Maiden Love." From Priscilla Jane Thompson, *Ethiope Lays* (Rossmoyne, Ohio: Published by the author, 1900), pp. 21–24; 25–26.

Susie Baker King Taylor

"On Morris and Other Island"; "Thoughts on Present Conditions." From Susie King Taylor, *Reminiscences of My Life with the 33d United States Colored Troops Late 1st S.C. Volunteers* (Boston, 1902), pp. 32–35, 61–62.

Clara Ann Thompson
"Uncle Rube and the Race Problem." From Clara Ann Thompson, *Songs from the Wayside* (Rossmoyne, Ohio: Published by the author, 1908), pp. 33–41.

Henrietta Cordelia Ray
"Verses to My Heart's Sister"; "The Enchanted Shell." From Cordelia H. Ray, *Poems* (New York: Grafton Press, 1910), pp. 61–63; 125–26.

Maud Cuney Hare
"Home Life." From Maud Cuney Hare, *Norris Wright Cuney: A Tribune of the Black People* (New York: Crisis Publishing Co., 1913), pp. 79–83.

Olivia Ward Bush Banks
"Voices"; "Fancies." From Olivia Ward Bush, *Driftwood* (Providence, R.I.: Atlantic Publishing Co., 1914), pp. 20; 15.

Georgia Blanche Douglas Camp Johnson
"The Heart of a Woman." From Georgia Douglas Johnson, *The Heart of a Woman and Other Poems* (Boston: Cornhill Co., 1918). p. 1.
"I Want to Die While You Love Me." From Georgia Douglas Johnson, *An Autumn Love Cycle* (New York: Harold Vinal, 1928), p. 42.
"Old Love Letters." From Georgia Douglas Johnson, *Share My World: A Book of Poems* (Washington, D.C.: Half-Way House, 1962), p. 10.
"Cosmopolite." From Georgia Douglas Johnson, *Bronze: A Book of Verse* (Boston: B. J. Brimmer Co., 1922), p. 59.

Sarah Lee Levy Lindo McDowell Brown Fleming
"John Vance." From Sarah Lee Brown Fleming, *Hope's Highway* (New York: Neale Publishing Co., 1918), pp. 16–21.

Charlotte Hawkins Brown
"Mammy": An Appeal to the Heart of the South (Boston: Pilgrim Press, 1919).

Angela Weld Grimké
"A Mona Lisa"; "Grass Fingers." From Countee Cullen, ed., *Caroling Dusk* (New York: Harper & Row, 1927), pp. 42; 38.
"At April." From Grimké Collection, Moorland–Spingarn, Howard University.

Zara Wright
"The Little Orphan." From Zara Wright, *Black and White Tangled*

Threads (New York: AMS Press, 1975), pp. 16–22. Originally published in 1920 by Bernard and Miller.

Mary Etta Spencer

"Little Silas." From Mary Etta Spencer, *The Resentment* (Philadelphia; A. M. E. Book Concern, 1921), pp. 7–13.

Lillian E. Wood

"The Cloud with a Silver Lining." From Lillian E. Wood, *"Let My People Go"* (Philadelphia: A. M. E. Book Concern, 1922), pp. 91–96.

Jessie Redmon Fauset Harris

[Rejection.] From Jessie Fauset, *Plum Bun: A Novel without a Moral* (New York: Frederick A. Stokes Co., 1929), pp. 70–81.

Nella Marian Larsen Imes

[The Abyss.] From Nella Larsen, *Quicksand* (New York and London: Alfred A. Knopf, 1928), pp. 283–95. Reprint. New York: Negro Universities Press, 1969; New York: Collier Books, 1971.